THE RIPPLE EFFECT

 volume 88

THE RIPPLE EFFECT

Gender and Race in Brazilian Culture and Literature

Maria José Somerlate Barbosa

Purdue University Press
West Lafayette, Indiana

♾ The paper used in this book meets the minimum requirements of American National Standard for Information Sciences—Permanence of Paper for Printed Library Materials, ANSI Z39.48-1992.

Printed in the United States of America
Interior template design by Anita Noble;
Cover template design by Heidi Branham;

Cataloging-in-Publication Data on file at the Library of Congress
978-1-61249-852-2 (hardcover)
978-1-61249-853-9 (paperback)
978-1-61249-854-6 (epub)
978-1-61249-855-3 (epdf)

*I dedicate this book to my mother, Dona Frida, whose
courage and resilience have always been
a source of inspiration.*

*This book is also for Larry. Because of his gentle ways,
I sing. Because of his tender touch, I dance.
Because of his warm embrace, I play.*

Contents

Contents

Acknowledgments

The Ripple Effect: Gender and Race in Brazilian Culture and Literature is a multifaceted project whose core foundation stems from analyses of materials I amassed from library and field research conducted between 2001 and 2018. During that time, some travel grants, awards, and research leaves were instrumental in my gaining access to resources housed in special or private collections, as well as garnering materials often unavailable in the United States. Thus, I appreciate the support of the Office of the Provost, the Office of the Vice-President for Research, and the College of Liberal Arts and Sciences at University of Iowa for granting me two research semesters (fall 2009, and spring 2016) during which time I collected and analyzed materials to map the role women have played in core arenas of Brazil's cultural and literary production. The 2018 CLAS Developmental Studies Hybridoma Bank (DSHB) award was invaluable in allowing me the means to travel to Brazil to collect materials at the archives of the Museu do Futebol in São Paulo. I am also very thankful to Drs. Pablo and Violet Recinos whose generous donations to my research agenda contributed to some of my travels to Brazil and in the United States to conduct interviews that I cite in this study.

I am also thankful to my students who motivated and challenged me to keep researching Brazilian popular culture and whose insightful discussions kindled my continuous interest in analyzing race and gender in *capoeira, carnaval,* soccer, and other Brazilian cultural manifestations. My special thanks to Anthony Bedel who worked as my research assistant in the summer of 2007 and located invaluable special materials for me. My sincere appreciation to Ahmed Hassanein, also a former student, whose generosity and expertise with technology were invaluable to complete some parts of this project. I am also grateful to Laura Graham who shared her expertise in cultural anthropology with me when we co-taught a Latin American Studies Senior Seminar on expressive cultures of Brazil, in 2004.

To analyze the growing participation of females in *capoeira* circles, I attended several workshops and *rodas de capoeira* as a guest observer and conducted a substantial number of interviews in Brazil and the United States between 2002 and 2016. Those experiences were invaluable to my assessment of women's contributions to *capoeira*. Thus, I am indebted to the *capoeiristas* who so generously shared their time and information with me, especially those with whom I conducted lengthy interviews: Frederico Abreu and Mestra Paulinha (in Salvador), Letícia Vidor Reis and Mestra Janja (in São Paulo), Mestra Cigana (in Rio de Janeiro), Mestra Marisa (in Chicago), and Mestra Luar do Sertão (in Tucson). To gather information for a discussion of women in soccer, I conducted research at the library and special collections of the Museu de Futebol in São Paulo. I want to express my gratitude to Julia Terin who helped me navigate the museum's collection and provided me with support to amass the materials I needed for this study. I am also indebted to Léa Campos for the long interview and the large amount of materials she shared with me in New York about her experience in soccer, in general, and as the first female FIFA referee, in particular. I also want to express my appreciation to Valéria Valenssa who met with me at her residence in Rio de Janeiro for an interview about her Globeleza trajectory and offered me access to, and copies of, books and video recordings housed in her private archive. Their collective generosity proved invaluable for the analyses presented in this study on *capoeira*, soccer, cultural shows, and televised performances. I am also grateful to the National Endowment for the Humanities for the 2001 summer stipend to collect *cantigas de capoeira* and work on representations of women in the lyrics of those songs. By amassing and analyzing those *cantigas de capoeira*, I took the first step toward the development of this larger study on gender and race as characterized in Brazilian popular culture.

Some of my earlier publications on *capoeira*, gender, and race served as a starting point for several discussions I present here. Those preliminary analyses were originally published in Portuguese. The sections from those publications used in this volume have been translated, modified, expanded, and adapted to fit the current discussions. I am thankful to the journals which published those articles for the rights to use portions of them. They are: "Capoeira: A gramática do corpo e a dança das palavras" published in *Luso-Brazilian Review* (vol. 42, no. 1, 2005, pp. 78–98), copyrighted by the Board of Regents of the University of Wisconsin system; "A mulher na capoeira" published in *Arizona Journal of Hispanic Cultural Studies* (vol. 9, 2005, pp. 9–28); "A representação da mulher nas cantigas de capoeira" which appeared in *Portuguese Literary and Cultural Studies* (vol. 19/20, 2011, pp. 463–77); and "As aves que aqui gorgeiam não gorgeiam como lá?: As abordagens raciais no Brasil e nos Estados Unidos" published in *Afro-Hispanic Review* (vol. 29, no. 2, 2010, pp. 237–62). Some aspects of the literary discussions presented in the second segment of Chapter Two were first published in *Chasqui: Revista de Literatura Latinoamericana* (vol. 32, no. 1, 2008, pp. 3–24). I am indebted to *Chasqui* for granting me author's use of all parts of the article. To the anonymous reviewers, I want to express my most sincere appreciation for their comments and suggestions.

Introductory Remarks

"Oh, Clear the Way"

The Ripple Effect: Gender and Race in Brazilian Culture and Literature provides the reader with a window into transformations that have taken place in Brazil's cultural, political, and historical environments from early twentieth century to the present day. It is with one eye on the present, another on the future, and always identifying the silhouettes and shadows of the past that *The Ripple Effect* examines literary texts and expressions of popular culture (*capoeira*, Candomblé, *carnaval*, the *mulata* profession, music, and soccer) to address the place and space that gender and race have had as binders of the discourse of the national identity. To accomplish that, it analyzes the negotiation of cultural boundaries, underscores political incongruities, discloses historical ambiguities, and examines social ambivalences. To reveal some paradoxes and double binds regarding race and gender dynamics, *The Ripple Effect* examines what is ideologically at play in the slippery variables of the concept of a national identity, and it discusses gender and race as cornerstones and points of conversion in Brazilian culture and literature. It probes into Brazil's "ambiguous process of modernization"[1] by describing the implications that laws and policies established in the 1930s and 1940s had in shaping the core and contours of morality that intend to silence women's voices and limit their choices.

To illustrate and contextualize the influence that writers had in scrutinizing cultural and social mores, this study includes numerous references to, and close readings of, literary texts (prose and poetry), and analyses of lyrics of songs from *capoeira* and the greater Brazilian music repertoire. The discussions of literary texts included in this work are based on two larger premises:

1

a) how effectively female writers examine and question the gender dynamics of the time; and/or b) how compellingly literature and other arts can document cultural norms, not just as faithful reflections or reliable catalogues of life, or even as mere agents of social changes, but also as complex constructions or representations of social values, ideas, and belief systems. Since literature lies at the intersection of several discourses, it is a valuable resource to examine social phenomena, traditions, cultural mores, and the management of culture as a political, social, and historical enterprise. By often reframing ideas and concepts through parody, irony, allusions, intertextuality, and multiple points of view, literary texts can connect different circumstances of the human experiences and offer diverse perspectives on how to approach or analyze political power, social and cultural dogmas, and historical facts. At times, they also work as a critical paradigm that provides clues, references, and suggestions on how to break away from cultural limitations or challenge traditional concepts and ideas. In this aspect, the literary texts discussed in *The Ripple Effect* illustrate and enhance the discussions on cultural expressions of Brazil.

The title and structure of this study were inspired by the verbal implications and the visual imagery of the ripple effects that Francisca Edwiges Gonzaga (better known as Chiquinha Gonzaga, 1847–1935) created in 1899. She cast a stone on the waters of Brazilian popular culture when the reveler group Rosa de Ouro commissioned her to compose a song for their *carnaval* parade. The result was the *marchinha*[2] "Ó, Abre Alas" ("Oh, Clear the Way"):

> Ó, abre alas
> Que eu quero passar
> Eu sou da lira
> Não posso negar.
> Rosa de Ouro
> É que vai ganhar.[3]

> Oh, clear the way
> Let me get through
> I am a musician
> I am not going to deny it.
> Rosa de Ouro
> Will win the competition.

The title/opening verse of the song is quite telling because, on a literal level, it expresses Rosa de Ouro's request for bystanders to open the way for the group to parade on the streets of Rio de Janeiro. At a symbolic level, it can also communicate Gonzaga's efforts to have the emerging popular musical genres (*maxixe* and *samba*), *carnaval* festivities, and African-derived celebrations recognized as part of the fabric of Brazil's national identity. The lyrics of the song can also be interpreted as a veiled reference to Gonzaga's personal history of struggles to be accepted as a female musician and an Afro-Brazilian composer at the end of the nineteenth century. In addition, in a larger sense, "Oh, clear the way" has the makings of a slogan that could be used to advocate for women's access to public space and the ability to exercise their rights as full-fledged citizens in Brazilian society.

Gonzaga was a pioneer on many accounts. She worked to convey respectability to less-valued musical rhythms, many of which were developed by the uneducated, poor, black, and brown population. Her talent earned her the reputation of an esteemed composer and musician, her fight for racial and social equality prompted recognition as an important social activist, and her courage and audacity earned her the label of a rebel. At the age of twenty-two, six years into an arranged marriage, she left her husband (who had forbidden her to play any instrument) to pursue a musical career. She performed at a diversity of sites ranging from illustrious theaters to venues deemed unsuitable for women of "good families" (Diniz 62). She managed to gain the respect of her peers who acknowledged her talent and shared the stage with her at a time when the division of public (male) and private (pious female) spaces was rigidly observed. Yet, her audacity was costly because she lost some personal rights and acquired the stigma of a non-conforming woman. Some of her other accomplishments comprise efforts to fight for the abolition of black slavery in Brazil (1888) and shoulder the leadership of a campaign to institute copyrights for musicians and composers (Diniz 14, 99–134). Edinha Diniz argues that Gonzaga's personal and professional trajectory was inevitably connected to Brazil's historical path and to the transformations that were taking place in the newly formed Republic (1889). Focusing on her taste in music as a type of insubordination, or a way to protest the overpowering patriarchal system, Diniz concludes that:

3

> Não era muito diferente desobedecer um pai, um marido ou uma norma imposta. Ao mesmo tempo que se libertava, ela libertava a música. A sua obra distingue-se pela observância do que rodeia, da captação do que é próximo ... e desta forma produz uma originalidade, dando à música um toque brasileiro. (161)

> It was not much different to disobey a father, a husband or an imposed norm. As she liberated herself, she also liberated music. Her work was distinct in that by observing what is around her, she encapsulated her surroundings and, as a result, created original material, lending to music a special Brazilian diction.

Gonzaga was such a talented musician and composer that, on November 26, 1914, the First Lady of Brazil, Nair de Teffé, breached protocol and invited her to perform during a diplomatic reception at the Palácio do Catete in Rio de Janeiro (Diniz 205). She played the rhythm *maxixe* (known as the Brazilian *tango*) which was popular with the lower strata of Brazilian society, but not sanctioned by the ecclesiastic authorities and other guardians of codes of conduct on the grounds that its dance choreography was licentious, and its rhythm had African-derived origins. Commenting on how discriminated *samba* and *maxixe* were at the time, Bryan McCann writes that they were "considered the lowest of the many popular genres in Rio ... and therefore the least worthy of sophisticated musical embellishment. And both genres, in different periods, were subjected to repressive measures by authorities cracking down on the disorder of the downtown dance scene" in Rio de Janeiro (44). No wonder that, the day after the diplomatic reception at the presidential palace when Gonzaga played one of her compositions, the *maxixe* Corta Jaca, the senator Rui Barbosa was so distressed by her performance and the First Lady's "bad taste" that he took to the Senate floor to comment on the "unfortunate" choice of entertainer and musical genre for such a significant event (Diniz 204–05).

In 1925, in recognition for her talents and activism, the Sociedade Brasileira de Atores Teatrais ("Brazilian Society of Stage Actors") conferred on her the association's highest honor (Diniz 14). When she died, ten years later, at the age of eighty-five, she had cleared the way for many "insubordinate" women to question the rules of patriarchy. By then, the sounds of her music had echoed in the streets of Rio de Janeiro, and her librettos had traveled from the smallest and humblest houses of entertainment to the most prestigious stages in the country. Gonzaga also challenged patriarchy and refused to be confined to the social mores of the time. For her courage to dare to assert her individuality and pursue her talents (despite so many retaliations), she can be considered a forerunner of the first wave of Feminism in Brazil. She was also an ardent reformer who engaged in cultural practices and used them as tools for ideological and social transformations. In the last decades of the nineteenth century, Gonzaga accomplished revolutionary creative acts and social activism that paved the way for women to engage in avant-garde movements such as the intellectual revolution that the first phase of Brazilian Modernism (1917–1930) epitomizes. In the decades following the Week of Modern Art in 1922,[4] writers and visual artists craftily adopted and recreated European models, introducing a steady flow of aesthetic experimentation into their works. Gonzaga's daring to experiment and her lasting contributions to Brazilian music are similar to the creative endeavors of the modernist writers, musicians, and visual artists of the first decades of the twentieth century.

To a certain extent, Gonzaga also set the example for female writers whose works remained outside the modernist canon. Her pursuit of a career at the turn of the twentieth century, social activism, and defiance of cultural mores predates some of the textual discussions addressed by non-canonical female novelists who wrote during the first decades of the twentieth century. Those works exemplify the efforts women made to circumvent cultural and literary traditions, and whose defiance can be considered a counter-revolution within the intellectual upheaval of Brazilian Modernism. As Susan Quinlan and Peggy Sharpe discussed in their critical edition of Adalzira Bittencourt's and Ercília Nogueira Cobra's compiled works, those writers were highly engaged in defending women's rights, and their texts articulated a strong defense of their ideological positions, and epitomized the rifts that existed within Brazilian Modernism (17).

Cultural Paradoxes and Double Binds

The Ripple Effect examines a variety of cultural concepts, theories, and rulings to draw a picture of the complex, ambiguous, and ambivalent mores of Brazilian society. It discusses how historical trajectories and political advocacies can impact popular culture and literary expressions. Yet, the reverse can also happen since literary and cultural studies often analyze contradictions, ambiguities, and disparagements. Using *capoeira* as a lynchpin to develop comparative argument, this study reveals how ambiguity has defined Brazilian culture. It communicates, for instance, that the swing movement of *ginga* (the foundational step of *capoeira*), and the art of *malícia* (astuteness and dissimulation) embody the same type of disguise that "cordiality" emblematizes. In routine interactions, Brazilians usually avoid lashing out at someone (*bater de frente*) and prefer to resort to other means to complain or confront people and circumstances by using "cordiality" to disguise intention, or maneuver situations. Such "cordiality," in many cases, masks a passive-aggressive style of social relations and traditions in which people prefer to manipulate others, rather than antagonize or oppose openly, because it can appear less hostile and tacitly more empowering.

Several scholars have analyzed "the middle ground of mediation" (Hess 10)[5] and *jeitinho brasileiro*[6] to discuss the complexity, conundrum, and ambiguity that dominate Brazilian culture in regard to social power. *Jeitinho brasileiro* represents a cultural system in which individuals use emotional recourses, and other means of persuasion, to flex the rules to obtain special favors and circumvent difficult situations. It also conveys ideas of disguise and refers to a special way of bypassing rules and social conventions in the intricate negotiations that form the collective discourse on Brazilian identity. David J. Hess writes that "it is in the vicissitudes of everyday Brazilian life that one uncovers the systematic conflict that makes it possible to understand the dialectic between the political events of the headlines and the hierarchy, and the personalism of the informal side of Brazilian society" (21). Those ambiguities and ambivalences so prevalent in Brazilian culture are intriguing and significant, particularly when analyzed against a gender and race backdrop. The ambiguity inherent in "cordiality," or nestled in the veiled maneuvering of a situation, is also a key component of both Brazilian social relations and the use of *malícia* in *capoeira*. Ben Downing connects the two aspects when he writes that if "*dar um jeitinho*" is to "give a little twist to things," *capoeira* is "a silky tissue of *jeitinhos*, of entrapments and Houdiniesque escapes from them" (556).

The Ripple Effect analyzes how "cordial" exchanges in everyday life in Brazil have been used to mask ambiguous relations of gender and race. As evidenced throughout this study, such ambiguity becomes a breeding ground for violence against women, regardless of race, social class, and education. This study also examines the process of inclusion and exclusion of the Afro-Brazilian population in the concept of a national identity (special attention is given to the *mulata* profession, the myth of the racial democracy, and the ideology of whitening). Brazil's cultural ambiguity is also unveiled in the discussions about gender and race in soccer, in the trajectory of the martial art-dance-ritual *capoeira* (from a prosecuted martial art to its consecration as "the Brazilian gymnastic"), and in the analyses of the lyrics of popular songs. Those songs are shrouded in innuendos, double meanings, riddles, and ironic inversions (in the case of *capoeira* chants), and camouflaged in poetic erudition, metaphoric connotations, and other sophisticated literary devices (often found in the lyrics of MPB songs). The analysis of Brazilian "cordiality" and its ambivalent characteristics also appears in the discussions of how women have used camouflage, *malícia*, and *jeitinho* to subvert the rules and establish a place and space for them in *capoeira* and in other manifestations of Brazilian popular culture.

In analyzing Brazilian ambiguity, in different aspects of popular culture and literature, *The Ripple Effect* addresses gender and race inequality, the struggles women have faced, and the victories they have landed. Were Gonzaga alive today, she would probably feel vindicated to see women holding important positions in public offices, pursuing careers beyond the limits of their households, making decisions about their sexuality, and participating actively in every segment of Brazil's national life. Nevertheless, she probably would also argue that, as encouraging as such accomplishments are, they have contributed to establish an erroneous belief in gender equality in Brazil. Most likely, she would challenge misconceptions that women no longer need to talk about resistance or debunk patriarchy because they have the right to vote and work, have an education, hold public office, and make decisions about their private lives. She probably would argue that, even if women now hold executive jobs, they are oftentimes paid less than men, and are likely to be passed over for promotions. As Brazil alternates between liberal and authoritarian political tendencies, and the government vacillates between protecting minorities and curtailing their rights, one may wonder how much the gender dynamics have actually changed in Brazil since Getúlio Vargas instituted the Estado Novo ("New State") in 1937, and signed into law many policies that restrained women's rights.

Gender and Race in the First Decades of the Twentieth Century

In the 1930s and 1940s, Vargas's regime advanced some of the previously established feminist agendas, and instituted new ones. The political, economic, and cultural changes implemented during his tenure were broad in scope and deep in reach. He created national steel and petroleum companies, instituted several political parties, and celebrated all things national, including African-derived cultural products with *samba* leading the way (Vianna 92). He also sought to unify Brazil by instilling nationalist pride and educating the population. To achieve that, he established a Ministry of Education which worked doggedly to promote nationalism in the newly centralized school system, and to accelerate the integration of European immigrants (especially those in the South) by demanding that Portuguese be the only language of instruction in schools (Burns 364). Interwoven in the framework of that era were social and political upheavals, government changes, and the development of a populist and nationalist project that seized the idea of a hybrid nation and the view of African-derived culture as a distinctive trait of Brazil's national identity. In this period, *carnaval* festivities—especially the neighborhood associations known as *escolas de samba*—received institutional support. In the mid-1930s, devotees of Afro-Brazilian religions were allowed the right to assemble, the martial art-ritual *capoeira* was elevated to the category of a Brazilian gymnastic, and *samba* became part of the national project of modernizing Brazil. In this context, as discussed in Chapter Two, Afro-Brazilian women were purportedly celebrated in literature and lyrics of songs as symbols of sensuality and a true expression of Brazil's racial democracy.

As part of efforts to unite and control the country, Vargas saw radio broadcasting as a useful means of disseminating "the official point of view" to all Brazilians (Burns 365). It was in this environment that the radio program *A Hora do Brasil* (also called

A Voz do Brasil), was implemented to inform, educate, and unite the people. The program was transmitted daily, from 1935 to 1962, between seven and eight PM as part of the government's determination to keep information under tight supervision. From 1939 on, *A Hora do Brasil* was under the direct oversight of the Departamento de Imprensa e Propaganda ("Department of Press and Advertisement/Propaganda"; McCann 20).[7] Radio stations were forced to broadcast *A Voz do Brasil* and air it at prime time; and loudspeakers were placed in public squares, lest someone had not made it home in time to turn on their radios. The cultural part of the program included Brazilian popular music, discussions of art and artistic projects in different regions, and information about touristic areas in Brazil. It also included political speeches—which addressed the working class directly—and radio-theater which created a space for dramatists who wrote historical plays. As McCann discusses, "When Getúlio Vargas assumed the presidency following the Revolution of 1930, his authority was tenuous"; therefore, to boost his governing power, "his new administrative cohort understood the imperative to reach and inspire a broad population with a message of inclusion and common struggle. Radio seemed perfect for the enterprise" (19).

Most people bought into the idea: *sambistas* were commissioned to compose popular songs whose lyrics reinforced the ideology of nationalism. Writers, musicians, historians, and sociologists such as Jorge Amado, Mário de Andrade, Cecília Meireles, Heitor Villa Lobos, Sérgio Buarque de Holanda, Antônio Cândido, and Gilberto Freyre acted as cultural mediators by adopting the hybrid culture as a liberating idea, and an ideological and symbolic construct of a Brazilian national identity (Vianna 90–92; Taylor 19; Squeff and Wisnik 132–90). Such a nationalist construct contributed to developing the image of a carefree nation in which the definition of exoticism and eroticism was intrinsically associated with music, *carnaval*, and "tropical" bodies. Brazil's stigmatized cultural identity (the *pardo*, resourceful, and playful country) seemed to define the people and the land. Such concept was reinforced by Carmen Miranda's unique performances and her role as an informal cultural ambassador in the United States (1939–1953), during which time she consolidated the idea of *samba* as Brazil's national rhythm (McCann 106–07, 146–49). Miranda was promoted as the Brazilian Bombshell, an image she cultivated with her flamboyant costumes, exuberant personality, and sensual dance movements to the contagious rhythms of *samba*. In addressing the cult of her personality, Kathryn Bishop-Sanchez pointed out that "the intense visual impact of her exaggerated, glamorous look ... created an exhibition of stylized effeminacy and excessive female sexuality" (2). As a result, the image of Brazil as a hybrid and exuberant tropical land of *samba*, tutti-frutti hats, and sensual moves enticed the imagination of foreigners and helped promote the image of the country as an erotic and exotic racial paradise (Gil-Montero 170–85).

The inclusion of *capoeira*, alongside soccer, *samba*, and *carnaval* in Vargas's nationalist project of the 1930s was, in some instances, a constructive undertaking. Even if the selection or invention of new characteristics for the country were simply a ploy to advance his nationalist and populist agenda, Vargas's desire to unify Brazil and commodify popular culture reaped some benefits. The *samba* rhythm and the lyrics of the songs contributed to emphasize the importance that race and popular culture played in building the concept of a respected racially-mixed nation (Vianna 65; Taylor 18). The ideology of Vargas's Estado Novo drew attention to cultural manifestations of African origin. However, as Hermano Vianna points out, the Vargas regime found itself at a crossroads: to create a cultural and political unity would require abandoning "the old ideal of 'whitening'" (the government sponsored idea of racial whitening by way of encouraging miscegenation) while selecting, or inventing, "national traits" to reformulate Brazilian national identity (113). The solution was "to embrace mestiçagem as a defining national trait" (Vianna 113). By validating traditions of African origin as unique features of Brazilian culture, the government conferred to those expressive practices an aura of authenticity and respectability which, in turn, had a positive influence on the general population's endorsement of those cultural practices (at least on a superficial level).

Vargas advanced the program of cultural nationalism and miscegenation and, initially, also supported a feminist agenda. The 1930 political revolution brought him to power as the provisional president who, at least in that initial stage of his term, appeared to be sympathetic to women's causes. He opened a space for Bertha Lutz who, upon her return from Europe, introduced new feminist ideas, was instrumental in organizing the Federação Brasileira pelo Progresso Feminino ("Brazilian Federation for Women's Progress"), and worked with her peers to argue for women's suffrage and other social and political rights. She was also part of a group of six Latin American activists who, in 1922, formed the Pan-American Association for the Advancement of Women. Of paramount importance to that wave of Brazilian Feminism was the fact that Luzt participated in drafting the new Brazilian constitution. She made substantial suggestions to promote women's causes and implement rights related to maternity leave, childcare, social security, gender equality, and a ban on violence (Marino 98). In February 1932, Vargas signed a decree enacting voting rights for women, a measure that in the Western Hemisphere was preceded only the by United States, Canada, and Ecuador (Marino 97). However, even though the emerging feminist movement initially found an opening to advocate for women's rights, that rapport with Vargas's governing body did not last long. Ilan Rachum informs that, from "July to September 1932, that is, between the establishment of woman suffrage and the election of the assembly, the state of São Paulo rose in revolt against the Vargas government, demanding an immediate return to constitutional procedures" (126). That revolt also mobilized a homegrown platform of solidarity in São Paulo during which time female supporters would sew uniforms, provide medical services, and operate a kitchen for soldiers. Different from the feminist movement led by Luzt that cooperated with the government, this group of women embraced opposition to the Vargas regime (Rachum 127).

Vargas's reprisal would soon be felt. In 1937, he retaliated against all opposing forces by closing congress and instituting a dictatorship. The new regime sent unambiguous signs of resentment toward women for having betrayed his trust: it shortened their campaign for equal opportunities by implementing several laws and initiatives that curtailed female rights and denied advancements to their cause. There were incremental punishments applied to women. In 1937, they were removed from consular posts and other offices they held abroad; in 1940 Vargas issued a presidential decree that "allowed a ten per cent reduction in the minimum wage of adult women in all the industrial locations"; and, in 1943, he signed another decree, "separating boys and girls in coeducational secondary schools" (Rachum 129). Vargas also limited women's choices on other fronts. A conspicuous example is a decree he signed in 1941 (Decreto-Lei 3.199, artigo 54) which prohibited females from practicing any type of fighting and sports considered "violent" (Bruhns 73). Sueann Caulfield has argued, when discussing the first four decades of the twentieth century, that for each step forward Brazilian women took, they were obliged to take another one backward since "the official ideology of state paternalism under dictator Getúlio Vargas after 1937, [was] an ideology sustained by a fevered rhetoric of 'organic' links between centralized state power, national honor, and the 'traditional Brazilian family'" (15). To curb the social upheavals, implement his populist experiments in the 1930s, and respond to the anxieties that those experiments created, "the Vargas regime reinvented honor as a mechanism for legitimizing authority" (Caulfield 15).

The feminist movement regained some momentum at the end of the 1950s when Vargas was no longer in power, but regrettably came to a halt again during the military dictatorship (1964–1985) established by the 1964 coup-d'état. The rulers reinforced Vargas's nationalist project by revisiting the concept of a "racial democracy" and focusing on the expressive cultures that could boost pride in the country's miscegenation and cultural diversity. That regime was committed to defending "the old Brazilian social values, and above all, the traditional patterns of the Brazilian family" (Rachum 130). The government's control over women's sexuality and lifestyles, their right to lead a public life, work in the profession of their choice, or even practice whatever sports they elected was ingrained on the blueprint of Brazilian society. A telling example is how the military regime reinforced the 1941 ban on several sports. To avoid gray areas and misunderstandings, in 1965, Marshall Humberto de Alencar Castello Branco, then president of Brazil, charted a longer and more explicit list of sports that were forbidden to women (Bruhns 73). Since those sanctions were not lifted until the late 1970s, the laws passed since the 1930s and 1940s had lasting and pervasive effects. Some of those prerogatives are, in many instances, still embedded in the makeup of the country, even though they may not be as readily noticeable because gender equality seems to be generally accepted as true. Such misconception masks conflicting relations of power, inequality, and double standards, and has worked as an undercurrent in Brazilian culture and lifestyle.

During the military dictatorship, the leaders used manifestations of popular culture to divert attention from their iron grip on politics. Critics of the repressive regime often theorize that the government's exaggerated emphasis on cultural programs was a manipulative tactic meant to distract the people from the regime's human rights violations.[8] It was during that time that, as part of its populist and nationalist agenda, the military rulers placed emphasis on soccer and *carnaval*, and promoted *capoeira* to the status of a "national sport" (L. Reis 144). The institutionalized support popular culture received during the military dictatorship is comparable to the efforts made by the Vargas regime to validate cultural manifestations of African origin as part of a hybrid nation proud of its miscegenation policies and "racial democracy."

Framework and Methodology

The Ripple Effect features an introduction, six subdivided chapters, a coda, notes, an index, and a bibliography. The discussions are organized in such a fashion that each part amplifies arguments that were introduced in previous segments, exemplifying the image that the title of this study conveys. Using *capoeira* as a point of connection, this text adopts a circular structure that resembles the rings formed in *rodas de capoeira* and *rodas de samba*. It blends field and library research to analyze the cultural paradoxes that lie underneath the layers of subtleties and the poetic undertones that guide *o jogo bonito* (as in *capoeira* and soccer), the syncopated rhythms of *samba* in *carnaval*, and the romantic overtures of the lyrics of popular music.

The discussions presented in *The Ripple Effect* are informed by works, in various disciplines, that have addressed Brazilian cultural production, or analyzed the country's historical and political development. Thus, significant to the embryonic stages of this study were Waldeloir Rego's 1968 groundbreaking study of *capoeira*, Hermano Vianna's text on *samba*, race, and nationality, and Heloisa Turini Bruhns's historical overview of *capoeira*, soccer, and *carnaval*. A host of other publications have added to my laying the theoretical foundation for this study. I am especially indebted to Sérgo Buarque de Holanda' discussion of "cordiality" in *Raízes do Brasil*, Thomas Skidmore's skilled analysis and precise writings on race, and E. Bradford Burns's insightful overviews of

Brazilian history. Texts by Gilberto Freyre (on the African influence in Brazilian culture), Teófilo de Queiroz Junior, Affonso Romano de Sant'Anna, and Roberto DaMatta (on women, food, and sex) also became reliable sources in the initial phases of this project. Those scholarly productions and theoretical paradigms contributed to my building a preliminary foundation from which I concocted an interdisciplinary line of research to navigate the ambiguities of gender and race in Brazil. In the initial stages of my research on *capoeira* chants as popular poetry, I also found a niche in studies that address the lyrics of Brazilian songs, or confer literary and cultural significance to the popular form of narrative poetry (*literatura de cordel*) originated in Northeast Brazil and sold as chapbooks at farmers' markets and fairgrounds. Those scholarly undertakings have validated those popular cultural manifestations and showcased the importance of preserving cultural archives that the lyrics of *capoeira* songs exemplify.

Chapter One, "Mapping Asymmetries," is divided into three segments that discuss facts and cultural specifics implemented in the first four decades of the twentieth century in Brazil. It addresses the politics of culture that allowed the government to pass laws and implement policies that had lasting effects on the gender dynamics in Brazil. The first segment of this chapter ("The 'Ambiguous Process of Modernization'") maps the ambiguity related to sexual morality embedded in the process of the country's modernization. This part references Caulfield's research on sexual morality, gender, and legal discourses, Susan K. Besse's study about gender inequity, and the discussion of women's rights as presented by Jude E. Hahner. These three also discuss how conflicting the arguments about Feminism and the definition of femininity were at the time. Their studies lent me a threshold from which to foster an analysis of how and why the Brazilian government passed laws that curtailed women's rights and prevented them from participating in certain forms of social interaction.

The second section ("The Literary Counter-Discourse") addresses creative texts by writers who highlighted female experiences and advocated for their rights in the first four decades of the twentieth century. By defying the traditional definition of "femininity," and denouncing the cultural and social parameters of the time, those writers contributed to an understanding of the reach the patriarchal discourse had at the time. Their texts offer compelling samples of a feminist counter-discourse, from the 1920s to early 1940s, and illustrate the theoretical discussions presented in the previous segment. They reveal the opinions of women writers who lived during that period, and who witnessed and felt the constraints (and the ripple effects) of those laws and policies. The authors and texts discussed are: Ercília Nogueira Cobra (*Virgindade Inútil: Novela de Uma Revoltada*), Patrícia Rehder Galvão (*Parque Industrial*), Adalzira Bittencourt (*A Sua Excia.: A President da República no Ano 2500*), and Lúcia Miguel Pereira (*Amanhecer, Em Surdina*, and *Maria Luiza*).

The last portion of Chapter One ("The 'Defense of Honor' Theory") addresses the argument which was often used in courtrooms to acquit men who committed femicide, a practice rooted in Portuguese colonial laws that, in Brazil, lasted until 1991 when it was ruled unconstitutional. It relates to discussions presented in the Coda and in other areas of the manuscript that examine domestic violence and other types of physical and psychological abuse still present in Brazilian society. To exemplify the reach and effect of such practices, this part focuses on the homicide of socialite Ângela Diniz and analyzes the series of femicides that became headlines in the 1970s and 1980s. This segment also discusses how Jorge Amado represents "the cruel law" in his best-selling novel, *Gabriela, Cravo e Canela*.[9] The discussions of violence against women in this segment of Chapter One pave the way for the analyses of similar topics in other areas of *The Ripple Effect*. For instance, it establishes a discursive complementarity with the textual analyses of representation of women in *capoeira* chants and lyrics of Brazilian popular music, and women's trajectory in soccer and *capoeira* circles as discussed in Chapters Three, Five, and Six.

Chapter Two, "The Erotic and Exotic Lure," focuses on race as a symbolic binding factor of the nation's identity. It blends feminist and cultural study theories to analyze how *mulatas* are represented and discussed in Brazilian music, literature, and the media. The first segment of this chapter ("Race as a Cultural Binder") presents an overview of race in Brazil, addressing selected comparative discussion of race between Brazil and the United States. It also focuses on two expressions that have become staple terms when talking about race in Brazil: the "ideology of whitening" and the myth of the "racial democracy."[10] To examine how and why those concepts became an integral part of popular culture and the Brazilian imaginary, this part also serves as a notional foundation for the subsequent divisions of the chapter. The second segment of this chapter ("The 'Made-in-Brazil' *Mulata*") discusses how and why a race category became a profession intended only for *parda* women (the *profissão mulata* merges race, gender, and sexuality into a professional category). It examines historical and social contexts (from colonization to the present) to analyze the ideologies that continued to foment such representation of Afro-Brazilian women. To appraise the contradictions, ambiguities, and ambivalences inherent in the Brazilian social and cultural scenario, it also analyzes the traditional representations of Afro-Brazilian women in some lyrics of songs, television commercials, mini-series, and contemporary poems.

The last segment of this chapter ("*Carnaval*: Tokens Mistaken for Wonders") addresses gender, race, and eroticism in advertisements of *carnaval* parades in Rio de Janeiro. It analyzes how women's sensuality and sexuality—as conceived in that environment—can be critically analyzed as tokens of a racial democracy. It offers a case study of the Globeleza character (a play on words meaning "Globo's beauty"), focuses on Valéria Valenssa's career and performances, and presents close readings of the vignettes produced during fourteen consecutive years by Globo Television Network to advertise *carnaval* celebrations. It also includes information from an extensive interview I conducted with Valenssa, and analyses of video recordings and printed materials from her private collection. My research differs from the traditional studies on *parda* women in Brazil because it establishes connections between a *mucama* (a mistress slave and lady-in-waiting) in colonial days and the *mulata* profession of contemporary times. To corroborate my findings, I analyze poems and lyrics of songs by contemporary writers and lyricists (most of whom are Afro-Brazilians) who also establish the connection between *mucamas* and *mulatas*. The literary examples that analyze Afro-Brazilian women's place in Brazilian society include poems by Affonso Romano de Sant'Anna ("Mulher"), Sônia Fátima da Conceição ("Passado Histórico"), and Edimilson de Almeida Pereira (a segment from *Caderno de Retorno*). There are also references to Jorge Amado's *Gabriela, Cravo e Canela*, and analysis of lyrics from the Brazilian repertoire of songs. Those discussions serve as channels, or connecting passageways, to examine gender and race in soccer in the following chapter.

Chapter Three, "Women in Soccer," is also divided in three segments. The first part (*"Futebol:* The Brazilian Passion") presents an historical overview of the development of the sport in Brazil, quotes from Carlos Drummond de Andrade's poem, "Futebol," which confirms the Brazilian gusto for soccer. It also analyzes the different opinions about the sport as presented by the authors Henrique Maximiliano Coelho Neto and Afonso Henriques de Lima Barreto. The second part of this chapter ("Let Me Play") examines the ways in which the discourse of masculinity affected the perception of and attitudes toward women's participation in sports and fighting games. Until the 1980s (when substantial cultural and political changes took place), the majority of conservative families would oppose their daughters practicing soccer for fear that it would thwart their "feminine condition," that is, young females could become mannish in their appearance. This part reviews the pseudo-scientific discourse on which those fears were founded. It also includes discussions about Vargas's policies to circumscribe women to the private space of the family. Those policies and the intense propaganda about the need to safeguard the female body to fulfill the mission of motherhood substantially reduced women's opportunities in sports.

The last part of this chapter ("The Soccer Museum") discusses the collection of artwork and video recordings of Museu do Futebol in São Paulo, and the history of women in soccer. It also presents a case study of the referee Léa Campos. The discussions included in the last two segments of Chapter Three reverberate in Chapter Five, which analyzes how families also dreaded the idea of their daughters playing *capoeira* because it was not only considered a violent sport, but also a marginal practice and/or a substandard form of cultural expression. Even though the National Council of Sports did not explicitly include *capoeira* in the list of forbidden sports, until mid-twentieth century it was trademarked as an Afro-Brazilian activity practiced by hooligans, rogues, and outlaws, and (similar to soccer) was considered a "man's activity," thus deemed unsuitable for the feminine physique.

Chapter Four, *"Capoeira: Jogo Bonito, Jogo de Dentro, Jogo de Fora,"* provides an overview of the fight-dance-ritual and draws some comparative analyses with other expressions of Brazilian popular culture. This chapter contextualizes *capoeira*'s development, examining how and why it was confined to the space of academies, reached universities, and became an international "cultural product." It is divided into three segments: "Mediating the Body's Spatiality," "Navigating the Cultural and Historical Space," and "The 'Double-Talk': The Interactive Space." This chapter analyzes *capoeira*'s development, practice, performative and ludic aspects, and the status it received as a cultural artifact. It also discusses terminologies, examines performative aspects (body movements, music, and the lyrics of the songs), offers insights into the debates about *capoeira*'s origin and development, and reflects on the two major styles of *capoeira*. It traces the history of *capoeira* from colonial days to the present and examines some subtle forms of resistance used to navigate cultural and political spaces. It also analyzes *capoeira*'s close connection with Candomblé.

By analyzing the historical, cultural, religious, and interactive space that *capoeira* occupies, and by searching for a common denominator with other Brazilian popular cultural manifestations, Chapter Four sets into motion some thoughts and debates about gender in *capoeira*, building a sustained momentum for what constitutes the core of the last two chapters. To illustrate discussions related to race and gender and how stigmatized *capoeira* was at the turn of the twentieth century, Chapter Four analyzes the 1890 novel, *O Cortiço* ("*The Slum*"),[11] by Aluísio de Azevedo, and Oswald de Andrade's poem "O Capoeira,"[12] published in 1925.[13] It also includes lyrics of *capoeira* songs (analyzed as samples of popular poetry) to highlight some of the key points discussed. Those chants also serve as connecting threads that link this chapter to other parts of *The Ripple Effect*. This chapter further discusses a short text by Machado de Assis (in which he analyzes how the population of Rio de Janeiro feared *capoeiristas* who formed *maltas*, that is, unruly and violent groups, at the end of the nineteenth century), and compares Machado's discussions to the anxiety that *funkeiros* (those associated with *bailes funks*, or funk parties) created in the *cariocas* in the 1980s and 1990s.

Even though the large female presence in *capoeira* in Brazil and abroad has already produced positive changes and motivated women to challenge inequalities, the temporal and spatial gap between male and female players continues to impact gender relations. To evaluate women's struggles and accomplishments, Chapter Five, "Women in *Capoeira*," analyzes their trajectory in this martial art-dance-ritual, discussing not only the rules of engagement, but also the *bonafide* recognition they have received lately. It is divided into three segments, the first of which ("Crafting a Space") includes references to, and opinions of, female *capoeiristas* of different races, social backgrounds, and economic and educational standings when discussing female's involvement in *capoeira*. The second division, "Neither Frills nor Symbolic Representations," centers on female *capoeiristas* who have reached the level of *mestras* or *contra-mestras* (high-ranking female teachers) in Brazil and in the United States. It also analyzes the supporting role women have played in *capoeira* academies, and pays a tribute to several *mestres* who taught and supported female *capoeiristas* and helped them advance through the rankings. The last segment, "Agents of Cultural Transformations," addresses representative samples of women in *capoeira* circles and the contributions they have given to change the gender dynamics in *capoeira*. It presents an introduction of the cultural, social, and political changes that took place in Brazilian society, between late 1960s and 1990s, to appraise how those changes influenced female inclusion in *capoeira* circles. It analyzes their discipline, efforts, and patience to gain skills and resilience with which to compete with male peers for a place and a space in *capoeira* circles. As exemplified in this chapter, every year, new *mestras, contra-mestras,* and *professoras de capoeira* continue, as Luís da Câmara Cascudo would infer, in his figurative language, the tradition of the "African mermaids" (Quianda, Quituba, and Quiximbi who represent endurance, cunning, and courage) and their "Mediterranean sisters" (*Geografia* 157–58). Women *capoeiristas* also take inspiration from historical figures such as the Angolan Queen Nzinga Nabandi Ngola (1582–1663) who fought and temporarily expelled the Portuguese in the seventeenth century. Cascudo believes that each slave ship that arrived in Brazil carried within it the strength and rebelliousness that the Angolan Queen bequeathed to her subjects (*Made* 40). He also observed that the historic legacy of defiance that Queen Nzinga represents has always been a symbolic component of practices of African origin in Brazil (*Made* 40). Female *capoeiristas* have strived to incorporate Nzinga's purported strategies into their teachings and have used the queen's name in their *capoeira* ventures (the Orchestra Nzinga de Berimbaus, for instance). Most of the women cited or discussed in this volume have also continued the tradition established by Chiquinha Gonzaga as they strive "to clear the way" for new generations.

Chapter Five examines the larger trajectory of women *capoeiristas*, focusing on *mestras* from different geographical areas in Brazil and the United States. The Brazilian *mestras* discussed or referenced in this study are from Bahia, Brasília, D.F., Minas Gerais, Pará, Rio de Janeiro, and São Paulo, and the majority of them are of African descent. Some of them are fully engaged in underprivileged Afro-Brazilian communities, even though they live and work in what could be considered "elite" settings of Brazilian society. They are anthropologists, historians, sociologists, and political activists whose work has contributed to boost *capoeira*'s importance in Brazil and abroad. Included in this study, are also references to *mestras* who never made it to, or past, a high school level of education. Regardless of their social and educational status, their presence in *capoeira* circles has contributed to change the general perception of the gender dynamics in the *rodas*. I also include references about Brazilian *mestras* who immigrated to the United States and currently teach *capoeira* in San Francisco, Chicago, and New York because of their unique contribution to disseminate the practice of *capoeira*. Two *mestras* quoted in this study were born in the United States, but they were trained by Brazilian *mestres*, have kept a close connection with Brazil, and served as role models for other women in *capoeira* circles. The scope of this study did not allow for a presentation of statistical details or the achievements of female *capoeiristas* worldwide, and/or the analyses of their trajectory in different stages of their training. By choosing to focus on *mestras* (rather than attempting to collect statistical samples of every country where women play *capoeira*), this chapter highlights the trajectory of those women who have removed roadblocks, paved the way for other female *capoeiristas*, and have contributed to establish healthy gender dynamics in *rodas*.

Chapter Six, "Women in Brazilian Popular Music and *Capoeira* Songs," presents close readings of those musical texts. It is divided into three interconnected segments: "Representations of Women in Song Lyrics," "The Verbal Codes of Difference," and "The *Bonafide* Place and Space of Women in *Capoeira* Chants." The chapter offers a comparative analysis of *capoeira* songs and samples of the repertoire of Brazilian popular music, focusing on representations of women. It also provides close readings of *capoeira* chants composed by females. Since the lyrics of a number of conventional *capoeira* songs are borrowed from the public domain, the contextualization of their meanings and references to other aspects of expressive cultures of Brazil were central to the development of this portion of the study. By examining the poetic features of *capoeira* chants, particularly when comparing older and contemporary songs, this chapter also evaluates the power language has—the "agency of words" as Alessandro Duranti has labeled linguistic performativity (16)—to convince, obscure, or frame reality. This part also analyzes how language can be used to combat discourses that seek to dominate. In addressing how women are represented in songs, and the role that women *capoeiristas* have played in changing gender dynamics, this chapter also functions as a connecting piece with the initial discussions of Chiquinha Gonzaga and Brazilian music.

The Ripple Effect follows the tradition of comparative and interdisciplinary works. It crosses analytical borders and adopts a cohort of tools and theoretical paradigms to analyze literary texts, lyrics of songs, dance performances, and *rodas de capoeira*. By combining library and field research, and using discourse analyses, case studies, and close readings of texts and contexts to discuss gender and race in Brazil, this work intends to broaden the critical focus and the methodological scope of previous scholarship on the topics. The analyses presented in this study also rely on information gathered during interviews, and observations of special ceremonies and workshops. In the interviews cited in this study, women expressed concerns about double standards, discrimination, violence, and other forms of male dominance in *capoeira* circles and in Brazilian culture in general. Whenever possible, I incorporate their points of view into those reflections. In examining violence against women, I also reference scholars who have studied the importance of politics in establishing laws intended to protect victims of sexual assault, or how adverse political changes have curtailed women's prerogatives.

The Ripple Effect makes references to Feminism in Brazil from early twentieth century to the present, but it is not a theoretical study of Feminism. This volume reveals women's changing place in Brazilian society, their fight for equal opportunities, the victories they have reaped, and the challenges they still face. It embraces conceptual expressions such as "hegemonic masculinity" (certain characteristics and practices prescribed as appropriate or

21

ideal for all men) and "emphasized femininity" (a type of femininity that renders females as naturally kind, caring, and fragile) as Milestone and Meyer have interpreted (20). Included in the theoretical discussions are Sylvia Walby's thoughts on "public patriarchy," a type of domination that uses institutional power, governmental agencies, and the ecclesiastic institutions to enforce male power (19–20, 101–02, 147–48). This study also adopts the concepts of masculinity and "symbolic violence" as presented by Pierre Bourdieu. It borrows from the terminology used by Besse, Caulfield, and Hahner, and in their discussions of how public and private patriarchy joined forces to define women's roles in Brazil during the first decades of the twentieth century. The arguments raised throughout this study are constructed around the concept of a "practiced space," defined by Michel de Certeau as a space that has cultural and symbolic dimensions, resulting from social and performative interactions (117). Thus, *The Ripple Effect* offers a view into several areas of Brazil's culture, presenting critiques of deep-seated ideologies of its society.

Most of the books about *capoeira* have a didactic purpose: they are designed as manuals to teach how to play the game or give simplified information about its origin, development, and cultural importance. A few volumes have an academic public in mind and address *capoeira* from an historical perspective, or study its music, choreography, and dance movements. Quite often *capoeira* songs are compiled into book chapters, websites, and other published venues, but are not systematically discussed, organized, or analyzed in terms of their thematic references and gender and/or race representations. Although the presence of women in *capoeira* circles has increased substantially in the last decades, to date, there is not a single comprehensive study, in English or Portuguese, which systematically analyzes their trajectory in the martial art-dance-ritual. *The Ripple Effect* intends to bridge some of those gaps and open the way for future discussions, by offering a multifaceted, comparative, and interdisciplinary analysis of *capoeira*, in the context of other cultural and literary manifestations, and placing it in the ideological and symbolic construct of Brazil as a hybrid nation.

Throughout this writing, I presented discussions suitable for an academic setting, while offering information that could also make *The Ripple Effect* attractive to a broader readership. With that in mind, I translated and explained words and expressions in Portuguese, provided cultural and historical information, and made other pertinent references. In citing titles, passages, or the lyrics of songs, I also included the original Portuguese version accompanied by an English translation to create the opportunity for bilingual readers to evaluate the linguistic nuances of the original texts. Unless otherwise indicated, the translations to English of quotations, titles, and expressions that were originally published in Portuguese or Spanish are mine. Allowing for how broad in scope, and how theoretically diversified *The Ripple Effect* is, I believe academics and lay readers interested in Brazilian culture and literature, and other related areas of study (such as Latin American studies, the African diaspora, and Women's Studies) may find it of interest. The analyses of texts and contexts presented in *The Ripple Effect* articulate a panoramic overview of the Brazilian processes of cultural and literary production. Such considerations serve as a roadmap for a better understanding of how gender and race play out in Brazilian popular culture, and in *capoeira*, in particular. *The Ripple Effect* makes a concerted effort to highlight women's accomplishments, convey their diversified views and insights, and raise questions that could keep the debates on gender and race afloat.

Chapter One

Mapping Asymmetries

The "Ambigious Process of Modernization"

Developed in the nineteenth century under the guidelines of a
society ruled by the coffee barons of São Paulo and other plantation owners, the concept of nationhood in Brazil was recon-
figured in the early decades of the twentieth century. With the
abolition of black slavery in 1888, the fall of the Monarchy, and
the proclamation of the Republic in 1889, the idea of development, growth, and modernization impregnated the political,
social, and economic agendas of the country. Still heavily influenced by positivistic ideas, the governing authorities of the new
Republic strove to adopt prerogatives that would advance the
concept of "order and progress" inscribed on the Brazilian flag.
Changes in immigration and racial policies, the recruitment of
European workers to replace slave labor, and the modernization of the means of transportation by investing in railroad
construction were some of the innovative aspects of the time
(Burns 259–60). With São Paulo playing a leading role, coffee
production rose to a staggering 77% of the world's total sup-
ply and "the influence of coffee extended beyond the realm of
economics into both national and international politics" (Burns
262). Even though there was a strong desire to modernize the
country and jurists had already rewritten some of the old codes
of honor that dated back to colonial and imperial times, in the
first four decades of the twentieth century, Brazilian society was
solidly structured around a "paternalistic and hierarchical social
order" (Caulfield 9). Caught in the ambiguity of the process of
modernization in Brazil, reformers wanted change, but were
concerned about losing their power. This ambiguity, Caulfield
argues, constructed a muddled discourse of modernity which

25

was often expressed through a double standard: when applied to men, it was considered in positive terms (a "progressive rationality"); when applied to women, it was defined in terms of "loose morals and a dissolute lifestyle" (99). As a result, she writes, "this gendered conception of modernity worked symbolically to justify the tutelage of the feminized popular masses by male intellectuals" and "to justify women's subordination to men" (99).

In the early decades of the twentieth century, the patriarchal discourse used several strategies to control women's voices, curtail their choices, and discipline them. The state ideology (which was endorsed by the powers that the domestic and religious structures represented), public wariness, and critical oversight contributed to allow for the implementation of laws designed to "protect" women from what was construed as their immature or inconsequential ways. Those involved in writing policies and passing laws resorted to strategic measures to accomplish their objectives, including penalizing disobedient females by denying them access to several professional fields, deciding where they could work, and establishing a code of conduct to regulate what was considered proper and improper behavior for them. In this environment, it is not surprising that an "honor code" was enforced, the "defense of honor" argument was sustained and, in 1941, the Decree-Law 3.199, which regulated women's access to sports, was issued. The decree established tighter control on Brazilian women's bodies by banning them from participating in any type of fight, or practicing certain sports considered "violent" or deemed unfit for the feminine physique. It patronized, criminalized, and severely limited women's options in terms of sports and leisure activities. Such criminalization was so widely accepted and enforced that it was reiterated and expanded in 1965, during the military dictatorship, and the ban was not revoked until 1979, during the *Abertura* period, when the despotic grip was relaxed, and Brazil slowly returned to a democracy.

In the first half of the twentieth century, women who defied the status quo, or challenged the traditional cultural norms, were perceived as posing a threat to the fabric of Brazilian society. Well into the 1930s, even after women had won the right to vote and had made significant advancements in securing teaching jobs and other positions in public service, they were still "warned not to allow the exercise of their 'rights' [to vote, work, run for office] to interfere with the performance of their most essential familial 'duties'" (Besse 10). They were informed that their rights should not prevent them from fulfilling their seemingly "natural" role as household managers, intelligent socialites, and child bearers. There was such a pervasive contempt for women's civil rights and a widespread fear that they would challenge the conservative morality of the time that taboo subjects such as prostitution, abortion, birth control methods, and sexual emancipation did not generate public discussion, and Feminism was ridiculed (Hahner 123, 150, 152–53). In attempting to tame the feminist movement and keep it circumscribed within the conventional boundaries of "acceptable" behavior for women, avid antifeminists and political conservatives directed their attacks on the liberal feminists and strategically used ridicule to intimidate women. Hahner examines several instances in which educators, the police, and the media punished females by having them arrested or subjected to verbal humiliation for demanding equal rights or challenging the conventional morality of the time (150–53).

Similar arguments appear in Besse's study about gender inequity in Brazil in which she discusses how the political and social apparatus contributed to establish a negative perception of women who defied the moral standards of the time. She asserts that educators, physicians, lay Catholic organizations, lawmakers, jurists, labor unions, and government agencies worked together to avoid the dissolution of customs in order to "protect" Christian families from degeneration (1–2). Those involved in creating laws and policies "campaigned to 'regenerate' the family and to elevate it (with women at its center) as the primary and essential social institution, capable of fostering economic modernization while preserving social order" (Besse 2–3). To project a modern image, the State sent an ambivalent message by also condemning husbands who exercised despotic power over their wives. However, it was a tongue-in-cheek attitude, since the State joined forces with educational, medical, religious, and social organizations to enforce a discourse embedded in pseudo-scientific values that could lend credibility to the repressive system they endorsed (Besse 6). A case in point is that much of the materials published at the time aimed at convincing women "that men sought modest and dignified women for their wives: women who would willingly restrict their social lives, refrain from ostentatious or frivolous behavior, and work hard to become competent housewives" (Besse 69). Therefore, on the surface, the discourse of modernity and its applications seemed to protect women, but underneath the superficial layer simmered the suggestion that females were unable to, or incapable of, making their own decisions as independent thinkers and decision-making adults, a judgment that infantilized and/or crippled their image.

Even though the State and staple institutions used their power to control women and make decisions for them, they also needed female cooperation for their supremacy to work well. As R. W. Connell and James W. Messerschmidt have argued (in an unrelated context), for powerful groups to succeed in attaining and upholding dominance over other groups, and for an agenda to come into play effectively, it is necessary to have "cultural consent, discursive centrality, institutionalization, and the marginalization and delegitimizing of alternatives" (846). In some instances, it also requires cooperation from groups that work from within a movement as is the case with the "official" Feminism of the 1920s and 1930s which embraced the ambivalent prerogatives adopted by the State. The organized feminist movement of the early decades of the twentieth century included a host of women who were not only well educated, but, in numerous cases, also professionally and politically accomplished. They fought for and made significant strides in several areas: they gained better access to education, had more employment opportunities, could vote, and benefited from legal recourses and institutional reforms (Besse 165). They were instrumental in raising their peers' consciousness about civil and political rights and fought hard to legitimize female activities in public spaces. However, as Hahner has argued, those feminists were "neither radical in their goals nor militant in their tactics" and their movement "grew more conservative as it became more respectable and acceptable by the ruling elites" (180). The conservative feminists did not support the counter-discourse of the liberal feminists, aligning themselves with the patriarchal order. In many ways, they acquiesced to the system in hope of being included, respected, and accepted by the male leaders. In such a cultural, social, and political scenario, libertarian feminists were often ignored, mocked, or prosecuted (Besse 165). Consequently, by embracing some patriarchal tenets, the women who adopted the official Feminism weakened their movement as a whole and contributed for it to become increasingly traditional. Those attitudes had lasting repercussions on the way Feminism was (and still is) perceived in Brazil by the general public. (For a number of people "feminism" is a "dirty word," and is often overridden and berated as "lesbianism," perceptions that stigmatize both gender and sexual preference.)

The anarchists and the libertarian feminists of the first decades of the twentieth century established a counter-discourse by criticizing the organized/official Feminism's silence on key issues such as divorce, sexual freedom, and female proletariat. That counter-movement also criticized the conservative Feminism's acceptance of the subordination of women within the family, especially the importance attached to chastity, which was so crucial that when in doubt, middle-class families paid doctors to verify their daughters' virginity. Throughout the 1920s and 1930s, medical and legal discussions and publications about complacent hymens were common, and verification of a woman's virginity was an acceptable practice. Such an intrusive procedure remained "a powerful means not only of validating deflowering complaints, but also of disciplining young women" (Caulfield 121). Throughout the country, in religious and lay conservative circles of Brazil, the importance given to women's virginity and chastity was paramount and lasted well into the 1970s, especially in middle-class homes, and in less industrialized and/or more conservative areas of the country. Females had little or no recourse to file complaints because most men accused of rape or other sexual crimes "were either acquitted or released without trial" (Caulfield 2). Impunity for other acts of severe violence against females (such as wife-beating or murder) was also often discarded on the grounds that those crimes "were committed 'in a justified state of uncontrollable passion,' which everyone understood meant that the man had acted 'in defense of honor'" as Caulfield contends (3). Such honor, as she further explains, "not only survived in twentieth-century law," but also gained prominence, and "'modernized' the legal defense of honor" (4–5, 9). Yet, not all women were silenced or intimidated by the tight patriarchal control. It was during this time that many female writers voiced their concerns. No other cultural or artistic production offered a more detailed criticism of the androcentric grip than some novels written by females who adopted a liberal form of Feminism. Their texts detailed the blueprint of the control patriarchy exerted over women's physical and symbolic space in Brazil.

The Literary Counter-Discourse

A substantial number of scholars, writers, and artists channeled their prodigious sparks of creativity to defining new aesthetic grounds in the first decades of the twentieth century in Brazil. Without the efforts and the courage of all those who challenged the old views and helped establish new creative patterns, Brazilian literature and other artistic expressions would not have so easily developed a unique profile and an aesthetic maturity capable of securing a special place in the country's history and in the world. While scholars do not always agree on the dates and phases of Modernism (the avant-garde literary and artistic movement of the first decades of the twentieth century), they concur that signs of change were already evident. In 1912, the writer Oswald de Andrade introduced European futurist ideas in the literary and artistic circles of São Paulo, and in 1917, the visual artist Anita Malfatti displayed her work in a solo exhibition. (Monteiro Lobato published a blistering review of the exhibition which he considered too different from the norm. His narrow-minded views of art impacted her career negatively.)[1]

In the first years of the movement, the modernists' longing for new venues of artistic expression fueled an intellectual revolution that kept an eye on Europe while rooting their creative endeavors in Brazilian traditions and culture. In that environment, the leading modernist group, the organizers of the Week of Modern Art in 1922, sought to "cannibalize" foreign cultures and ideas and blur the division between popular culture and erudite knowledge. In its longing for creative freedom and in their desire to contribute to national development, the modernists focused on Brazilian people, nature, and society. Striving to incorporate national elements in their artistic endeavors, they turned to African and indigenous cultures, and replaced old Brazilian values and obsolete forms of artistic expression with ideas and techniques imbued in the period's definition of progress. In concert with the political and economic instability that dominated the decades between the two World Wars, their hybrid discourse and diversified agenda challenged institutional views, implemented new literary directions, and modernized Brazilian artistic environments. They questioned the literary establishment and artistic environments in Brazil and channeled their creative energy to contribute to the definition of a national identity. Hence, their intellectual venture was rebellious in form, audacious in content, and nationalist in orientation.

Most studies of Modernism in Brazil have focused on the merits of the movement's diverse creative productions. A few scholars, however, have championed the need to analyze the movement in broader terms to insert it into a social and historical context. Wilson Martins, for instance, argues that Modernism was larger than a literary school or an intellectual period; it was "an epoch of Brazilian life inscribed within a wide social and historical process, the source and result of transformations which far overflowed aesthetic frontiers" (7). In a similar vein, Randal Johnson contends that one of the tasks facing critics of Brazilian Modernism "is to broaden and deepen the analysis, resisting limiting canonical interpretations based solely on aesthetic criteria or Eurocentric conceptions of modernism" (210–11). He maintains that the movement should be reinserted in "its objective socio-historical context" and scholars should examine the movement's "different sub-currents, tendencies, and practitioners in terms of their diverse articulations and affiliations with the social and ideological ground" (Johnson 210–11). More recently, works by Idelber Avelar, Christopher Dunn, and Marshall C. Eakin have analyzed it as a counter-discourse or included it within a larger historical and cultural perspective, oftentimes discussing questions related to class and race. Although those studies have increased the field of vision, added latitude to the understanding of the significance of the movement, and contributed to diversify the theoretical approaches to analyze Brazilian Modernism, for the most part, the literary production of women is not a central concern in those studies.

An examination of books on literary history, encyclopedias, anthologies, and textbooks reveals that narratives written by women were rarely anthologized, discussed, or cited until the 1980s. While literary critics occasionally praised some women writers, and even though there were a few female poets whose verses became popular before and after the Week of Modern Art, broadly speaking, progressive women writers were not taken seriously, and seldom was the work of a woman novelist recognized or praised. In the last decades, however, there have been an increasing number of literary critics who have taken a feminist and/or revisionist approach to analyze the project of modernity in Brazil. They have highlighted the canon's omissions and inconsistencies and the exclusion of women writers from the mainstream literary scene of the 1920s and 1930s. To correct discrepancies, some scholars have retrieved texts from obscurity, placed their writing in the larger historical, social, political, and literary context, and analyzed their bold views and innovative styles. They have republished, discussed, and/or translated the works of Bittencourt, Cobra, Galvão, and Pereira which did not receive the critical acclaim they deserved at the time.[2]

A number of conservative critics and literary historians such as José Veríssimo, João Ribeiro, Andrade Muricy, and Tristão de Athayde have dispelled what they label as "the myth of discrimination" against women writers in Brazil by citing Francisca Júlia da Silva Münster, Gilka Machado, Cecília Meireles, and Henriqueta Lisboa as prototypes of successful writers who published before and after the Week of Modern Art. However, even if there was an opening in the Brazilian literary community for those women poets, the themes and subjects they addressed did not challenge the state of affairs. The poetry published by Lisboa, Meireles, and Münster focused on ethereal themes and their verses are often analyzed as mystic and/or didactic. Meireles remains the emblematic woman poet of schoolbooks and anthologies. While the quality of her poems is indisputable, it is also true that literary critics have often used words such as *noble, discrete, airy, delicate, fluid,* and *suave* to describe her poetry (cf. Hulet 120). Machado is another poet who is sometimes cited as an example that there was no discrimination against women writers, regardless of their thematic choices. However, as Nelly Novaes Coelho's research reveals, throughout her publishing career, Machado "fought against a general animosity," and her books did not receive the recognition they deserved because her themes included erotic desire, and she openly questioned bias against women (228). Other literary critics mention Júlia Lopes de Almeida as a prototype of a female fiction writer whose books were widely read, and cite her as an example of the fair treatment women received in the literary establishment. Yet, as Darlene Sadlier contends, Almeida was read mostly because she presented quaint and "charming portraits of wives, mothers, and life in the home" (575).

Texts by Bittencourt, Cobra, Galvão, and Pereira are anarchically different from the *noble, discrete, airy, delicate, fluid,* and *suave* poetry of the period or the charming description of family life. Similar to the literature published by avant-garde male writers and anarchists of the period, these authors discussed multiple operations of power, located sites of struggle, created modes of resistance, and analyzed the junctures where cultural, social, and historical differences are articulated. The difference is that, embedded in the women's innovative style, themes, and narrative techniques were messages intended to raise consciousness and instill a sense of selfhood. For instance, they questioned the roles women were expected to play as mothers and wives in "modernizing" the nation, and overtly addressed topics considered taboo at the time (women's right to a fulfilling sexual life, virginity, abortion, birth control methods, lesbianism, prostitution, and rape). By casting light on the hypocrisy of the religious mentality of the time, and by describing the protagonists' refusal to accept religious paradigms of obedience and abnegation, their novels refuted myths and archetypes (the Virgin Mary, for instance) which contributed to alienate women from their rights. Hence, by fashioning an anarchic counter-discourse in the 1920s and 1930s, they established a contrapuntal position within the newly formed modernist cultural and literary agenda.

Cobra and Galvão voiced their concerns forthrightly by calling the social and historical order into question, and analyzing the fluid structures of class, gender, and race. They used their texts to campaign against the treatment of women as sexual objects for male consumption, condemned violence, and incited women to emancipate their own bodies through the liberation of their sexuality. They also analyzed female prostitution, sickness, and suicide as the result of oppression, poverty, and lack of formal education. By openly discussing sexuality and directing attention to the social, cultural, political, and economic function of the human body, their works also struck numerous blows against patriarchal maneuvers and sexual taboos, and condemned the way families participated in the control of female bodies. In this instance, their thoughts are akin to contemporary theories by Marxist feminists that have analyzed the body as a social and political construction in which the institution of family, domesticity, and work reproduce the sexual division of labor.

Cobra can be considered a modernist writer not only because her style is unmistakably experimental and unconventional, but also, and precisely, because she proposes a revolution in social mores capable of modernizing the country (R. Q. Cobra 4–6). Following a similar line of thought, Susan Quinlan and

Peggy Sharpe argue that the subject matter Cobra discusses is anarchically subversive, thus fitting the revolutionary tenets of 1920s Modernism (28–30). In her texts, Cobra uses humor, parody, and mockery to satirize conservative views and question "acceptable" moral values of the time. The attention Cobra pays to topics concerning women's health, education, and sexuality also establishes a dialogue with other female modernist writers of the period, particularly with Galvão. Considering the audacious topics Cobra presented in her 1927 *Virgindade Inútil: Novela de uma Revoltada* ("*Useless Virginity: A Dissent Novella*"), it is not surprising that it was considered dissolute. As she mentions in the prefatory note of the second edition, governmental-sponsored censors prohibited the circulation of the 1924 edition of her book-length theoretical essay, *Virgindade Anti-higiênica: Preconceitos e Convenções Hipócritas* ("*Unhygienic Virginity: Prejudice and Hypocritical Conventions*"), on the premise that it was pornographic and degraded the morality of the time (109).[3] Her publications underwent state scrutiny because of her thematic choices. Based on interviews she conducted with Cobra's relatives, Maria Lúcia de Barros Mott states that, in the 1930s, Getúlio Vargas's special police interrogated Cobra several times because her inflamed discourse was considered potentially dangerous to the regime. Rejected by her family and fearing prosecution and imprisonment, she changed her name and moved to the state of Paraná, in the South of Brazil, and in the later stages of her life, moved to Argentina (Mott 99).

Virgindade Inútil's plot presents an undeniable urgency or impatience in its fast-moving chapters, and an anarchic use of language and characterization. The novel attacks the government's indifference regarding public health, education, and moral issues and gives a sardonic description of Brazil as Bocolândia ("A Fool's Republic"). Using irony, parody, and double-entendre, Cobra objects to the country's ambiguous discourse and paints a graphic description of the double moral standards of the time. A case in point is a passage in which the narrator discusses the discrimination unmarried women ("spinsters") and prostitutes suffer in a society that values marriage as the supreme measure of women's respectability and worth. The narrator seizes the opportunity to underscore the hypocritical values attributed to marriage and the economic contract it represents by revealing that, even though the protagonist is an intelligent, pious, and educated young woman, the doctor to whom she had been promised in marriage calls off the wedding when her family faces bankruptcy. Rebelling against social and moral conventions, the hypocrisy of family values, and the importance attached to virginity, still a minor, Cláudia flees from home and willingly loses her virginity to a stranger during a train trip. When the family locates her, she is submitted to a medical-legal exam to check whether she is still a virgin and is subsequently committed to an asylum to be "rehabilitated." Cláudia's rebellious actions expose the double standards and blind spots of the morality of the time, revealing the conundrum of the "ambiguous project of modernity" (as Caulfield would argue) that focused on "progress" while excluding non-conforming and liberal women from its core propositions. The protagonist's life story is also described as a project of self-discovery. As Cláudia strives to define herself as a woman and a citizen in a society dominated by conflicting and duplicitous values, her epistemological desire to learn how to challenge the social and moral values of her time becomes her utmost anthological quest.

In tandem with Cobra's texts, Galvão's 1933 novel, *Parque Industrial: Romance Proletário* (published in English as *Industrial Park*, 1993) addresses feminist topics forthrightly, revealing little ambivalence or disguise in intentions. Most of the characters are anarchists and proletarian women placed against the background of São Paulo's growing bourgeois class. Galvão's text underscores the stark polarities between classes and the feminization of poverty represented by the increasing number of female factory work-ers and slum dwellers. The narrative harshly satirizes São Paulo's female bourgeoisie, attacking ideological precepts and issues related to wealthy, intellectual, and white women who adopted or sided with the premises of the "official" Feminism (Besse 164; Unruh 197). David William Foster argues that Galvão depicts females "who inhabit a range of margins of society because of their conditions as prostitutes, women of color, immigrants, and the destitute and dying," and "women who are agents of a savage capitalism because they are in a position to exploit other women" (27). Questioning the conservative definition of womanhood and the parameters set to control female sexuality, Galvão envisioned the need for social, economic, and political transformations that would allow female subjects to take control of their bodies. In this instance, she criticizes the conservative Feminism for adopting patriarchal values and ridicules women's naiveté, or their lack of understanding that selecting their own careers and making personal family choices should be a right, not a patriarchal concession.

The chapters and dialogues of *Parque Industrial* are short, and the narrator's intrusions and comments are punctuated with exclamation points indicating the ironic tone Galvão adopts in the novel. The text promotes ideological transformations and emphasizes a dialectic discourse with Marxist overtones, describing the oppression of the working class in São Paulo, when the city was deeply committed to its process of industrialization. The titles of every chapter illustrate these points: they focus on factory workers; denounce the dismal socioeconomic conditions the working class experienced; and address class struggle, division of wealth, economic surplus, public health and education, and political unrest. In addition, Galvão goes beyond other socially committed writers of the time who also discussed organized labor, division of class, and poverty, by treating gender concerns as a social issue. She also challenges the status quo and questions the moral rules of the time by addressing sexual taboos more directly and placing their characters outside the family circle (Owen 71). Galvão relies on her faith that a fair distribution of wealth and an equitable stratification of social, economic and political power can change all relations, including the dynamics of gender. Her discussion of domination and exploitation, as it relates to gender and class, predates one of the platforms of late twentieth-century Feminism which draws attention to the (oftentimes conflicting) partnership between Marxism and Feminism.

Paralleling the social and racial struggles that the novel emphatically describes, there is also a sexual tension which is expressed not only through the linguistic urgency of the short sentences, but also in the choice of vocabulary, and in the allusion and/or metonymic references to sexuality. Similar to Cobra's criticism of the code of honor concerning female chastity and virginity, Galvão includes a passage in *Parque Industrial* that discusses how parents joined force with lawmakers, jurists, and doctors to enforce the paramount importance of virginity to safeguard the virtuous space of the family. The passage describes Dirce (a young, rebellious, and wealthy woman) who was examined by a doctor because her father suspected she was no longer a virgin. In the chapter "Instrução Pública" ("Public Instruction"), Galvão questions the importance given to virginity by describing the sexual tension existent in schools between male teachers and female students, and the potential for sexual abuse in those places. She extends the rape metaphor (of the male teachers brazenly entering the classrooms) to discuss the exploitation of workers by the bourgeoisie and describe the violence and intimidation perpetrated by those who represent institutions of power and authority (such as the police, family, church, and legal and medical Systems). She also depicts the actions of a young, rich, and bored man who entertains himself by raping and impregnating an impoverished adolescent, and then abandoning her to fend for herself and suffer dire consequences. Galvão finds an effective way to reflect on the reality of people who live beyond the gates of São Paulo's mansions, especially those who populate poor neighborhoods, prostitution houses, and/or work in factories. In those instances, her choice of vocabulary is harsh and cold like São Paulo's industrial park.

In discussing the lack of critical reception of Galvão's novel, K. David Jackson finds it telling that "although equal to the radical social criticism in novels by Oswald de Andrade and Jorge Amado, writers later considered central to nationalist concepts of literary modernism," Galvão's novel was hardly noticed or "was not mentioned in any subsequent major history of Brazilian literature" (126). Foster also shares this interpretation, commenting that the academic establishment showed lack of interest in a woman's proletarian novel, published when literature addressing working-class topics was popular (32–33). The flimsy critical reception that *Parque Industrial* received at the time can be attributed to Galvão's account of women's voices, and her politicization of themes considered taboo subjects such as labor exploitation, syndical organization, and sexuality (Jackson 126; Foster 32–33). Those topics fell outside the conventional framework of subjects women usually addressed in their texts. While Galvão's literary talent is undeniable, the media ignored her texts, focusing on her personal life, and paying attention to the ways she challenged the moral limits of the time. The media discussed the uninhibited way she dressed and talked, her participation in political protests, arrests, and involvement with the Communist Party (Besse 181–83; Boaventura 151–64; Jackson 115–53; Risério 19–21; Unruh 196–98).

Galvão is a revealing example of the slanted process of inclusion and exclusion of women in the early phases of the modernist movement. The fact that she embodied Paulo Menotti del Picchia's fanciful project for a modernist "muse" is sometimes confused with a positive critical reception of her texts. Vicky Unruh captures this misunderstanding and argues that the radical modernists adopted the young and irreverent writer, transmuting her into "the performing New Woman of *antropofagia*, the embodiment of its primitivistic aesthetic," a status substantiated by the poet Raul Bopp who "rechristened her as 'Pagu'" and "celebrated her 'come-and-go body'" (195). Fear of exclusion or persecution, or the need to fit in, may explain why she accepted the "modernist muse" position while fostering her "own critical ambush of *antropofagia*" (Unruh 217). This fear may also explain her problematic relationship as a woman and a writer with the Communist Party, a relationship so riddled with double standards that she published *Parque Industrial* under the pseudonym Mara Lobo to avoid clashing with "the authoritarian directives of the Communist Party in which she was attempting to hold an honorable place" (Foster 33). In a way, she found herself in an ambivalent position: she craved the sense of belonging that the avant-garde artists and the Communist Party provided, while simultaneously criticizing them. She strove to be taken seriously as a young Communist, while questioning some of the Party's dictates and, in her writing, she explicitly parodied her male literary peers (Oswald de Andrade, for instance, with whom she was romantically involved).

Similar to Cobra and Galvão, Bittencourt also innovates literarily, and her 1929 text *A Sua Excia. A Presidenta da República no Ano 2500* ("*Your Excellency: The President of the Republic in the Year 2500*") exhibits a penchant for parody, satire, and ironic humor. The novel is also stylistically and linguistically innovative in that it presents a form of anarchism attuned with the discourse of the modernist avant-garde. In the introductory pages, she warns that the narrative deviates from the established literary models because it is highly experimental with form and plot, defies genre classification, and may be read as a criticism of Brazilian society, a pedagogical tool, or a fictional work. To achieve a chameleonic and episodic quality, the novel draws on several genres, presents cutting-edge narrative techniques, utilizes linguistic and stylistic devices, experiments with spatial dislocation, and implements frequent temporal shifts. Therefore, comparative to works by her contemporary male peers, *Sua Excelência* also innovates in aesthetic experimentation, literary devices, and narrative structure, fitting well into the modernist agenda of the 1920s and 1930s.

The ultramodern and ideal society that Bittencourt describes seems, at times, so implausible, and darkly humorous that it fits into a tongue-in-cheek framework of a futuristic Brazil. Her narrative devices (such as her frequent use of superlatives, exclamation points, and her satirical comments) support this argument. Her novel describes a highly industrialized and technological country governed by Mariângela de Albuquerque, a twenty-eight-year-old woman, who is elected Brazil's first female president. The fact that it would take Brazil nearly six centuries to reach the condition of a "superior culture" and have a female president may also be interpreted as a derisive comment on the country's steadfast "progress." The narrative voice also pledges a woman's right to vote and compete in the job market, campaign for education, advocate social and political rights for women, and criticize the government's indifference to Brazil's poor and illiterate citizens. The text also focuses on the effects of the state's intervention into the private sphere of the family, discusses the Catholic Church's compliance with patriarchal maneuvers, and addresses the negative influence that the Eugenics movement had in women's lives. (A case in point is the description of Mariângela's suffering because she has to order the execution of a famous and talented painter with whom she is in love because he is disabled.) In addition, the novel questions laws which limit females' social mobility and berates the cynicism of politicians who voted for and/or campaigned against women's emancipation.

Sua Excelência's plot describes the summit of an advanced and eugenic society,[4] highly controlled by the State. In that society, women have some privileges (for instance, they can be elected to the highest office of the country), but, even in the year 2500, countless generations of future mothers are required to enroll in the State-sponsored institution called Escola das Mães ("Mothering School"), an institution designed to teach women the chores and zeal of motherhood and wifehood. The institution's primary goal is to turn them into pious and obedient wives and to lead them into believing that an unswerving dedication to raising their children is the largest (if not the only) major contribution a woman can make to develop a great nation. The author questions the dominance of ideas riddled by a tyrannical ethos and by a fascist system of values and mocks references to women treated and/or described as "the angels of home" (177). In this instance, Bittencourt's analysis of the roles women were expected to play is in line with Bourdieu's theoretical discussions about the reasons for the exclusion of women from the realm of serious things and public affairs. For him, they were "confined to the domestic universe and the activities associated with the biological and social reproduction of the lineage" so that they could play their "feminine" role in society (*Masculine* 97).

Quinlan and Sharpe offer informed analyses of how Bittencourt discusses Eugenics, motherhood, and Feminism in *Sua Excelência* (19–20, 24). They interpret the novel as a sign of her alignment with the Feminine Republican Party of the 1920s and 1930s and consider that her definition of womanhood is ambiguously entangled with the social and biological theories of her time. They also discuss the novel as a utopian discourse, an illustration of the tenets of Marinetti's Futurism, and an emblem of the modernist agenda. Débora R. S. Ferreira follows this line of thinking as she asserts that Bittencourt's "national utopia is constructed following totalitarian, eugenic, and fascist principles" (52). While appreciating their readings, I undertake a different approach by analyzing Bittencourt's text as a parody of the "advanced" and eugenic society of the future, and by analyzing the narrative's subtle, but derisive tone, as signs that the author undermines the very principles the narrator so painstakingly works to establish. In my view, Bittencourt's use of ambiguity has a camouflage effect that masks the narrative's sarcastic penchant and establishes the text's propositions as a double discourse. For instance, the narrative voice indicates that, even in 2500, nearly six centuries beyond the time of the novel's publication, women would still need to comply with the obligation to prime Brazilian society for greatness by fully applying themselves to their "subliminal" role of mothers. The sardonic and/or parodic tone of the narrative also undermines patriarchal parameters by discrediting the bylaws, hygienic precepts, and rational norms which stemmed from the scientific discourse of the time. It also reveals the absolute control of the State over the family structure as it compares the discrepancy between having a young woman as president while every female is subject to the state-imposed rules of the "Mothering School" which epitomizes the sublimation and the de-realization of women as individuals.

The reading of the text as a parody also allows for an understanding of *Sua Excelência* as a counter-discourse of the futuristic project of Modernism (championed by Oswald de Andrade, following the tenets of Marinetti's Futurism). Bittencourt highlights the dismal and dehumanizing effects of ultra-modernization by using a diversity of narrative techniques that serve to disguise the narrator's piercing criticism of the loss of individual freedom at the hands of a totalitarian regime. She also uses an ambiguous and ambivalent discourse to mock the notion of a racially, socially, economically, and politically "developed" Brazil of 2500. Even if the author hides behind the veil of parody to avoid the direct critical approach taken by Cobra and Galvão, her parodic analysis of Brazilian society offers a sound literary illustration of the view of womanhood as a sort of "intertext,"[5] or a "subtext," culturally inscribed by the patriarchal discourse. Her criticism of Brazilian society (as she predicts it to be six hundred years into the future) echoes the theoretical commentary historians, social scientists, and literary critics present of the ambiguity of the patriarchal order as it relates to women's causes.

Similar to the position adopted by her peers, Pereira also discusses race, class, and gender discrimination, and strives to raise women's political responsiveness in her novels. In *Maria Luiza* (1933), the narrator criticizes the lack of social, economic, and moral opportunities for women and examines the cultural, social, and political changes at the turn of the century, revealing that, decades after the abolition of slavery, racism and the white elite's slave-holder mentality were still prominent in that society. Pereira centers the story on a love triangle and mocks the elitist and Marxist discourse of Maria Luiza's lover. The narrative focuses on the protagonist's powerful sexual attraction to a man who offers her the novelty of exciting intellectual conversations and a gratifying sexual liaison, and thus breaks with the prevailing romantic notion that fulfilling sex for women can only exist if it is intertwined with love. This aspect of the novel echoes the proposition Cobra presents in *Virgindade Inútil*, in which she establishes that "physical love is as necessary to a woman as eating and drinking" (44).[6] Such an interpretation was quite a scandalous assessment for the 1920s and 1930s, but a groundbreaking interpretation of women's rights. For instance, their views predated Sharon Hite's celebrated report on female sexuality, published in 1976, by approximately half a century.

Pereira discusses the protagonist's longings, fears, struggles, doubts, and reveals the character's desire to subvert and undermine the moral standards of the time by rebelling against her rigid up-bringing. She also affords the reader the opportunity to hear the protagonist's own version of her infidelity and her analytical take on the motivations for such a marital escapade. Maria Luiza also undergoes phases in which, driven by shame and self-reproach, she transfers the guilt she feels about her infidelity to her husband's incapacity to please her sexually, or by rationalizing that she committed adultery because of her "weak feminine nature" (207). This last argument also indicates that she struggles with the ideology she has internalized during her process of socialization in which she was taught to denigrate her own sex, or nature, to become subservient to the cultural, economic, political, religious, and social domains of her society. Pereira grounds the narrative energy in the contradictory values that Maria Luiza wants to reconcile: the protagonist is often caught between her sense of duty to her role as a mother and a wife, and the burning desire to free herself from those bonds. By examining Maria Luiza's wavering thought process and moral dilemma, Pereira also exposes deadlocks and the blind spots of the patriarchal discourse to which women also subscribe.

Pereira uses the narrative technique of constructing and de-constructing arguments to decide who or what led Maria Luiza to commit adultery. In the process, she showcases the protagonist wrestling with her guilt feelings, and longing to find an excuse, or an explanation for her behavior. Such literary strategy of rationalization and the dubious process of self-validation/condemnation bear some similarities to the characterization of Bento in Machado de Assis's *Dom Casmurro*. In that novel, Machado takes every opportunity to highlight Bento's weak character, paranoia, and obsessive nature, while also intermittently suggesting that Capitu may have been unfaithful to her husband. Pereira picks up from where Machado left off and adds a unique female perspective to her novel: in some ways *Maria Luiza* reads as a literary response to Bento's account, especially because, unlike him, she learns to take responsibility for her own acts. At the end of the novel, the protagonist finally realizes that agency comes at a price; she learns that true liberation requires the courage to examine moral codes and question old-fashioned values, but it also means facing the consequences of the choices one makes.

Also published in 1933, *Em Surdina* ("*In a Whisper*") centers on the protagonist's refusal to marry for convenience, and the negative connotation that aging has for females. To communicate the need for change, she constructs a pedagogical character to speak from one generation to the next as Cecília mentors her young niece on how to develop modes of defiance. Although she knows that resistance cannot efface strategies of power completely, she expects to teach the youngster to strengthen her position in the family circle by locating and challenging sites of oppression. She hopes to instill in her the desire to overturn or, at least, minimize social, institutional, and sexual discrimination in order to build a more self-governing future for her and forthcoming generations. This novel presents another significant analytical focus as Pereira highlights the impact that aging has on the depreciation of women in society. The narrative voice compares the social opportunities that a bachelor has in contrast to the dismal realities of a single woman and evaluates the double standards applied to male and female sexual choices. The concerns Pereira presents in this text resonate with Gari Lesnoff-Caravaglia's theorizing about the concept of aging for women in Western societies in which he considers that the word bachelor "connotes something of freedom, a sexually fulfilled life, or at least a life full of many kinds of social opportunities," while the words "spinster" and "old maid" refer to a woman who supposedly "failed" to attract a husband (17).

Pereira describes Cecília's uncle as a middle-aged, handsome bachelor on vacation from his diplomatic post in Europe who becomes the most coveted male in town as he charms the young women and amuses himself with the patriarch's expectations that he will propose to one of their daughters. By comparison, at the end of the novel, Cecília is a single, twenty-nine-year-old woman (nearly half her uncle's age), whose prospects of receiving another marriage proposal are quite dim. Her circle of family and friends pity and censure her for having challenged the status quo because they cannot understand or sympathize with the fact that twice she turned down the opportunity to marry, missed the chance to validate herself as a member of society, and placed her body at the margins of reproduction. In their eyes, her defiance and resistance to comply with social and familial roles epitomize her as an untrained and inadequate woman. Therefore, by comparing the social choices Cecília and her uncle had, and by emphasizing the gendered double standards of the time, the novel establishes a piercing criticism on the ways society views female aging and sexuality.

Published in 1938, the novel *Amanhecer* ("*Awakening*") discusses the relationship that a provincial young woman (Aparecida) develops with a militant Communist named Antônio. In this text, Pereira returns to the failed partnership between Feminism and Marxism that she had introduced in *Maria Luiza* but presents a new variant. In analyzing the emotional underpinnings of their relationship, Pereira makes a keen critical commentary on how male intellectuals of the time who were militant communists, anarchists, or socialists would often theorize against stratification of class, social rights, equal distribution of wealth, and other topics of oppression, but resisted the idea of truly integrating gender issues into their theoretical precepts. Antônio reflects on the callousness of the bourgeoisie, and the hypocrisy of the Church, and raises Aparecida's consciousness about class polarities in Brazil. He awakens in her the desire to break away from her provincial lifestyle, coaches her on the need to have an education and a career, and warns her about the danger of depending on marriage for financial stability. In addition, he makes a concerted effort to tutor her about women's rights and prerogatives and educates her about sexual liberation. However, he cannot follow his own teachings and behaves as an arrogant intellectual who not only patronizes her, but also plays games to keep her bound to his personal power. Cristina Ferreira-Pinto analyzes this characteristic of *Amanhecer*, arguing that Aparecida had assimilated an ideology that renders women inferior to men and dependent on their goodwill and, because of that, she could not become a strong person, find existential meaning in herself, or establish an equal and sustainable relationship with Antônio (57). Although Aparecida defies several conventions and rules of Brazilian society at the time, she cannot free herself from the "Penelope complex" as she sits and waits for him to rescue her, or to add meaning to her life. The last sentence of the novel (which ends in a question mark) seems to problematize her sexual and emotional relationship with him, and also indicates an embryonic consciousness-raising process taking place as the protagonist realizes that the concept of an identity springs from the ability to develop a personal history that is not only interlocked with others, but also removed from situations of fierce dependency.

In Pereira's three texts addressed in this study, she establishes an environment in which her characters wrestle with profound emotional and moral crises as they attempt to define themselves and analyze their roles in the family. While she shares with Bittencourt a less abrasive form of criticism, thematically, she supported ideas which are closer to those proposed by Cobra and Galvão. Pereira also argues against social conventions and institutions, discussing the social and cultural production of sexuality. Her texts question the historical and social process, and probe deep into questions of gender, race, divisions of wealth, and religious dogma. Like her peers, Pereira politicizes the private sphere of the family, disempowering the hierarchy that the roles of wifehood and motherhood precipitate. In their quest for self-knowledge, her female characters also analyze the cultural, religious, and social contexts which their conflicts reflect and/or describe. However, her position, in relation to gender issues was ambivalent and contradictory. As a novelist, Pereira berated patriarchal beliefs by creating liberal characters that searched to establish an identity as full-fledged citizens and rebelled against hypocrisy, domination, and double standards. But, as a literary critic, she aligned herself with the male conservative group and undermined the accomplishments of other female writers.

Rachel de Queiroz remains the only female novelist of the 1930s whose texts received critical and public acclaim, and appropriately, she earned a place in the Brazilian Academy of Letters (in 1977 she became the first woman to be elected to that institution). Her early novels focus on social issues concerning the Northeast region, a literary trend so popular at the time that Fred P. Ellison, among other critics, considers that it defined the Brazilian novel in the 1930s. In examining the feminization of the national discourse in Queiroz's novels, Joanna Courteau argues that in her first three novels,[7] the female protagonists challenge the patriarchal discourse, but only superficially. Courteau explains that ambivalence by submitting that, even though there is an attempt on the protagonists' part to question the status quo, they do not really subvert the dominant precepts of the time because the protagonists of her early novels crave maternity and domesticity as a grounding center for their life experiences (750). Considering the arguments that Besse, Caulfield, and Hahner present that what it meant to be a feminist was an issue of great contention from the 1910s to the 1930s, and that women described as anarchists and libertarian feminists threatened the popular imagination, it is not surprising that, given her privileged position in the male-dominated literary environment and the Communist Party, Queiroz distanced herself from any association with radical Feminism. Aligned with a centrist movement on women's issues, like many intellectual women of the time, the novelist rejected the ideas expressed by liberal Feminism and even snubbed the "feminist" label on the grounds that there had never been discrimination against women in Brazil (Ferreira 89). She endorsed the organized Feminism of the 1920s and 1930s which "negotiated a minefield"[8] with the patriarchal discourse, that is, women would win access to education, employment, and suffrage, but, in turn, would leave the core principles of patriarchal morality untouched. In other words, women would have the right to vote, work, and run for office if those activities did not interfere with their roles of household managers and child bearers, as Besse would argue.

To a certain extent, it is possible to compare Queiroz's professional trajectory as a novelist to Pereira's as a literary critic. The former was the truly acclaimed female novelist of the 1930s and the latter was the only female literary critic in Brazil who was fully accepted into academic circles of the time. As a literary critic, Pereira complied with male-defined rules, adopted her male peers' attitude, and ignored female authors almost entirely because she did not believe that they contributed significantly to the development of Brazilian literary tradition. As Elizabeth A. Marchant concludes, for Pereira "to assert her voice as a woman and a literary critic, she was required to participate in a discourse that served to erase women's voices" (18). It is ironic that, despite the high aesthetic quality of her novels, they were undermined by the reactionary mentality that she also represented. Hence, Pereira seems to have played a double role: as a critic she aligned herself with the "bearded academy" (Marchant's expression), but as an author she challenged the status quo. Considering that the institution of Family was the pillar on which patriarchy built its moral arguments, her characters tender progressive views by critically analyzing the hypocrisy of conventional marriage, and the notorious concept of prostitution as "a necessary evil," that is, a way to protect honest and pious single women from the irrepressible forces of male sexual drive. Thus, it is possible that Pereira's candid analysis of the standard arguments of Brazilian society can have negatively impacted the reading public's opinion and the critical reception of her texts.

As their narratives reveal, Bittencourt, Cobra, Galvão, and Pereira problematized crucial issues in women's struggles against oppression and contributed to the expansion and understanding of cultural and aesthetic frontiers. These novelists incorporated the modernist avant-garde agenda and ethos into their narratives while simultaneously subverting the established discourses. They articulated new ideological grounds by offering literary alternatives to the models of the time and broadening the feminist discursive focus to include discussions of age, class, and race. Their insightful and unconventional narratives also contributed to a more diversified framework of the period by enhancing the debate on gender relations and dramatizing the process of cultural, social, political, and literary dislocation imposed on women. These four authors added a unique accent to the polyphonic voices of Brazilian Modernism and substantiated a counter-discourse within the literary and theoretical framework of the 1920s and 1930s. Their narratives also contributed to survey the role gender played in the establishment of a national identity and drew attention to women of color and several other underprivileged segments of society.

For their perceptive way of analyzing female polyphonic voices, Cobra and Bittencourt (in the 1920s) and Galvão and Pereira (in the 1930s) are instigators of progressive forms of feminist critical thinking. The "protocol of entanglement"[9] that their polemic views established reveals their contrapuntal positions and contributes to expose the double-binds and blind spots of the sanctioned Feminism of the time. Their narratives added a fresh perspective to Brazilian literature and added weight to liberal Feminism by addressing the politics of the "official" movement and pluralizing it by insisting that class, race, and age are the catalysts of different experiences for women. They examined the politics of cultural practices, censured the ascending social, intellectual, and economic classes for their lack of concern for others, and criticized the government's indifference to the less-privileged population. Their texts also defended the right to education, equal rights and opportunities, better working conditions, and improved social provisions for all citizens. They refuted double standards, questioned the institution of marriage as devised at the time, ridiculed role playing in the dynamics of gender, and emphasized the importance of education for women's emancipation from the androcentric grip. In summary, they not only fought for the choice to work, vote, select a career, and practice any sport, but also rejected traditional social structures, questioned the motivation of time-honored institutions, and rebelled against the constraints placed on women's bodies and sexuality. As the six novels discussed reveal, patriarchal societies customarily enforce binary differentiations, emphasize the division of labor, and establish structures of power and male domination, both at home and in public spheres. They often measure virility and appraise masculinity by the emotional, physical, economic, and social control men have over their families and estates.

The "Defense of Honor" Theory

The tight control patriarchs had in defining morality in the earlier decades of the twentieth century, and the parameters used to define masculinity in traditional environments, played a key role on how women were, and still are, perceived in Brazil. If chastity and virginity were associated with honest and single women, masculinity and virility became milestones used to define what it meant to be a man in Brazilian society. Embedded in the definition of an "honorable" woman in Brazil was the strict supervision and enforcement of female fidelity, virginity, and chastity. Female adultery was also construed as proof that a man failed in his role as the guardian of private virtues and thus it could be a serious blow to his identity as a male, and potentially destabilize the parameters by which he and his peers judged him superior, smarter, and stronger than the opposite sex. To safeguard male "honor," for centuries, societies around the world have used harsh methods to punish female infidelity. Feeling betrayed, demoralized, humiliated, and defeated on their own turf, men could counter-attack by shaming females in public, expelling them from the family, or approving their killing.

For conservative branches of society, the concept of honor for men and women are quite dissimilar, a difference that Bourdieu highlights as he distinguishes two types of gender-related honor. He contends that, for a woman, honor "can only be defended or lost, since her virtue is judged successful by her virginity and fidelity," whereas for a "real" man the concept of honor is not attached to sexuality, but rather to "pursuing glory and distinction in the public sphere" (*Masculine* 51). Such glory and distinction would not be attained in Brazil if a man was considered a *corno* (cuckold), in which case he would fear the opinion of his peers who could interpret the woman's infidelity as a sign that he was incapable of exerting power and authority over his household. (Significantly there is not a commonly accepted, or used, feminine counterpart for the Portuguese word *corno*.)[10] The image of an unfaithful wife (or a fiancée, and even a lover) can still have damaging effects on a man's pride, especially in highly conservative circles of Brazilian society because female infidelity is considered an act of defiance, or civil disobedience that can denigrate his reputation. To rectify the act of a woman's infidelity, lessen the negative impact it could have on his reputation, and thus remedy the situation, a man could exercise his "right and duty" to clear his reputation by inflicting cruel treatment (including death) on the women who dared to challenge the status quo. As discussed in the Coda, the news in Brazil is still peppered with references to femicide (*femicídio*) and other types of gender-related violence.

A woman looking for love or sex outside her house could also raise suspicions about her partner's virility or his ability to please her sexually. Either case could be interpreted as a testimony of a man's malfunction as a virile male. Female unfaithfulness was perceived as such an overpowering attack on a man's identity that the only way to defend his manhood and restore respectability to the family name was "to wash his honor in blood" (*lavar a honra com sangue*), in other words, to practice "honor killing." The "defense of honor" theory was often used in Brazil, until 1991, to excuse and sanction men's violent behavior when their wives or partners deceived them romantically and/or sexually.[11] Such an extreme measure had two main goals: to prevent the public from casting doubt on a man's sexual performance and prowess, and set an example for other disobedient females, sending them a memorable warning about the dangers of such audacity. To excuse men's cruelty, it was necessary to shift the blame to the other side, that is, explain female infidelity as a perversion, a genetic or hereditary malfunction. Like weeds to be plucked out of a flower bed, the "malformed" and sinful women would be eradicated for the benefit of social order, and men would perform an act of "goodness" to society by preventing the "disease" from spreading to future generations.

In Brazil, male infidelity fell (and still falls) into a different category. It often codifies a feeling of power and entitlement that adds a positive connotation to the myth of the daring adventurer or conqueror whose expertise in the art of lovemaking makes him desirable to females and envied by his peers. An unfaithful husband often expects his wife to forgive his extra-marital adventures and improve her appearance so that he will be more interested in staying at home. Typically, men are not alone in this kind of thinking: it is not unusual for women to side with this point of view and go to extremes to look sexy to keep their men faithful and at home. Even in the new millennium, women are still expected to show their capacity to forgive by ignoring or pardoning their husbands, lovers, or fiancés when they betray them sexually. This behavior has a constant presence in *telenovelas* in Brazil, since those serialized dramas often indoctrinate the population that, for the wellbeing and sanctimony of the family, women should exercise forgiveness when their husbands or partners are unfaithful. Considering how vastly popular those dramas are and how they have contributed to "normalize" behaviors, the popular endorsement of those views reveals that male infidelity is not considered a social problem; forgiveness is presented as an essential part of the feminine psyche.

One of the best literary examples of the social, cultural, and legal implications of "the defense of honor" theory can be found in Jorge Amado's popular novel *Gabriela, Cravo e Canela*. It takes place in 1925, in the small port city of Ilhéus, Bahia, the hub of the rich cocoa plantation owners. The novel's thematic overtone is the definition of "progress." In his notional definition of progress, Amado includes cultural, economic, literary, gender, racial, political, and social changes. Central to the novel's plot is the discussion of how important the removal of the port's sandbar is to the progress of the region since it prevents large ships from docking, negatively affecting the exportation of cacao. The sandbar also becomes a metaphorical reference to a hegemonic masculinity that delays cultural and social progress in the city by treating women as second-class citizens. Amado navigates the social landscape of Ilhéus describing the patriarchal grip as a catch-22 situation and analyzing "the cruel law" (as Amado labels honor killings) as an impediment to the region's modernization. Amado's narrator seems to side with theories that explain male privilege as "a trap" because such concession places every man in a perpetual state of tension, having to assert and defend his manliness at all costs, in all circumstances.[12] By discussing the double standards of morality, the definition of masculinity and virility, the division of public and private spaces, and focusing on the dissolution of obsolete customs, Amado questions the social, cultural, and legal parameters of such a patriarchal society.

Central to the novel's thesis is Amado's repudiation of the notorious argument that a man had the right to kill a woman to defend his honor. Even though it was not part of the Penal Code, the "defense of honor" was a frequent and successful argument that lawyers used to acquit their clients in Ilhéus. Amado's narrator questions the norm that had allowed rich plantation owners not only the right to rule over their land with devastating determination, but also to subordinate their families, workers, and townspeople to the power and authority of their skewed perception of rights and prerogatives. Amado's novel reveals that, if a woman's adultery (or even the hypothesis of unfaithfulness) could lead men to commit violent acts, a male's infidelity was approached from a completely different viewpoint. Male infidelity was a source of pride because it also stressed a man's dominance as an alpha-male and could prove to his peers that he had power, control, and territorial dominance. In this sense, comments uttered by Amado's narrator analyze the concept of manliness in a manner similar to Bourdieu's concept of "relational notion," described in *Masculine Domination* as "construed in front of and for other men against femininity, in a kind of fear of the female, firstly in oneself" (53). Amado also discusses the different types of punishment applied to mistress women (in the novel they are young, pretty, and economically underprivileged females) who dare to be unfaithful to the older, married men who support them.

Confronted with a situation in which Gabriela was unfaithful to him, Nacib (who was a foreigner and did not seem to have fully absorbed the moral standards of Ilhéus) did not feel comfortable executing the "defense of honor" code of conduct that would give him the "right" to kill his wife. As a result, he found himself at a difficult crossroad: if he did not kill Gabriela, he would become the laughingstock of the town and probably lose his male customers (he owned a very centrally located and popular bar where all the important townsmen congregated). Since Gabriela was a *parda* young woman from the countryside who had no proper documentation (her birth certificate was falsified for her to marry Nacib), his friends and clients advised him to declare the document invalid and nullify the marriage. However, to prove his manliness, he still needed to apply the treatment reserved for concubines who were considered not worthy of having a man "wash his hands in blood." Thus, Nacib beats up Gabriela and expels her from his home.

In real life, half a century after Amado's description of Ilhéus society, the practice of "honor killing" became a widespread practice in all social echelons in Brazil. It was particularly ironic because its heyday happened at a time when the government boasted about the re-modernization of the country during the "economic miracle" of the 1970s. In analyzing the dynamics of Brazilian society at the time, and the reasons why so many murders of affluent women took place, it seems that the deciding factor was their challenging the status quo and awakening their husbands' jealousy or fear. (Most of the high-profile cases were women who were financially independent, occupied positions in public spaces, and interacted with a large number of people.) The most notorious case of the "defense of honor" in Brazil happened in 1976 when Raul Fernandes do Amaral Street, commonly known as Doca Street, murdered his lover, the thirty-two-year-old socialite Ângela Maria Fernandes Diniz. The legal interpretation the defense lawyers used made the trial notorious and was widely publicized in the national and international news. Diniz was a wealthy woman who was legally separated (*desquitada*)[13] from her husband whom she married at the age of eighteen and with whom she had three children. When their *desquite* was officiated, her influential husband won custody of the children because, as a *desquitada*, Diniz was considered unfit to raise them. Therefore, even if it was possible for women to be legally separated from their husbands, a number of females dreaded the stigma associated with the label because their lifestyle would be scrutinized, and their reputation was bound to be smeared. They would be regarded as sexually liberated women (*mulheres fáceis*), which meant that—since they did not have a husband to control them—they would be prone to promiscuity. In the public eye, *desquitadas* were women who were not dedicated enough to make their marriage work, did not put the well-being of their children above their own personal aspirations, or did not abide by conventional moral standards. *Desquitadas* who did not win the right to raise their children were stigmatized as failed mothers and women incapable of fulfilling their higher duties to the nation. In analyzing the ways in which *desquitadas* were categorized, Mary del Priore elucidates that in the Brazilian environment of that time, *desquitadas* (as well as women who were separated from their husbands) were placed at the same moral level of prostitutes, and would be blamed for any problem their children might have in school (*Mulheres,* 230). As a consequence, to avoid stigmatization or clouding their children's future, most women remained in unhappy or abusive marriages, especially if they could not support themselves. It is worth noting that a man's reputation was not subject to such disgraces because, as previously discussed, the concept of honor for men was differentiated.

When Diniz met Street, he was legally married to Adelita Scarpa, an affluent woman from São Paulo, with whom he had a three-year-old son. Three months before the murder, Street left his wife to live with Diniz, a decision that produced negative public opinion. She was described as a homewrecker, a sinner who deprived a child of his father's companionship. Thus, it is not surprising that when Street murdered Diniz, a number of media reports on the crime were unfavorable to her and sided with his version of the events. The media covered the crime extensively and, in many instances, put Diniz on trial: instead of a murder victim, she was portrayed as a woman unfit to be a good mother and wife, a socialite who loved parties, used drugs, cherished her independence, and was sexually uninhibited. In other words, they claimed that she got what she deserved.

Street's defense lawyers accused Diniz of being engaged in homosexual lovemaking and dissolute behavior, and used such arguments to convince the jury that she was prone to immoral behavior, and that he killed her to "rightfully defend his honor" (*Mulheres* 208). According to the court records, the lawyers also claimed that she had offended him by calling him a *corno* and suggesting a *ménage-à-trois* with a female German tourist who was visiting Brazil at the time. However, as a witness for the prosecution, the cleaning lady who was at the house when the crime happened painted a different picture. Her deposition revealed that Street murdered Diniz because she terminated their relationship and demanded that he leave her beach house in Búzios, a resort town in the state of Rio de Janeiro. According to the housekeeper, in a rampant rage, he drew a pistol from his briefcase and fired four shots at close range to the upper part of her body, disfiguring her face and killing her instantaneously. Priore writes that, as Street's lawyer explained during the trial, the fight began as a fit of jealousy, an attempt on his part to protect his reputation because Diniz tended to compare him to her other lovers (*Mulheres* 208). Disputing Street's version of the crime, and disagreeing with the verdict, Diniz's friends claimed that he already had a history of domestic violence, and that he was a forty-five-year-old *bon vivant* who often lived off the money and prestige he acquired by associating himself with wealthy and socially affluent women. Therefore, they argued, the motive for the crime could also have been his anger at her for terminating the relationship and cutting off his source of income. The fact that he was carrying a gun in his briefcase when he went to her house in Búzios raised suspicions about the argument his defense team used that the murder was an act of uncontrolled passion, a spur-of-the-moment case, the result of fear of losing her because he loved her too much.

Brought to trial in 1976, Street never denied the murder, but the jury sided with his defense team and acquitted him on the grounds of the "defense of honor" argument. To convince the jury, his defense lawyers presented a three-pronged argument that shifted the blame entirely to Diniz: a) they asserted that she had offended the virtues of the Brazilian family; b) she had humiliated him so much that his only choice to save his "honor" was to murder her; and c) he shot her because he loved her too much and could not bear the thought of living without her. Street's legal defense team banked on the fact that conservative circles of Brazil would endorse such killing. The arguments they used implied that, if Street did not react, he would be seen as an individual who was morally deformed, and a socially debilitated person who did not have the strength, or the sagacity, to control his household. It seems that such arguments sounded quite convincing because, in Street's first trial, the crowd (made up of males and females alike) that had been waiting outside the courtroom gave him an ovation as he left the Court House a free man (Priore 208). Considering that Street was no bastion of virtue, and that he was still married at the time of the crime and thus, by definition, was unfaithful to his legitimate wife, the jury's deliberation was tainted with double standards. Consequently, there was no defense of his "honor" (in the most meaningful sense of the word), but rather the defense of his masculinity and/or his lifestyle, and the reinforcement of the patriarchal order. Street's version of the crime motive, the lawyers' defense argument, and the jury deliberation reveal how embedded Brazilian society was—and in some cases still is—in values that, as previously discussed, had been established to exercise control over women's bodies and lives. The definition of honor by which they abided during the trial is rooted in the concepts established in Brazil during colonial times, enforced during Vargas's Estado Novo, and not ruled unconstitutional until the last decade of the twentieth century.

However, not everyone applauded the verdict. The protesters against his acquittal paraded the streets of Brazil carrying banners with the motto: *Quem ama não mata* ("*One Does Not Kill a Loved One*"). Although there were widespread objections from women in Brazil and sympathizers with their cause, it was not until 1979 that Street was retried and condemned but spent merely three and a half years in prison. In 2006, he released a book called *Mea Culpa: O Depoimento que Rompe 30 Anos de Silêncio* ("*Mea Culpa: The Testimony that Breaks 30 Years of Silence*") in which he gives detailed information about meeting Diniz, his extramarital affair, why he left his wife and child to live with her, and how he killed her. As it was made public during Street's trial and acquittal, the impunity sanctioned by the "defense of honor" argument raised questions about the conservative circles of Brazilian society that, to safeguard patriarchal rules and protect a cold-blooded killer, disguised "honor killing" as an act of morality.

The economic hardships of the 1980s and 1990s contributed to put women in the work force in large numbers, balancing the power in households, or at least minimizing the strict division of labor and the separation of private and public spaces according to gender categories. However, in most cases, there was not an inversion of the workplace (men doing domestic chores while women held jobs outside their homes). Quite often, women had double shifts: they would work outside the home, and come back in the evening to cook, clean, take care of the kids, and pay the bills. Priore elucidates that "in 1995, one in every five Brazilian families was led by women who doubled their functions by taking care of the family and pursuing a career" (*Mulheres* 229). Such a change was the direct result of large reforms that had occurred in Brazilian society, especially the role divorce played in freeing the involved parties to break the ties of marriage, and lawfully marry again. Slowly and reluctantly, branches of the Brazilian government let go of the overpowering grip that the Catholic Church exerted on society regarding laws of marriage and, pressured by a substantial number of female voters, divorce was approved in 1977.[14] By 1995, the number of legal separations had risen to 21%, a good indication that religious dogmas and family traditions were losing their power to influence the lifestyle of Brazilian families (*Mulheres* 231). It took nearly two decades, after divorce became legal in Brazil, for the shame associated with the status of a "divorced female" to begin to fade away.

The period comprising the turn of the 1970s and the beginning of the 1980s heralded a revision of the concept of masculinity in Brazil which "coincided with the consolidation of the LGBTQ movement, divorce laws, the beginning of the massive incorporation of middle-class women within the wage labor force, and the marked decadence of the ideal man promoted by the military regime" (Avelar 49). However, considering the larger number of "defense of honor" cases and acquittals of men who perpetrated them, the revisionist argument of masculinity was not extensive or all-embracing. As Priore remarks, in the second half of the 1970s and 1980s, male violence against women increased considerably, permeating every echelon of Brazilian society. The crimes that called more attention were those committed by wealthy and well-educated men who interpreted the feminist advances in the areas of work, education, family relations, and sexuality as threats to the stability of the patriarchal status quo (208–09). The list of honor killings from mid-1970s to early 1980s is long, and all men who perpetrated the crimes used the "defense of honor" argument and were acquitted. In 1980 alone, just in the city of Belo Horizonte, six high-profile women were murdered, including the executive Eloiza Ballestros Stancioli, whose death was based on the suspicion of her infidelity (*Mulheres* 211).[15] Most of those victims were career women, financially independent, young, and able to redo their lives if they were to separate from their husbands. Numerous other cases never made it to mainstream media and the statistics seem to focus on affluent females because the deaths of women who lived on the fringes of society were not considered great or unusual news capable of making prime time newscasts or agitating public protest in the same way that the killing of upper middle-class or rich women would. To a certain extent, the changes in cultural codes that took place in the late twentieth century have contributed to destabilizing the hegemonic notion of masculinity and alter the rules concerning previously acceptable standards of behavior. In the environment of the political opening and adjustments brought about by fast-changing means of communication, the concept of masculinity has undergone questioning and reformulation. However, as discussed in the Coda, violence and femicide still run rampant in Brazil, and Afro-Brazilian women are even more susceptible to experiencing those cruelties.

The Erotic and Exotic Lure

Race as a Cultural Binder

The extensive mixing of races in Brazil has fascinated scholars who have often traced parallels with the United States. Historically speaking, in the United States racism was founded on biology (one-drop rule), while in Brazil stigmatization and discrimination were based on phenotype, that is, there was a veiled preference for Caucasian physical characteristics (Nogueira 287–308). In the United States, the Jim Crow laws guaranteed the separation between blacks and whites, and under the one-drop rule, African Americans with no visible signs of African ancestry would still be considered black, and would be punished for violating seg-regation laws or crossing the color line and trying to "pass" for white.[1] Unlike African Americans, Afro-Brazilians did not need to circumvent the laws by pretending to be white, or negate African ancestry, because the "mulatto escape-hatch"[2] and the absence of institutionalized forms of discrimination afforded many Afro-Brazilians opportunities unavailable in the United States.

While, for the most part, the United States adopted a bi-racial system of classification, Brazil embraced a pluralistic system, based on "physiognomic characteristics and degrees of pigmenta-tion" (Toplin 137). The popular expression *dinheiro embranquece* ("money whitens the skin") illustrates the argument that, rather than racial discrimination, Brazilians usually hold a class preju-dice, in which case skin color is not an impediment for class mo-bility (Toplin 140). To be considered black in Brazil, one should not have any percentage of white ancestry, otherwise he or she would fall into other racial categories such as *pardo/a, mulato/a, moreno/a,* and numerous other classifications. This informa-tion was confirmed in a 1976 study conducted by the Brazilian

Institute of Geography and Statistics (IBGE) to respond to the needs of the people who complained that the five racial categories (white, black, brown, Indian, and Asian) that had been previously used to classify the population were insufficient to describe the variety of existent skin colors. Attempting to respond to the people's complaint, the IBGE conducted a survey and collected 134 self-identifying terms, many of which just described physical appearance (Instituto Brasileiro de Geografia e Estatística 386).

Howard Winant presents a revisionist reading of race categorization in Brazil and the United States. He reveals that the Brazilian racial complexity and the American bipolarity have undergone changes because "race has taken new forms in both countries as a result of new conflicts and new perceptions about racial identity, racial politics, and the very meaning of race in everyday life" (99). Winant observes that in the contemporary United States "racial identity is being transformed from dualistic to multipolar, in the case of minorities," while in Brazil, "black identities are becoming more dualistic (as opposed to continuous)" (106). As an example, he cites the "color line," which used to play a defining role in racial identity in the United States and has eroded now (106). Even though biracialism was the verifiable measure to define race classifications in the United States, in reality not all people were distinguished or treated just in terms of that bipolarity. It is a fact that light-skinned African Americans historically received a more preferential treatment than those who were darker. Robert Brent Toplin concludes that "out of America's own subtle sliding scale of racial values came a socioeconomic pattern that resembled the Brazilian situation in many ways. The once popular American saying 'If you are white, you're right; if you're brown, stick around; if you are black, stay back' would be understood by many Brazilians regarding their own society" (148).[3]

A number of scholars have examined the slippery nature of race categories in Brazil by discussing, for instance, how the word *mulata* (a *parda* woman) is oftentimes interwoven with the term *morena* (technically a brunette, olive-skinned woman). For Eakin, this exemplifies "the fluidity and ambiguity of Brazilian color categories" and how "all skin tones are in the eye of the beholder" (109).[4] Natasha Pravaz wonders if the term *mulata* is not simply "a privileged signifier in a large paradigmatic chain of associating cultural terms such as *cabrocha, morena,* and *baiana,*" terms that can "denote 'black woman' or 'light-skinned black woman' and are inscribed in Brazil's complex system of racial classification" ("Brazilian" 116). Adele Fátima, one of six young women that Oswaldo Sargentelli recruited for his original "show *de mulatas*," in 1971, in the night club Sucata in Rio de Janeiro (Sargentelli 37–40), is considered a *morena* by most people. It remains to be determined if her success (in Sargentelli's shows and as a model) owes much to the fact that her phenotype (lighter skin color) links her to the concept of *boa aparência*. The infamous concept of "good appearance"—which signals a lighter skin tone, straight or softly curled hair, and thin lips and nose—was so widely accepted or used in Brazil that it was included in job advertisements. Individuals who had "good appearance" were generally given preference when competing for employment, housing, a school spot, or other social and professional opportunities. Roberto DaMatta calls this veiled way of discriminating "racism the Brazilian way" (*Relativizando* 61), a practice that survived to the end of the twentieth century, even if it was not as conspicuous as it was in the 1950s and 1960s. The concept of "good appearance" finds a counterpart in the theory of *um defeito de cor*" ("a color defect"), as children would be categorized when born with a darker complexion or other physical characteristics that could indicate non-white ancestry.[5]

Although guided by different principles and ways of categorizing and addressing race, both the United States and Brazil considered the black race a "problem" to be solved (Roosevelt 410). In the United States, white supremacists fought hard to keep the Caucasian population "untarnished," while in Brazil miscegenation was already so prevalent that, in the beginning of the twentieth century, the alternative was to encourage interracial marriages to accelerate the process of "whitening" the population. Since the identification of a person's race in Brazil is mostly determined by phenotype rather than ancestry, it was believed that miscegenation would dilute blackness to a point that most of the population would eventually be considered white, or almost white, by Brazilian standards. The white elite and the governing authorities hoped that through miscegenation, by the third generation, the children of interracial marriages would have lost most of the physical characteristics that could categorize them as direct descendants of African slaves. An illustration of such theory hung on the walls of the National Museum of Rio de Janeiro. The 1895 canvas by Modesto Brocos y Gómez, *A Rendenção de Can* ("*The Redemption of Ham*") portrayed three generations affected by interracial mixing. At the back of the painting, Brocos y Gómez painted an older black woman and, in the center, he positioned a *parda* mother holding a light-complexioned child on her lap and sitting next to a white European companion/father of her child.

By the end of the nineteenth century, the large Afro-Brazilian population of both sexes had already successfully tiptoed its way past many racial and social crossroads. In the beginning of the twentieth century, the number of mixed-race individuals was high and, it was not uncommon for them to have formal education, or occupy some important positions in areas of political, military, literary, and artistic milieus. Consequently, miscegenation, the fluid racial interactions, the absence of racial segregation, and a certain preference for interracial sexual relations at the lower strata of society contributed to the pervasive image of Brazil as a racial democracy. Caulfield summarizes such discussions by stating that "Brazilians' supposed tolerance, or even predilection, for interracial sexual relations was central to the theory that the population was 'improving' because of the 'whitening' effect of miscegenation" (146). As she further explains, these "contradictory ideas became pillars of nationalist ideologies of left and right in the 1920s and integral elements of the corporatist authoritarianism that eventually prevailed in the state policy in late 1930s" (146). Theodore Roosevelt rightfully predicted in 1914, during his visit to Brazil, that miscegenation would become a disseminated practice at the economically lower branches of Brazilian society, whereas the elite would remain mostly white since interracial marriages were not as common at that social and economic level (411). Nevertheless, as Thomas Skidmore, Carl N. Degler, Florestan Fernandes, and Thales de Azevedo, among others, have discussed, even if interracial marriages were not as common in the upper levels of Brazilian society, between 1900 and 1920, the ideology of whitening became popular in all strata of society because it was reaping social benefits and creating a desirable effect. By embracing a laidback attitude toward interracial marriages or co-habitation, the population could become whiter and be conceived as more modern and prosperous.

Thus, from the late 1890s to the first decades of the twentieth century, the established order bet on miscegenation to whiten the population hoping that it would make Brazilians look more "civilized" and socially more fluid. Miscegenation could provide another advantage: it would establish a positive image of the country as a flexible and harmoniously organized society that had a superior ethical attitude toward race (especially in comparison with the United States). This is an aspect that the newspaper *O Paiz* promoted on June 14, 1920, describing Brazil's lack of discriminatory laws and the absence of hateful attitudes toward people of color as a strong indication of the moral superiority of its people (Caulfield 258, n. 2). The prospect of having a mostly white nation delighted the elite, and the *pardo* and black population also saw benefits because the ideology of whitening could accelerate their inclusion in society. The "mulatto escape-hatch" created a racial bridge between whites and blacks in Brazil, and a cultural and social ease so pervasive that it became part of the definition of the country's national identity, celebrated in all arts and popularized in the twentieth century. A case in point is the popular 1939 song "Aquarela do Brazil" ("Watercolor of Brazil") by Ari Barroso which overstresses the beauty and assets of Brazil, describing it as the land of the *mulato inzoneiro*" ("the good-looking mulatto"), and the *morena sestrosa* ("the beautiful brown girl").[6]

It was not just Brazilians who applauded the ideology of whitening and embraced the concept of a racial democracy. Scholars have examined reports and other writings of American travelers and researchers who, until the 1950s, were enamored with the absence of racial violence and legal segregation in Brazil, and who considered the Brazilian model as a viable, or superior, alternative to standards in the United States.[7] David J. Hellwig reveals that even African Americans saw Brazil as a model of racial democracy that should be emulated by the United States (18). To illustrate his point, he compiled twelve articles written between 1914 and 1926 which praised the Brazilian racial model. Most of them were published by African American thinkers in journals and magazines destined for a similar reading public (Hellwig 35, 45, 48, 52, 58, 82–83). In the 1930s, the effects of the Great Depression contributed to halt such publications presumably because people took fewer trips abroad, or because there was less money to invest in the publishing business (Hellwig 87). In the 1940s, the topic gained considerable attention again. France Windance Twine mentions that a study conducted by Donald Pierson (which concluded that racial issues were not a deciding factor in social opportunities in Brazil) and E. Franklin Frasier's research (which also praised the country's racial dynamics) are good samples of how a positive image of the Brazilian harmonious racial interaction continued to draw foreign attention (7).[8] In commenting about why, in the 1940s, African Americans assumed Brazil was a racial democracy, Patrícia de Santana Pinho concludes that they were misguided by their country's racial classification. As she discusses, "one of the reasons both Brazil and Cuba then became known as versions of racial paradise for African American travelers is due in part to how they, informed by the US one-drop rule, mistook mulattoes, several of whom were occupying high social and political positions, for blacks" (25).

In the 1930s and 1940s, Gilberto Freyre's publications played a significant role in validating the concept of a Brazilian racial democracy. He wrote extensively about the African impact on Brazilian culture, and his texts, particularly his 1933 *Casa Grande a Senzala* ("*The Masters and the Slaves*," 1946 translation), influenced the definition of Brazil as a race-embracing democratic republic. Vianna construes that *The Masters and the Slaves* broke with previous ways of analyzing Brazilian culture because Freyre argued that miscegenation played a positive role in distinguishing Brazil as a nation that embraced racial equality (43). Freyre also promoted the importance of African-derived cultural manifestations, considering them the sincerest expression of Brazilian culture (Vianna 278). Even if Freyre did not coin the expression "racial democracy,"[9] from the 1930s to the 1950s, his influence on cultivating the idea of miscegenation as evidence of lack of racism contributed to propagate the idea of a racial egalitarian society in Brazil. Therefore, cultural products like *samba* and Afro-Brazilian cuisine became powerful symbols of diversity and inclusiveness and were integrated into Vargas's populist agenda. The government also included *capoeira*, soccer and *carnaval* into the nationalist project of the late 1930s and 1940s which contributed to validate several forms of popular cultural. For Eakin, "while samba became the symbol par excellence of *mestiçagem*, in popular music, *carnaval* emerged in the 1930s and 1940s as the principal ritual showcasing the Freyrean vision" (90). By streamlining manifestations of African origin into the concept of a national identity, Vargas's policies affected those cultural productions in Brazil positively, and drew attention to some unique features of popular culture (Taylor 18). However, as Vianna argues, the Vargas regime found itself at a crossroad: to elevate practices of African origin—most of which were prosecuted and forbidden until the mid-1930s— and embrace the idea of a Brazil mestizo par excellence it would require abandoning "the old ideal of 'whitening'" (113). The way to work around this conundrum was to make those practices of African origin and the idea of *mestiçagem* significant by convincing intellectuals and the white elite to adopt the cause. Even if the idea was not homogeneously accepted, it gradually took root and became the trump card used to advocate the notion that, as a racially-mixed society, Brazil was morally superior (especially when compared to the United States) because it was more inclusive and open-minded. In analyzing the impact of Vargas's policies, Vianna contends that "Brazil was perhaps the first country in which mestiço pride and elements of urban popular culture combined to create a widely consensual national identity" (113).

Vargas's ideological project and populist policies of the 1930s and 1940s were revisited and reformulated by the 1964–1985 military dictatorship (Chauí 90, 99). From the late 1960s to early 1980s, popular culture became part of the ideology of a national integration which the authoritarian regime implemented. In this political environment, during the so-called "economic miracle years" of the 1970s, the dictatorship used popular culture to promote an image of Brazil as a joyful, sexy, carefree, and fast-developing country. Echoing Vargas's dogmatic bent and nationalist guidelines, the authoritarian government reinforced the concept of a racial democracy by focusing on several popular traditions that could nurture and inspire the sense of pride in Brazil's cultural and racial diversity. By officially linking popular culture to national identity, the governing authorities provided the masses with a coping mechanism, diverting attention from the regime's pervasive atrocities against human rights and/or its callous censorship against freedom of the press and speech. At that time, the country witnessed a substantial growth in the demand for and appreciation of African-derived popular culture. It was then that *capoeira* was promoted to the status of a "national sport," soccer was Brazil's *jogo bonito*, and *carnaval* festivities exuded sensuality, creativity, and fun. The government used a diversity of cultural productions to sew together the image of unity in diversity.

The "Made-in-Brazil *Mulata*"

Brazilians have traditionally given a remarkable importance to sex in defining themselves as a people because, as Richard G. Parker notices, "individually and collectively, most of them derive their sense of identity from a positive perception of their sensuality" (8). The exotic and erotic lure of the Afro-Brazilian woman, established in colonial and imperial Brazil, contributed to foment existing sexual stereotypes about Afro-Brazilian females. Freyre's tireless descriptions and analyses of *parda* women as sexual partners is a legacy that remains alive because the theorizing of national identity in Brazil still includes references to gender, race, and sexuality/sensuality (S. Costa 42). Lélia Gonzalez (229–35) traces the myth of the *parda* woman's unhinged sensuality/sexuality and their everlasting disposition for sex to the practice of selecting female African descendants to work as *mucamas* in the plantation houses. According to Gonzalez, when the term *mucama* (a Kimbundu word meaning "mistress slave") made its way into the Portuguese language, it gained some additional meanings. It was still used to refer to young women of African ancestry who were selected to be special concubines and perform sexual favors for slave owners and younger males of the families, but it also referred to those who were assigned lighter domestic chores and/or kept company with the lady of the house (a lady-in-waiting). *Mucamas* often found themselves in ambiguous situations: if they did not fulfill expectations, they could receive physical punishment or be sexually abused; if they engaged in sexual affairs with the slave owners, they could be submitted to attacks of jealousy by white mistresses. Most *mucamas* adapted to the situation and took advantage of the system, in some cases, they managed to maintain long-lasting relationships with white men of the household (Giacomini, *Mulher* 23–28). Thus, it was not unusual for *mucamas* to utilize their social and intermediary position in the house—as retainers and as a source of sexual pleasure—to negotiate better living conditions, or even their freedom. It is in this context that the Afro-Brazilian women's social and physical mobility also contributed to disseminate the idea that they were highly skilled in the art of lovemaking.

In colonial days, white men avoided criticism from their families and/or ecclesiastic authorities for their dissolute behavior, licentious conduct, or moral double standards by blaming *parda* women's ardent temperament. By categorizing them as irresistible creatures whose lack of moral values, bewitching charm, and a tantalizing sexuality seduced them, they reversed the argument. These are some characteristics that Freyre details in chapters four and five of *The Masters and the Slaves*, when he analyzes the African impact on sexual and family life in colonial Brazil, and traces the deployment of the myth of the Afro-Brazilian woman's everlasting disposition for sex (278–476). He writes that scholars such as Raymundo Nina Rodrigues and José Veríssimo contributed enormously to disseminate such ideas. Rodrigues championed the concept of "the lascivious hybrid woman" by describing her as "an abnormal, sexually super-excited type," while Veríssimo considered her a "'dissolvent of physical and moral virility'" (Freyre, *Masters* 402). In Freyre's opinion, there were also other major contributing factors to such stereotyping; namely: a) the impact that popular songs had on disseminating ideas about the *parda* women's lust and sensuality; b) fear of homosexuality; c) the imposition of virginity to white, unmarried women; and d) the role travel narratives played in describing Brazilian lifestyle and costumes. The songs of the colonial period often referred to the Afro-Brazilian women's allure and sinfulness, most probably because those females did not have to abide by the strict moral, religious, and social codes forced on white females.

For historical and social reasons, black and white women had fewer opportunities than the brown population to overtly express their sexuality and sensuality. White women were excessively guarded before and after marriage, and black women were overridden as unattractive, oftentimes overworked and too tired to engage in lovemaking. The belief that brown women had an everlasting disposition for sex was also born out of a fear of homosexuality that permeated every plantation house. As Freyre discusses, to avoid mockery and secure heirs, parents made heterosexual intercourse an integral part of their boys' rite of passage from childhood to puberty, or from puberty to adolescence. They crafted opportunities for their sons to be sexually initiated by slave women, usually young, charming, and well-groomed *mucamas*. The lighter the skin, the more probability a slave had of being chosen for such a position. Therefore, the standards by which masculinity was measured, and progeny was secured, depended heavily on the acceptance and glorification of men as womanizers and procreators, most often at the expense of Afro-Brazilian women. The third category to which Freyre refers is the strict Catholic and patriarchal codes of honor, morality, virginity, and chastity for women of the upper social class. As a result, Afro-Brazilian females become the repository of the white men's lust, and indirectly protected the virtues of white damsels.

The topic has drawn the interest of literary critics, historians, anthropologists, and social scientists. For instance, Parker contends that, for most Brazilians, "the *mulata* possesses a charm and attractiveness unimaginable in any other woman anywhere else in the world" (153). Queiroz Júnior traces the development of that myth in songs and literature, discussing the important role that literary texts played in establishing the mestizo woman as an aesthetic and sexual symbol of Brazil.[10] John Burdick's work also examines the experience of women of African descent in Brazil and discusses "the color of love" and "the *mulata* and *morena* in the courtship arena" (26–50). In tracing and examining the long-standing association of mixed-race women, food, and sex, Sant'Anna argues that literary texts popularized the image of the Afro-Brazilian woman as someone who is always "good in bed and in the kitchen" (*O canibalismo*, 19). Sant'Anna questions the rules of erotic-racial-economic endogamy and exogamy by describing how those texts dramatize the play between the white women who could become spouses, and the *parda* females who should be mistresses and thus be "eaten," that is, laid (*O canibalismo*, 19). To this day, examples of the association between *parda* women, sex, and food abound. Several incarnations of oversexed Afro-Brazilian women who cook well appear in novels, poems, songs, films, television programs, advertisements, and jokes. In those venues they are also linked to certain flavors, smells, and exotic spices which, when combined, connote their sensuality and eroticism.[11]

DaMatta also analyzes the metaphors of eating and having sex in *O Que Faz o Brasil, Brasil?* (*"What Makes Brazil What It Is?"*). He gives several accounts of situations in which eating is used as a reference for having sex, an indication that women are considered food to be savored. The comparison also applies to homosexual relationships where the terms "active" and "passive" are often used (51–64). As DaMatta summarizes his analyses:

A relação sexual e o ato de comer, portanto, aproximam-se num sentido tal que indica de que modo nós, brasileiros, concebemos a sexualidade e a vemos, não como um encontro de opostos e iguais ... mas como um modo de resolver essa igualdade pela absorção. (60)

A sexual act and the act of eating, therefore, are so entangled that they reveal how we Brazilians conceive sexuality, not as an encounter of opposite and equal sexes ... but rather as a hierarchy in which the one who eats swallows the one eaten.

The representations of women as "edible" substances so prominent in novels such as Jorge Amado's *Gabriela, Clove and Cinnamon* and *Dona Flor and Her Two Husbands*, and Aluísio de Azevedo's *O Cortiço* also appears in *telenovelas*, and songs. Those texts emblematize the longstanding admiration in Brazilian society for texts and contexts that link women to mouthwatering food and spicy sex (especially in reference to women of color). DaMatta endorses this cultural trend when he considers that "Gabriela revoluciona com as armas que possui: seu corpo, seu tempero, sua comida, seu cheiro de cravo e seu sabor de canela ("Gabriela revolutionizes by using her body, cooking abilities, and appealing to the senses with the taste of exotic food"; *O Que* 112). The same type of associations can be found in television commercials. For instance, in 2002, to advertise a beer brand during *carnaval,* a computer-generated advertisement established a visual connection between a brown body and a dark beer bottle. The commercial began with a *morena* dressed in a skimpy bikini, dancing *samba* on the top arch of the *sambódromo,* Rio de Janeiro's five-block amphitheater built especially for *samba* parades. (The amphitheater is crowned by a large concrete M that has been popularly interpreted as a reference to the word *mulata.*) For about thirty seconds at a time, the intermittent image of the woman's body and the beer bottle complemented and supplemented each other, shape-changing to the frenzied rhythm of the *carnaval* songs. The connection between the pleasure of drinking beer, and the visual delight of watching the seducing body, was unmistakably clear as the image of the brown beer bottle and the *parda* woman and its gustative-visual-sexual discursivity sustained a voyeuristic pleasure.[12]

Telenovelas offer another source of promoting the benefits of miscegenation and racial democracy and depicting women of color as symbols of Brazil's sexuality, sensuality, and culinary talents. Banking on the fact that the concept of an all-inclusive national identity is popular, television networks in Brazil—with Globo leading the way—have aired a string of serialized dramas that connect food and sex with brown women because it is a topic that still appeals to viewers. Of special significance are Globo's *telenovelas* that air at prime time because they are broadcast at a time when they reach a large number of viewers. A good example is *O Clone* ("*The Clone*"), a *telenovela* aired in 2001–2002, in which Solange Couto played the role of Dona Jura. She had the emblematic part of the *parda* woman who used any excuse to have a party, dance, flaunt her wiles, and display her outstanding cooking abilities. She owned a bar in São Cristóvão, a working-class neighborhood of Rio de Janeiro, and her culinary abilities and the festive environment of her commercial establishment were so impressive that they attracted customers from all social classes, including VIPs who became regulars.[13] In real life, at the age of sixteen, Couto became one of the Afro-Brazilian women who were part of Sargentelli's 1969 pioneering show of *mulatas* (Dalevi).[14] In the scene taped on April 12, 2002, Sargentelli lent his prestige to his former *mulata* by visiting her bar to savor her exotic food while interacting with Afro-Brazilian women dancing *samba*. Ironically, and sadly, Sargentelli was overtaken by the emotion of reconnecting with Couto in an environment that reminded him of the first group of performers he promoted and suffered a heart attack at the age of seventy-eight while still at the studio.[15] As distressing and unfortunate as this news was, it seemed to reinforce the idea that brown Afro-Brazilian women possess an irresistible, arresting, and dangerous sex appeal, all of which combined with exotic and spicy foods could prove too strong for the weak heart.

The sensuality of the Afro-Brazilian woman is a concept so embedded in Brazilian cultural ethos that it guarantees a captive audience. In 2003, Globo launched *Da Cor do Pecado* ("*The Color of Sin*"), another prime time *telenovela* showcasing a beautiful brown Afro-Brazilian woman (Taís Araújo) who was an excellent cook/restaurant owner, romantically involved with a white man. The title of the *telenovela* undermines any positive projection of her character because *pecado* is closely associated with seduction, temptation, and promiscuity, and the title suggests that those character deviations are genetic blueprints (resulting from the color of her skin). Since the interest in the topic is pervasive, in the *telenovela America* (2005–2006), Couto was cast again, this time as Dalva, a *samba* dancer who embodied the concept of the "made in Brazil *mulata*," and reached international recognition (or so she claimed) by dancing in European night clubs. Twelve years later, when her mother (who was her child's caretaker) died, Dalva returned to Brazil to reveal the name of the boy's father so that he could raise him, and she would be free to return to Europe. While she waited for the right moment to make her announcement, Couto's character boasted about her lifestyle in Europe and graced Vila Isabel's dance floors with her *samba* skills. Dalva reinforced several stereotypes regarding Afro-Brazilian women: she embraced the *mulata* profession, was oversexed, and uninterested in raising her child because she was unfit for motherhood (supposedly a pious and sanctimonious quality which a true *mulata* would not have). Although Couto played an important part in *America*, her role withstood the racial ambivalence of the Brazilian social system which promotes women of color as national symbols of sensuality and sexuality, gastronomy, and cultural ambassadors of *samba* and *carnaval*, but does not deviate from those roles.

In the 2007–2008 prime time *telenovela Duas Caras* ("*Two Faces*"), Globo added a little twist to the plot by raising awareness about the dangers of signing up to "dance *samba*" in Europe because of the extensive trafficking of women and prostitution rings. The plot introduced Faustina, a woman who disappeared for a few years and returned to Brazil as countess Finzi-Contini. In the fantasy realm of the *telenovela*, she met an old nobleman in Italy who rescued her from prostitution and slavery, married her, named her the sole heir of his immense fortune, and died shortly after. To educate Afro-Brazilian women about the perils of attempting to pursue the *mulata* profession in Europe, and end up enslaved in a prostitution ring, she established an NGO in Brazil. Although the *telenovela* draws attention to a very serious and real problem, it still idealizes the *mulata* profession by conveying the idea that, even if the chances are slim and the price is high, beautiful and young Afro-Brazilian women can climb the social ladder by dancing *samba* and marrying rich European counts. Since, for the most part, Globo's *telenovelas* have a purported social, cultural, and didactic agenda, *Duas Caras* also educated the population about racial respect and tolerance, by having the characters use politically correct terms, and by highlighting the perils of a racist society, and the importance of cordial race relations. However, while the *telenovela* reveals the racial ambivalence often found in Brazilian society, and questions Brazil's racial democracy, it also reinforces the ideology of whitening by presenting several inter-racial marriages (as a solution to correct or eradicate racism). The theme is recurrent. A case in point is the 2017–2018 *telenovela*, *O Outro Lado do Paraíso* ("*The Other Side of Paradise*"), which offered discussions about racism, presented interracial couples, and cast an Afro-Brazilian woman in the role of a good cook. The positive change in *O Outro Lado do Paraíso* was that the character moved out of poverty, not by dancing *samba* or embracing the *mulata* profession—as presented in previous *telenovelas*—but by working her way out of poverty, attending law school, and becoming a competent judge. Thus, the brown Afro-Brazilian woman is one of the most celebrated, discussed, and stereotyped female character. She appears in travel accounts, paintings, songs, films, television programs, cultural shows, popular sayings, and in modern time, she is featured in advertisements, and sought after for sex tourism.[16]

Visual artists, musicians, and intellectuals in the first decades of the twentieth century adopted the concept of *mestiçagem* and celebrated the "made-in-Brazil *mulata*." A case in point is Emiliano Di Cavalcanti, one of the most prestigious painters of Brazilian Modernism, who asserted that, by definition, *mulatas* have to be Afro-Brazilians because they are living proof of the country's policy of miscegenation, symbolize the concept of "Brazilianness," and thus represent a "national product." In explaining why he painted Afro-Brazilian women so frequently, he confided that, for him, as a symbol of Brazil, the *parda* woman holds a racial and social intermediary position; she also likes music and soccer: "Para mim, a mulata é o símbolo do Brasil. Ela não é nem preta nem branca. Nem rica nem pobre. Ela gosta de música e futebol" (qtd. in R. Rosa). Di Cavalcanti's definition of a *mulata* goes beyond a race category to express what she likes and dislikes, establishing her as the measure of real Brazilianness. Such concept continued to expand and became so polyvalent that since the late 1960s the word *mulata* has acquired other meanings. It has been used, for instance, to refer to young females of African ancestry who make a living dancing *samba* in night clubs or tourist spots (Sargentelli 44, 70–71), advertising *carnaval* on television, traveling in dance groups, or participating in sex tourism. Thus, the term *mulata* can refer to a *parda* woman, but it can also denote a profession embraced by Afro-Brazilian females who master the art of *samba* dancing to perform in public spaces.

In his autobiography *Ziriguidum*, Sargentelli recalls that, in 1969, during a *roda de samba* (a *samba* gathering) at a bar, he was brainstorming with friends for an idea to produce a cultural show when he suddenly thought of the word *mulata*, inspired by the traditional *carnaval marchinha*, "O Teu Cabelo Não Nega" ("Your Hair Does Not Deny It") that his uncle, Lamartino Babo, popularized in 1931 (37). In the song, the lyric voice identifies a brown Afro-Brazilian woman by her phenotype (her hair) and invites her for a night of lovemaking:

> O teu cabelo não nega, mulata
> Porque és mulata na cor
> Mas como a cor não pega, mulata
> Mulata, eu quero o teu amor.[17]

> Your hair reveals, *mulata*
> That you are a mestizo woman
> But since skin color is not contagious,
> *Mulata*, I want your love.

The song harbors notions of color prejudice and a cordial racism as it informs that the male considers it acceptable to have the Afro-Brazilian female as a sexual partner only because race is not contagious or sexually transmittable, in other words, he does not run the risk of becoming racially compromised and, consequently, socially impaired. In analyzing the lyrics of "O Seu Cabelo Não Nega," Pravaz writes that "a close look at the syntax and semantics of the song might give us a clue into the reasons why the Carnivalesque march has come to be considered one of the most important recordings of Brazilian popular music and one of the most successful Carnival songs of all time" ("Imagining" 53).

Sargentelli banked on the conventional description of Afro-Brazilian women as hybrid, licentious, and sensuous figures, and in 1969, produced and directed a "*mulata* program" in which he featured only young and beautiful Afro-Brazilian women (Sargentelli 37–52). While he is not responsible for the pervasive stereotyping regarding Afro-Brazilian women, and while he borrowed and adapted the idea for his shows from performances that featured white women in Brazil and Europe, Sargentelli takes credit for having shaped the contours of the "made-in-Brazil *mulata*," and for having put his signature on a new profession (39). As he acknowledges, he modelled his shows after Carlos Machado who had previously produced similar programs for the night clubs Night & Day and Casablanca. The difference is that Sargentelli decided to include only Afro-Brazilian females who he hand-picked to showcase the concepts of miscegenation and a racial democracy as they danced to the *samba* rhythm (Sargentelli 39).[18] In his autobiography, Sargentelli confides that his career as a *mulatólogo* ("*mulata* producer") began after the 1964 military coup d'état, when the authorities considered his radio and television shows subversive and forbade him from working as a journalist. Ironically, he found a niche for his new career in the government's cultural and political agenda that elected *carnaval*, soccer, *capoeira*, and other lay and religious festivities as representative samples of Brazilian cultural identity (Sargentelli 43–47). He and his associates opened night clubs in Rio de Janeiro (Sambão, Sucata, and Oba, Oba), and he directed a cultural show which consisted of stand-up comedy routine, and Afro-Brazilian women parading their bodies dressed in scant bikinis, dancing *samba* in impeccable postures to the feverish rhythm of *carnaval* music. As seasoned performers accustomed to dealing with captive audiences, they were aware of the power of their bodies, exuded sensuality, and exchanged vibrational energy with the public.

Sargentelli was so successful in his new professional endeavor that, in addition to the three night clubs in Rio de Janeiro, he and his associates opened other similar venues in São Paulo and Porto Alegre, and in 1974, developed a touring company called "Oba, Oba" (Sargentelli 44, 70–71).[19] To staff his performances, he recruited up to forty women who worked for him at different night clubs. He also promoted the show in Europe, calling it "Sargentelli e as Mulatas Que Não Estão no Mapa" ("Sargentelli and the Out-of-This-World Mulatas"; Sargentelli 37–52). He successfully sugarcoated his stand-up comedy and musical program with the ideological argument that, by choosing only Afro-Brazilians to perform in his shows, he was promoting "Brazilianness" and creating job opportunities. He personally selected the women whose age group ranged from sixteen to twenty-five years old, most of them from economically challenged neighborhoods. To be selected, they had to conform to the parameters and definition he outlined in an interview in which he explained that "*Mulatas* have thin waists, thick thighs, naughty little-girl faces, good teeth, and very good smell; they shake and jiggle, making everyone's mouth water" (Dalevi). Sargentelli's definition of the made-in-Brazil *mulatas* does not describe them racially; it adopts a misogynist and mercantile concept presenting them as objects of desire and consumer goods. In some ways, his selection criteria reproduce the colonial model that slave owners would use to pick Africans in the slave markets or choose *mucamas* to work in the plantation houses.

Sargentelli's cultural shows became so popular that they generated a series of copycats. To meet the demand of the tourism industry, several night club programs and folkloric groups began recruiting experienced *mulatas* for their programs, shows, and cultural events which, in turn, led special groups in Rio de Janeiro to train candidates for the *mulata* job. As Sônia Maria Giacomini mentions, those courses prepared young, pretty, brown-skinned women—who were also skilled *samba* dancers—to become competitive in the market ("Aprendendo" 213–46). They learned choreography and how to apply makeup, acquired some sophisticated norms of etiquette and posture, mastered the art of seducing/engaging an audience and, at the conclusion of the course, received a certificate. The list of the attributes and skills that Giacomini compiled reveals that for *mulatas* to be tall is a plus, and to be construed as a *mulata* one should also be responsible, keep appointments, arrive on time for rehearsals, and groom the body well, similar to the requirements for a modeling profession.[20] Pravaz distinguishes between *passistas* who do not charge for their dancing talents and usually parade during the *carnaval* festivities, and *mulatas*, "women who engage in dancing the samba in a commodified spectacle and receive some form of remuneration" ("Imagining" 48).[21] Such distinction can be used as a general way of discussing the *profissão mulata*; however, it does not account for the fact that one category does not eliminate the other. For instance, Valéria Valenssa and Adele Fátima offer two outstanding samples of how malleable these categories are. As illustrated in Roberto Faustino's video recording *Escolas de Samba:*

O Espetáculo. A Documentary of Rio's Carnaval, Globeleza Valenssa embodied the *mulata* category and was a *passista* in *carnaval* parades in Rio de Janeiro and São Paulo. Adele Fátima was both part of the group of six women selected by Sargentelli to dance *samba* in his first *mulata* show, and a famous *passista*, holding the coveted position of *madrinha da bateria* ("*carnaval* queen").

As seducers of audiences, *mulatas* resemble erotic dancers, and walk a tight rope between a belly dancer and a prostitute. As far as the economic and social gains that performing jobs or media attention can bring, the *mulata* profession could be compared to the work of Victoria's Secret models, although not considered as glamourous. The *mulata* coaching in Rio de Janeiro that Giacomini discussed resembles the preparation that Venezuelan women receive to compete in international beauty pageants, or geisha training in Japan. It can also be argued that Couto, Valenssa, or the other "made-in-Brazil *mulatas*" have jobs similar to Las Vegas showgirls, or even *Playboy* bunnies. In all these professions there are similarities as to the use of the body and the endorsement of the exploitative model. Nevertheless, even if images of white women (fashion models, for instance) are part of the concept of a sensual Brazil, the *parda* women have an additional task: they are the emblematic tokens of a purported racial democracy and a brown nation. The *mulata* is described as a symbol of Brazil, and as such, she holds the key to the understanding of the significance that sexuality-sensuality and eroticism-exoticism plays "within the paradoxes of Brazilian life, within the double standard of a patriarchal tradition developed in a slaveholding society," as Parker contends (153). In no other cultural manifestation in Brazil have women of color manifested their dance skills so vividly or projected a sensual image so deliberately than during the *carnaval* season. In *Carnivals, Rogues, and Heroes*, DaMatta discusses Rio's *carnaval* parades as a representation of the complexity of Brazilian culture (61–82). His interpretation of Brazilian *carnaval* presupposes a symbiotic harmony of gender, race, and class in which people intermingle democratically on the streets, and invert relations of power by moving from the margins to the center during the parades, projecting the image of a country united in its liveliness and exuberance. However, as the "*mulata* profession" exemplifies, the image of a hybrid, resourceful, and playful country also promotes a quest for identity through the exotic and erotic experience and overlooks the ambiguities prevalent in gender and race relations in Brazil.

Carnaval: Tokens Mistaken for Wonders[22]

Since the mid-nineteenth century, *carnaval* festivities have been associated with masks and costumes which have been popular in Brazil. It was then that the first bands and adorned floats paraded on the streets of Rio de Janeiro, and the revelers marched or danced to the sound of instruments and *carnaval* songs. Since 1928, *samba* schools (associations that parade during *carnaval*) have taken to the streets of Rio de Janeiro with their dazzling displays of colors, costumes, and floats, creating a visual extravaganza rivaled only by the fast and contagious rhythms of the musicians and dancers.[23] The participants in the *samba* parades usually live in shantytowns or impoverished neighborhoods, but dress up in lavish costumes, create elaborate floats and choreography, and put on an unmatched show for national and international spectators. It is in the media-controlled and monitored environment of *carnaval* parades that the image of the *mulata* comes forth as a national product, an erotic ideal, and an intrinsic part of "the sensual ethos"[24] of Brazilian life, in general, and of the *carnaval* season, in particular.

Such a symbolic representation was highlighted in the early 1990s when Globo Television Network created the character Globeleza ("Globo's beauty") and selected Valéria da Conceição dos Santos (who adopted the stage name Valéria Valenssa) to play the role. The first step in that direction happened in 1989 when she entered a beauty pageant, The Tropical Girl, a variation of The Girl from Ipanema contest. Valenssa did not win the competition because, she argues, the title is traditionally awarded to a Caucasian beauty, and she was "the only black woman in the pageant" (Bergallo and Duarte 44). Analyzing her professional transformation, she considers that, in a way, she won a larger and more important beauty pageant because the Tropical Girl contest gave her the visibility she needed to be noticed by Globo executives (Valenssa, "Personal interview").[25] She competed with more than 100 women from São Paulo and Rio de Janeiro and won the audition to become the face of Globo's advertising campaign for *carnaval* parades, in 1990 (Valenssa, "Interview" by Barbosa; Bergallo and Duarte 45). In 1993, Globo's producers re-invited her to star in the Globeleza's promotional vignette, and she signed a long-term contract with the network, becoming its *carnaval* ambassador-at-large (Valenssa, "Interview" by Barbosa).

For the next fourteen years the two main designers—Hans Donner, from Austria, and his first wife Sylvia Trenker, from Switzerland—created the drawings that were rendered on Valenssa's body. The "costume" that she wore for Globo's vignettes, and occasionally to parade with the *samba* associations, consisted of decorative body paint and a thin strip of surgical tape that partially covered her pubic area. The chromatic code the designers developed to market the Globeleza character explored the visual appeal of a few designs in glittering, water-resistant colors painted on her body. Donner and his team fashioned an arresting image of Globeleza by drawing different geometrical designs on Valenssa's body. The media followed those developments closely and applauded every representation of Globeleza, focusing on the artistic aspects of the designs and on her construed sensuality. Her performance established a "libidinal investment"[26] as it reinforced the imperatives and urgencies of a specific discourse that established the "lure of desire" and "lure of mimetic reflection,"[27] with the purpose of enticing viewers to watch Globo's broadcast of *carnaval* celebrations.

For a decade and a half, during the *carnaval* season, in ten to fifteen second television spots, Valenssa performed as Globeleza, and graced the front pages of popular magazines and internet sites. Her performance aimed at inducing viewers to watch the network's advertisement of parades and other *carnaval* celebrations. In doing so, the network construed an erotic enterprise to represent the Brazilian seductive energy (Petrini 130). The intermittent fleeting images of Valenssa's body parts dancing to the rhythm of a catchy jingle functioned as a provocative and flirtatious performative device that teased the viewers, inviting them to piece together her body in movement. Set to enrapture the viewers in the message of unity in diversity, the Globeleza vignette combined visual, acoustic, and linguistic effects to establish a connection between cultural production and national identity.

The language of traditional jingles is catchy and simple, the verses rhyme, they last just a few seconds, and are intended to advertise consumer goods. Intent on reaching a pre-established market and generate commercial success, Donner and his team set the Globeleza image to an engaging tune composed by Jorge Aragão. The Globeleza jingle delivers the message connecting the *mulata* body, national product, and *carnaval* celebrations:

Vem pra ser feliz,
Eu tô no ar, tô Globeleza,
Eu tô que tô legal
Na tela da TV,
No meio desse povo,
A gente vai se ver na Globo.[28]

Come to be happy.
I am on air, I am Globeleza,
I am doing just fine,
On the TV screen,
In the middle of the people,
We will see each other on Globo.

By presenting variations on a theme every year, Globo built a cultural dynamic with viewers, simultaneously re-asserting old meanings and introducing new visual parameters. For instance, in 2000, Brazil celebrated the 500-year anniversary of the official "discovery" of the country, and themes related to the land, its peoples, and Portuguese colonization dominated the *carnaval* festivities. Apparently, in the spirit of celebrating the indigenous people of Brazil, Globeleza wore a stylized headdress and her body was painted to resemble the designs imprinted on the bodies of the indigenous women the Portuguese encountered, and which Pero Vaz de Caminha detailed in a long letter he wrote to Dom Manuel, the King of Portugal, between April 26 and May 7, 1500. Caminha informed the monarch that, on their way to India, the Portuguese fleet had found a new land. He offered a meticulous account of the people, their surroundings, and lifestyle, and described how captivated he felt by the people's natural ways of living and the looks of their bare bodies. He explained that their attire consisted mainly of body paint, headdresses, and pieces of bones pinned to their lips and earlobes.

In referring to women, he described their physical attributes in very complimentary terms, paying special attention to one of them whose body was rounded, well-shaped, and painted from top to bottom with a special tincture of different colors. Caminha had equal admiration for the fertility of the land, the abundance of water, and good weather.[29] His letter became the first historical document and literary text about Brazil, and provided an intellectual synthesis and a gendered interpretation of the land and the people the Portuguese encountered. Thus, it must have escaped Donner and Globo's executives that their thematic choice was ideologically telling. They reproduced the colonial model by connecting Valenssa's body painting and headdress to the designs the Portuguese colonizers admired on the bodies of the indigenous women they first encountered in Brazil, and whose original coastal cultures were decimated in less than a century after the "discovery."

In 2002, Donner and his design team decorated Valenssa's body with twelve stylized butterflies which the media interpreted as a creative novelty because it connected her to nature and presented a light and fluid design that contrasted, in a positive way, with the geometrical format of several other drawings previously imprinted on her body. The butterflies were hailed as symbols of her lightness, representations of the fluidity of her dance movements, markers of her sensuality, and an indication of a more evolving pattern. In this case, the free-floating lightness that the butterflies represented could also purportedly embody the volatility of the *mulata* body in the general consensus of race and sexuality in Brazil. It could further, and ultimately, be interpreted as embodiment of the malleability of Brazilian racial relations, and the dynamics of social mobility that *carnaval* represents. In the 2003 *carnaval* season, another significant variation occurred because Valenssa was pregnant with her first child. To offer the viewers something original, Globo compiled images of her previous performances to present the *carnaval* vignette and surprised the spectators by ending it with the image of an expectant Globeleza in the nude. Valenssa mentions that she received several letters from women who thanked her for performing the Globeleza character while noticeably pregnant. Those letters expressed viewers' support and gratitude for her bold gesture and contribution to demystifying taboos about pregnancy and sensuality (Valenssa, "Interview" by Barbosa).

The letters Valenssa received from her fans corroborate the information that Célia Abicalil Belira collected in large urban centers in Brazil for her study on photography, pregnancy, sensuality, eroticism, and the space of the expectant body in Brazilian society. Belira discusses the changes that have taken place since the actress Leila Diniz was photographed sunbathing in a small bikini while pregnant in the 1970s (411–23). In sync with new waves of Feminism in Brazil, in the 1980s and 1990s, "the aesthetic of pregnancy" challenged the traditional patterns of behavior that

associate expectant mothers with modesty and piety. To disseminate the new aesthetic and win public opinion more easily, several
famous models and actresses agreed to pose in the nude, or in
semi-nudity, in advanced stages of their pregnancies, for photos
on front pages or covers of reputable newspapers and magazines
such as *Jornal do Brasil* and *Pais e Filhos* (Belira 421). This new
visual received the readers' positive acceptance, and the images of
pregnant-nude women contributed to create a "space of eroticism"
for expectant mothers, establishing new standards for the evaluation of sexuality and sensuality (Belira 421). In this cultural context, it is easy to understand why several women believe Valenssa
contributed to improve their self-esteem and advance the feminist
cause in Brazil.

While it is not an overstatement to say that social, racial, and
sexual categories in Brazil are malleable, it is also true that the
borderline between having a prudish attitude toward the body
and allowing it to be exploited in commercial ventures is fuzzy
and often overlooked. A case in point is the definition of sensuality expressed in the popular magazine *Revista Época* which, in
2000, elected Valenssa "the natural heir of the feminists from the
60s and 70s" (1). It theorizes that she had become the prototype
of an emancipated modern woman who "takes control over her
body without letting go of seduction" (1; see also Moreno 44–46).
Such discourse contributes to create a social and cultural displacement since the image that is promoted—a feminine and feminist
woman is the one who is not afraid of exhibiting or displaying her
body—masks an ideology of marketing, and reinforces the notion
that "femininity" should always be attached to the word "sexy,"
both in its metaphorical associations and in its explicit connotation of arousing, or tending to arouse, sexual desire. It seems that
only in this context can the *mulata* profession be considered a
career for emancipated women.

When she became pregnant for the second time, Globo used
the advanced technology of a studio in Los Angeles to produce
a digital replica of Globeleza (Valenssa, "Interview" by Barbosa).
To avoid recapping the same kind of image that had already
been aired in the previous *carnaval* season, Donner taped the
vignette when she was still in the early stages of her pregnancy
(Valenssa, "Interview" by Barbosa). Aired on January 11, 2004,
the advertisement displayed a computerized adaptation of her

performance. In comparison with previous vignettes, the virtual Globeleza looked highly manufactured, robotic, cartoonish, and stiff, an image that resembles the structure and material on which the concept of Globeleza was built and first aired in 1991. (As described by Donner in his autobiography, *Hans Donner e Seu Universo*, before Globo assigned a real person for the *carnaval* advertisement, it used a cardboard design and a stylized mannequin for the commercial).[30] Having consistently chosen Afro-Brazilian women to advertise its *carnaval* programs, Globo fabricated the misconception that women of all races have equal opportunities in the corporation.

As Valenssa discusses, her role as Globeleza opened some doors for her to pursue entrepreneurial ventures. Complementary to her job as the Globeleza character, she attempted a performative career as a singer and dancer by participating in a show organized by the group É o Tchan, in São Paulo, and joined the show Ela Brasil, in Garden Hall, in Rio de Janeiro (Valenssa, "Interview" by Barbosa; Donner 194; and Bergallo and Duarte 95–103). From 2000 on, Donner designed products stamped with the Globeleza brand—jewelry, a lingerie collection, a video recording, and a calendar—to be sold during the *carnaval* season (Valenssa, "Interview" by Barbosa).[31] In the video recording *Aprenda a Dançar Samba com Valéria Valenssa* ("Learn How to Dance *Samba* with Valéria Valenssa"), she introduces herself as "the symbol of Brazilian *carnaval*" and discusses the process of producing and taping Globeleza's vignettes. During the footage in which Valenssa gives *samba* lessons, the video production intertwines her body and dance movements with images of Rio de Janeiro (especially the sinuous patterns of Copacabana and Ipanema sidewalks, and the curvaceous landscape of the city that the Guanabara Bay and the mountains Corcovado and Pão de Açúcar exemplify).[32] The connection Donner makes between Valenssa's body and Rio's sites is remarkably similar to the associations Caminha presents in his letter to the king of Portugal in 1500 in which gender, race, ethnicity, and sexuality become markers of cultural and ideological spaces. Thus, Donner helped Globo perpetuate its neo-colonial model and economic agenda by selling the images of his wife as the hybrid, sensual *mulata*, and by collapsing the difference between her (exotic) body and the (tropical) landscape of Rio de Janeiro. When some people in

Brazil and abroad criticize him for masterminding the promotion and sale of his wife's naked images, he justifies and defends his choices. For him, nudity is a beautiful and sensuous enterprise that must be shared. As he explains, Valenssa is not really naked because her skin color works as a sort of formal dress that covers her entire body:

> Certa vez, estava com um engraxate na rua, acabando de dar o brilho nos meus sapatos, quando ele me perguntou referindo-se a Valéria: "Seu Hans, como é que você consegue mostrar sua mulher daquele jeito?" Não é só no Brasil que isto acontece. Jornalistas estrangeiros passam por aqui e, depois de tomar um pouco de intimidade, acabam fazendo a mesma pergunta ... Sinceramente só posso dizer que acho a Valéria tão deslumbrante, que não é justo guardá-la só para mim ... A cor da sua pele já é uma vestimenta, um traje de gala." (180–81)

> Once, I was having my shoes shined when the shoeshine boy asked me a question in reference to Valéria: "Mr. Hans, how do you have the courage to display your wife like that?" It is not just in Brazil that I get this type of question. As soon as foreign journalists who are traveling around here get acquainted with me, they ask me the same question ... Honestly speaking, I find Valeria's beauty so stunning that I do not think it is fair to keep it just for myself ... The color of her skin is already a type of clothing, a fancy evening gown.

His comments indicate that he does not seem to perceive, or chooses to ignore, that by foregrounding Valenssa's nudity as a symbol of the erotic, exotic, and sexual Afro-Brazilian woman, he is not only denigrating her as a woman but also an entire race category. By weaving her image into a larger ideological complex (the ideology of whitening and the myth of the race democracy), he links gender, race, and identity, and consequently fragments her subjectivity. In attempting to erase Valenssa's nakedness, Donner's constructed discursivity creates a reverse effect. By establishing her body and race as emblematic tokens of Brazilian *carnaval,* and construing Valenssa's race as a sort of attire, he discloses his perception of race and gender. Such a comment also displays the estranged logic of a white foreigner and his neo-colonial sexual-racial politics and establishes a roadmap for the discourse of "otherness" (the different, exotic, and erotic). Hence, metaphorically speaking, Donner has tattooed his Globeleza with the discourse of "the piccaninny" (the other/the conquered),[33] and has confined her to the display of a construed sensuality that fits the traditional pattern of a slave-holding mentality.

In 2005, after Valenssa had played the Globeleza role for more than fourteen years, the network decided to replace her. Although Globo terminated her contract, Valenssa still appeared on the pages of its official site until 2006. During that period, the network kept an interactive site, where visitors could stimulate their voyeuristic cravings by drawing and painting on Valenssa's virtual, stark-naked body. The digital model moved to the sound of the *samba* rhythm creating the illusion of an interaction and enticing spectators to clothe her body physically and emotionally. From 2005 on, Globo introduced new faces: Aline Prado, Giane Carvalho, Nayara Justino, and Éricka Moura filled the Globeleza position (Bergallo and Duarte 91, 116). Justino starred as the new Globeleza in 2013, but her term was short-lived (C. Gomes). She believes the network acquiesced to viewers' complaints that she was "too dark" to play the role, and in the following year a lighter-skinned *mulata* was selected for the Globeleza position (C. Gomes). This episode reveals "a sliding scale of prejudice"[34] and a range of skin color for *mulatas*. As previously discussed, it also reinforces the concept of "good appearance," which can function as a measurement during job selection.

In analyzing the relationship between the field of cultural production and national identity, Jen Webb asserts that "the fragments of the concept of a 'nation' can be welded together, at least momentarily, by the representation of 'us' in story or performance or visual forms" (157). This is the concept that Globo adopted in 2017, when it changed the Globeleza's image and, for the first time since 1990, the character wore a costume and danced with other performers who represented several regions of Brazil. The new vignette flashed quick images of folkloric costumes and regional *carnaval* celebrations and reunited them into the picture of an energetic, beautiful, and centripetal Globeleza surrounded by the regional representations, all dancing to the jingle: "No meio desse povo / A gente vai se ver na Globo" ("In the middle of the people / We will see ourselves in Globo"). In commenting on Globo's choice to end the era of Globeleza's nudity in the *carnaval* vignettes, Valenssa seems nostalgic and saddened because she believes that the beauty of Brazilian women is no longer held in high esteem: "A beleza da mulher brasileira não é mais valorizada" (*Extra,* n.p.). However, she also acknowledges that *carnaval* culture has changed and gives Globo credit for adapting to the new reality.

Valenssa finds the changes that Globo's executives made in the *carnaval* vignette very radical, but she also opines that the network is attempting to catch up with the cultural transformations that have taken place in Brazil in the last decade: "Se essa mudança foi tão radical é que eles também estão tentando acompanhar essas mudanças" (*Extra,* n.p.). When discussing pursuit of fame, financial gain, success, and her professional *mulata* ventures, Valenssa does not question Globo's ulterior motives in casting only Afro-Brazilian women as Globeleza, or her husband's Svengali behavior. She appears to be content with her *mulata* career, the financial benefits it brought her, and the spotlight she enjoyed dancing *samba* on many Brazilian and European stages (Valenssa, "Interview" by Barbosa). She confides that her desire to work as a *mulata* goes back to her childhood dreams when she aspired to be hired as "Sargentelli's *mulata,*" ascend socially, and marry "a blue-eyed man" (Bergallo and Duarte 27–29).[35] With regard to the public display of her body, she considers it a type of "artistic nudity" as in visual arts (Valenssa, "Interview" by Barbosa).

As Valenssa's comments reveal, she does not seem to realize that *globelezas* and other "made-in-Brazil *mulatas*" are tokens of a national identity mistaken for wonders of a racial democracy. Valenssa and the other women who work in the *mulata* profession find themselves in a no-win situation: the marketing techniques that producers of *mulata* shows bring them many benefits, but to climb that social and economic ladder they become an object of sexual voyeurism, and a new version of a the colonial *mucama.* Analyzing the question from a different angle, Valenssa contended that it is also important to consider how difficult it can be to rebuff the opportunity to ascend socially and become well known in the entertainment industry, especially because there are fewer prospects for women of color (Valenssa, "Interview" by Barbosa). She used autobiographical details to make this point and justify her choices, explaining that she was born and raised in Pavuna, an underprivileged neighborhood on the outskirts of Rio de Janeiro, and did not have many opportunities to study or advance socially (Valenssa,

"Interview" by Barbosa). As she argued, it is enticing for anyone, regardless of race or gender, to exchange menial jobs, or subservient positions (she worked in telemarketing), for the opportunity to hold high-paying jobs, and to be known far beyond the frontiers of one's national territory (Valenssa, "Interview" by Barbosa; Bergallo and Duarte 58).

In her analysis of space, subjectivity, gender, sexuality, and the politics of identity, Kathleen M. Kirby writes that "it is precisely when the space of the body coincides with the space of ideology that [symbolic] violence can occur" (13). However, as she further analyzes, for symbolic violence to occur it needs consent; that is, women must agree to be "woven into a larger ideological complex," by endorsing the system that "tears apart their subjectivity" and defines them by the surface of their bodies (13). Webb presents a similar analysis of symbolic violence, discussing it as an ancillary form of aggression that is dangerous specifically because it is misrecognized and accepted as something that is natural, or "the way things work" (25). In tandem with Kirby's and Webb's theoretical discussions, critics of the *mulata* profession see it as a form of concealed violence. For instance, in coining and discussing the label and ideological formula "*mulata* cordial," Sant'Anna argues that women who agree to have their race and bodies exploited for financial gain contribute to mask racial and social conflicts (*Canibalismo* 41). Mariza Corrêa adopts a similar point of view to analyze the development of the *parda* woman's pride in *mestiçagem* and uses the term *mulatice* as a critical way to refer to the attitude of Afro-Brazilian women who embrace the *mulata* profession uncritically (47–48). Pravaz adopted Corrêa's neologism to argue that it would be simplistic to interpret those performers as mere victims of an oppressive system, "not only because of the immense delight women take in showcasing their talents, but most importantly because *mulatice* is understood by many as a source of racial pride itself" ("Brazilian" 133).

When Afro-Brazilian women sport the "made-in-Brazil *mulata*" trademark with pride and zeal, they overlook the fact that those engaged in the creation and development of the *mulata* profession treat them as commodities. They do not seem to realize that, by endorsing the system that exploits them, they transform their bodies into a one-dimensional paradigm sized to fit into the symbolic map of a mixed-race nation. By uncritically accepting the *mulata* profession, Valenssa and other Afro-Brazilian women assimilate and endorse that model of exploitation and become complicit with the system that undermines their individuality and denigrates their race and gender. For them, the *mulata* profession is considered an enviable award, an emblem of power, or a sign of inclusion into the entertainment industry. The females who adopted this profession also have a counterpart in the famous *parda* women characterized in Brazilian literature and popular songs as symbols of sensuality and sexuality. Their descriptions can be found, for instance, in the poetry of Gregório de Matos e Guerra (1636–1696) whose irreverent and satirical poems spared no social class in Bahia, and reserved for brown Afro-Brazilian women his sharpest criticism because, in his opinion, they were untrustworthy creatures whose unrestrained sexuality and thriving promiscuity could only harm a man (Queiroz Junior 33).[36]

The concept of a sensual and unreliable brown Afro-Brazilian woman is repeated in Azevedo's *O Cortiço ("The Slum")*.[37] Published following the aftermath of the abolition of black slavery in Brazil, the end of the Bragança Monarchy and the proclamation of the Republic, *O Cortiço* captures social, political, and cultural transitions. It documents the social changes of the time, presents a grim picture of Rio de Janeiro's urban society, and summarizes the upheavals of a convoluted society and a city swollen by the influx of urban migration (mostly displaced freed slaves and soldiers returning from the Canudos War), and the inflow of European immigrants who were brought to Brazil to replace the black work force. Following the deterministic bent of the time, the text summarizes the best expression of Brazilian Naturalism in its description of the appalling reality of tenement dwelling in a city infested with dire poverty, serious public health issues, and bulging housing problems.[38] It focuses on themes of displacement, migration, immigration, racial stereotyping, and prejudice as it presents a variety of characters from different backgrounds, races, and ethnicities. The main character, however, is the tenement itself, a collective entity that exerts a powerful negative influence on all people who dwell in it. The novel presents a stereotypical picture of the mixed-race population of both genders, describing them as flawed human beings. Firmo (the *capoeirista*) and Rita Baiana (the *samba* dancer) are represented in the novel as conspicuous examples of Afro-Brazilians who hold an intermediary racial and social position and, because of that, do not pledge alliance to any group. Consequently, their ambiguity and character ambivalence portray them as undeserving of trust (they are intelligent, sensual, and physically attractive, but are also arrogant, unfaithful, selfish, and prone to deceiving). As Barbara Browning discusses (in another context), "the so-called *mulato* capoeirista is a figure moving between categories. He exists at the anxious point of contact between blacks and whites. And while that point of contact was sexualized in the body of the *mulata* sambista, it is made violent in that of the capoeirista" (96).

The mixed population of African descent was often described as people who upheld little or no racial allegiance and withstood low moral standards. As for Afro-Brazilian men, they emblematized untrustworthy individuals who were prone to violent and mean behavior and, therefore, needed to be feared. The gendered perception of race was stigmatized in the image of *parda* females because they allegedly possessed a bewitching charm and a boundless sexuality as evidenced in the characterization of Rita Baiana. In addition to her conspicuous sensuality and sexuality, Azevedo added a few more ingredients to his formula: Rita Baiana is beautiful, happy, sociable, and dances *samba* well. Her name also adds a touch of "authenticity" to her racial profile as it refers to someone from Bahia (the cradle of the African diaspora in Brazil), and indirectly connects her to the Afro-Brazilian women described in Matos's poetry. Thus, Rita Baiana reproduces some of the stereotypes that Matos made popular in the 1700s and establishes new typecasts. Azevedo portrays her as a trickster, someone whose seductive powers and unbridled sexuality sow unrest and stir discord. The combination of those characteristics—which are more noticeable when she dances—ruins the lives of men bewitched by her charm and has a decimating effect on Firmo and Jerônimo (the Portuguese immigrant who leaves his family because of her).

Inspired by Azevedo's character, in 2011, John Neschling and Geraldo Carneiro composed the song, "Rita Baiana,"[39] in which they catalogue and inflate a long list of stereotypes associated with her everlasting disposition for sex. While Azevedo's narrative is told in a third-person narrative voice, Neschling and Carneiro's song presents a first-person female voice explaining to the man of her affection why she is so voluptuous. The lyric voice describes the overwhelming sexual need that afflicts her as a heavy burden, a form of slavery, a biological trap, an illness triggered by the tropical climate of Rio de Janeiro.

Olha, meu nego,
Isso não dá sossego.
E se não tem chamego,
Eu me devoro toda de paixão.
Acho que é o clima feiticeiro,
Do Rio de Janeiro que me
Atormenta o coração.

Listen, my dear,
This feeling gives me no break.
When I do not make love,
I burn in passion.
I think it is caused by
Rio de Janeiro's bewitching climate
That torments my heart.

In a way, her explanation reproduces the old mentality that it was nearly impossible for a male to resist the sensuality and sexuality of the *parda* woman because it is so uncontrollable that not even she can tame or avoid it as described in the following verses:

Eu nem consigo pensar direito,
Com essa aflição dentro do meu peito.
Ai, essa coisa que me desatina,
Me enlouquece, me domina,
Me tortura e me alucina.
E me dá
Uma vontade e uma gana dá
Uma saudade da cama dá.
Quando a danada me chama
Maldita de Rita Baiana.

I cannot even think straight,
'Cause I feel so afflicted.
Ai, this feeling unhinges me,
It drives me crazy, it dominates me,
It tortures me and makes me crazy.
It gives me
An uncontrollable desire
And a craving for a bed.
When this sexual craving calls me
Rita Baiana is doomed.

This song was also recorded and made popular by Zezé Motta, a well-known singer and a distinguished black actor in Brazil. By lending her voice, prestige, and fame to popularize the song, Motta reinforced several stereotypes addressed in the song "Rita Baiana." Yet, it was not the first time that Motta embraced formulaic roles designed for Afro-Brazilian women. For instance, she played the leading role in the 1976 film *Xica da Silva*[40] which focuses on the life of an Afro-descendant woman named Francisca da Silva de Oliveira, better known as Chica da Silva (1732–1796), who lived in the mining town of Diamantina during the gold and diamond rush. The film caricatures Silva's life by focusing on her construed bewitching charm, burning sexuality, and her occasional grotesque attitudes and behaviors. A case in point is the refrain of the thematic song ("Xica da, da, da Silva")[41] which is a play on words: *da* from her name Chica *da* Silva, and *dá* from the conjugated form of the verb *dar* ("to give"). Both words are pronounced the same way and the pun, intended to provoke laughter, reveals the hidden Brazilian discourse of gender and sex. That is, in addition to the traditional meaning it has, in colloquial Brazilian Portuguese the verb *dar* can also mean the act of willingly consenting to having sexual intercourse. The word *da/dá* is repeated and thus emphasized throughout the song's refrain which is played at every sex scene, or when it is suggested that Silva knows some powerful sexual tricks capable of holding any man to her side. The focus on her sexuality submits the idea that her eroticism might have been the only gift she had and the single reason such an influential white man selected her to be his long-term companion.

Silva became the slave and mistress of the richest and most powerful white man of the region who freed her six months later and, disregarding the colonial laws, co-habited openly with her for fifteen years, and helped her raised their thirteen children until he had to move to Portugal for business reasons (Furtado 15–20). In her historical account of Chica da Silva's life, Júnia Ferreira Furtado questions several myths about her sexual allure by focusing on her sense of empowerment, the attention she gave to her children's education, and the respect (or fear) she earned as the richest woman in Diamantina. However, as Furtado also mentions, to gain such a prominent place in a slave-driven society, Chica endorsed some of the ideologies of the white society that had enslaved her. She also had African and Afro-Brazilian slaves, adopted manners and values sported by the upper echelons of Diamantina's society, and used dissimulation to be part of the social circles that had previously scorned her (Furtado 17).

In a conversation with Henry Louis Gates Jr. in her residence in Rio de Janeiro—when he was filming the documentary *Brazil: A Racial Paradise?*—Motta described the racist comments she heard when she auditioned for the movie *Xica da Silva*. She confided to Gates that the producer and/or the director did not want to cast her because she was considered "too black" and not beautiful enough for the part.[42] She had to fight hard to play that leading role. Motta also rightly complained about the lack of opportunities for black women to work in cinema and television; however, by accepting the role, or insisting to play parts that depreciate or mischaracterize her peers, Motta reinforced the status quo. The part she played in the film *Xica da Silva*, and her choice of recording and performing the song "Rita Baiana" during the popular television program *Fantástico* did not contribute to advance Afro-Brazilian women's causes. Motta does not seem to realize that the entertainment industry continues casting stereotypical roles exactly because women will compete fiercely to play them.

But not all are gray areas in terms of race in Brazil. A number of poets and musical groups have adopted a judicious position in reference to the "mulatto escape-hatch," the *parda* woman mystique, the "cordial *mulata*," and the myth of racial democracy. They reiterate the criticism voiced by activists, cultural anthropologists, historians, and sociologists who often analyze the ambiguous relations of race and gender in Brazil. The poet and anthropologist Edimilson de Almeida Pereira is one of those writers who turned his attention to such topics. For instance, his book-length poem, *Caderno de Retorno* ("Notebook of a Return")[43] addresses historical silences and revisits individual and collective memories related to the Portuguese colonization and black slavery. The poetic voice connects past and contemporary discourses, and links local and global spaces by analyzing movements of migration, immigration, and slavery. Pereira draws a literary picture that spills beyond Brazil's frontiers as he reconfigures the social and cultural position of several minorities on the "skin-map" of a globalized world. The following stanza is a catalyst of emotions for the narrative voice and a compass for the reader to navigate the ambiguous characteristics of race relations and the myth of racial democracy in the ambiguous landscape of Brazilian society:

Tenho doze anos.
Ao entregar a roupa limpa,
me indicam a entrada de serviço
mal iluminada.
O menino deliza o hades das garagens
Adivinha a campaminha em braile.
A cozinha abre a porta
(até quando fará os mesmos gestos?)
sorri recolhe as peças
e mergulha outra vez
no Brasil colonial.
Será o dublê de mucama que
areou vasilhas
sábados a fio?
e engomou por força o próprio destino?
(Pereira 208)

I am a twelve-year-old delivery boy.
When I hand over the clean clothes,
they point to the poorly lit
service entrance to me.
The kid glides through the garage's darkness
And blindly fumbles in search of the bell.
The cook opens the kitchen door
(until when will she repeat those gestures?)
smiles and receives the clothes
and once again she recedes
into colonial Brazil.
Could she be a mucama's double who
shined dishes
Saturdays on end?
and was obliged to press her own destiny?

The verses cited above analyze the emotional experiences of a twelve-year-old boy who is entrusted with the task of delivering a bundle of cleaned clothes to one of his parents' clients. At the front door of the house he is reminded to use the "service entrance" which is located at the back of the house. (The *entrada de serviço* and *elevador de serviço*, which a number of critics consider a veiled form of *apartheid*,[44] are ambiguous and ambivalent spaces found in higher-end and middle-class homes and apartment buildings in Brazil.)[45] To reach the "service entrance," he must go through the unlit space of the garage. At this point there is a reference, in lower case, to the mythological Hades ("O menino deliza o hades das garagens"), connecting the dim garage to the underworld and alluding to the dark space of separation between the front and back doors where the "service entrance" is located. The garage suggests not only the physical dark space he has to traverse to reach the "service entrance," but also the emotional and intellectual crossing he must undergo for his rite of passage to take place (the recognition of social and racial differences). In arriving at the "service entrance," he looks at the smiley Afro-Brazilian woman who opens the kitchen door and receives the clothes. At that moment, a shift in narrative voice takes place, marking the loss of childhood innocence.

Like a mythological quester, he reaches the zenith of his apprenticeship when—face-to-face with the smiling female servant and her submissive acceptance of her fate—he begins to question the passageways of Brazilian history and the myth of the racial democracy. Pereira conveys this change by having the twelve-year-old poetic voice—which addresses the reader in the first person of discourse at the beginning of the stanza—transmute into an enquirer/narrator who uses the third person of discourse to raise questions about the Brazilian racial and social systems. Pereira compares the role the woman plays as a servant in modern Brazil to how *mucamas* behaved in the big plantation houses in the colonial past. Bemused by the fact that she looks happy, the adult-poetic voice ends the stanza with incisive questions about how unaware Afro-Brazilian women who work as domestic servants are of their exploitation in the social and economic strata.

In the poem "Mulher" ("Woman"), Sant'Anna also invites the readers to look at historical facts, this time to evaluate the traditional moral codes and the amalgamation of gender, race, and sexuality in colonial Brazil. He paraphrases a popular saying that associated women's social and sexual function in the domestic structure, a construct that Freyre discussed in *The Masters and the Slaves*.[46] The following verses elucidate Sant'Anna's (95) parodic interpretation of it, calling attention to the fact that not much has changed in Brazilian society since then:

> Lá está ela: como no tempo do avô
> numa tríade exemplar:
> a mãe preta no eito,
> a mulata no leito,
> a mãe branca no lar.

> There she is: just like she was in old times
> in a prototypical triad:
> the black woman in the fields,
> the mestizo woman in bed,
> the white mother at home.

A similar revisionist analysis appears in the poem "Passado Histórico" ("Historic Past") by Sônia Fátima da Conceição in which she questions the racial-sexual-biological generalizations of black and *parda* women. As the poem illustrates, usually the black woman is not considered sensual or beautiful, and the *parda* female is mischaracterized as too sensual to be a good worker. She points out the historical silences that disregard the *parda* woman's capacity to work and omits that she was also submitted to the rules and punishments of the slave system. Those historical omissions also hide the black female's physical attractiveness and sex appeal as discussed in "Passado Histórico" (118):

> Do açoite
> da mulata erótica
> da negra boa de eito
> e de cama
> (nenhum registro).

> Of the whipping
> of the erotic mestizo woman
> and the black woman good at working
> and in bed
> (there are no records).

The poems by Sant'Anna and Conceição are thematically in sync with Angela Gilliam's discussion of Freyre's theoretical views about the contribution women of color have given to Brazilian society. In her critique of Freyre, Gilliam sees "the need to visualize the burden of slavery from the perspective of the slave woman," and labels his concept of *mestiçagem* "the-Great-Sperm-Theory-of-Nation-Formation" because she believes Freyre "degrades the Afro-Brazilian women by postulating their roles as perennial sex objects" ("Women's" 226–27).

Tinkering with two different voices, in the poem/song "Mulata Exportação" ("Made-in-Brazil *Mulata*"), Elisa Lucinda also captures and highlights some paradoxes of Brazilian history and culture. Using a call and response technique, the two poetic voices establish a contrastive tone between past/present, male/female, and white master/black slave. Even though the text is, at times, structured as a discursive play of thesis and antithesis, the message it conveys goes beyond a mere set of oppositions because it also highlights historical intersections, social interplays, and the struggles of forces that those conflicts reflect and/or describe. The first part of the poem is told from a slave-owner mentality and a male-controled point of view that pokes fun not only at women, but also at any type of Afro-Brazilian resistance. For instance, the male voice ridicules the cultural opposition the *malês*[47] represented in Bahia, from 1827 to 1831, when they organized insurrections, openly challenging Catholicism and the slaveholding system. The following fragments of the first part of the poem corroborate such readings:

> Rebola meu bem-querer
> Que eu sou seu improviso
> Seu karaoquê
> [...]
> Vem ser meu folklore,
> Vem ser minha tese,
> Sobre nego malê.

> Swing your hips, honey
> For I am your improvisation,
> Your karaoke.
> [...]
> Come be my folklore,
> Come be my thesis,
> On Afro-Brazilian *malês*.

In the second part of the poem, Lucinda emphasizes the complex and ambivalent position that race, gender, sexuality, and sensuality have acquired in Brazil. Embodied by a female voice, this segment offsets the male ideological position by presenting a counter-discourse that questions the general perception of Afro-Brazilian women as products owned, bought, or sold as sexual objects. In the second part of "Mulata Exportação," the poetic voice warns that the injustices of the slave system cannot be erased in modern-day by simply hiring a *parda* woman to dance *samba* in cultural shows, night clubs, or to play stereotypical roles on television or in cinema:

Olha aqui, meu senhor:
Eu me lembro da senzala
E tu te lembras da casa grande.
Vamos juntos, sinceramente,
Escrever outra história.
Digo, repito e não minto:
Vamos passar essa verdade a limpo
Porque não é dançando samba
Que eu te redimo ou te acredito.

Hear me out, sir:
I remember the slave quarters
You remember the plantation house.
Let's together, in an honest way,
Rewrite history.
I say it, I repeat, and I do not lie:
Let's be clear about something
It is not dancing *samba*
That I redeem or believe you.

Brazilians' heightened awareness of their sensuality and sexuality adds captivating liveliness and *joie-de-vivre* to their lifestyle, yet it also helps promote a superficial image of the country (which the *mulata* profession epitomizes). The song "Mucama," released in 1994 by the musical group Cidade Negra,[48] examines some of these aspects. To draw a comparison with the behavior of *mucamas*, it analyzes how Afro-Brazilians (male and female alike) appear to be unaware of how exploited they are. The lyrics of the song compare the discrimination Afro-Brazilians undergo in modern days to the way slave owners treated Africans and their descendants. However, the lyrics of the song also stress their co-optation with the system that exploits them. The song berates Afro-Brazilians for assimilating ideas, moral codes, patterns of behavior, and values steeped in the colonial ideological paradigm. It censures them for appearing to be satisfied with the cultural norms and social system as long as they can watch television, participate in *carnaval* festivities, dance in cultural shows, function as sexual toys, or accept the position of provisional icons of a cultural identity. In addressing the role the *parda* women have in this cultural scenario, the lyrics of the song criticize them for endorsing practices that subjugate them (for instance, the fierce competition to play the Globeleza character).[49] The song criticizes both the promoters and the performers who are involved in the ambivalent form of inclusion of *mulatas* into the national imaginary as sexual symbols, and their exclusion from other significant aspects of Brazilian cultural identity. It censures all of those who engage in, endorse, and foster the consumption of women's bodies as advertising tools or consumer goods, as the following verses reveal:

> Mucama na cama do patrão
> Me chama, me chama de negão:
> Paga salário de pão,
> Mas come o que a população
> Não come.
> O que se espera de uma nação
> Que o heroi é a televisão?
> Que passa todos os seus meses mal,
> Melhora tudo no Carnaval?
> Eu só vou te usar,
> Você não é pra mim,
> Já temos outra pra botar no teu lugar.
> Pirlimpimpim!
> (Cidade Negra, faixa 1)

> *Mucama* in the boss's bed
> Call me "big black"
> The pay is chicken feed,
> But the boss eats what
> The crowd does not.
> What can be expected of a nation
> In which the hero is a television set?
> It suffers during the whole the year,
> And everything gets better during *carnaval*?
> I am just going to use you,
> You are not good enough for me,
> We already have another one to replace you.
> Pirlimpimpim!

The rap part of the song addresses the Afro-Brazilian working class whose dreams of social and economic growth only materialize in *carnaval* costumes, music, and dance. It characterizes the Afro-Brazilian population as a type of lady-in-waiting and a slave mistress (*mucama*) who continues to be exploited but seems content to abide by the rules: "E o povo-mucama continua sorrindo." The song also reveals that the "made-in-Brazil *mulata*" concept masks domination and stigmatization, and the *mulata*

97

profession is a concession made to the patriarchal ideology and a slaveholding mentality. The criticism about the passive attitude of the Afro-Brazilian population is most evident when the poetic voice censures them for their lack of social ambition and higher aspirations, and for accepting scraps of food, small pieces of land, and stray bullets, clear references to the dire violence so prominent in the shantytowns of urban centers in Brazil.

> Mucama que nada exclama,
> Que não se inflama,
> Que não reclama,
> E se acalma vendo novela.

> *Mucama* who does not say anything,
> Who does not get upset,
> Who does not complain,
> And calms down watching *telenovelas*.

In 2002, the rap artist Nega Gizza (Gisele Gomes de Souza) released the album *Na Humildade* ("*In Humility*") in which she addresses questions related to race, citizenship, division of wealth, violence, gender, and the myth of a racial democracy. Nega Gizza is a resident of a *favela* ironically named Parque Esperança because it is a place where there is no park or hope. The first song of the album, titled "Filme de Terror" ("Horror Movie"), presents a litany of problems that afflict the impoverished and (mostly) black and *pardo* population of Brazil (poverty, hunger, lack of decent housing, violence in the *favelas*, and empty promises by politicians). It also lists police persecution and brutality, a staggering division of wealth, separation of physical and social space (the rich people live near the beaches and the poor up on the hills). As Frederick Moehn has analyzed the thematic contents of *Na Humildade*, "her album presents a black woman favela resident's perpective on rap, race, class, miscegenation and Brazilian citizenship. It is a subject position she regards as alienated by the discourse of miscegenation, and deprived of the full complement of rights associated with modern citizenship in the West" (116). The first lines of the song sarcastically introduce stereotypes of a tropical and carefree mixed-race country and establish a dialogue with the songs and poems previously mentioned:

País da democraca racial
Da mulata exportação
Brasil! nação feliz, um país tropical
País da pedofilia, futebol e carnaval
Brasil que nos condena a viver
Como animal irracional
Vamos fingir que vai passar
Vamos fingir que é natural.

Country of racial democracy
Of the made-in-Brazil *mulata*
Brazil! happy nation, a tropical country
County of pedophilia, soccer and *carnaval*
Brasil that condemns us to live
As irrational animals
Let's pretend it will go away
Let's pretend it is natural.

As the examples discussed reveal, revisionist poets, composers, and activists addréss stereotypes, historical omissions, taxonomies, social immobility, and paradoxes that feed into the ambiguous racial system in Brazil. Their texts illustrate that they often work hand-in-hand with historians, cultural anthropologists, and sociologists to review assumptions, question misleading concepts, and debunk the idea of a Brazilian harmonious synthesis of racial diversity. In a number of ways those texts reveal hidden conflicts and uneven layers of society. The poems and songs discussed in this chapter also criticize Afro-Brazilian women for partaking in the exploitative enterprise that contributes to stigmatize Brazil as a country of erotic utopia. They illustrate the efforts made to raise awareness in the Afro-Brazilian population, in general, and women in particular, about the dangers of becoming symbolic representations of a national identity. Their criticism also reiterates Renato Ortiz's discussion that, if the idea of a mixed-race Brazil presumably makes it possible for everyone to recognize each other as part of a national identity, it also conceals racial conflicts by acting as an ideological formula that slackens national consciousness (*Cultura* 44, 94). Ortiz construes that the ideology of syncretism, which *mestiçagem* and the concept of a racial democracy symbolize, masks stratified class and race divisions and presupposes the idea of a society where conflicting relations of power do not exist (*Cultura* 95). And, as is examined in the following chapter, no other Brazilian cultural manifestation can translate the image of a country where those conflicting relations of power are downplayed to a minimum than soccer.

Chapter Three

Women in Soccer

Futebol: The Brazilian Passion

In an endorsement of Edilberto Coutinho's book of short stories, *Bye, Bye, Soccer*, the literary critic and writer Silviano Santiago offers an overview of the importance *futebol* has acquired in Brazil. He considers that the game "should be understood primarily as a metaphor for the human condition," and summarizes the thematic focuses of Coutinho's narratives in equally passionate terms: "To free oneself from fear, to fully participate in the game of life, to lose oneself in the kingdom of fantasy without borders, to surrender to the element of change in one's life, these are some of the themes that appear in Coutinho's short stories."[1] In *Soccer Madness*, Janet Lever addresses some of the social and cultural reasons why sports, in general, and soccer in particular, have become vastly popular worldwide. She contends that a sport can contribute to integrate a nation because it can be shared by "people of different social classes, ethnicities, races, and religions" (19). In just a few decades after it was formally introduced in Brazil, soccer had already won the hearts and minds of the people. As early as the 1930s, it was already a professional activity, gradually played throughout the country in schools, on beaches, fields, vacant lots, backyards, and streets, in part because it is a relatively inexpensive sport and can be played anywhere (Levine, "Sport" 239). In analyzing why soccer became a passion and spread rapidly from region to region in Brazil, Robert M. Levine considers that the sport not only "provided a common language of experience to an increasingly mobile population lacking national symbols," but it also "offered group loyalty, emotional release, and a technical knowledge which could be mastered without schooling or pedigree" ("Sport" 236).

Informally, soccer was first introduced to Brazilians in 1864 "by British sailors on shore leave" (Levine, "Sport" 233). Formally, it was presented by the Brazilian-born Charles Miller (from Scottish father and English mother) when he returned from England, in 1894, with soccer balls, a guidebook, and a bourgeois tradition from England, "a gentlemen's sport" at that time (Santos 12; Eakin 172). Miller was instrumental in founding the São Paulo Athletic Club (organized in 1902), where he played until 1910. The sport was also popularized in Rio de Janeiro by Oscar Cox. In 1903, two new soccer clubs appeared: Fluminense in Rio de Janeiro and Grêmio in Porto Alegre, and in 1904, Belo Horizonte followed suit by establishing the Sport Club. In the 1910s, small neighborhood soccer clubs called *clubes de esquina* ("corner clubs") began taking root. Corinthians Paulista was the first popular club to gain prominence; afterwards there was a proliferation of teams that appealed to the masses (Santos 11–14). Levine summarizes the historical trajectory of soccer in Brazil, proposing four evolving and distinct phases:

> *Futebol*'s history falls into four broad periods: 1894–1904, when it remained largely restricted to private urban clubs of the foreign-born; 1905–1933, its amateur phase, marked by great strides in popularity and rising pressures to raise the playing level by subsidizing athletes; 1933–1950, the initial phase of professionalism; and the post-1950 phase of world class recognition accompanied by elaborate commercialism and maturity as an unchallenged national asset. ("Sport" 234)

In Brazil, soccer has been used to foment nationalism at home and as a commercial and political tool abroad.[2] Its cultural significance can be measured by how it has contributed to the Brazilian Portuguese lexicon, and how it is represented in visual and performance arts, and in literature and music (Scarinci).[3] There is no shortage of literary, academic, and mass marketed books, and articles on soccer's history, development, and importance. A case in point is José Miguel Wisnik's analysis of the cultural significance of soccer in which he discusses Pier Paolo Pasolini's comparative assessments of soccer and literature. As he explains, for Pasolini, the style of soccer played by Germans and Englishmen resemble a realistic prose; the way the Italians play can be consider a form of "aesthetic prose"; and South Americans, especially Brazilians, play soccer as if they were writing poetry (207). The following excerpt from Carlos Drummond de Andrade's poem, "Futebol," underscores Pasolini's views and lauds soccer's importance in Brazil's national imaginary:

> Futebol se joga no estádio?
> Futebol se joga na praia,
> Futebol se joga na rua,
> Futebol se joga na alma. (13)

> Should soccer be played in a stadium?
> Soccer should be played at the beach,
> Soccer should be played on the street,
> Soccer should be played on the soul.

The representation of soccer in literature, however, is not a new phenomenon. As Leonardo Affonso de Miranda Pereira (198–205) discusses, it goes back to 1908, when Coelho Neto published the novel *Esphinge* in which he introduced a very fit character, an Englishman named James Marian, who practiced tennis and "foot-ball" regularly.[4] If soccer appeared just as an isolated reference in that novel, by 1912, Coelho Neto's attention to the sport had grown substantially, to a point that he joined the Fluminense Futebol Club and, three years later, wrote the club's fight song. From then on, he adopted soccer as his true passion. Basing his admiration for soccer on eugenic principles and the regenerative qualities of sports, Coelho Neto saw in it the potential to improve the physical and mental characteristics of Brazilian people because he believed it would make them stronger, more disciplined, and prone to developing a sense of collectivity. But soccer was not the only sport or gymnastic that Coelho Neto thought could help discipline the Brazilian "character." Throughout the nineteenth century, and in the first three decades of the twentieth century, the general public perceived *capoeira* mainly as a type of martial art, and a physically challenging exercise. Such aspects of *capoeira* caught Coelho Neto's attention whose interest in the fight-ritual dates back to 1910 when he lauded it as an excellent gymnastic. In 1928, he published an article ("O Nosso Jogo"; "Our Game") praising its merits and proposing a pedagogical use for the African-derived fight-ritual. He argued that *capoeira*'s movements could contribute to

103

harmonize body and mind and suggested it should be adopted as a national sport taught in schools and military academies (Coelho Neto 89–94).

In 1918, Coelho Neto's unswerving admiration for "foot-ball" drew the attention of the Afro-Brazilian writer Lima Barreto who opposed the increasing crescent popularity of soccer on the grounds that the players of large and important clubs were mostly white, the game was foreign and elitist, and it used terms such as "corner kick," "club," "goal," "offside," "pass," "penalty kick," and "team."[5] (In the first decades of the twentieth century, soccer was initially played by white men, in elite clubs, and by the employees of the British companies established in Brazil.) An intellectual dispute broke out between Coelho Neto and Lima Barreto who called attention to the fact that the black and mestizo population were not allowed to participate in important matches. Leonardo Pereira condenses Lima Barreto's opinion on the subject as follows:

> Vendo nos sócios dos grandes clubes os herdeiros dos antigos senhores de escravos, Lima enxerga no futebol uma das formas de continuação da dominação exercida, durante décadas, pelo regime escravista ... Longe de projetar através do futebol o futuro do país, vendo-o como um "regenerador da raça brasileira" como fazia Coelho Neto, Lima Barreto enxergava nele apenas a continuação de um passado de diferenciação. (216)

> Considering the members of large clubs to be heirs of slave owners, Lima sees in soccer a way to preserve the forms of domination that slavery had imposed ... Far from seeing in soccer the capacity to project the country into the future, "invigorating the Brazilian race," as Coelho Neto had advocated, Lima Barreto could only see the continuity of a past based on differentiation.

Lima Barreto's resentment was exacerbated in 1921, when the president of Brazil, Epitácio Pessoa, banned the participation of black and brown Brazilians from the national team that would go to Argentina to compete in a championship. The writer rose to the occasion, commenting on the unfortunate decision of the president which he considered an attempt to hide the fact that Brazil had a large mixed-race population (L. Pereira 214). Elected as a blessing by some and a curse by others, soccer became so predominant that, by 1922, even Lima Barreto recognized the sport's popularity by conceding that membership in a "foot-ball club" was a must for people of all walks of life (L. Pereira 217). For workers, however, soccer was not a way of disciplining the body (as Coelho Neto envisioned), or a mechanism of social alienation (as Lima Barreto asserted), but rather a leisure activity, a ludic experience. Around 1920, workers who usually had a membership in one of the small "foot-ball" associations also took interest in *carnaval*, another activity that was becoming quite popular. During the *carnaval* season, members of the "corner clubs" began requesting permission from the police for their groups to parade the streets of Rio de Janeiro as a form of combining entertainment and advertisement. For them, carrying their soccer club banners when dancing *samba* in the parades was another way to gain more visibility and attract members to their "corner clubs" (L. Pereira 220–21).[6]

Numerous media sports commentators and writers have claimed that the creativity and swing of Brazilian soccer style can be traced to the rhythms and choreographies of *samba* and analyzed it as an art form that transformed players into soccer artists. The players' agility and dance-like movements have also been associated with movements in *capoeira*. There are, for instance, similarities between *ginga*, the swing movement of *capoeira*, and the rhythmic movements of soccer, which seasoned Brazilian players perform during the game to dribble past their opponent, showcase their artful skills, and advance to the goal area.[7] (Didi, Pelé, Garrincha, and Marta are some of the most conspicuous examples of players who embody the style of playing that characterize *futebol-arte*.) Comparisons between similar ways of playing *capoeira* and soccer, or dancing *samba*, are not new; they can be found in Freyre's 1930s writings that connected the Brazilian style of soccer to African-centered cultural expressions (Barreto 235). Freyre cited Brazilian soccer as another sample of "tropical hybridity," and popularized the idea of a "foot-ball *mestiço*" in an article that he published in 1938 in *Diário de Pernambuco*. He considered that the Brazilian players had developed a unique style of playing that resembled *ginga* and *samba* dancing. For Freyre, when contrasted with the European style of playing, Brazilian soccer amassed unique qualities such as elements of surprise, malice, and spontaneity: "Há alguma coisa de dança ou capoeiragem que marca o estilo brasileiro de jogar futebol, que arredonda e adoça o jogo inventado pelos ingleses" ("It has *capoeiragem* which sets apart the Brazilian way of playing soccer, a way of playing that rounds and sweetens the game"; "Foot-ball" 4). Thus, during his lifetime, Freyre became the most expressive voice to consider *mestiçagem* a key factor in the development of *futebol-arte*. Mário Filho's 1947 pioneering work on race in Brazilian soccer (*O Negro no Futebol Brasileiro*, for which Freyre wrote the preface), added additional weight in validating Brazilian *mestiçagem* and racial democracy, and connecting it to soccer. There is also the positive impact that Vargas's policies had on validating all African-derived cultural products (with *samba*, soccer, and *capoeira* in the forefront) in the 1930s and 1940s.[8] Ana Paula da Silva observes that if, on one hand the government's incentive contributed to promote and sanction cultural practices, on the other hand, it also "provided a convenient stage for the dramatization of the Estado Novo ideology of miscegenation, with ethnically and regionally rooted cultures losing their specificities and being absorbed within the Brazilian culture whole" (7).

Even though DaMatta does not refer directly to *capoeira*, he compares soccer to *samba* dancing, refers to *jogo de cintura* (to move the beltline with ease and elegance), and discusses elements of improvisation, which he considers "a metaphor for the so-called art of *malandragem*" ("Sport" 107). Thus, his description of an elegant soccer game includes many aspects of *malícia* (trickery, astuteness, evasiveness), a fundamental part of a well-played *capoeira* game. (In *capoeira*, evasion and *malandragem* often supersedes direct confrontation, similar, for instance, to a good dribble in soccer.) By the time Brazil won the FIFA World Cup for the third time (1970), it was considered that the country had developed a special way of playing soccer: *o jogo bonito*, or *futebol-arte*.[9] The beautiful game had acquired the respect of fans throughout the world who marveled at the grace of the players on the field. It is the grace and elegance of the body movements of soccer that caught Drummond's poetic insight when he compared the players' skillful dribbles and jumps with dance steps. The following excerpt from his poem "Futebol" describes soccer as an artistic performance, a fundamental expressive manifestation of Brazilian culture. Drummond portrays the players' leaps and bounds poetically. For him, the bodies moving on the soccer field defy gravity because in their leaps and bounds, they draw magical sketches in the air and become an object of art: "São vôos de estátuas súbitas,

/ desenhos feéricos, bailados, / de pés e troncos entrançados" ("There are flights of sudden statues, / fairy designs, ballets, / of feet and braided trunks"; 13).

But *mestiçagem* has not always been a source of pride in soccer. For most Brazilians and soccer analysts, the worst tragedy in the history of Brazilian soccer was the 1950 World Cup when Brazil, the favorite to win the championship, was tied with Uruguay in the final match. In Simoni Lahud Guedes's assessment, the sad experience of losing the title in 1950 transformed race into a scapegoat, and the loss into a national drama that was never completely forgotten because, regardless of the outcome of a match, a national team is always considered a living symbol of a nation: "Todas as vezes que um grupo de homens escolhidos como os 'melhores' veste a camisa da seleção brasileira de futebol, eles se transformam, para o bem ou para o mal, num símbolo vivo da nação" ("Every time a group of men chosen as the 'best' wears the shirt of the Brazilian football team, they become, for better or for worse, a living symbol of the nation"; 55). The Brazilian goalie, Moacir Barbosa Nascimento (known simply as Barbosa), was unable to defend a penalty kick and Uruguay won the final match, on Sunday, July 16, 1950. That date is popularly known as *o dia que o Maracanã chorou* ("the day Maracanã stadium cried"). The frustration and humiliation that became entrenched in Brazil's collective memory had the makings of a myth that begged for a plausible explanation (Abrahão e Soares 19–20). The *parda* Barbosa and his race were blamed for his "fault," or inability to secure a victory for Brazil. Many considered it an act of "treason," and some posed questions about his masculinity. Barbosa carried that burden and stigma for the rest of his life.[10] Stereotypical gender configurations in Brazil consider sports that are played using the hands (volleyball and basketball, for instance) to be less masculine than those in which the players can only use their feet (as in the case of soccer). In this context, when frustrated with the performance of a male goalie, the crowds at stadiums diminish his importance by suggesting he is effeminate. In a discussion of gender, race, soccer, and nation building, Marcos Alves Souza highlights these discussions, and analyzes the ambiguous position male goalies have in the national imaginary because they touch the ball with their hands. He writes that for a goalie to fail to intercept a ball is often interpreted as "falta de masculinidade e virilidade, ou também desvio moral, pois [o goleiro] está ali para defender a sua "cidadela" ("lack of masculinity and virility, and also a moral deviation, since [the goalie] is there to defend his citadel"; 147).[11]

In 1954, once again, with the majority of the national team made up of *pardos* and blacks, the loss to Hungary was blamed on the "inferior" race, unable to stand up to strong Europeans. Brazil has had other losses in World Cup championships as well, but the emotional effect of the humiliating loss to Germany during the 2014 FIFA World Cup can only compare to the 1950 loss. For Eakin, "The *Mineirazo* of 2014 will probably now go down in the country's football annals as an embarrassing bookend to the *Maracanazo* of 1950" (186). It does not seem, however, that public opinion and/or commentators have blamed *mestiçagem* for that last disastrous performance. In analyzing the possible causes for such a poor execution, Eakin connects it to the transition from *futebol-arte* to a globalized conglomeration of "styles of play from around the world" (187). He also presents a comparative assessment between Brazil's 1950 and 2014 losses. In 1950, he contends, the population of Brazil was "mostly rural" and amounted to fifty million people; the country relied on radio and newspapers for broadcast and publicity, and the sport "had just a couple of decades with professionalization" (186). In 2014, the country was in a completely different position: it had an "overwhelmingly urban" population which had surpassed the two hundred million mark; Brazilian society had become "completely saturated with television broadcasting, a vibrant film industry, and radio"; and, since 1958, it had won the World Cup five times (186). But, once again Brazil lost at home, and *mestiçagem* could no longer be blamed for it. "The *seleção* may continue to be *mestiço*," concludes Eakin, but it does not "mean that they share a style of play that one could label *futebol mestiço* or *mulato*" (187).

It saddens fans around the world that Brazil has increasingly lost the unique style that established its *futebol-arte*. The era of the *futebol-arte* seems to be gone by now, largely because of the enticement of a globalized market that promised and delivered economic and social opportunities of unprecedented dimension. Players are no longer bound by national borders or styles of playing; they have had to adapt their styles to the different clubs where they play in great rotation and, consequently, the "Brazilian" style of the game has changed (Eakin 187). Some of the most noticeable differences, as Wisnik argues, include a "more intense focus on physical and athletic training," and "a more brutal body-to-body play to undermine free-form styles" (208). He also contends that those adjustments changed "the texture of the game," which now displays "some of the jarring disruptions of American football and rugby and much of the strategic planning of the game of chess" (208). Thus, in its globalized form, Brazilian soccer seems to have lost the artistic propensities and, metaphorically speaking, has become increasingly similar to "a type of essayistic prose" that aches to have some poetry (Wisnik 209). Despite the 2014 catastrophic loss and a national ego severely bruised, there is still a lingering hope of becoming *hexacampeões* (receiving the World Cup trophy for the sixth time).

"Let Me Play"

It is intriguing that, although soccer tournaments often unite people from different social classes, races, and genders, until 1979 Brazilian women were not allowed to play soccer in a sustained and legal way. In analyzing the history of female presence on the fields as players and/or referees, one wonders why women did not seem interested in playing, or were excluded from the game, and what historical and political background can shed light on the reasons for their lacunae. It seems that one of the reasons for their exclusion from the game is the discourse of masculinity that shaped Brazilian society in the 1930s and 1940s, and which affected the perception of and attitudes toward women in sports, professional, and cultural activities. This gendered socio-cultural discrepancy can be traced to the conservative belief that the symbolic as well as the concrete spaces that *futebol* occupies belong primordially to men. For a vast majority of fans, soccer has been deemed a male sport, a fact that is emphasized by the public reaction to and attendance at women's matches, and the lack of technical and/or financial support females receive from club owners, sponsors, and the media.

Historically speaking, one date seems to have sealed the fate of Brazilian women in some sports and limited their range of choices for four decades. On April 14, 1941, through the Decree-Law 3.199, Brazil's president, Getúlio Vargas, signed into law the country's National Council of Sports (Conselho Nacional de

Desportos, CND), establishing the rules and regulations for sports in Brazil. Article number 54 addressed women and instituted that:

> Às mulheres não se permitirá a prática de desportos incompatíveis com as condições de sua natureza, devendo para este efeito, o Conselho Nacional de Desportos baixar as necessárias instruções às entidades desportivas do país.[12]

> Women will not be allowed to practice sports that are incompatible with their nature, and the National Council of Sports should establish a precise list of forbidden sports and ensure that those lists are sent to the institutions engaged in teaching or practicing sports in the country.

The 1941 decree was ratified on May 26, 1965 by decree number 4.638, article number 7, and signed into law by Castello Branco, then president of Brazil. As specified in the law, the National Council of Sports deliberated on its position, adding more specific language: women were not allowed to practice any type of fight, soccer, polo, weightlifting, or baseball (Bruhns 74; Taffarel e França 239). The decrees which prohibited women from practicing sports deemed unfit for their nature could be considered examples of "public patriarchy" as defined by Katie Milestone and Anneke Meyer (10).[13] The parameters the Brazilian government used to limit women's participation in sports and martial arts were based on antiquated ideas of a feminine mystique, or the fragility of the female body which, it was proclaimed, needed to be safeguarded for procreation because it was destined to fulfill women's primary function of motherhood. In both instances, the government joined forces with the legal and medical discourse (supported by family values and religious prerogatives) to promote a pseudo-scientific discourse that specified that women's bones were more fragile, their center of gravity was lower, their hearts and lungs were smaller, and their nervous system was weaker; therefore, their bodies were not fit to practice sports that require strenuous physical exercise. In other words, lawmakers and family members believed or, at least conveyed the message, that they were protecting women, and helping them live longer and happier lives by staying home, raising strong and healthy children, and contributing to the greatness of the nation as pious mothers and wives.

Prior to the 1980s (when there were substantial cultural and political changes in Brazil), the majority of conservative families still feared that the practice of soccer and *capoeira* could not only threaten their daughters' "feminine condition"—they could become mannish in their appearance—but also subject the family to the humiliation of having a daughter adopt such a marginalized practice (in the case of *capoeira*), or a violent sport (in reference to soccer). The media also played a role in disseminating ideas contrary to the practice of female soccer, adopting the pseudo-medical discourse emphasized by the Vargas regime (1930s and 1940s) and during the military dictatorship (1964–1985). It was not until 1983 that the norms for women's soccer in Brazil were put in place, and they began organizing teams, while struggling to find sponsors and win public approval. In 1991, FIFA established the Women's World Cup. Since then, the team has accumulated a substantial number of collective and individual trophies. Marta Vieira Silva, for instance, has thrilled fans around the world. Writing about her for the *New York Times*, in 2007, Michael Sokolove described her performance in highly admiring terms. In talking about her ability to play *futebol-arte* flawlessly, and her sense of empowerment and control when in possession of the ball, he depicts her movements in sensual and poetic terms: "Every part of her body seems trained to touch it, stop it, spin it, push it through some small space or set it up, just so, to blast it by a goalkeeper."

The current female national soccer team has won several awards and prizes for Brazil; however, the players still face prejudice from family members, authorities, the media, and the general public. Such attitude has discouraged women (especially from the middle class) from practicing the sport, or electing it as a career choice (since most of the players come from impoverished backgrounds and see in soccer an opportunity for social ascension). In addition, those women who persist and become players often encounter difficulties: it is hard to find sponsors (or even a team to play on);[14] and they are often discredited and stigmatized as unfeminine, or failed attempts to imitate men. As a result, in past decades, the media, the players, and the clubs have felt the need to sugarcoat women's participation in national and state leagues to attract the public and sponsors for the events. (In 2001, the state championship was sponsored by Pelé Sports & Marketing).

To attract a masculine public to the matches, find sponsors, and draw media attention, the organizers of the championship established beauty and sensuality as the main criteria in the selection of women players (Bruhns, Goeller, Knijnik, Romero). Enny Vieira Moraes and Maria Odília Leite da Silva Dias argue that female soccer in Brazil falls into the category of *excentricidade* (192). Considering that the Merriam-Webster dictionary defines "excentric" as a variant spelling of eccentric, and that the word originates from "ex-center" (meaning placed outside the center or not centrally located), it seems safe to imply that the vast majority of Brazilians still consider female soccer a novelty, an eccentricity, an exotic form of entertainment, or an acquired taste.

In a comparative analysis, female volleyball is very popular, and the national team has collected a steady string of victories (also in beach volleyball). The popularity that volleyball enjoys could be tied to the fact that it was not included on the list of sports banned/ratified in 1941/1965. It was allowed in schools and clubs as part of women's physical education programs or activities, and it is played with the hands, not the feet, and thus deemed more feminine. Brazilian female volleyball players are usually less muscular than soccer athletes and often wear tight-fitting uniforms, all of which may play a part in the popularity the sport enjoys. This seems to be the opinion of Joseph (Sepp) Blatter, who was president of FIFA from 1998 to 2015, and who vexed some prominent European women players, in 2004, by suggesting that, to attract more interest to female soccer, women should play in tighter shorts and in "more feminine clothes like they do in volleyball" (BBC Sport).[15] His sexist comment reinforces the cultural decoy of the exotic and erotic lure in activities that involve women in public spaces.

The politics of Brazilian *futebol* reveal that, from the 1980s to early 2000s, it was commonly expected of female soccer players to sweeten their performance with a touch of sensuality. A telling example is a soccer match that took place in the Clube Hípica Paulista, in October 1991, in the city of São Paulo. According to the news reported by *Folha de São Paulo*, the match revealed the interest of the *elite paulistana*, the affluent segment of São Paulo's society that attended the match played by women who worked as models for *Playboy Magazine* and the Ford Modeling Agency. The event was not open to the public, and the proceeds were channeled to charitable organizations. Thus, the focus of attention was not the sport itself, but rather the shapely and firm bodies, and the attire they wore. In the article titled "Mulheres disputam futebol sem empurrões e cusparadas," in October 1991, a journalist reporting for the newspaper *Folha de São Paulo* describes the match in terms of the players' beautiful legs, and their tight and stylish uniforms:

> A chuteira é trocada por tênis importados e o calção dá lugar a sainhas e bermudas de lycra. Os corpos são firmes—esculpidos em aulas de ginástica, hipismo, vôlei. Os cabelos são presos com fivelinhas, laços e lenços. (Qtd. in Bruhns 76)

> The cleat is exchanged for imported tennis shoes, and the shorts gave place to mini-skirts and spandex Bermuda shorts. The bodies are firm—sculpted in aerobic classes, equestrianism, and volleyball. The hair is held up with small clips, bows, and scarves.

Focusing on the physical appearance of players, the reporter presented a linguistic pun to describe his perception of the match. For him *o jogo bonito*" ("the beautiful game") became *um jogo bonito de se ver* ("a game that is pleasant to watch"). In this case, representationally, the soccer match lost its characteristics of the *futebol-arte* because it no longer placed emphasis on style, improvisation, and creativity, or highlighted the technical or aesthetic aspects of the game. The superbly elegant moves and maneuvers commonly found in "the beautiful game" became permeated with connotations of voyeurism. In her analysis of the news about that match, Bruhns considers that the aesthetic of the game was intertwined with the players' looks and outfits, which reflected the image of a certain standard of feminine beauty, and which is also usually associated with a certain social class or distinction (76).

The fascination with women's bodies as "a sociocultural artifact"[16] is quite prevalent in Brazilian culture. The "cult of the body" (a pervasive and endemic Hollywood type of search for eternal beauty and youth) scores high in every corner of Brazilian society and permeates all social classes. It has been analyzed by anthropologists, sociologists, and historians who have discussed the increasing attention that the human body has received as a key element in defining identity.[17] It was also exploited both by the organizers of matches and by the female players, or referees, who have internalized the concepts of beauty and sensuality.[18] In this context, the importance that the shapely female body has as a seductive asset (the coveted object) is also used in sports for personal gain and to generate income. The most striking example is Ana Paula da Silva Oliveira who has worked as an assistant soccer referee since 1999. In 2007, she posed nude for the July edition of Brazilian *Playboy Magazine*, a move that sparked some controversy. The media claimed that she received nearly a quarter of a million dollars for the photos, and some attribute her fall from grace from FIFA's and CBF's list of referees to this *faux pas*.[19] Since then she has worked as a football commentator, a reality TV star, and has returned to working as a referee in lower divisions. This reveals the social and cultural paradoxes existent in a country that has had a difficult time coming to grips with the idea that women can (not only emblematically) represent the larger discourses of the nation. It also reveals Brazil's ambiguous and ambivalent position in defining its own role in a fast-changing world, perhaps because the traditional segments of society feel that to embrace new assertions and abandon outdated perspectives can disrupt the order. These examples illustrate the place that female players hold in the eyes of the media, the contradictions existing in Brazilian society, and how sensuality—as a determining factor in the concept of femininity and Brazilian identity—has downplayed women's involvement in the most popular sport in Brazil.

There have been some positive changes lately. For instance, Globo Television and other networks in Brazil have opened space to advertise the Women's World Cup, not as an *excentricidade*, but as an example of a sport well played. In 2019, Globo aired a documentary about Marta Vieira Silva's professional life (Globo Reporter, May 31), and on June 30, included a segment about the performance of the Women's National Team in the 2019 FIFA World Cup on the Sunday television program *Fantástico*. The sport's commentator reserved for them a good dose of respect and consideration by showing a clip of a game, and emphasizing that, despite having lost on a penalty kick, they played well and Silva was a *tour-de-force*. One of the best moments of that segment—which revealed an encouraging place that the Women's National Team had gained in the media—was when the commentator reminded viewers that the Men's National Team (Seleção) had also lost to France in 2006, in exactly the same way. Another sign that positive changes are taking place is the references to females in the Museu do Futebol.

The Soccer Museum

On September 29, 2008, the city of São Paulo was awarded a soccer museum (Museu do Futebol), the brainchild of José Serra, the state of São Paulo's then governor. Located under the concrete bleachers of the stadium Pacaembu, Corinthias's headquarters, it is a daring project, intent on telling the history of this sport in Brazil and connecting it to numerous historical and political facts and personalities. The Museu do Futebol keeps its current permanent exhibits on two floors.[20] The first is divided into six halls: Exhibit A is labeled "Grande Área" ("Large Area") and houses a collection of pins, toys, stamps, and figurines, objects that comprise an endearing retrospective (*memória afetiva*) of Brazilian soccer. Exhibit B is "Bola no Pé" ("A Ball on the Foot"), an interactive exhibit about children playing soccer; and Exhibit C, named "Sala dos Anjos Barrocos" ("Hall of Baroque Angels"), presents information about players who transcended expectations and earned outstanding spots in Brazilian soccer. It also pays tribute to twenty-seven players, two of whom are women: Maraildes Maciel Mota (Formiga) and Marta Vieira Silva, the only woman, according to the exhibit, to be invited to imprint her foot in the sidewalk hall-of-fame outside the Maracanã stadium in Rio de Janeiro. Exhibit D ("Sala dos Gols"; "Hall of Goals") presents information and photos about the best goals and dribbles by Brazilian players. Sala E ("Rádio"; "Radio") pays homage to radio journalists and commentators and addresses the importance the radio played in broadcasting soccer to the entire nation in the 1930s and 1940s; and F ("Sala da Exaltação"; "Hall of Exaltation") features the cheering and passion of organized fan clubs.

The second floor of the museum is considered an historical axis (*eixo histórico*) and includes the "Hall of Origins" ("Sala das Origens") which lodges photographs from mid-nineteenth century to the 1930s. It features materials that address the history, development, and professionalization of soccer in Brazil. The second hall ("Sala dos Heróis"; "Hall of Heroes") discusses Brazil's racial and cultural *mestiçagem* in the 1930s and 1940s. The video recordings, posters, photos, and other information amassed in this hall give information about *mestiçagem* in popular music, visual arts, dance, gastronomy, and soccer. There are posters of poems (by Carlos Drummond de Andrade, for instance), reproductions of Tarsila do Amaral's paintings, and testimonials by renown intellectuals such as Sérgio Buarque de Holanda and Gilberto Freyre offering their endorsement of soccer and *mestiçagem*. It also features some black or *pardo* players such as Leônidas da Silva and Domingos da Guia. There is a hall dedicated exclusively to present detailed information and praise (in video recordings, statements, photos, and memorabilia) about the five World Cups that Brazil won. The hall named "Sala do Rito de Passagem" ("Hall of the Rite of Passage") exhibits recordings and discussions about the unforgiven loss to Uruguay in 1950, and the shame/defeat (7x1 loss to Germany) in 2014. Another entire hall is dedicated to Pelé and Garrincha; and the last one, "A Dança do Futebol," ("The Dance of Soccer") offers information, video recordings and photos of Brazil's celebrated style of playing soccer (*futebol-arte* or *football mulato*) that, as previously discussed, has also been associated with the choreography of *samba* and *capoeira*. It allows the visitors the opportunity to review some of the best moments of Brazil's *futebol-arte*.

In 2015, three additional visual displays (Futebol Feminino, Pioneiras, and Plasticidade) were added to the hall "A Dança do Futebol" to showcase the trajectory of women in soccer. The video materials included in the section "Futebol Feminino" discuss the history of prohibitions and discrimination against women in soccer. They inform about the first two Women's International Competitions that took place in Italy in 1970, and in Mexico in 1971, and add a touch of historical scrutiny by reminding visitors that, while women worldwide were playing in those competitions, females in Brazil were still not allowed, by law, to practice soccer. This recording also reveals that the governing authorities had control over women's bodies and their use of public space, even before Law number 3.199 went into effect in 1941. To illustrate such information, it recounts an episode that took place in 1940, when the team Primavera Futebol was not allowed to travel to participate in a tournament in Buenos Aires and Montevideo. Stopped just before their departure, the players were told they were grounded because they were minors (even though they had their parents' permission to travel). Other recordings, however, emphasize that women often challenged the authoritative discourse, and when possible, escaped the watchful eye of the Brazilian government and their families to play soccer (albeit in a very small number, played at neighborhood clubs, in beneficent events, or as exotic circus attractions).

The second video recording, "Pioneiras" ("Pioneers"), show-cases information and interviews with several women who paved the way as players, sport commentators, referees, or who worked for club organizations. This recording also reveals women's deter-mination. As it points out, the 1941 prohibition was unable to fully deter women from playing soccer because several clubs were formed in numerous states, among them the Araguary Atlético Clube, in the interior of Minas Gerais. The Araguary team was composed of adolescents (the average age of sixteen) who would play mostly beneficent games. Wherever they went, their matches would fill up stadiums, and they had an enviable fan club for the time. Quite often they would play a preliminary game before the scheduled male game. They traveled outside Minas Gerais always in the company of two of their mothers and their coach, Ney Montes. (Newspaper clips confirm their presence in Belo Horizonte and Salvador; they were also invited to play in Mexico but could not accept because they would not have permission to leave the country.) The team had already undermined the rule of law for an entire year (1958–1959) by the time it gained headlines in larger newspapers. By then, their existence became too obvious to be ignored by the authorities, and the team was disbanded. Yet, women continued to play in other parts of the country in friendly matches or to raise money for charity. In 1959, Clube Pacaembu organized its first female match to raise money for a hospital, and São Paulo's City Hall granted the team approval to play.

The section "Pioneiras" also makes references to other women in journalism, in executive positions in club organizations, coach-ing small teams, and working as referees. For instance, there is information about Marlene Mathews who, in 1991, became the first female president of Corinthias, in São Paulo, one of the largest and most prestigious soccer clubs in Brazil. She paved the way for Patrícia Amorim, who was the president of Clube de Regatas do Flamengo (2009–2012), a prominent soccer club, in

Rio de Janeiro. But, as featured in this section of the Museum, Léa Campos (Azaléa de Campos Micheli Medina) is the woman who made most of the newspaper headlines in the 1970s for her work as a referee and for managing to convince the then President of Brazil to authorize the accreditation of her referee certificate. Therefore, little by little, women found ways to crack the system code. Yet, it was not until 1979 that the ban was lifted completely, and even so, it still took another four years for the Conselho Nacional de Desportos to define the rules for the practice of female soccer in the country.

The third recording, "Visibilidade para o Futebol Feminino" ("Visibility for Female Soccer"), discusses the prominence of Brazilian women in soccer, and traces the history of the female National Team, which was organized in 1988 and included players mostly from the team Radar (Rio de Janeiro), and some athletes from Clube Juventus (São Paulo). The team took part in the first female championship organized by FIFA (International Tournament of Women's Soccer) in China. There is a spatial and temporal gap of sixty-one years between the first participation in a FIFA World Cup by the Brazilian male National Team (in 1930), in which they finished in sixth position, and the female National Team (in 1991) in which they earned a well-positioned third place. Therefore, it is impressive that, less than a decade after they were allowed to form a team and search for sponsors, the Brazilian Women's National Team returned home with a trophy. In 2005, to celebrate their sustained achievements, the Brazilian Post-Office issued a commemorative stamp featuring female players. The Museu do Futebol also highlights the history of women in soccer, presenting a substantial number of exhibits in "Sala de Curiosidades" ("Hall of Curiosities"). The printed information is accessible in Portuguese, English, and Spanish, and the well-organized displays present material about women playing or involved with soccer from the nineteenth century to the 1930s.[21]

The Museu do Futebol showcases oddities in "Sala das Curiosidades," in what seems to be an intentional effort to reveal the paternalistic and, sometimes misogynist, approach that was taken regarding women and soccer. But the curators balanced the displays by contrasting exhibits that highlight the historical devaluation of women in soccer with some of their most daring achievements (for instance, exhibit number 143 shows a woman sewing a skirt to play ball, another playing ball wearing a skirt as early as 1919; there is also information that, also in 1919, women were organizing tournaments in England). Exhibit 164 indicates that there was some involvement of Brazilian women in clubs, but only as supporters: it displays a picture of a woman named Leonor who, in 1938, represented female support at the matches during the World Cup, in France, by attending the games as Rainha do Vasco (ambassador of the Rio de Janeiro team). "Wall C" also presents information to potentially educate visitors about the involvement of women in soccer in Europe and Brazil. Exhibit number 210 presents a photo of a Brazilian women's team during the inaugural match of the field lighting of the Municipal Stadium of Pacaembu, São Paulo, on May 17, 1940. The female team from Rio de Janeiro, Cassino Realengo, played against S.C. Brasileiro, in a preliminary match before the clubs from Rio de Janeiro and São Paulo met. Exhibit number 226 presents information about a match by Brazilian women that took place on June 23, 1940. Number 265 displays copies of newspaper clips, in Rio de Janeiro, in 1922, about a woman who was allegedly acting as a referee in a soccer match, and a cartoon satirizing such an "unusual" event.

The exhibition seems intent on educating the public about historical, political, and cultural discrepancies. Before women could play soccer on fields, stadiums, or beaches, they were featured in circuses,[23] and their performances were considered anomalous and eccentric events. On Wall H, exhibits number 427 and 428 present photos and newspaper information advertising the attraction of Circo Irmãos Queirolo and Circo Garcia.[24] One special match that took place on November 25, 1930, in Rio de Janeiro, caught the attention of the press because ten women formed two teams to play each other representing Brazil and Uruguay. Thus, female soccer was introduced not as a sport, but rather as an eccentric and exotic act, a somewhat grotesque form of entertainment. The news published in *Jornal do Brasil* (as referenced in the museum exhibit) describes the women as *adestradas* (tamed), a word usually used to denote animals that perform at a circus, and at other similar types of extravaganza.

The Soccer Museum also displays numerous paintings, prints, newspaper clips, and reprints of cartoons that reveal that the female association with soccer was not taken seriously. In many instances, female players were objects of mockery. Wall H displays

119

copies of FIFA's collection of Fred Spurgin's humorous illustrations about women playing soccer.[25] Those drawings comprise a set of four postcards from the 1890s that reflect the attitudes of the mentality of the time. Exhibit H8.1 is titled "A Fine All-round Player," a play on words intended to refer to the picture of a curvaceous female body wearing shorts on a soccer field. H8.2 is a drawing of a woman dancing on the field while the men are having fun at her expense. The postcard is titled "Playing the Game with the Boys." Exhibit H8.3 presents a woman applying makeup during a match while the male players stop the game to watch her in disbelief (the postcard is titled "Making up for the Other Players"). H8.4 presents a man and a woman dressed in similar jerseys and the underlying legend: "A Football Match! Oh! What a Game It is!"

To describe the public opinion about women in soccer, the Museum also exhibits a copy of an infamous letter written by José Fuzeira (dated April 25, 1940) to then President Vargas complaining about the large number of young women who had been playing soccer in Rio de Janeiro, São Paulo, and Belo Horizonte. He was concerned about the damages it could do to the bodies and psyches of Brazil's future mothers and urged the President to take some measure. It remains unknown if Vargas read or answered the letter or took Fuzeira's complaints seriously. However, a year later (April 14, 1941) Vargas signed the Decree-Law No. 3.199 into law that outlined exactly what Fuzeira had suggested. It seems that Mr. Fuzeira was one of the countless Brazilian citizens and government authorities who were heavily influenced by eugenic theories devised in Europe at the end of the nineteenth and first decades of the twentieth centuries.

Gertrud Pfister writes that the medical profession in Germany "felt authorized to speak on almost all aspects of women's lives," including gymnastics and sports. For doctors, men were the norm and the right measure, while women were depicted as "deviant," "deficient," and "incomplete" (194). She also cites Johannes Müller's theory that women were physically disadvantaged because they had "smaller lung capacity, smaller heart volume and smaller number of red blood corpuscles" (194). Pfister informs that to convince the population that motherhood should be the main objective of a woman's life, doctors claimed to have "objective knowledge, stated with the full authority of medical science"

(192). The pseudo-scientific discourse of the time was developed from three main premises. The "vitalist theory" asserted that the human organs could store only a limited amount of energy and, thus, women should channel it to procreation. There was also the belief that the uterus needed to be protected because it was "the most vulnerable and endangered part of the female body" and "excessive physical exercise was claimed to have an inhibiting effect on the development of the pelvis and, as a result, cause difficulties during childbirth" (Pfister 192). There was also the theory developed by the prominent gynecologist Dr. Hugo Sellheim who asserted that "men had strong, taut muscles while women had loose, slack ones," and an attempt to tighten the muscles of the female abdomen and pelvis could lead to severe difficulty in childbirth (Pfister 193).

Pfister addresses the widespread fear that physical exercise would make women "physically and psychologically more masculine" and, consequently, less interested in heterosexual relationships and, therefore, "masculinization" could deviate them from fulfilling the most essential purpose of womanhood: to be a mother (193). She concludes that such theories were also developed out of fear that the "masculinization" of women's bodies, via strenuous physical exercise, could threaten the established "division of labor and, consequently, the dominating structure of society" (194). The medical discourse often used "anthropometrical measurements" and banked on the fact that women were oftentimes "afflicted by ailing health during menstruation and pregnancy" to generate the consensus that they were the "weaker sex" (Pfister 185). Doctors also theorized about female's physical and mental "fragile" nature to establish the myth that their nervous system was not as strong as men's. However, as Pfister concludes, "deformities of the spine, anemia, shortness of breath, fainting, weak nerves, and hysteria" could have been a result of the "living conditions of the women of the time" (186).

Those theories conveniently overlooked the fact that women's "frailty" could also have been caused by lack of proper exercise. Their "nervousness" could also have been related to their lack of personal choice (they were often entrapped in marriages of convenience, having to serve and obey older men chosen for the expediency of their parents, or restrain themselves to the confinement of the private space of the house).[26] Thus, their "hysteria" could have been triggered by boredom, malnutrition, and a number of other factors unrelated to genetic predisposition. This is a point that Michel Foucault raises in his historical account of the roots of madness in which he analyzes the concept of hysteria and hypochondria categorized as "mental illnesses" by the medical establishment. He credits Thomas Willis's study for having "liberat[ed] hysteria from the old myths of uterine displacement" (144). Foucault writes that, for Willis, "the idea of hysteria is a catchall for the fantasies, not for the person who is or believes himself ill, but of the ignorant doctor who pretends to know why" (138).

Speaking from her own experience, the soccer referee Léa Campos addresses the struggles she underwent to challenge concepts rooted in pseudo-scientific ideas that guided the actions of citizens (like Mr. Fuzeira) and lawmakers (like President Vargas). She is featured in the Museu do Futebol because her accomplishments were extraordinary at the time, particularly when it is taken into consideration the social and cultural limitations she faced as an aspiring woman athlete. In the 1960s and 1970s, she lived in Belo Horizonte, a city still quite provincial at the time. As she outlined in an interview, Minas Gerais is a state traditionally rooted in family values, tradition, and religion, a place where the foundations of the infamous organization Tradição, Família e Propriedade (TFP)[27] were strong and widespread. Thus, she had to overcome many obstacles to be the first woman in the world to receive a FIFA certificate to referee soccer matches (Campos).[28] She became involved with sports at an early age, and in 1967, challenged the opinion of her family and social circles by taking an eight-month-long course at Federação Mineira de Futebol to become a soccer referee.[29] However, upon concluding and passing the classes, she was unable to receive the certificate (Campos). According to her, João Havelange, then president of CBD (Confederação Brasileira de Desportos; "Brazilian Football Confederation") was unyielding in his opposition to certify female arbitrators because he did not think women had the bone structure to play or referee soccer matches. Campos proved him wrong by undergoing a medical examination and evidencing her physical stamina, but he remained skeptical, and she had to wait until 1971, nearly four years after having completed the course, to have her certificate accredited by CBD (Campos). In the meantime, she refereed friendly matches (which the authorities would not bar) and, in 1970 and 1971 worked as a sports commentator at the radio station Mulher, and TV Nacional, in Brasília (Campos).

As she details in a 2016 interview, also in 1971 she received an invitation to referee a FIFA match in Mexico for the International Championship of Female Soccer. She considered it a unique opportunity to showcase her talent and advance her career, but to accept the invitation she would need to have Havelange's authorization for her to participate in the match, and for CBD to officially certify her diploma (Campos). Considering how adamant Havelange was in his refusal to recognize her credentials, she looked for creative solutions. She confided her frustration to some high-ranking officials in Belo Horizonte's branch of the Army who sympathized with her cause. Breaching protocol, they informed her that the president, General Emílio Garrastazu Médici, would be making a one-day visit to Belo Horizonte, and perhaps he could intercede on her behalf. *O jeitinho brasileiro* came in handy as she used her connections[30] to secure a five-minute meeting with President Médici on July 17, 1971, during which time she explained to him why she needed the accreditation of her referee certificate (Campos). She asked him to bend the rule in her favor by using his power and influence to convince Havelange to validate the certificate that she had earned in 1987, and bequeath her permission to travel to Mexico to officiate the FIFA match (Campos). She confides that the general listened to her attentively and instructed her to meet him for lunch on the following Monday, in Brasília. She complied, and on July 19, 1971, after the meeting, she flew to Rio de Janeiro on a military plane carrying with her a handwritten letter written by the president, commanding Havelange to sign the certificate and give her permission to go to Mexico. Initially hesitant to obey, Havelange finally caved in, and turned the event to his favor. He called in the press to witness two historical events: the accreditation of a female referee diploma, and the permission for her to officiate a FIFA international match (Campos). On July 18, Pelé had played his last game in Maracanã stadium, before retiring from Seleção, and foreign journalists were still in Rio de Janeiro when her certificate was accredited. Such an event also made national and international news (Campos).

In 1974, Campos's ascending career was interrupted when she nearly lost her left leg in a serious traffic accident. The bus on which she was traveling to referee a game in Três Corações hit a truck and, as a result, she spent two years using a wheelchair, and underwent a large number of surgical interventions to reconstruct her leg (Campos). Even though she regained mobility, her rising career as an arbiter lost momentum and intensity. But her efforts were not in vain. By the time the 1941 and 1965 decrees were lifted, in 1979, she had paved the way for a number of other women to follow in her footsteps (such as Sílvia Regina de Oliveira, Ana Paula Oliveira, and Regildênia de Holanda Moura). However, despite the occasional breakthroughs for women, male soccer still holds a privileged position in the national imaginary while female soccer, in a larger context, is primarily considered a departure from the norm. These discrepancies reveal the complex negotiations of everyday life in Brazil in terms of gender (similar, in some instance, to the same negotiations regarding race and social class), which are influenced by the collective discourse on Brazilian identity.

The good news is that the social and political changes that have taken place since the 1980s in Brazil have contributed to women feeling more valid and becoming more involved in soccer. The successful profiles of Brazilian women recruited to play on foreign teams have also played a key role in changing the negative perception of women in *futebol,* at least in the most open-minded spheres of Brazilian society. As a result, there has been a larger involvement of Brazilian women in sports, even though the number of them playing soccer is very small when compared to the massive numbers of male players in Brazil. Their acceptance on international professional teams has also grown in the last decade because Brazilian players such as Marta, Formiga, Kátia Cilene, and Pretinha were recruited to play abroad. The prestige, respect, and salaries they earned abroad have positively influenced how their families and the general public reassessed their careers and have created a larger interest for the sport. Famous male players, most of whom come from less privileged social classes, receive royal treatment when they win a World Cup, or a medal in the Olympic Games, and are hired to play on prestigious European teams, idolized by the media, and emulated by children. The families of female players have hoped that their daughters have the same benefits. Hence, changes in the politics of culture, economic benefits, and the feminist movement have opened a space for women in this sport, although the battles they have won have not bypassed the obstacles they still have to overcome.

In a broader context, the metaphor of a *ginga* and the chore-ography of *samba* are representative samples of social and cultural maneuvers (Bruhns 131–48; Rosa 208–09). Such maneuvers can also describe the techniques women have used to trick the male-controled system and perform in the Brazilian game of socio-cultural relations. Guedes makes that association when she connects *futebol-arte* to other expressive cultures of Brazil (referencing Afro-Brazilian dances and rituals, in general, and citing *samba* and *capoeira*) specifically because they require, in her words, a *requebrar feminino*—a feminine way of swaying the body (51). Thus, metaphorically speaking, women in Brazil have assimilated the flexibility of a *gingado* and the choreography of *samba* to play soccer. They have also adopted *o jeitinho brasileiro*, that special way of bending the rules without breaking them, as social and cultural maneuvers to dribble through a male-controled system and perform in the socio-cultural arena of sports. Since the laws that forbade females from practicing "violent" sports were in place for nearly four decades, women had a spatial and temporal disadvantage when compared to male participation in soccer and *capoeira*. Despite this and other obstacles and constraints, their persistence is paying off. In less than four decades, nearly half of the *capoeira* players in the world are female, the number of *mestras* and *contramestras* (highest rankings in *capoeira*) continue to increase, and the Brazilian Women's National Soccer Team has brought home an enviable number of trophies. Marta ("Pelé in a Dress," as the media refers to her) has been elected the best player in the world six times, a matchless feat thus far.

Chapter Four

Capoeira: *Jogo Bonito, Jogo de Dentro, Jogo de Fora*

Mediating the Body's Spatiality[1]

The martial art-fight-dance-ritual *capoeira* combines elements of musical and theatrical performance, and functions as a recreational, aesthetic, and professional system.[2] To impart the notion that it is not merely a physical training or a performative act, most *mestres* (the most advanced teachers of the art) and other committed players highlight the holistic aspects of the game, often describing it in terms of its physical, musical, verbal, ludic, and ceremonial composition.[3] Akin to priesthood, the art of learning and practicing *capoeira*'s body-mind-spiritual connection demands from high-ranking devotees a lifetime commitment. Traditional *capoeira* aficionados frequently portray *rodas* (the human circles formed to carry on the game-ritual),[4] as sites encased in *axé*, a Yoruban word that means "life force" or "vital energy."[5] Such a connection contributes to attach spiritual ties to the game and establish an association with other African-derived forms of expressive cultures in Brazil. As engaged players describe it, a *capoeira* circle is a catalyst of different energies, and a space of corporeal, linguistic, social, and historical mediation in which *capoeiristas* can learn to project poise, practice respect for the other players, and develop a deep sense of mindfulness. They can also learn to balance tensions, and harness emotions to curb the violent aspects of the game/fight. Thus, zealous adepts usually depict the process of mastering *capoeira*'s philosophical principles, movements, instruments, and songs as an all-inclusive, ritualistic enterprise. The result is a polyphony of interconnected voices that distinguish *capoeira* from other martial arts.

The magnetism of a *capoeira* game owes much to its visually seductive components and to an interactive system in which the participants choreograph their movements in sync with the rhythms of the instruments. The players also remain attentive to the messages contained in the lyrics of the songs which can be used to regulate the mood of the players and moderate the pace of the game. The steps, syncopated rhythms, and words of the songs create an ambiance in which the players engage in the art of playing *capoeira* while the spectators may feel mesmerized by the compelling fluidity of the *roda*. Such interactive and improvisational aspects might help explain why the verb of choice to refer to *capoeira* is *jogar* (Browning 88; Downing 546; Lewis 2), a multifaceted Portuguese word which connotes the meaning of entertainment, suggests the lightness of dance, and implies the essential competition of a match or combat.

Accomplished *capoeiristas* oftentimes base their definitions of the *capoeira* game on the interactive principle of a dialogue in which ideas can be accepted as well as questioned and refuted, rather than as a debate in which contestants attempt to win an argument by questioning and/or discrediting others. Greg Downey follows this line of argumentation as he considers that a *roda de capoeira* presents a series of interconnected elements in which the call-and-response movements form "a conversation in which the answer to a question is, in itself, a new question" ("The Interaction" 12).[6] Analogous to the exchanges of a chess game, seasoned *capoeiristas* use astuteness, calculated moves, and improvisation to advance or close the game. Each move can lead to a series of other moves in which the players combine creativity, grace, and resourcefulness with skillfulness, alertness, and insight to establish a corporeal dialogue with their partners/opponents. Ben Downing takes the parallel between the interaction in a *roda de capoeira* and a conversation/ dialogue even further by relating a *capoeira* game to literary texts. For him, "Each game, like each poem, fiction, or essay, involves a thousand half-conscious decisions of lexicon and syntax, tallying up (one hopes) to the *capoeira* correlative of a signature 'voice'" (560). Borrowing from the beauty and elegance of Brazilian soccer, Downing also uses the expression *jogo bonito* to describe the *capoeira* players' spontaneous and graceful response to each other's movements.[7] The expression was first used to refer to Brazilian soccer matches, or any game in which the players perform elegant moves or dribbles, and there is little or no display of violence. Nick Harper claims that Stuart Hall coined the term and Pelé (Edson

Arantes do Nascimento) popularized it.[8] In seeking to play a "beautiful game," whilst facing the ambiguity and ambivalence of their double role, *capoeiristas* learn to walk a tightrope, so to speak, in which they scrutinize intentions, respond to unexpected moves, strive to balance emotions, and keep the ludic aspects of the game without over exposing themselves.

As the players tune in to the process of the game, rather than to the end result, they craft opportunities to evade the strikes and neutralize the opposing force, negotiating a place and space in the *capoeira* circle. When highly aggressive moves and other types of violence occur in *rodas de capoeira*, the players seem to lose perspective of the ludic aspects of the game, becoming deaf to other voices and blind to playful interactions. To discourage aggressive behaviors, *mestres* and other high profile *capoeiristas* warn that such engagements can transform a potentially creative dialogue into an arrogant monologue. Cautioning against the use of senseless violence—when players strike the partner viciously or endeavor to dominate by means of force—they also advise that unnecessary aggressive maneuvers and violent moves strip the game of its playful elements, and transform the *roda* into a fighting arena, similar to a boxing ring. To reinforce such a standpoint, they teach their students to avoid exhibitionism, and warn against engaging in a struggle of forces. They impart the notion that the game is a libertarian process in which the players develop the ability to center themselves so as to find their point of reference both in *capoeira* circles and in the world. Thus, besides helping their students acquire technical skills and learn the minutiae of the game, *mestres* also feel the need to teach their apprentices the ethical principles established in the development of *capoeira*. As Nestor Capoeira asserts, "By its own nature capoeira is a mirror of life, a mini-theater where people stage and dramatize archetypes of situations, relationships, and energy exchanges" (*Roots* 18). Letícia Vidor de Sousa Reis is one of the scholars who discusses the *roda* as a catalyst of energies and an arbitrating center that resembles the world. She confers special meanings to certain movements, endowing them with the status of a symbolic cultural resistance. For instance, she analyzes the *aú*, and other inverted movements of *capoeira*, as part of a social microcosm, in which such movements are symbolically used to subvert the dominant hierarchy and represent rebellious paradigms of social and ethnic relations in Brazil (174).

A *roda de capoeira* also provides the players with the opportunity to learn how to use *malícia*, a word that embodies positive and negative traits: it can mean playfulness, astuteness, intelligence, and good judgment, but also sneakiness, deceit, and trickery (Lewis 49; Downey, *Learning* 123). Such a range of meanings might help explain why *capoeiristas* refer to the game as *malandragem*, the art of disguise and roguery. Accomplished players become experts in using *malícia*, not only to neutralize violent or mischievous behaviors, but also to trick the arrogant, unwary, or inexperienced contenders into revealing their vulnerabilities. However, to master that art well, players have to exercise a delicate balance between excessive scheming and deceptiveness. To instruct on how and where to draw that line, Nestor Capoeira resorts to the Brazilian expression "malandro demais se atrapalha," meaning that "when one tries to be too clever or smart, instead of confusing his opponent, he confuses himself" (*Little* 33). As he asserts, as soon as the *capoeirista* becomes obsessed with the idea of outsmarting others, they forget how to apply *malícia*, and turns the game into a mere calculated plan of attack. He offers an abridged account of the how to recognize and use *malícia* in the game and in life:

> It may be said that *malícia* has two basic aspects. The first is knowing the emotions and traits—aggressiveness, fear, pride, etc.—which exist in all human beings. The second is recognizing these traits when they appear in another player, and therefore being able to anticipate the other player's movements, whether in the *roda* or in everyday life. The player who is *malicioso* is able to dodge under an opponent's kick and prepare for a counterattack or a takedown before the assailant finished what he started. In everyday life, he should be able to recognize the real human being that hides beneath the social mask of someone he has just met. (Little 33)

In the song "Essa Arte" ("This Art"), Mestre Barrão not only illustrates Nestor Capoeira's analysis of *malícia*, but also goes a step further as he associates the act of playing *capoeira* and using *malícia* with the contrite reflection of a prayer bequeathed by ancestors:

> Essa arte me encanta,
> Eu não quero mais sair.
> Oh! Bendita capoeira,
> Que vem dos nossos ancestrais.
> [...]

Cada salto é uma reza,
Cada reza é uma canção.
E o que faz levar vantagem
É a malícia do negão.

This art enraptures me,
I no longer want to leave.
Oh! Blessed *capoeira*,
That our ancestors bequeathed to us
[...]
Each jump is a prayer,
Each prayer is a song.
The black man's astuteness
Gives him some advantage.

In general, the movements of *capoeira* can be grouped into attack, defense, and evasion which form the fundamental steps of the game, determine the position of players in the *roda*, and set the direction the interaction will take. In addition to the key movements, there are various kicks and takedowns used to open the game, trick the opponent, unsettle the other's confidence, and strike the partner/adversary. Numerous publications (in print and online) aim at teaching students how to master the art of *capoeira* playing, and offer detailed accounts of the movements and kicks of *capoeira regional* and *angola*.[9] Besides *ginga* (the opening step of *capoeira*, a back-and-forth, side-to-side swaying movement) there are three other basic movements in *capoeira*: a) *negative* which is played in a more erect position in *regional* and closer to the ground in *angola*; b) *rolê* which is also performed at ground level and could be used to transition from the floor to a standing position and to escape incoming attacks and protect more vulnerable areas of the body; and c) the *aú*, a cartwheel, the inverted movement that "makes the *capoeirista* very unpredictable" (Capoeira, *Little* 65–70). *Ginga*, which is executed standing up, helps maintain the equilibrium and the interactive process of the game.

Easily recognized by its languid cadence and repetitive nature, *ginga*'s deceptively simple motion emblematizes a ludic mediation, and translates the ambiguity and *malícia* of the *capoeira* game. In tracing the roots of the word, Nei Lopes shifts the connection to Africa by providing several terms from the Bantu languages (*junga*, *jingala*, *jinga*, *yenga*) that share similar phonetic sound structures with *ginga,* and which also convey the idea of a spinning, circling, or oscillating movement (109). Portuguese dictionaries add other meanings to it. For instance, in the sugar cane mills of colonial and imperial Brazil (1500–1889), the word *ginga* also referred to a mug or pail that, tied to a long pole, was used to transfer the sugar syrup from one large boiler to another. In the decantation process, the slaves had to incline their bodies to reach the boilers, without leaving their position or losing balance. That movement is also called *ginga.* Additionally, the word refers to an oar fitted to the gunwale of a rowboat used for water propulsion. Rowers generally reach toward the stern to insert the blade of the oar in the water, and lean back, toward the vessel's bow to propel the movement. The forward thrust and backward pull—which is also named *ginga*—resembles the opening movement of *capoeira.*

Despite the fact that all of those oscillatory movements and rocking motions bear a resemblance to the foundational step of the *capoeira* game, and could be related to slave work in colonial Brazil, there is no clear-cut evidence that the *capoeira* movement was named after the pail or the oar, or if the tools were named after the swaying movements that slaves made around the sugarcane boiler or in a row boat. Thus, it seems sensible to conclude that the origin of the word *ginga* is African and it has been used to represent different ways of rocking the body in Brazil. In contemporary and informal Portuguese, *ginga* has acquired larger metaphorical dimensions; for instance, it refers to a certain way of swaying the body which simultaneously produces a vigorous cadence and a loose and flexible movement. To have *ginga* is similar to displaying *jogo de cintura* (an expression that, in its literal sense, refers to the ability to sway your hips, to have flexibility at the beltline, a stride often associated with rouges and *capoeiristas*). Metaphorically speaking, both *ginga* and *jogo de cintura* denote the ability to adapt to new, unexpected, or changing situations; in other words, to use flexibility in the game and in life, or a way to maneuver through social structures and relations of power.

When tension emerges in a *roda de capoeira,* the mood of the game changes, and the body movements become faster, trickier, and frequently malicious. Oftentimes, the players are caught in an adrenaline surge that allows their egos to take control, and consequently, lose sight of the holistic aspects of the game. In those cases, it is common for the group leader to attempt to control the belligerence by slowing the rhythms of instruments and selecting songs that caution against the use of gratuitous force. The slower pace of the music serves to decelerate the game intensity and gives the players a brief chance to rest from the strenuous physical and mental exercise. During that time, and in other less intense parts of the game, the players walk in a counterclockwise motion known as *a roda do mundo* ("the wheel of the world") or *a volta ao mundo* ("a turn around the world"). The reverse rotation also gives them an opportunity to halt briefly to center themselves and reflect on the direction the *roda* is taking, and address the problems created when power play and inflated personalities begin to interfere with the playful aspects of the game. Additionally, that pause allows them time to analyze the symbolic meanings of the game (which combines elements of performance, partnership, and constructive competition). It also gives them a chance to reinitiate the game and inject a lighthearted attitude and a mindset attuned to the higher principles of the game. Actually, the word *volta* also implies a "return to" a beautiful game, a connotation that adds another metaphorical layer to the interpretation. Similar to her analysis of the inverted movements of *capoeira*, Reis places a *roda do mundo* or *volta ao mundo* in a larger context, and interprets the anticlockwise movement as an historical counter-discourse because it may prompt the players to think of *capoeira*'s origins and development and reflect on the resistance, subversion, and insurrection that the struggle against slavery and oppression emblematizes (165–74). While such an interpretation has its merits when contextualized in an historical reading, some players simply analyze the *volta ao mundo* as a pause for them to collect themselves, cool down their heated emotions, and restart the game in a more playful way.

The players' corporeal maneuvers doggedly negotiate a physical and mental space inside and outside the *capoeira* circle which the expressions *jogo de dentro* ("inside game") and *jogo de fora* ("outside game") convey. The two terms refer to the loops that are formed to play and/or watch a game and function as boundaries set to protect the players from unwelcome interruptions. The *cantiga* "Jogo de Dentro, Jogo de Fora" ("Inside Game, Outside Game") offers a meaningful sample of *capoeira* songs that emblematize the physical, spiritual, and symbolic spaces that the two expressions represent. It emphasizes the need to find the perfect equilibrium between playing as teammates and fighting as competitors:

Jogo de dentro, jogo de fora (Coro)
Jogo bonito é o jogo de Angola.
Jogo bonito, berimbau e viola.
Valha-me Deus, minha Nossa Senhora.
(Public domain; qtd. in Bola Sete 142)

Inside game, outside game (Chorus)
Angola's game is the beautiful one.
Beautiful game, *berimbau* and viola.
Help me God, Our Lady.

Taking a larger context into account, Lewis believes the reference to inside and outside circles works as "a metaphor linking
the two spheres, as in the phrase 'take a turn around the world,'
which becomes a technical term for circling the ring" (193). Floyd
Merrell offers a different interpretation and suggests that one way
to analyze the expressions *jogo de dentro* and *jogo de fora* is to associate them to the two major styles of *capoeira* (*angola* and *regional*).
For him, *jogo de dentro* is "inside play, down low, low and close
to the other partner, ready to dish out a dose of *malícia*," which
angoleiros are prone to associate with their *capoeira* style, whereas
jogo de fora can be more closely related to *capoeira regional* in that
it is played "standing up at a distance, maneuvering arms and legs
up and down" (93). Regardless of the interpretation presented, the
inner circle offers a protected environment for the players and, at
a metaphorical level, it represents the physical, mental, emotional,
and spiritual boundaries that exist within and beyond the *roda*.
The tradition of associating the way *capoeiristas* behave in the "inside game" to how they live their lives (the "outside game") is part
of the ethical principles by which enlightened players guide their
teachings and engagement in the *rodas*.

In traditional *capoeira* circles, when preparing to initiate the
game, the players squat near the *berimbau*, focusing their attention
on the rhythmic sound of the instrument. (*Berimbau* is the leading
instrument in *capoeira*; it originated in Africa and is composed of a
gourd resonator and a single string stretched across a long-bowed
pole.) Such a display of reverence attests to the *berimbau*'s symbolic and metonymic representation of African traditions, a notion
that is corroborated by the numerous allusions found in *capoeira*
chants. A case in point is "Cavalaria," a song in which Mestre Bola
Sete (José Luiz Oliveira Cruz) teaches the history and philosophy

of *capoeira*, offers an overview of the Afro-Brazilian resistance, and discusses the key role the *berimbau* has played as a musical instrument and a symbol of resistance to enslavement:

> Berimbau chama,
> A roda inicia
> No mato, numa clareira.
> É hora de alegria.
> De repente ... um toque,
> Gritos ... correria ...
> A Guarda Nacional,
> A Cavalaria.
> Tudo se transforma,
> Tudo é terror,
> Luta violenta,
> Não se sabe o vencedor.
> Capoeiristas lutando
> Ao lado da razão.
> Cavalaria foge,
> Fugindo da obrigação.
> Capoeiristas vitoriosos,
> Feridos, mas contentes.
> A capoeira continua, camarada!
> Vamos em frente!
> (Bola Sete 83)

> *Berimbau* calls
> The *roda* begins
> In the woods, in a clearing.
> It's time to be happy.
> Suddenly ... a rhythm,
> Cries ... running ...
> The National Guard,
> The Calvary squadron.
> Everything changes,
> Everything is terrifying,
> Violent fight,
> It is hard to tell who the winner is.
> *Capoeiristas* fighting
> On the right side of the law.
> The Calvary squadron flees,
> Running away from its duty.
> *Capoeiristas* declare victory,
> They are hurt, but content.
> *Capoeira* continues, comrades!
> Let's move ahead!

Three names are the most common terms used to refer to the *berimbau*: a) *gunga*, which has the largest gourd resonator and a deep tone, functioning as a bass and played by the *mestre* or the leader of the group; b) *médio*, which offers an intermediate pitch and high notes, and maintains the beat; c) and *viola* or *violinha*, which determines the rhythmic variations of the songs. In discussing the beats and analyzing the *berimbau's* rhythmic complexity, Downey contends that "even though the most virtuosic musicians depend on the same three tones, improvised performance can become extraordinarily complicated, with staccato delays, syncopation, and subtle shading of the instruments timbres on a basic toque" (*Learning* 90). In this aspect, the *berimbau's* rhythm can be compared to a *ginga*, the foundational step of *capoeira*, which, in its repetitive swaying motion, can also be mistakenly described as ordinary in appearance, but which requires perfect balance and a steady swaying motion. In addition to the *berimbau*, *capoeiristas* also learn how to play *caxixi* which is a small percussion instrument of African origin that consists of a closed basket filled with seeds or other particles, and which accompanies the *berimbau*. In most *capoeira* circles, the participants play *atabaque* (a large drum also used in religious ceremonies of African origin), *reco-reco* (a metal or bamboo scraper), *pandeiro* (a tambourine), and *agogô* (a double cowbell).[10]

In his study of the development of the *berimbau* in colonial Brazil, Richard Graham traces the instrument's origin to Kongo/ Angolan musical bows, namely, "the *hungu* of Luanda and the *mbulumbumba* of Southwestern Angola" (2). He concludes that "by the end of the nineteenth century, the *berimbau* had shed its initial association as a beggar's instrument, re-emerging in the socially powerful context of the *capoeira* wrestling game" (6). Basing his interpretation on information found in travel narratives and the drawings of foreign artists of the Brazilian colonial and imperial periods, Rego favors the hypothesis that instruments and songs were not used in the first stages of *capoeira's* development in Brazil, and argues that the precise dates when instruments became part of *rodas de capoeira* are inconclusive and debatable at best (59–60).[11] Siding with Rego, Assunção discredits studies that have manipulated records to connect instruments and songs to the genesis of *capoeira* because he believes there is no reliable evidence of the specific point in time when the *berimbau* became an intrinsic part of the game (7). However, it seems likely that slaves and other Afro-Brazilian descendants used the sound of the *berimbau* to warn players of impending danger, when masters, foremen, plantation overseers, bush captains, and other supervising authorities would approach the sites where they played *capoeira* (Rego 35). Following the abolition of slavery, *capoeiristas* also continued to draw on the *berimbau's* sound to announce an impending police arrival, or the approach of special armed forces that targeted *capoeira* groups (Assunção 110–12, 161–62; Capoeira *Little*, 39–44; Downey, *Little* 88–99; Rego 35).

Two major *berimbau toques* ("beats") called "Aviso" ("Warning") and "Cavalaria" ("Mounted Calvary Corps") corroborate the argument that musicians would place themselves in a lookout position and played the instrument to inform *capoeira* groups of impending prosecution (Lewis 151; Rego 35, 60). While there are controversies regarding the time and space when instruments became a vital part of *capoeira* circles, most researchers and instructors have chosen to underscore the significance the instruments have had to the performance of the game and the crucial role the *berimbau* plays as the leading instrument of a *roda de capoeira*. Other researchers analyze its rhythms, beats, and tones, often addressing the misleading simplicity of its musical variations, and its "slight dissonance" as Lewis describes the rhythms of the *berimbau*. Catherine Evleshin highlights its significance as the chief instrument of a *roda*, stating that, in addition to controlling the rhythm, the *berimbau* directs "the speed, the emotional intensity, and even the style of the game" (13).

Considering the significant role that the music has had in *capoeira* circles, it seems logical that *mestres* use *capoeira* songs to teach the rules of the game, monitor the *roda's* energy and development, warn against escalating violence, and remind the players of the principles of *capoeira*. The songs can function as mood moderators, or as tools with which to placate the players' dangerous impulses and alleviate the tension in the *roda*. They also serve the purpose of healing the pain of bruised egos and are instrumental in defining the artistic and philosophical principles of the game and help control the energy of a *roda* by commenting on or explaining the game. Hence, they have a disciplinary and didactic purpose, and connect the players' movements and rhythms of the instruments to a larger historical meaning as when the lyrics of the songs trace a rudimentary history of the African diaspora in Brazil, or evaluate the corporeal, social, and religious mediation in *capoeira* circles. The lyrics of the songs also include aphorisms and riddles which communicate symbolic meanings and function as a form of linguistic astuteness. In that sense, learning the metaphorical significance or the symbolism embedded in the aphorisms and riddles is somewhat equivalent to learning how to use *malícia* in the physical game.

A good example of how to use the lyrics of the songs as a teaching tool can be found in "Eu Vou Ler o Beabá" ("I Am Going to Read the Alphabet"), a public domain song cited by Mestre Bola Sete in which the lyric voice describes the *berimbau*'s physical structure, rhythmic variations, composition, and beats. The song also discusses the instrument's historical function in the game, and offers a representative sample of the reverence all *capoeiristas* have or should have as the following verses exemplify:

> Eu vou ler o BE-Á-BÁ,
> O BE-Á-BÁ do berimbau.
> A moeda e o arame
> E um pedaço de pau.
> A cabaça e o caxixi,
> Aí está o berimbau.
> Berimbau é um instrumento
> Que toca numa corda só.
> Pra tocar São Bento Grande
> Toca Angola em tom maior.
> Agora acabei de crer:
> O berimbau é o maior.
> (Bola Sete 89)

> I am going to read the alphabet
> The *berimbau*'s fundamentals.
> The coin and the wire
> And a good stick.
> The gourd and the caxixi,
> There you have the *berimbau*.
> *Berimbau* is an instrument
> Played on a single string.
> It plays São Bento Grande
> It plays Angola in major tone.
> I no longer have any doubt:
> The *berimbau* is the best.

As the game unfolds, the *berimbaus* establish the rhythm, the other instruments follow suit as bodies advance and retreat, speaking a corporeal language laden with improvisations and attuned to the rhythm of the instruments and the meaning of the lyrics of songs (they are usually classified as *ladainha, chula, corrido* and *quadra*). *Ladainha,* a long litany and an introductory narrative, is mostly sung in *rodas* of *capoeira angola.* A *mestre,* or someone who has earned enough respect from the community, or received permission to vocalize the *ladainha,* intones it in preparation for the opening of the game. During its performance, no physical action takes place so that the players can focus on the meaning of the words and the message they convey. The *chula,* which follows the *ladainha,* is shorter, but can also pay homage to the game, praise God, mention infamous *mestres,* instruct about moral values, and describe social, historical, and cultural situations. Everyone in the inner and outer circles can sing the *corridos,* the short songs that have a more accelerated rhythm and accompany the body movements. In addition, there are *quadras* (four-verse stanzas) that Mestre Bimba developed for *capoeira regional.* Although this division is helpful, it is important to remember that such categorization bears a didactic purpose only, and variations in style, size, and content occur regularly; for instance, in most cases, *chulas* and *corridos* fall into one single group. Thus, a firm division between the types of songs is debatable, particularly because most of the traditional songs were not composed specifically for *capoeira.* Considering historical facts and cultural mutations, Rego warns against the risk of assigning strict classifications to the songs because it is difficult to distinguish songs composed for *rodas de capoeira* from those adopted from the public domain (89). Most of the traditional *capoeira* chants can be traced to Brazilian popular music (folkloric songs, and the lyrics of *modinha* and *samba*). Generations of *capoeiristas* have borrowed from popular culture and have taught those *cantigas* for so long that they have become part of the *capoeira* tradition.

Orality has played a significant role in the preservation and transmission of songs and it also became a defining factor in the variances found in the lyrics of the songs.[12] Conventional *capoeira* songs belong to an oral tradition (roughly speaking, until mid-twentieth century they were rarely found in print), and have no restricted intellectual property. Therefore, it is as difficult to pin-point the dates on which the conventional songs were composed as it is to verify with absolute certainty the transformations their lyrics have undergone. For instance, though references to slavery and police repression often appear in traditional *capoeira* songs, it would be hasty to assume that those allusions reveal the historical epoch in which they were composed because several recently com-posed songs emulate the themes and the linguistic traits of older songs, especially when making historical references. Identifying songs composed more recently is not a difficult task because they can refer to *mestres* who are still alive, address modern and contem-porary social and cultural issues, define and distinguish *capoeira angola* from *capoeira regional*, and lately have addressed women as players. Usually, the composers of traditional songs (those that are public domain or drawn from the popular archive) are unknown, but the lyricists of new *cantigas* (published in books, *capoeira* magazines, CDs, and websites) take ownership of the songs, a tendency that makes it easier for researchers to verify dates or the approximate time of composition.

The lyrics of the songs often reflect the choice of vocabulary and grammar of the spoken Portuguese language. This linguistic characteristic has led purists to disregard their poetic aspects, and argue that those chants lack erudition, or linguistic sophis-tication. However, a meticulous reading of the lyrics of the songs discloses a complex range of meanings and poetic maneuvers, often concealed in the verbal folds that a plurality of meanings can convey. Quite often the songs offer an assortment of allusions and meanings that are hidden behind the veil of analogies, inversions, *double-entendres*, metaphors, metonymies, parodies, and ironies. While the songs have the pragmatic function of moderating the mood of the game, the ludic and poetic discourse embedded in the figurative language also highlight the creative and improvisational features both in language and in the movements of the bodies, and thus provide *double-entendres* and ironies which serve to high-light the ambivalent characteristic of several aspects of the game. The linguistic traits and figures of speech found in *capoeira* songs work simultaneously to reveal and hide meanings and contribute to establish an interactive dialogue in a *roda*. The songs become part of a larger discourse that incorporates body movements, language, and musical sounds, and in which bodies and the words communicate with each other to express new meanings through improvisation and versatility.

Using a linguistic analogy, Lewis argues that the songs invert the traditional "hierarchy of verbal/nonverbal relations," and "serve as contextualization cues for action in the ring, similar to the way raised eyebrows or curled lips can affect the meaning of linguistic utterances" (12). Stylistically speaking, literary devices and tropes found in *cantigas de capoeira* also serve a function comparable to the role *malícia* plays in the dynamics of the game. The lyrics' simplicity works as a disguising device that veils aesthetic complexities. In that aspect, they share a commonality with the seemingly "plain" movements of a *ginga*, the misleading "minimalist" tones of a *berimbau* beat, and the "shyness" of the closed-in movement of an *aú* in *capoeira angola*. In terms of their thematic contents, the songs can mention Bahia's folklore, describe cultural behaviors and traditions, and analyze conceptual views of the world. They offer a singular view into gender relations, and prompt a comparison with the thematic foci of other songs in the repertoire of Brazilian music. They refer directly, or sometimes just allude, to Brazilian social, cultural, or historical aspects, and pay homage to African and Afro-Brazilian popular heroes such as Zumbi (the leader of Quilombo dos Palmares, the largest community of escaped slaves in colonial Brazil). They also describe instruments, assert codes of conduct, reaffirm philosophical principles and moral values, revere *capoeira*'s renowned *mestres*, praise the Christian God, Catholic saints, and the African orishas.

Some groups of *capoeira* in São Paulo, even those who play *capoeira regional* such as Capitães d'Areia and Cativeiro, have joined the *angoleiros*' attempts to "reafricanize" *capoeira* by bestowing upon the players an aura of guardians of African ancestries and traditions in Brazil (L. Reis 141–61). Mestre Bola Sete is a sound example of a practitioner who endeavors to "reafricanize" *capoeira* by connecting it with Candomblé and other practices of African origin. His *ladainha* "Orixás da Bahia" ("Bahian Orishas") offers a good sample of *capoeira* chants that praise the Afro-Brazilian cosmology, establishes correlations between the ritualistic process of *capoeira* and sites of worship, and showcases the religious syncretism of Afro-Brazilian religions and Catholicism. The lyrics of the song pay homage to the deities that best symbolize the artistry of the *capoeira* game: Oshosi (the nimble and dexterous hunter),

Shango (the exuberant and courageous god of thunder and lightning), Oya (the goddess of the forests who represents bravery and impulsiveness), Ogum (god of metallurgy and war, a symbol of violence and virility), and Eshu (the trickster, the guardian of the roads, and Ogum's companion):

> Xangô, rei de Oyó,
> O Exu é mensageiro,
> Omolu, Senhor São Bento,
> Oxóssi, santo guerreiro.
> Iansã das tempestades,
> Janaína, rainha do mar,
> Nanã, Iyabá Senhora,
> Mãe de todos os orixás.
> Ogum, o deus da guerra,
> Oxalá, santo de fé,
> Olorum, o rei supremo,
> O Senhor do candomblé.
> (Bola Sete 80–81)

> Shango, King of Oyó,
> Eshu is the messenger,
> Omolu, Master São Bento,
> Oshosi, the warrior saint.
> Oya, of the tempests,
> Yemoja, queen of the oceans,
> Nana Bukulu, Iyabá Mistress,
> Mother of all orishas.
> Ogum, god of war,
> Obatala, the saint of faith,
> Olorun, the supreme king,
> The Master of Candomblé.

The reference to Eshu, in the second verse, does not seem gratuitous since Mestre Bola Sete acknowledges the entity's status as an emissary. Considering that Eshu embodies a multiplicity of meanings and represents an efficient communication gateway between humans and orishas, Henry Louis Gates Jr. describes him as a skilled interpreter who can be simultaneously "the messenger and the process of interpretation" (*The Signifying Monkey* 7, 21–23, 252–53).[13] Eshu embodies good and evil, and connects the physical and spiritual realms. He is also the master of crossroads and a trickster; therefore, it is not surprising that a number of *capoeiristas* see in Eshu a mirror-image of themselves (Rego 39, 42, 80, 146–47, 180, 236, and 256). Equally duplicitous, crafty, seductive, transformational, and flexible, Eshu and *capoeira* players can be recognized and/or stereotyped as highly resourceful personalities who can use creativity, seduction, and *jeitinho* to accomplish their goals.

In a song named "A Árvore da Mandinga" ("The *Mandinga* Tree"), Mestre Bola Sete registers *capoeiristas*' veneration for and identification with Eshu who is an entity that lives on the fringes of society, and suffered social and cultural exclusion in the process of acculturation in Brazil. He was demonized by missionaries who mistook his enormous phallus—which in Africa symbolizes fertility—for an unbridled sexuality (Ortiz, *Morte* 127). As suggested in the song "A Árvore da Mandinga," the entity would protect escaped slaves because he was a trickster who could do *mandinga*, sympathize with their cause, and protect them from prosecution, physical abuses, and even spiritual assaults.

> No tempo da escravidão
> Quando nego matou sinhá
> Foi na árvore da mandinga
> Que o nego foi morar.
> O feitor passava perto
> Não podia enxergar
> Procurava o nego escravo
> Que matou sua sinhá
> Exu, santo malandro,
> Messageiro dos orixás
> Protegia o nego escravo
> Que cansou de apanhar.
> (Bola Sete n.p.)

> During slavery times
> When a black man killed the white lady
> It was at the mandinga tree
> That the black man would hide.
> The foreman would go by
> And could not see him.
> He would look for the black slave
> Who killed the lady of the house.
> Eshu, a rouguish saint,
> Messenger of the orishas
> Would protect the black slave
> Who got tired of being beaten up.

143

Ma as the Mandinka which is part of the Mali Empire.[14] Widely used in Africa and in the Americas as a synonym for sorcery (Schaffer 321–69), the concept of *mandinga,* which originally meant "magic" or "spell," is still used in Candomblé's religious ceremonies (Harding 22–37). As indicated in Bola Sete's song, *mandinga* also had its meaning extended in *rodas de capoeira* where it is interchangeably used with the word *malícia.* The exchangeable use of *malícia* and *mandinga* connotes the players' hidden or inner power which allows them to disguise intentions, trick, and confuse the opponent and is often interpreted as a form of sorcery. It also reflects their astuteness and ability to prove themselves smarter than their competitors in the *roda* and in life.

Players are profoundly conscious of the ambivalence found in *capoeira* (game/fight), and recognize the need to keep an impenetrable and indestructible body (*corpo fechado*) and ward off their magnetic field from attacks.[15] To establish a corporal, emotional, and mental dialogue with others, they have to heighten their attention; yet they must also work within the ambivalence of the game by closing their physical body and magnetic field to avoid being tricked or hurt while playing. To "close" (that is, protect) their bodies from material and spiritual harm, believers in Candomblé and *capoeira* circles wear amulets and/or beaded necklaces. The song "Vamos Jogar Capoeira" ("Let's Play *Capoeira*") by Mestre Bola Sete illustrates and defines the concept of *corpo fechado* as the energetically impermeable, sealed, or armored body. He offers a prime example of the interconnected practice of *capoeira* and Candomblé and discusses the advantages of closing off one's magnetic field when playing *capoeira.* He honors Besouro, one of the greatest *capoeiristas* of all time, and a marvel in his own right. The legend goes that Besouro developed such a *corpo fechado* that he could skillfully trick or fight the police, or simply magically disappear in front of their eyes.[16]

> Vamos jogar a capoeira
> Como manda a tradição
> Jogo de dentro, jogo de fora
> É o jogo de Angola.
> Capoeira, meu irmão
> É o exemplo do Besouro
> De Santo Amaro da Purificação
> Que tinha o corpo fechado
> Quando fazia uma oração

E saía vadiando,
Enrolando pelo chão
Na roda de capoeira
Dava um aperto de mão
Era um jogo mandingueiro
Não machucava o companheiro
E nem batia sem precisã
Mas a polícia o temia.
No momento da ação,
Quando ele se benzia,
A todos ele vencia
Com seu santo de guarda.

Let's play *capoeira*
As tradition requires
Inside game, outside game
It is Angola's game.
Capoeira, my brother,
It is the example set by
Besouro from Santo Amaro da Purificação
The one who had a closed-off body
When he prayed
And was engaged in playing *capoeira*
Rolling on the ground.
In a *roda de capoeira*
He would shake hands
It was a game played with mandinga
He would not hurt a partner
And would only strike if needed
But the police feared him.
When in action,
He would cross himself,
He would defeat everyone
With the help of his guardian angel.

Mestre Bola Sete composed several other songs that establish the connection between the practice of *capoeira* and Candomblé. In "Timbuera" ("Cashew Nut"),[17] a long chant he wrote to praise Pessoa Bababá, the player who first introduced him to *capoeira* in the Tororó district in Salvador, he describes the dark basement in which, away from the repressive and watchful eyes of the police, he learned the fundamentals of the fight-ritual. The choice of *timbuera*[18] for the title of the song provides a telling image of the place and space *capoeira* used to occupy in the Brazilian cultural and social environment. Comparing *capoeira* to a cashew nut/

seed that grows outside the core of the fruit, Mestre Bola Sete describes the process of exclusion that *capoeiristas* suffered and depicts the art of playing *capoeira* as a marginalized activity that needed to be conducted in hidden areas to avoid prosecution. He also contextualizes the historical trajectory of *capoeira* by referring to slavery and the repression to which players were subject. The stanzas cited below underscore Bola Sete's recollections of his lessons in *capoeira* and the foundational values that his first instructor imparted to him. The references to "campo de mandinga" ("field of magic") and "feitiço" ("spells") allude simultaneously to the religious aspects of the words and the connotations of learning the art of *malícia*, or disguise, in *capoeira*. The dark basement, the hidden space, where he first studied the *capoeira* moves reminded him of *senzalas* (the slave quarters of colonial Brazil). To brighten the place so that they could practice, Pessoa Bababá would light a few candles at the corners of the room. The image of the flickering flames in the dark recess of the basement also works as a metaphor for the development of *capoeira* as a form of cultural resistance, illuminating the dungeons of history that slavery represents.

> Era um campo de mandinga
> No meio da escuridão
> Com uma vela em cada canto
> Em cada canto um lamento
> Relembrando o sofrimento
> Do tempo da escravidão
> Brigar contra um não tem graça
> Já lutou com sete praça (sic)
> Não tem feitiço que ele não desfaça
> É capoeirista de raça
> Que gosta de tomar cachaça
> Na porta do botequim.
> (Bola Sete 24)

> It was a field of mandinga
> In darkness
> A candle lit in every corner
> In each corner a lament
> Would remind us of suffering
> From slavery times
> It is not fun to fight one single person
> When he has fought seven soldiers
> He can undo any spell

He is a true capoeirista
Who likes to drink sugarcane rum
At the bar door.

As Paul Christopher Johnson analyzes it, Candomblé devotees believe that, as a porous mass, "the body cannot resist incursions by sickness, misfortunes, unwelcome entities, or the malevolence of enemies" (126). For this reason, he explains, devotees developed several practices such as "herbal bathing, ritual scaring, amulet wearing, and initiation" to ward off detrimental forces and thus secure the body's unity by closing its magnetic field (126). "Closing the body" not only prevents unwanted external energies from taking over one's magnetic field, but as Johnson reminds us, it also precludes a porous body from leaking *axé*, a person's magical energy or life force (126). The need to "close off" one's body in religious rituals of African origin is intended as a defense mechanism against attacks, or contamination, from uninvited entities of the supernatural world. Thus, learning how to close off one's physical, mental, and spiritual bodies is part of the special ceremonial treatment that devotees must undergo to become an initiate in Candomblé. Downey offers a compelling explanation of how and why *capoeiristas* need to learn to balance the acts of playing the game and avoiding reacting too quickly to a movement or gesture that may look like a provocation (*Learning* 146).[19] His research indicates that "numerous similarities exist between 'closing the body' in Candomblé and what *capoeiristas* hope to accomplish in the game. In both cases, practitioners fear an atmosphere rife with dangers, believe the body is porous, and even see 'wounding' (or learning by falling) as a way to close the body" (146). However, as Downey also points out, "For all the similarities, differences are marked. Candomblé devotees, for example, believe that rituals can permanently close the body and thus bring increased protection," while *capoeiristas* find the need to "respond to the body's openness with constant diligence, without hope that one single act or posture might make the body less permeable" (146).

Capoeiristas who are also affiliated with African traditions connect the expression *corpo fechado* to the religious rites and ceremonies of Afro-Brazilian traditions designed to grant physical and spiritual protection to their devotees. *Capoeira* players use the expression *corpo fechado* to connote working on one's defense on many levels. At the physical plane, to avoid being hurt, they become skilled at using hands and arms to protect the most vulnerable parts of the body (face, neck, chest, and lower torso).[20] At the emotional and mental levels, by learning to use astuteness and disguise, players project poise, reassurance, and a sense of invulnerability. They broadcast a level of confidence that others often sense as outright power and tight control over their personal space and, consequently, such display of confidence functions as an armor intended to keep other players at bay. Protective strategies are often described or mentioned in *capoeira* songs, and the expression *corpo fechado* has become an integral part of *capoeira*'s vocabulary. To wrap *capoeira* in mystic content, and transform it into a highly symbolic enterprise, quite often *capoeiristas* underscored the connections between their art form and African-derived religious expressions (L. Reis 188–94). Mestre Bola Sete, for instance, confers to *capoeira* a sense of mystery or a metaphysical quality, placing it at the level of a quasi-religious practice. Consequently, Candomblé and *capoeira* have a symbiotic and historical relationship as far as some ritualistic practices are concerned.

The song "O Berimbau de Bola Sete" ("Bola Sete's *Berimbau*") gives a telling account of how the *mestre* connects his religious affiliation with his craft by bestowing upon the leading instrument of *capoeira* the symbolic role of calling for divine guidance and protection. The two stanzas below highlight the duplicitous nature of his *berimbau* (used as a musical instrument and a symbol of magic force and protection). As the song illustrates, learning how to protect one's magnetic field can heighten the players' awareness of their personal power and help them develop an acute awareness of their surroundings which are great assets for *capoeira* players:

> O berimbau de Bola Sete
> Tem sete laços de fita
> E o seu nome gravado
> Com uma letra bem bonita.
>
> Tem um amuleto bem amarrado
> Lá no alto da biriba
> Pra guardar e fechar o corpo
> Do mestre capoeirista.
> (Bola Sete 29)
>
> Bola Sete's *berimbau*
> Has seven ribbons

And his name engraved on it
In a beautiful handwriting.

It also features an amulet tightly tied
To the top of the wooden bow
To close off
Mestre capoeirista's body.

To ensure a *corpo fechado* in Candomblé, devotees undergo training and blessings, and wear a *patuá*, an amulet like *bolsas de mandinga*, the protective pouches Brazilians wore around their necks in the eighteenth century. At the time, the Roman Catholic Church prohibited *bolsas de mandinga* because they were considered a form of sorcery,[21] even if the concept of guarding a person's magnetic field also exists in popular Catholicism.[22] To become a fully-functional protective instrument, a *mandinga* pouch or *patuá* needs to be consecrated by a religious authority or by someone with magic power, in the same way that a scapular (*escapulário*) needs to be blessed by a clergyman. To date, Catholic devotees wear medals, crosses, rosaries, and devotional scapulars, all-purpose forms of protection which are guaranteed by a favorite saint, Jesus, or the Virgin Mary. In *capoeira* circles, it is also a practice to wear a necklace, or a *patuá*, to safeguard the bearer from malicious attacks in the *roda* and in the world (Almeida 74). In that sense, the *capoeiristas'* necklaces offer them a form of protection similar to the defense devotees receive when wearing a *patuá* or scapular.[23]

In *Mestre Bimba: Corpo de Mandinga*, Muniz Sodré provides a biographical account of the *mestre*, and shares substantial information on the existing connections of *capoeira* rituals and the Afro-Brazilian belief systems. He reveals that Mestre Bimba adopted the Solomon Sign (*Signo de Salomão*, popularly referred to as *Cinco Salomão*) for his *capoeira* academy, but implemented some changes, adapting it to other religious configurations. The objective of selecting Solomon's star as an emblem for his *capoeira* academy was, in Sodré's words, "algum modo de convocar as virtudes da ponderação física e mental para não se perder no jogo da vida e da roda" ("a way to summon the virtues of physical and mental poise and moderation to avoid getting lost in the game of life and in the *capoeira* circle"; 58). In his search for absolute protection, Bimba recreated Solomon's star by intertwining two triangles to represent equilibrium in *rodas de capoeira* (Sodré 58). In addition,

149

he placed a cross within the circle, in his belief that it could represent either Jesus of Eshu's crossroads (Sodré 58). Mestre Bimba also had strong connections with Candomblé where he was under the patronage of two very powerful orishas: Shango, representing the divine force that drives a *protégée* to shine in the world, and Yemanjá, the Goddess of the Waters (Sodré 94).

In a number of houses of worship of Umbanda and in some variations of Candomblé, Yemanjá is characterized as a mermaid dressed in blue and white (the colors commonly associated with her in Brazil). She is widely revered in numerous public festivities throughout the country and is considered, as Armando Vallado summarizes her role, the sentinel or guardian of the waters of the sea, and the "great African mother of Brazil" (163–95, 199–218). The references to Yemanjá and/or mermaids in *capoeira* songs—especially the ones written by lyricists affiliated with Afro-Brazilian religions—connect the empowerment of women that Yemanjá represents and the mastery of seduction that mermaids and sirens symbolize to *malícia* in *capoeira*. The song "Sereia"[24] ("Mermaid"), recorded by Mestre Limão, refers to Yemanjá and Ogum as protectors and advisors and offers a good example of how closely connected several *capoeiristas* are to the guiding principles of Afro-Brazilian religions.

> Eu sou filho de Ogum
> Sobrinho de Yemanjá
> Tanto faz se tou na terra
> Tou nas águas ou tou no mar
> Ó Sereia …Ó Sereia …
>
> Uma criatura linda
> Que canta na beira do mar
> Vestida de azul e branco
> O seu nome é Yemanjá
> Ó Sereia … Ó Sereia …
>
> I am Ogum's child
> And Yemanjá's nephew
> It does not matter if I am on land,
> Water, or the ocean
> Oh! Mermaid … Oh! Mermaid …

A beautiful creature
Who sings at the edge of the sea
Dressed in blue and white
Her name is Yemanjá
Oh! Mermaid ... Oh! Mermaid ...

Mermaids use the persuasive charm of their songs to seduce sailors and other navigators, and then, annihilate them by taking them to the deep realms of the waters they inhabit. *Capoeiristas* also use their songs to lure other players into the *roda* and apply the art of *malícia* to take down an opponent/partner. These two aspects are outlined in the following stanzas from the song "Sereia":

Sereia, criatura linda,
Que encanta os homens assim
Cantando na beira do mar
Forçando eles pararem
Ó Sereia ... Ó Sereia ...

Pela doçura do teu cantar
Eu me vejo obrigado a parar
Ó Sereia ... Ó Sereia ...

Num dia de lua cheia
Tava sentado junto ao mar
Quando de longe ouvi
O canto de uma sereia
Ó Sereia ... Ó Sereia ...

Mermaid, pretty creature,
Who charms men
Singing at the edge of the sea
Forcing them to stop
Oh! Mermaid ... Oh! Mermaid ...

Your singing is so sweet
That I feel compelled to stop
Oh! Mermaid ... Oh! Mermaid ...

On a full-moon night
I was sitting near the ocean
When I heard far away
A mermaid's song
Oh! Mermaid ... Oh! Mermaid ...

In the introduction to a collection they organized, Linda Phyllis Austern and Inna Naroditskaya write about sirens and their sisters as "the most elusive and paradoxical of all creatures" (1). As they further explain, sirens have taken numerous configurations: "they are disembodied demons of darkly water depths, night club performers of modern city, celluloid angels, zoological finds, carved capitals, consort of Chinese sky-gods, and the frame for the string of an Irish harp ... One of the few qualities that draws them together is their music" (1). In many legends, their singing is described as sweet and enticing, but also conniving, tricky, and dangerous, characteristics that the Portuguese expression *canto de sereia* exemplifies. In *capoeira* songs, the expression *canto de sereia* alludes to the game itself in which one player may charm or bewitch the other into a *jogada* that proves to be a dangerous trick. The enticement to play, the ambiguity embedded in the game, the desire to lure the other into a move—only to outsmart the other player—are all skillful uses of *malícia/mandinga* that could describe *um canto de sereia* and typify *um jogo bonito*. Thus, the image of Yemanjá looming large over the ocean waters as a protector and, as a mermaid, is significant for many *capoeiristas*. The players believe that she lends her musical talents and seductive wiles to them, which gives them the confidence to enter the *roda* knowing how to use music and *malícia* as strategic playing devices.

In the song "Sereia," the lyricist also invokes Ogum. As Zeca Ligeiro describes the deity, he is "the god of iron" and "the lord of war"; he is "stormy," has a "bellicose temperament," "lacks patience," and "his dance is warlike" (108). Ogum is the prototype of a violent, feisty, arrogant, and impulsive person, but he also represents people who fight for their objectives and do not give up easily (Verger 95). In some traditions, Ogum is considered a son of Yemanjá (Berkenbrock 240), and he gets along with Eshu who is his best companion (Bastide, *Candomblé* 179–81). Primarily a trickster, Eshu is duplicitous, crafty, seductive, transformational, and flexible. For the reasons mentioned above, *capoeira* players often find a symbolic connection with Eshu and/or Ogum, entities that can defend, protect, open the roads and the channels of communication, but who are also prone to play pranks and behave surreptitiously, or act arrogantly and/or violently (Rego 146–47).

In Brazil, Eshu has a female counterpart, Pomba Gira (also identified as Pombagira). The word derives from Bonbogirá, the name given to Eshu in houses of worship of Candomblé de Angola of Bantu origin (Prandi 140). As discussed in Chapter One, in the beginning of the twentieth century in Brazil, social zealots strove to redefine a code of honor and morality for women to establish a tighter control over their bodies, sexuality, and lifestyle. It was in this period that Umbanda was first organized, in Niteroi, as a hybrid religion that combines African traditions, elements of Roman Catholicism, and religious practices of the indigenous people of Brazil. At that time, Pomba Gira (an entity whose concept in Brazil blends African, European, and local mythologies) was incorporated into Umbanda's pantheon. In analyzing Pomba Gira, Kelly E. Hayes describes her as a "holy harlot," an entity that symbolizes "the quintessential femme fatale, [and] the perilous seductress depicted in pulp fiction and film noir" (4). For Hayes, she is "possibly evil, definitively dangerous," and "embodies a uniquely Brazilian envisioning of femininity's dark side" (4). As an ambiguous and ambivalent figure that personifies positive and negative characteristics, she is both esteemed and feared and could evoke an image of how players position themselves in *capoeira* circles.

In the Brazilian cultural landscape, Pomba Gira's powers and charm transcend religious settings. In the popular imagination, she is respected for her "feminine" powers, but also despised for her extravagant vanity, unbridled sexuality, and elemental power. In a sense, Pomba Gira's flirtatious personality, licentiousness, and power of seduction could characterize her as a precursor of the women who embrace the *profissão mulata*. It could also be connected to the way the *parda* women are described in Brazil in literature, music, and visual performances, from colonial days to the televised rendition of contemporary *carnaval* parades (as discussed in Chapter Two). Pomba Gira is fiercely independent, boisterous, and assertive, qualities that make her sought after to resolve contentious issues pertaining to love affairs, money, power, and other comparable needs and wants. She often uses vulgar language and debauchery, and as a headstrong and commanding woman, "defies patriarchal criteria of feminine respectability" and shatters "established norms of conduct and moral action," as Hayes describes her and summarizes her actions (8–9). In that sense, the pioneering female *capoeiristas*, at the end of the nineteenth century and in the first decades of the twentieth century, who were indicted in the police records and rebutted in newspapers as women of ill-repute,

153

strong and uninhibited fighters, and prone to disorderly conduct, could be associated with her.

In addition to the numerous specialized Umbanda publications about Pomba Gira and the countless references to her name in Brazilian music and poetry, there are several other literary, artistic, and performative examples of works that feature her in a central role. She has been showcased in novels, a play, a *telenovela*, and a musical production in which she was typified as a Brazilian gypsy.[25] Such a range of musical, literary, cinematic, legal, and cultural productions has contributed to her popularity. Her power and popular appeal were also highlighted in a courtroom in a widely publicized murder case in which she was accused of having offered ill advice to a woman during an Umbanda séance session (Contins and Goldman 103–32). As described in *The Summer of Pomba Gira* (a 2009 novel by Oleander Main), Pomba Gira's fame of protecting and empowering females has reached the United States, probably as part of the culture that waves of Brazilian immigrants brought to the United States in the 1980s and 1990s.

But it is not just women who can be associated with Pomba Gira. Studies connect male *capoeiristas* with her as well. As Eshu's female cohort, she also embodies the concept of *malandragem* (roguery, trickery, and street smarts). Additionally, because she is quite accomplished in the art of disguise, dissimulation, and seductive powers, she symbolizes *malícia*, a cornerstone of *capoeira* playing. Thus, the concepts of *malícia* and *malandragem* that are often associated with *capoeiristas* can also be connected to the imagery that Pomba Gira, gypsies, and mermaids have in the Brazilian cultural imaginary. (A gypsy is one of Pomba Gira's seven depictions or avatars.)[26] In citing an example of *capoeiristas* doing "their *mandinga*, magic spell" when participating in *capoeira* circles, Nestor Capoeira makes an explicit reference to Pomba Gira by asserting that, although her influence in *capoeira* is not so obvious, her "bravery and cunning" determines "the ethics, the way of being and acting, of the *capoeirista*" (*Roots* 61). He also compares the mischievous moves between two players to her "malicious smile" and "debauched laughter" (*Roots* 65). Even though he does not refer to Pomba Gira directly, Merrell reports having often heard from "male capoeiristas that women are by nature superior in the fine art of Capoeira than men, since for survival value in a male dominated society they have been forced to become adroit dissemblers" (36).

As a hybrid and syncretic martial art-dance-ritual, *capoeira* also adopts elements of Catholicism, most noticeably in the lyrics of songs that refer to or invoke saints (especially the Virgin Mary, Saint Anthony, Saint Benedict, and Saint Peter), and uses vocabulary related to Catholic sacraments or rituals (such as *batizado*). Those references are not surprising, given that the Brazilian national identity was forged in religious and cultural syncretism, and that a large number of *capoeira* songs have their origin in folkloric and traditional popular songs. Quite often players make the sign of the cross as they squat at the foot of the *berimbau*, while waiting for their turn to enter the *roda*, a gesture that Browning connects to the *aú*, *capoeira*'s cartwheel, which resembles an inverted cross and is also considered the sign of Eshu's crossroads (111). The emotional involvement with the gesture of making the sign of the cross and kissing the thumb in *rodas de capoeira* is a form of preparation to play. Downey describes his own personal experience as follows: "Although it may 'mean' many things as a symbol, the gesture exists experientially at a crossroads between tension and readiness, as a *capoeirista* takes up a defensive stance in a perilous world" (150).

Navigating the Cultural and Historical Space

The interest in defining and analyzing *capoeira* as a dance, martial art, and a ritual has increased in direct proportion to its popularity worldwide. As a result, numerous book-length studies and scholarly articles have contributed significantly to an understanding of the game's origin and development, and to dismiss myths and essentialisms about *capoeira*, often in comparison with African combat games and their transformation in the Americas. For the most part, studies of *capoeira* describe it as a Brazilian martial art-dance-ritual and claim that Africans and their descendants combined an Angolan dance movement with other African fighting skills, to which songs and musical instruments were added, probably to disguise the elements of combat and competition and trick the watchful eyes of slave owners in colonial Brazil. Others describe *capoeira* as an exact replica of African ancestral foot and stick fighting. Another group sees it as a hybrid tradition, a creole practice, whose elements can be traced back to Africa, but have undergone transculturation and incorporated elements from various backgrounds and ethnicities.

Considering the lack of precise information or written documentation about the derivation of the game, it is not surprising that dissentions about the origins and development of *capoeira* have divided scholars, *capoeiristas*, and other interested parties. Most of them agree, for instance, that *capoeira* has African roots, although they differ in opinion about the exact time and space where it began, or on how to describe its growth in Brazil. The literary and artistic works of foreign writers and painters such as Henry Koster, Maria Graham, Johann Moritz Rugendas, and Jean Baptiste Debret, in the eighteenth and nineteenth centuries, remain the major sources of information about the onset of *capoeira* in Brazil. Their texts and drawings have given a sound contribution to its study as they documented their experiences of traveling through the country.[27] The majority of the studies that connect *capoeira* to its African roots also refer to Albano Neves e Souza's 1960s drawings which he sketched during a trip to Brazil. He found some similarities between *capoeira* movements and the moves and kicks of the Angolan zebra dance, called *N'Golo* (or the variant Engolo), a seventeenth-century African fight-ritual that was performed during the initiation of female teenagers into womanhood in which the contestants display great dexterity and perform acrobatic kicks (Assunção 23–24, 49–52, 192; Downey 218; Talmon-Chvaicer 19, 154–55; and Tigges 31).[28]

Some contemporary scholars have closely followed the line of research that *capoeira* is an offspring of *N'Golo*. M. Thomas J. Desch-Obi, for instance, analyzes *capoeira* as an African fight-dance transplanted to Brazil. He traces the origin of *capoeira* to *kandeka*, "a stick fighting contest" and "a slap-boxing match practiced primarily by young males" (34). Desch-Obi also finds striking similarities between the characteristic kicks in *capoeira angola* and "engolo's inverted kicks" which he believes "gave birth to a martial art" (4). While Desch-Obi presents a detailed and informative description of African rituals and dances, discusses combat games, and offers some comparative connections with diasporic rituals in the Americas, at times, he does not substantiate his claims. For that reason, countering Desh-Obi's arguments, historians such as Maya Talmon-Chvaicer and Matthias Röhrig Assunção consider his assertions as mythical or folkloric references. Talmon-Chvaicer builds an argument against Desch-Obi's proposition based on the fact that he limits the historic space to "a single performance, place, date, and people as the source of capoeira" (19). She maintains that, historically speaking, it sounds naïve to disregard the fact that the Congo-Angola population kept extensive "relationships of exchange" throughout the Atlantic Ocean during the slave trade and, therefore, it is likely that several "fighting techniques, war dances, and combat games reached Brazil and combined to form the basis of capoeira" (19). Assunção asserts that Desch-Obi oversimplifies a complex process by presenting "a 'monogenetic' origin of capoeira" and disregarding many other inverted movements of the fight-ritual (56). While Assunção acknowledges that, unquestionably, *capoeira* has African origins, he refutes the premises that it is an African brand, or a mere reproduction of *kandeka* or *engolo*, concluding that *capoeira* is a hybrid form developed in the Americas (55–56). He also disagrees with what he considers Desch-Obi's emphatic argument for "capoeira's Africanness" because such a position essentializes history and is likely "to homogenize the [African] continent and freeze its culture in a pre-modern and non-Western state of authenticity" (27). Gerard Taylor is equally critical of Desch-Obi's research and conclusions. Central to his argument is that Desch-Obi singles one myth among so many other convincing legends and oversimplifies it (291). However, balancing the two sides of the argument, Taylor also notices a few inconsistencies in Assunção's claim, especially his emphatic and overwhelming critique and dismissal of the fighting practiced by Ndongo, Imbangala, and Kondolese forces (276–81).

In his quest to explain *capoeira* as a mixed martial art of the Americas, Assunção also extends his criticism to any scholar who chooses to classify *capoeira* as a "Brazilian" martial art. He discards "anachronistic labels such as African or Brazilian," not only because he favors an interactive approach between form and context, but also because he banks on Paul Gilroy's discussion of the Black Atlantic to construe his defense of *capoeira* as a hybrid development in the Americas (2). Thus, he questions both "afrocentric perspectives" and the "Brazilian nationalist claims" (8) by arguing that "capoeira is a prime example of a 'counterculture of modernity'" (30). In building his thesis, Assunção presents an array of opinions from other experts who share his views. For instance, he mentions that, as far back as 1941, Melville J. Herskovits had already questioned the assumption that *capoeira* was a unique "Brazilian art," based on the fact "that he had witnessed similar combat games in the African continent and in several locations in the Americas" (23). To seal his argument, Assunção states that Herskovits's observation was overlooked for several decades because it did not suit the nationalist discourse of the time which highlighted *capoeira* as a unique Brazilian art form (23). Thus, Assunção concludes that *capoeira* is "neither Brazilian nor African but rather a transatlantic, creole development" (32), and illustrates his premise by mentioning several other combat games in the Americas, including *bassula, cufuinha, mani, moringue, morengy,* and *mrengé* that share some traits with *capoeira* (56–66).

Brazilians have also weighed in on the discussion about the origin of *capoeira*. Letícia Reis is one of the scholars who criticizes the emphasis on *capoeira* as a Brazilian martial art-dance-fight and concludes that the widespread indifference to analytical comparisons between the art form in Brazil and other countries of the African diaspora is the result of the need to showcase *capoeira* as a "truly" Brazilian martial art to fit the needs of Getúlio Vargas's populist and essentialist agenda of the 1930s and 1940s.[29] Aligning himself with Muniz Sodré's position, Nestor Capoeira refers to *mestres* Bimba (who elected Brazil as *capoeira*'s homeland) and Pastinha (who saw Africa as the cradle), and concludes that, as it is known now, *capoeira* is not practiced in Africa; for him, the "beginning is Brazilian" and "the 'principle' (the roots, the historicity, the myth) is African" (*Roots* 107–08).

Most scholars divide the history of *capoeira* into three chronological moments: a) a prosecuted art form (beginning of the nineteenth century until the 1930s); b) its legalization (1930s); c) and its institutionalization as a "sport" in the 1970s (L. Reis 3). Whether one follows such divisions, or not, the truth of the matter is that, in the 1800s, *capoeira* was considered a "contravention" and its practitioners could receive severe punishments (Almeida 25–27; Bruhns 24–38). From 1824 onward, the slaves who were caught playing *capoeira* were subject to whipping or hard labor such as working on road construction or could even be sent to distant islands (Bruhns 24–25; Soares, *A capoera* 44). *Capoeira* players were also repeatedly stereotyped as vagrants, and stigmatized as thugs, because they engaged in disorderly conduct, or were involved in violent fights with rival factions (Rego 291–302). Despite all the police vigilance and prohibition, after 1870, the practice of *capoeira* had already extended beyond the social limits of slavery and poverty since some socially affluent white people were also engaged in its practice (Bretas 61; J. Reis 6; Soares, *A capoeira* 43, 61, 230).

At the end of the nineteenth century and the first decades of the twentieth century, the public dreaded *capoeira* gangs or rings (*maltas*, as they were known in Rio de Janeiro), a fear the police fostered and overstated to help gain the population's support for their actions against *capoeiristas* (Bretas 57–64). As a result, the police and other authorities fiercely repressed *capoeira* circles in the earlier decades of the Republic (1889–1920) as part of the sanitization efforts to cleanse Rio de Janeiro physically, culturally, and socially (Holloway 129–40; J. Reis 24–60). In analyzing the "hidden history of capoeira," Talmon-Chvaicer writes that, as of the mid-nineteenth century, it was considered a public threat and as such "the municipal authorities, journalists, and scholars regarded *capoeiras* as violent and disruptive bandits" (61). Her research reveals that there was an ongoing effort to divest *capoeira* from its ludic characteristics by describing it only as a fight, to a point that it "was increasingly detached from its original music and dancing and was essentially a criminal activity" (61). However, such stigmatization and criminalization never deterred *capoeiristas* from playing in public spaces or organizing competitions. They "played capoeira in front of military and religious processions and mocked and derided public officials," all of which was made possible because "the masses admired them and enjoyed their performances" (Talmon-Chvaicer 61).

To lawfully prosecute players, the Cavalaria and Guarda Nacional (cavalry and special squadrons of the police force) classified *capoeiristas* and their groups or gangs as vagrants, hustlers, or outlaws, alleging that they violated Chapter IV, Article 295 of the Empire's Criminal Code, established in 1830, which outlawed those activities (Rego 291–93; J. Reis 24–45). However, such prosecution was a contradictory and unlawful decision since the right to assemble and habeas corpus were rights sealed in the 1824 Constitution which granted freedom of association to all emancipated Brazilians (Assunção 10). The stigma against *capoeira* remained alive and strong for many decades. The fear-based rejection of the *capoeira* craft in the nineteenth century and in the first decades of the twentieth century owes much to the fact that some individuals resorted to sharp *capoeira* kicks and would not hesitate to use edged weapons as powerful forms of defense

159

and attack. To justify prosecuting *capoeiristas*, authorities often cited the Penal Code (Decree number 847, chapters 202, 203, and 204, established on October 11, 1890) which criminalized vagrancy and/or disorderly conduct (Assunção 1; Rego 291–92; J. Reis 46–60). Because of the role the police played in raiding groups and in controlling, or attempting to eradicate *capoeira*, the police archives from imperial Brazil (1808–1889) and from the beginning of the twentieth century remain the most significant documental source about the history of *capoeira*. Those archives reveal that, to control social disturbances or riots, the authorities charged recalcitrant *capoeiristas* with the label of vagrants in which case *capoeira* players could receive a punishment of two to six months in prison (Assunção 94; Rego 298–314). Such practice survived until the mid-1930s when, for political and strategic reasons, Vargas's regime legitimized popular cultural expressions such as *carnaval*, soccer, and *capoeira* by integrating them into his nationalistic project (Almeida 31–32; Downey, *Learning* 170–77; Rego 316–17; and J. Reis 82–84).

Several examples of Brazilian popular songs and literature reveal *capoeira*'s ambivalent nature (defense/attack, game/fight); in some cases, they include verbs such as "kill" and "die," and mention the use of edged weapons.[30] The popular song from public domain, "Quem Vem Lá" ("Who Goes There"), confirms the tradition of carrying a scarf around the neck and a razor in the pocket which was associated with the image of the rogue or rustler (*malandro*) and also connected to *capoeiristas*:

> Montado a cavalo,
> Fumando charuto,
> Coberto de luto,
> Sou eu Brevenuto.
> Eu venho gingando,
> Chinelo arrastando,
> Lenço no pescoço,
> Navalha no bolso.
> (Public domain; qtd. in Rego 98–99)

Ridding a horse,
Smoking cigars,
Dressed in black,
I am Brevenuto.
I sway and swing,
I drag my flip-flops,
A scarf on my neck
A razor in my pocket.

Waldeloir Rego reports having had a conversation with Mestre Bimba (Manoel dos Reis Machado) in which he learned that the *mestre* would instruct his followers to drape a silk scarf around their necks as a protective device. He believed they would be safer because a blade would not cut through pure silk, the material of which those imported scarves were made (Rego 43). Mestre Bimba further explained that, by wearing the scarf, *capoeiristas* did not run the risk of being stigmatized as fighters in Salvador and, therefore, could escape police prosecution since it was common for men to drape a scarf around their neck to prevent sweat or dust from staining their shirt collars (Rego 43). By conveying to his students the slick imagery of a razor touching the silk scarf, without tearing through it, or wounding a *capoeirista*'s neck, Bimba prompted his pupils to think creatively. In this case, a figurative language construed the ambivalence of *capoeira* (fight/game) and imparted the idea that the smooth quality of the silk scarf proves more efficient than a lacerating razor blade. Even though Mestre Bimba was pragmatic and was not prone to resort to symbolism, metaphors, and riddles to teach his students, it is significant that, in this case, he conveyed the metaphor of the silk scarf to teach the students to recognize and learn that is easier, safer, and more effective to use *malícia* (trickiness, cleverness, an awareness) to protect the body than to resort to a direct blow, a violent kick, or a weapon. Hence, in associating the lightness and astuteness of *malícia* to the soft, yet resilient, characteristic of the silk scarf, Mestre Bimba seems to have considered the ethical and downy aspects of the game, and the mediating feature of controlling emotions to avoid vicious moves and dodge a fight.

Vicente Ferreira Pastinha, the founder of *capoeira angola*, would also illustrate the lessons he wanted to impart to his students, by telling stories of *capoeiristas* who would hide blades in the extremities of their instruments, including his own habit of carrying "a little sickle that could be mounted on the *berimbau* transforming the instrument into a powerful weapon in case of a street fight" (Assunção 154). The following stanza of the song "Berimbau" corroborates the fight aspects of *capoeira* to which Mestre Pastinha refers, and which can highlight the game's ambiguous roles. Composed by Baden Powell and Vinicius de Moraes, this song is one of the most significant examples of how two highly regarded musicians introduced Afro-Brazilian cultural elements into the mainstream music of the 1960s:

> Capoeira me mandou
> Dizer que já chegou
> Chegou para lutar.
> Berimbau me confirmou
> Vai ter briga de amor
> Tristeza, camará.

> The *capoeira* player sent me
> To announce that he has arrived
> He has come to fight.
> The *berimbau* assured me
> There will be a lover's quarrel
> How sad, my friend.

To rationalize the implementation of slavery and/or colonialism, during their expansionist period and slave trade maritime exploration, the Portuguese fostered theories that Africans and their mixed-race descendants were lesser beings who should be feared, mistrusted, and disciplined because they were prone to aggressive and/or promiscuous behavior. The fact that slaves oftentimes rebelled against mistreatment, and would aggressively fight for their lives, contributed to the development of several stereotypes associated with African descendants and their cultural heritage in Brazil. As previously mentioned, the concept of a dangerous *capoeira* player, and the notion that *parda* women were oversexed and promiscuous, are steeped in Brazil's colonial past. It is true that the fear-based rejection and prosecution of *capoeira* owes some to the fact that the ludic characteristics of it were repressed during most of the eighteenth and nineteenth centuries, when the martial art aspect of the game were more prominent. However, it is also true that in the beginning of the twentieth century *capoeiristas* in Rio de Janeiro had formed groups that spread fear in the population.

It is exactly the concept of a cunning, street-smart player that Oswald de Andrade, one of the best representatives of the first phase of Brazilian Modernism (1922–1930), presents in his poem, "O Capoeira." Although the element of fighting in Andrade's poem reinforces the concept that *capoeira* can be a violent game, the poem describes the *capoeirista*'s brawl not as a struggle for dominance between rival groups, but rather as a counter-discourse to assert his mobility right (thus questioning the Penal Code which criminalized *capoeiristas* for vagrancy). "O Capoeira" tenders a highly confident player who launches a preemptive attack on a policeman. In the brief exchange of words between the *capoeirista* and the policeman, Andrade captures both the verbal and cultural tensions, and provides evidence that the confident and clever *capoeirista* is physically and emotionally better equipped to dominate the policeman and subordinate him to his prowess and fighting dexterity:

> —Qué apanhá sordado?
> —O quê?
> —Qué apanhá?
> Pernas e cabeças na calçada.
> (Pau Brasil 87)

> —Want to be beaten up, cop?
> —What?
> —Want to be beaten up?
> Legs and head on the sidewalk.

Andrade's quest to promote *capoeira* as a valued Brazilian cultural expression was subversive in its own right because at the time he wrote the poem the African-derived fight-ritual was still considered an underground activity and represented a subaltern segment of Brazilian society. Even if the poem does not directly address the laws that forbade the practice of *capoeira*, it pokes fun at them by using the slanted venue of parody, and by presenting an ironic tone to delegitimize police raids that acted proactively to avoid unruly behavior, or imprisoned *capoeiristas* for vagrancy. By doing so, Andrade also discredits the legitimacy of the Penal Code which stigmatized and criminalized *capoeiristas* and curtailed their freedom of movement.

"O Capoeira" inverts the hierarchical order by subjecting the absent-minded and unwary policeman to the authority, control, and skills of the *capoeira* player, and thus Andrade pays homage to a martial art-dance-ritual that, until mid-1930s, was forbidden on the grounds that it was a dangerous attack/defense practice and a menace to the social order. The *capoeirista*'s defiance of the policeman's authority finds a counterpart in Andrade's linguistic and artistic insubordination (as one of the *modernistas* who led the 1920s and 1930s artistic movement). "O Capoeira" highlights what *mestres* and other respected leaders of *capoeira* teach and emphasize: the duplicitous nature of the fight-ritual which is intended as a ludic activity, but also commonly used as a form of self-defense or attack. By presenting the *capoeirista* as someone who is able to react and think faster than the policeman, the lyric voice also casts doubt on the selection and training of policemen at the time. (Numerous jokes and popular stories attest to the fact that Brazilians used to regard police officers, especially those occupying the position of *soldado* as undeserving of much respect because those in low-ranking levels on the police force, were usually filled in by men who supposedly could not qualify for a better job.) Additionally, the poem introduces the *capoeirista* as a good representative of the vernacular language (the "real" Brazilian Portuguese). Considering that language is often used as a tool to establish class distinctions in Brazil, by adopting an unschooled form of language, Andrade confers to spoken Portuguese a unique literary space at the time. In this sense, the lyric voice exemplifies in this poem one of the tenants of the first phase of Brazilian Modernism: to revolutionize literature by narrowing the wide gap between spoken and written language so prevalent at the time. By selecting an underground activity as a thematic concept and endorsing it as a sample of a significant component of Brazilian culture, Andrade upended some prejudicial perceptions of the time, and underscored the *capoeiristas*' defiance of the norms, most likely to showcase such acts of insubordination as a form of cultural resistance.

The poem's irreverent tone also illustrates the avant-garde trends that characterized the first three decades of Brazilian

Modernism, and especially the Week of Modern Art in São Paulo, which strove to highlight Brazilian culture, language, and people. In some ways, the *capoeirista* attack on the policeman is similar to Andrade's defiance of traditional values and obsolete cultural models that he highlighted in his 1928 "Manifesto Antropófago" ("Cannibalist Manifesto"). As a prominent intellectual, Andrade was an agent of change, and one of the architects of the loud and defiant artistic expressions that the avant-garde literary tendencies of Modernism represented in its introductory phase. He was also a symbolic actor, a surrogate-of-sorts for the recalcitrant artists and writers of the first phase of Brazilian Modernism who overturned old patterns and norms and validated Brazilian popular culture. Following the tenets of the movement, Andrade searched for Brazil's national identity in its peoples and cultural expressions and lent his prestige as an acclaimed author and financially affluent intellectual to a marginalized, but defiant, Afro-Brazilian cultural practice. The poem showcases the *capoeira* player's courage to challenge the policeman as a sign that he was confident that his martial art could invert the seat of power the police represented.

The dexterity of *capoeira* players, the violence of the game, the fighting of rival factions and the fright they produced in the population were also detailed and, at times, exaggerated in Azevedo's *O Cortiço*. A substantial part of the novel addresses the perils associated with challenging *capoeiristas* who were prone to incite riots, provoke others, and engage in disorderly conduct. The novel describes them as cunning players who outsmarted opponents, escaped police prosecution, and mastered the use of razors. As depicted in Azevedo's novel, *capoeiristas* use of violence and edged weapons contributed to heighten the population's fear. Firmo, for instance, is a street-smart, overconfident, squanderer *capoeira* player who is identified by his swing (a way of swaying the body usually associated with rogues and ruffians). He is a dexterous fighter and a dangerous enemy who joined the *capoeira* group Gayamus (also known as Carapicus) when he was still in his teens. When Cabeça de Gato, a rival *capoeira* group, was formed in another tenement, fights broke out between the two gangs, terrorizing the population.[31]

Azevedo's realistic and colorful description of Rio de Janeiro's social and racial composition at the end of the nineteenth century reveals a sharply divided and, paradoxically, entangled society in which *capoeiristas* were fiercely prosecuted by the police, but also contributed to patrol the police excesses against common citizens.[32] Azevedo devotes a good portion of *O Cortiço* to describing rival *capoeira* gangs (*maltas* as they were known) which also operated as police surrogates in the tenements, offering protection to small businesses and the population during public festivities, and serving as a shield against police brutality and other abuses of power. Depicted in the book in a number of ways (as thugs, gang members, and social protectors), *capoeiristas* also embodied courage and a fearless commitment to their art and to the cult of their personality. The *capoeiristas* displayed treacherous fighting skill, could easily kill or mutilate their opponents, get out of a brawl unscathed, and escape the police.

The newspapers took notice of such unruly behavior. For instance, Machado de Assis wrote about the violence imparted by *capoeiristas* in Rio de Janeiro, analyzing the role newspapers had in amplifying such fright. From 1883 to 1886, he contributed a newspaper column, titled "Balas de Estalo," for the newspaper *Gazeta de Notícias*. One of those chronicles (published on March 14, 1885) was about *capoeira*, the behavior of *capoeira* players, and how newspapers contributed to spread panic in the population by publicizing how they used razors and other weapons to intimidate the public. In analyzing the level of violence that *capoeiristas* had spread, and how terrorized the population of Rio de Janeiro was of them, Machado used one of his trademarks, the analysis of human nature, to assess the situation, and concluded that the reason they were so vicious was because they craved attention. They were narcissists who sought adulation and notice, and suffered from *erotismo de publicidade*. Machado highlights how self-absorbed *capoeiristas* were and how they also use songs for self-aggrandizement. The solution to the problem was, in Machado's opinion, for newspapers to stop talking about *capoeiristas*:

> Capoeira é homem. Um dos característicos do homem é viver o seu tempo. Ora, o nosso tempo (nosso e do capoeira) padece de uma coisa que podemos chamar—erotismo de publicidade ... Aqui tocamos no ponto essencial ... Recorre à navalha, espalha facadas, certo de que os jornais darão notícias das suas façanhas e divulgarão os nomes de alguns. (443)

> *Capoeira* is man. One of the characteristics of human beings
> is to live according to his time. Well, our time (ours, as well as
> that of the capoeirista) suffers from one thing called—eroticism
> of publicity ... And here we touch on the crucial point ... He
> resorts to using razors and knife stabbing randomly because he
> is sure the newspapers will print the news about his prowess and
> will showcase some of their names.

A similar type of fear materialized at the end of the twentieth century. In analyzing the "demonization and glorification of funk" music in Rio de Janeiro, the violence of gangs, and the widespread fear of *funkeiros* in the 1990s, João Freire Filho and Micael Herschmann focus on how the media stigmatized two million *funkeiros* who live in impoverished areas, even though the vast majority of them never committed a crime (232). They criticize major newspapers, magazines, radio, and television "for spreading and legitimating labels, thereby, collaborating decisively toward disseminating moral panic" (223). They contend that by incessantly talking about *funkeiro's* violence, *arrastões*, robbery, and their connection with organized crime, the media contributed in large scale to create a generalized anxiety in the population. The fear of *funkeiros* escalated, they inform, when the media linked them to the collective form of stealing called *arrastões*,[33] and with narcotrafficking and criminal organizations (229–238). Freire Filho and Herschmann highlight how ironic it was that, if the enduring campaign run by newspapers, radio and television stations to disparage Rio Funk created a widespread fright in the population, it also increased the popularity of "'young *funkeiros*' lifestyle and cultural production among social groups situated way beyond the hills and domain of Rio de Janeiro" (225).[34] Hence, the media perception of *funkeiros'* behavior is similar to the newspaper opinion of *maltas*, groups of *capoeiristas* which terrorized the population of Rio de Janeiro at the turn of the twentieth century.

The "Double-Talk"[35]: Interactive Space

In its efforts to manipulate public opinion and find common ground to define a national identity, Vargas's administration increased funds for education and established new government agencies to carry on culturally related projects. Those projects "encompassed not only the preservation of cultural patrimony, but also support for 'patriotic causes' such as physical education" (Assunção 19).³⁶ The emergence of the nationalist agenda put forth by Vargas's reorganization of the New State (Estado Novo) in the 1930s, the centralization of the education system, and his populist and nationalist agenda all contributed to revitalize folklore and cultural history which, in turn, promoted *capoeira* to the status of a Brazilian "national sport" (Downey, "Domesticating" 1–32; Taylor 21–22). In analyzing the emphasis on physical education in the early decades of the twentieth century in Brazil, Taylor mentions that "the Vargas government strove to imitate other countries such as Germany and the United States where there was a systematic emphasis on physical culture, and organized sports were established at universities and high schools, and practiced by members of the upper and intellectually accomplished classes" (20–21). Thus the Vargas regime contributed substantially to confer on *capoeira* the status of a desirable cultural product, or as Taylor asserts, "during Brazil's Estado Novo, for the first time since the eighteenth century, the *capoeirista* was not the immediate target of police repression," and after 1930, the 1890 law that prohibited the practice of *capoeira* was not enforced; as a consequence it was easier to legalize *capoeira* (Taylor 17–20).

In 1932, to escape police persecution, win respectability for *capoeira* as a "serious" athletic activity, and engage the middle class in the process of legitimizing an Afro-Brazilian cultural space, Mestre Bimba opened an academy and named it Centro de Cultura Física Regional ("Regional Center of Physical Culture") in Salvador, Bahia. He figured that, to be easily recognized as a contributing asset to the agenda of a national identity, among other things, his method of *capoeira* needed to receive recognition from the State. Consequently, he established a new identity for *capoeira* by strategically organizing it into a regimented structure to which he added a few new moves and steps. To effectively counter preconceived notions and stereotypes about *capoeira*, Mestre Bimba understood that it was necessary to craft a method and set up some objective measurements for it. He removed *capoeira* from the streets and projected it as "the Brazilian national gymnastic" for which he created a manual displaying a strict sequence of kicks, strikes, and other moves (Almeida 32; Assunção 19–20; Rego 291–92). To add even more credibility to his cultural center, Mestre Bimba named it a "school" which he registered, in

1937, in the Inspetoria do Ensino Secundário Profissional ("Bureau of Technical Schools"), realizing a long-lived dream of some segments of Brazilian society (Abreu, *Bimba* 29; Lewis 32; Rego 268–70, 282). In his method and manual of playing *capoeira*, Mestre Bimba included movements in which the players can touch each other (the standard *golpes ligados* or *cinturados*), introduced some kicks taken from other martial arts, US boxing techniques, and adapted elements from African-derived dances or fighting styles, such as *maculelê* (Rego 33). Emulating the graduation system of other martial arts, Mestre Bimba used colored scarves to mark his students' progress from one level of skills to the next. He based those advancements on the players' learning curve, training, experience, and general knowledge of *capoeira*'s history and philosophy.

Mestre Bimba was attuned to the political changes that had been taking place under Vargas's administration. By removing *capoeira* from the streets and intentionally associating it with physical education, he bestowed an aura of respectability and acceptance to his "regional" style. He transformed the ritual-fight into a gymnastic of sorts, a genre that, as he rightly estimated, seemed more familiar, domesticated, and thus less threatening to the white middle class, intellectuals, and ruling authorities. Intent on reaching a wider public and claiming legitimacy for it, Mestre Bimba modernized his style of *capoeira*. While Mestre Bimba's detractors accuse him of having marred *capoeira*'s tradition by changing its features and placing it in a controlled environment (as opposed to being played on the streets, at beaches, vacant lots, and parks which made it more democratic and less restrictive), his supporters argue that if *capoeira* had remained in open public spaces, it would have continued to be feared, prosecuted and, eventually, would have been completely criminalized, and/or nearly eradicated.[37]

Bimba's followers contend that he understood that, for *capoeira* to gain the credence it deserved, he needed to work from within the social and cultural mindset of the ruling elite. To make *capoeira* sustainable, Bimba recognized that it was imperative to circumvent social hostility by adapting it to fit the expectations and rules of the social order. He had to change some of the older misconceptions about *capoeira*; to do so he tamed and enveloped it in a cultural garment that would look familiar to the middle class, the segment of society most likely to be drawn to a gym (*academia*), and which could more easily afford the monthly fees (Assunção

128–149; Downey, *Learning* 61–63). He accomplished in practice what Sheyla Benhabib theorizes when discussing the struggles new social groups undergo, as the cultivation of "judgement of public sphere" (410). She argues that such forms of engagement contribute to establish an identity-based sphere that allows for "the epistemological as well as the political universal [to be] re-appropriated in a process of creative rejection and expansion" (410). Thus, in adopting the social and political rules of engagement of the time, Mestre Bimba identified a new way to help *capoeiristas* establish some form of collective identity.

Currently, *capoeira regional* (and its variations) can be easily identified because it is played in a more upright posture (the players usually strike each other at chest or head level), and the concept of "performance" can be quite important. A *capoerista* may interrupt the play, a practice known as *comprar o jogo* ("to buy the game") and the inside circle is wider in diameter (if compared to *capoeira angola*'s ring), most likely to allow adequate space for the players to perform athletic exhibitions and acrobatic movements. Considering that *capoeira regional* is a style played at a faster pace, and the participants use more aggressive movements, violence is more prone to happen (Esteves 126). In *capoeira regional* and hybrid styles, the participants also clap to accompany their singing. Feeling the pressure to earn a place and a space in the new market and establish themselves as valuable commodities in the field of physical education and recreational sports, the members of the Bahian diaspora looked for creative solutions. To market *capoeira* as a martial art, Mestre Bimba's followers upgraded his colored scarves to ropes (*cordão* or *corda*), to be worn as belts, as in karate or judo. Bimba's followers also instituted a *batizado* ("christening"). The term refers to the annual event organized by a *capoeira* group, usually coupled with *formatura* ("graduation," or the "changing of cords" for more advanced students in *capoeira regional*) to formalize their initiation as players into *rodas de capoeira*. It is considered by many as a rite of passage, and a validation of each student's individual efforts to learn the moves and attend classes regularly. Lewis describes a *batizado* in the following terms:

> In *Regional* academies, this event marks the first time a student is allowed to play in a *roda* to the music of the *berimbau*, and the student must begin by demonstrating his or her knowledge of the *sequências*, set sequences of required moves done with a

> partner. The focus of the event in all academies is when a stu-
> dent to be initiated plays *capoeira* with a master, usually not his
> or her own but one of those invited specially for the occasion
> and is ceremonially "taken down" in the course of play. (69)

The interaction with high-ranking players is a sort of pride for
the new students because it is seen as an "honor" (the invited *mestre* is similar in importance to a keynote speaker in conferences or
business meetings, or a featured performer). The presence of such
highly regarded individuals (and also the *capoeiristas* from other
groups who attend the *batizado*) benefits the whole group because
it exposes the members of one association to techniques and approaches from their peers, gives the students the opportunity to
interact with high-ranking individuals, and showcases each student's personal performative abilities. The "takedown" technique
during the *batizado* is meant to christen the new student (a rite of
passage in which the neophyte is "baptized" to the floor) when a
high-ranking *capoeirista* showcases their dexterity and knowledge,
and also projects their importance by making a move that surprises
the new student and takes him or her to the floor. The "takedown"
also has the symbolic meaning of teaching humility.

Other changes have occurred, and additional variations have
been implemented since Mestre Bimba first organized *capoeira
regional* in the 1930s. For instance, the system of ranking belts
is not uniform in terms of size or colors (some groups use the
colors of the Brazilian flag while others adopt hues that speak to
them in particular ways), or is standardized in terms of requirements to advance from one level to the next (Almeida 52–54;
Downey, *Learning* 104–05). Some studies analyze a diversity of
styles as byproducts of *capoeira regional*, or discuss the transformations that have taken place, *vis-à-vis* the social and political
environment of the late 1950s and early 1960s. During that time,
drastic transformations occurred in urban settings of Brazil and
capoeiristas had to adjust to the new environment, as Bira Almeida
(Mestre Acordeon) has discussed: "With all the changes in the
social and political structure of the country, my generation can
be considered the last of that which molded the saga of *capoeira
regional* in its present reality" (122).[38] The national and international development and spread of *capoeira* can be traced back to
the period between the 1960s and 1980s, when Mestre Bimba's
students migrated in large scale from Salvador to São Paulo and

Rio de Janeiro, and later to the United States and other parts of the world. In São Paulo, they found the need to make additional changes in the game to compete with the Asian martial arts which had already won the attention of the Brazilian middle class. It was at this time that the directors of academies, *mestres*, and others involved in teaching *capoeira* decided to homogenize, nationalize, and globalize it (L. Reis 125–61; Taylor 161–305). To do so, it was necessary to divest the game-fight-dance from its African heritage, transforming it into a Brazilian martial art, or the new Brazilian "gymnastic" as Reis describes it. Such labels conferred great social and cultural recognition to *capoeira regional* in Brazil and abroad.

Striving to emphasize *capoeira*'s connection with African roots, and to present a counter-discourse against Mestre Bimba's *capoeira regional*, in 1941, Mestre Pastinha established some ground rules for a new style of *capoeira,* and founded a sports center in Salvador that he called Centro Esportivo de Capoeira Angola ("*Capoeira Angola* Sports Center"). Even though Taylor raises questions about the widespread belief that Mestre Pastinha was the solo creator or organizer of the style of *capoeira angola*, he acknowledges that "undeniably it was Mestre Pastinha who, in the 1940s and 50s, persisted in the quest to establish a permanent base for the Centro Esportivo de Capoeira Angola in Salvador" (45).[39] In collaboration with some of his closest associates, Pastinha fomented the idea of cultural resistance and looked for support in the Afro-Brazilian community. His style differs from Mestre Bimba's in that it does not incorporate elements from other martial arts, the *roda* moves at a slower pace, and there is not a fixed sequence of movements which are performed closer to the ground. For instance, the *aú* in the *regional* style is "open" whereas in *angola* it is "closed" (Capoeira, *Little* 66). Additionally, the players have to keep a certain distance from each other; and if someone wants to enter the *roda*, they must wait until a player chooses to leave the circle, rather than "buying" the game.[40] Following African traditions, Mestre Pastinha used aphorisms, metaphors, and riddles to teach valuable lessons about the game and life (Almeida 1). Browning considers that "most everything Pastinha said is lyrical and indecipherable. But his ambiguity isn't without significance. It's strategic lyricism. Much of Pastinha's philosophy is embedded in the lyrics of the capoeira songs that he sang" (107).

Some other differences between *capoeira regional* and *angola* are also noticeable. For instance, the numbers indicate that it is harder to obtain the title of *mestre/mestra* in *capoeira angola*, in part because to climb the hierarchical ladder the novices are at the mercy of a highly subjective structure; namely, for an *angoleiro/a* to reach the highest level in the trade, the student depends exclusively on the *mestre*'s assessment, which often happens in consultation with other established members of the community who are also versed in *capoeira* (there is no use of *cordão* or *batizado* system).[41] That is not to say that hierarchy is inexistent or played at a minimum in *capoeira regional*, or that it does not have a say in promoting a *mestre*; it means that the use of belts and *batizados* to advance the students through the ranks seems to infer that *mestres* and instructors in *regional* have adopted a procedural evaluation system, based mostly on the skills the players acquire (similar to what happens in other martial arts). In this instance, *capoeira regional* may appeal more to people who have the need to gauge their learning progress since the belt system allows for a more objective measurement.

Capoeira angola seems to attract people who find in the slower, ritualistic, and dancelike movements a viable alternative to the dangerously fast kicks of *capoeira regional*. It also gained popularity with *capoeiristas* who did not like the changes Mestre Bimba had implemented and who sought a closer connection with Africa. Mestre Pastinha and his followers emphasize the need to focus on interaction, partnership, and dialogue; and although violence also occurs in *rodas* of *capoeira angola*, *angoleiros* oftentimes claim that they practice defense, rather than attack, and advocate the use of clever maneuvers, instead of what many call gratuitous force. The chant "Jogue Comigo com Muito Cuidado" ("Be Very Careful as You Play with Me") illustrates such discussions, drawing attention to the ambiguous and ambivalent characteristics of the game, and highlighting the penchant to play *capoeira angola* in a defensive mode. Yet, the lyrics also warn that, depending on individual input (for instance, if the opponent shows an arrogant or mean behavior), it can also be played offensively:

> Jogue comigo com muito cuidado!
> Você só apanha
> Se for malcriado.
> Se você não bater,
> Eu também não lhe bato.
> É o jogo de Angola, meu camarado!
> Seja manhoso,
> Mas não seja malvado.
> (Bola Sete 143)

Be careful in playing with me!
You will only be battered
If you behave badly.
If you do not hit me,
I will not hit you.
It is Angola's game, my comrade!
Be cunning,
Not mean.

Since the mid-1980s, many groups in São Paulo, Rio de Janeiro, and Salvador (and other large urban centers in Brazil) have made a concerted effort to create a greater visibility for *capoeira angola* by advertising its African connections. The pursuit of a more "authentic" form of *capoeira* that Mestre Pastinha's method represented also gained popularity because it resonated with the expansion of black militant groups in São Paulo,[42] in the 1980s, after Brazil returned to democracy. As *capoeira angola* became more popular, Mestre Pastinha's followers increasingly voiced their disapproval of Mestre Bimba's style and its variations. Some feel that the *regional* style has betrayed the original principles of the game and abandoned *capoeira*'s roots and traditions. They are prone to criticize *capoeira regional* for purportedly deviating from the principles of the game and transforming the *roda* into a ring for acrobatics and competitive purposes (Mestra Janja, "Contra-Mestre" 20). In some circles, especially in Brazil, there is a conspicuous tension and polarized opinion about the two major styles of *capoeira*. In such environment, it is not uncommon for players to refer to each other derogatorily or to strive to legitimize the "best" or the "true" style of *capoeira*. Rosângela Costa Araújo (Mestra Janja), for instance, one of the most prominent female voices in *capoeira* circles in Brazil and abroad, dismisses *capoeira regional* as an attempt to "whiten" *capoeira*, transforming it into a sport and a folkloric branch of the game, suitable for the elite's taste ("Sou" 42).[43]

Others would disagree with Araújo's protectionist approach. Merrell, for instance, who considers himself an *angoleiro*, exercises critical distance in his judgement, and questions the excessive isolationism and search for authenticity championed by the adepts of *capoeira angola*. He points out that the game offers a "conservative look" because the followers cling too closely to the African roots. He finds such position highly ironic because "a culture can hardly hope to revive its past in pure form and maintain it intact.

Tradition can be no more than an idealized version of an irretrievable past" (10). Since *capoeira angola* is played slower and closer to the ground than *capoeira regional* and its variants, it offers less visual stimulation or performative zest which draws criticism from practitioners of *regional* who complain that the movements in *capoeira angola* are unappealing and less aesthetically intriguing, and not as fiercely combative. Downey acknowledges that *capoeira angola* may not appeal to those who are looking for striking performative acts or want to use it for self-defense: "The aesthetic of Capoeira Angola is strange at a first glance. Its slow movements, quirky dance steps, unusual postures, and inverted acrobatics do not obviously appear strong, dexterous, or even martial to many observers," (*Learning* 186). A number of *angoleiros* would disagree with this view, drawing attention to the fact that *capoeira regional* puts too much emphasis on performance, and the gentler pace of *capoeira angola* requires a great deal of patience, cunning, and disguise which can be as effective in the game as the energetic maneuvers used in *regional* and mixed styles. This is a point that Merrell raises by discussing violence, exhibitionism, and acrobatic moves in *regional*, but also questioning the idea that *capoeira angola* is deceptively simple, slow, and less violent: "Among the smiles, playful gestures, and feigned taunts, there were moments of tight-lipped determination that suddenly set the play into a twirling cyclone of action" (10–11). Considering all alternatives, it would be too broad a generalization to describe *capoeira angola* as a non-violent style, and *capoeira regional* as mere acrobatics. In both types, kicks and moves can be used to highlight personal prowess, or to impose physical, mental, and emotional domination.

Offering a conciliatory point of view, Merrell gives his testimony that in the *rodas* in which he participated, both forms of *capoeira* "embodied game and play; both were creative and efficient, deceptive and aggressive, and flexible and rigid" (10). This is an opinion shared by Browning, who considers the dispute between the groups to be a senseless rivalry not only because the "apparent musicality always contains violent potential, and all aggression is transformed into dance," but also because both styles seem to be "in dialogue with one another, and speaking, finally, the same double-talk" (114). Thus, despite the friction between the adepts of the two styles, there are contemporary segments in Brazil, the United States, and in other countries that emphasize the similarities rather than the differences, and advocate blending the two styles into a hybrid format. In this case, there is a tendency to deem *capoeira* an arching category in which a preference for one style does not mean the rejection of the other. The *capoeiristas* who practice a mixed style of *capoeira* oft explain their approach as a version that combines fast, acrobatic moves from *capoeira regional* and slow moves from *capoeira angola* (merged to form *capoeira contemporânea* or *atual*). They emphasize how imperative it is for players to understand and experience the equilibrium necessary to maintain positive and negative energies, and to play graciously in both styles of *capoeira*. *Mestres* and other instructors who adopt this view highlight the dialogue, respect, and appreciation of differences. They believe that such behavior becomes an iconic representation of how players should behave not only in *rodas de capoeira*, but also in the wider circle of life.

Some of the distinctions between *capoeira angola* and *regional* do exist; however, it is important to remember that, even within each style, variations can occur, depending on the players' disposition and personality, and on the parameters the *mestres* assign to their group. Several cultural anthropologists, historians, and *capoeiristas* have criticized a bitter divide between the two styles because they believe there are as many different interpretations of each style as there as *mestres*. In any art form, school, and religion, leaders of the group impart their choices and perceptions on their followers who, in turn, develop their own personal styles or individual interpretations. This is an aspect that Browning highlights as she discusses that "capoeira styles vary greatly from one master to the next. If the whole premise of the game is not to block one's opponent but rather to take his movement in and invert it, then it is easy to see how apparently differing styles could be absorbed and modified by each other" (101). Jair Oliveira de Faria Júnior (Mestre Sabiá) also adopts this position. (He has worked with Frederico José Abreu in the *capoeira* center Ginga Mundo, in Salvador, to create a space in which different styles of *capoeira* can be learned and appreciated.)

As the discussions in this chapter exemplify, the history of *capoeira* reveals that, from colonial days to the twentieth century, it rose from an underground activity to become a national and international cultural attraction, and arguably one of Brazil's paramount cultural exports, second only to the popularity of the *bossa nova* rhythm in the 1960s. The legacy of the Brazilian diaspora contributed to the development of *capoeira* and its establishment in academies and working groups throughout the United States and in other countries. Scholars' interest in studying and writing about *capoeira* has also helped the fast growth of *capoeira* around the world. They have advocated the physical and mental benefits of practicing this martial art-dance-ritual and have lent their prestige to popularize its practice. Either for the ethical foundation of it (all people are equal in *capoeira*), or for pragmatic reasons (to maintain the number of students in the academies), group leaders have exercised a conscious effort to open the space for women to participate in the game. The presence of well-known Brazilian *mestres* who immigrated to the United States and numerous other parts of the world, or who give workshops for organized groups as special guests, has contributed enormously to attract both men and women to learn *capoeira*. As discussed in Chapter Five, a substantial number of women also participate actively in *capoeira* circles and a few have taken a leadership role. The social and economic success that Brazilian *mestras* have had in the United States (and in other countries as well) has also served as an incentive for other women to continue playing.

Chapter Five

Women in *Capoeira*

Crafting a Space

Scholars who embrace the theory that *capoeira* is an offspring or a continuum of an Angolan Zebra dance, *N'Golo*, often refer to the research done by the Brazilian folklorist, Cascudo, who established an intellectual dialogue with his African peers. Based on the information he garnered about *N'Golo*, Cascudo reached the conclusion that the movements of *capoeira* originated from that initiation rite, performed by young men to mark a female rite of passage. The fight-ritual had two coveted prizes: it would guarantee the winner the right to choose his wife from the pubescent females who were watching the games, and he would be excused from paying a dowry to his bride's family. As Cascudo describes it:

> Entre os Mucope do sul de Angola, há uma dança da zebra, *N'Golo*, que ocorre durante a Efundula, festa da puberdade das raparigas, quando essas deixam de ser muficuenas, meninas, e passam à condição de mulheres, aptas a casamento e procriação. O rapaz vencedor no *N'Golo* tem o direito de selecionar sua esposa dentre as novas iniciadas e sem pagar o dote esponsalício. *N'Golo* é a capoeira. (*Folclore* 184–85)

> In Southern Angola, the Mucope people traditionally celebrate *N'Golo*, the zebra dance/competition, which takes place during Efundula, the festivities regarding the girls' puberty ceremony, when those *muficuenas* become women and can marry and procreate. The male winner has the right to select his wife and is excused from paying a contractual marriage dowry. *N'Golo* is *capoeira*.

But even if *N'Golo* is accepted as a precursor of *capoeira*, and the evidence of women's presence in that initiation rite is undisputed,

179

females were not actively engaged in the fight-ritual. In essence, the female adolescents were twice removed from any position of power in *N'Golo*: first because they attended the games only as spectators, and secondly, and foremost, because they were the coveted prize of the competition, and thus the young men's objects of desire.

To tip the gender case in favor of the argument that women have always been part of *capoeira* circles, scholarly publications and other writings also refer to the female presence in *rodas de capoeira* in Rio de Janeiro and Salvador in the nineteenth century and in the beginning of the twentieth century. As Eugênio Líbano Soares discusses, *capoeiristas* would gather on Largo da Sé, in Rio de Janeiro, where women who sold sweets and other typical dishes (called *quitandeiras*) would set their stalls (*Negregada* 175). While a large number of females may have been present in *N'Golo* and around *rodas de capoeira*, they were mostly bystanders, or supporters. Defenders of the argument that women were always part of *capoeira* circles also refer to the eighteenth- and nineteenth-century drawings and narratives of Debret, Koster, Graham, and Rugendas and/or cite police records of the nineteenth and twentieth centuries. The police archives and catalogues of popular songs reveal that females had a key role in keeping urban slave culture alive as Ruth Lande described in *City of Women*. However, they also reveal that, until the late twentieth century, there was not a significant number of women playing *capoeira*, nor had they impacted its culture in a meaningful way.

At the end of the nineteenth century and in the first decades of the twentieth century, to enforce order and authority, city-sponsored raid groups persecuted *capoeira* practitioners for rowdy and violent behavior. To protect themselves, *capoeiristas* joined forces with Candomblé priestesses, street vendors, and prostitutes who also feared police hounding. In Salvador, *rodas de capoeira* were generally formed in places where *baianas* (street vendors dressed in large hooped, colonial-style white skirts, shawls, and turbans) would sell African-derived foods (Rego 297; Lande 249). Those females were inclined to support the men with whom they shared a social, cultural, or familial background. Women typically helped *capoeiristas* in two ways: a) since *rodas de capoeira* frequently happened near places where they had stationed their food stalls, it was easy for them to be on the lookout and warn *capoeiristas* when the police were approaching; b) they would also hide weapons (usually

a sharp blade) in their hair and/or bosom, and make those weap-
onries available to *capoeira* players whenever they needed them to
attack rivals or defend themselves (Rego 297). Hence, it became
less threatening for *capoeiristas* to practice their game on the premises where women had set up their stands. The exchange of favors
most likely helped both groups: the women acted as sentinels for
the men playing *capoeira*, but also profited by selling more goods
when a large crowd gathered around the *roda*.

Considering that *capoeira* and other African-derived cultural
expressions were persecuted, stigmatized, and considered inferior cultural practices, solidarity was a key factor for African
descendants to keep their heritage alive in Brazil. Yet, even if such
comradery reveals that they were accomplices, it does not indicate
that women participated in *rodas de capoeira*. They were present at
those circles, but primarily as tangential participants. The following *corrido* confirms the references to their presence near *rodas de
capoeira* as the adverb *aí* ("over there") indicates:

> —Dona Maria, o que vende aí?
> —É coco e pipoca que é do Brasil.
> Coro: Dona Maria, o que vende aí?
> (Public domain; qtd. Bola Sete 127)

> —Dona Maria, what are you selling over there?
> —It is Brazilian coconut and popcorn.
> Chorus: Dona Maria, what are you selling?

In discussing the absence of women in *capoeira* circles in the
nineteenth and early twentieth centuries, scholars have examined
some cultural factors that might have played a role in preventing
them from playing. According to Lande, in the 1930s and 1940s,
in Salvador and other areas of the Northeast in Brazil, women
generally wore long dresses or skirts (107). That type of garment
would have made it difficult for most of them to participate in
rodas de capoeira because of the inverted movements in which
legs go up and expose body parts, something unacceptable at the
time (Taylor 207). Yet, striving to reveal that women's presence
in *capoeira* dates back to early twentieth century (or even before),
other researchers have reached different conclusions. For instance,
to make a case that female *capoeiristas* are not a recent phenomenon, Antônio L. C. S. Pires republished a photo of two women

181

that was displayed in Mestre Bimba's academy in Salvador. Pires also analyzes their attire (baggy, shorter pants) which he describes as the type of "folkloric outfits" that *capoeiristas* in Bahia had begun to wear in the 1930s (293). In reporting the result of several meetings he had with female *capoeira* players from the Senzala Group—during which time he discussed with the participants the absence and/or presence of women in *capoeira*—Nestor Capoeira mentions that one of the associates referred to that same picture, reminding the group that "Bimba trained his daughters as capoeiristas" (*Little* 180). However, even if the two women were Bimba's daughters and he had trained them, the photo simply indicates that, occasionally, women entered the masculine circle of *capoeira* as active players and, in this case, because their father was a prominent *capoeirista* who had developed a special method to teach *capoeira*. They are the exception, not the rule.

Pires cites a police report, dated 1900, that uses the term *jogar capoeira* in reference to a woman who tried to protect herself using movements and kicks identified as such.[1] He concludes that, in Bahia, women who washed clothes professionally, or worked on the streets as artisans, *baianas*, and prostitutes were in permanent contact with male *capoeiristas* and, consequently, learned how to use a razor and the movements of *capoeira* and played with men in the *roda* (291). His conjectures are relevant, especially in the context of other references to women being taken into custody for disorderly conduct, participation in street fights, and use of razors and other weaponry. Other studies—conducted by Waldeloir Rego, Josivaldo P. de Oliveira, and Luiz Augusto P. Leal (in Salvador) and Soares (in Rio de Janeiro)—also report that police archives have information on women who were arrested for fighting and using razors. However, Oliveira and Leal did not find evidence that women who fought on the streets used *capoeira* kicks for attack or defense (134). Quite often the police records or newspaper stories described their fights as traditional hair pulling, slapping, or biting, and very few police records used the words women and *capoeira* in the same statement (Oliveira and Leal 147–48).

Oliveira and Leal refer to Salomé who, in the 1920s and 1930s, became well known for attending *capoeira* gatherings (*frequentar rodas de capoeira*) in Salvador. They reached the conclusion that she was a *capoeirista* on two premises: a) her name appears in a song quoted by Rego in which the lyricist asks where she is ("Cadê

Salomé, Adão / Salomé foi passear"; "Where's Salomé, Adam / Salomé went out for a walk"); b) Mestre Atenildo's recollection that she was famous for being feisty, fierce, courageous, and for her ability to sing *samba* songs and play *capoeira* (117–18). They also cite a woman, in Belém, who frequently appeared in police records and local newspapers. They mention an article published on November 21, 1876, "Que Mulher Capoeira!" ("What a Female *Capoeira*!"), which refers to a slave named Jerônima who was caught practicing it. There is also information about Liduína Alves Mascarenhas, identified in 1911 by the newspaper *Folha da Noite*, in Belém, as having used *capoeira* kicks to battle Maria José da Conceição (Oliveira and Leal 156–57).

In investigating the nineteenth century repression of *capoeiristas* in Rio de Janeiro, Soares found the names of two women (Isabel and Ana) who behaved like other ruffians of the time and were arrested for playing *capoeira* on January 29, 1897 (*Capoeira* 370). As he notes, the police records he consulted described them in a fashion similar to the other prosecuted figures of *capoeira*: they often fought when challenged or addressed unpleasantly, and felt the need to display their *capoeira* skills. However refreshing it was to find such references, Soares acknowledges that they are isolated cases and do not compare in any sizable measure to the large numbers of men practicing *capoeira* at the time. In an attempt to establish a record of women who were active in *rodas de capoeira*, in Bahia, the names of seven females are often cited for allegedly having participated in the game during the first six decades of the twentieth century: Maria Homem, Júlia Fogareira, Maria Cachoeira, Maria Pernambucana, Maria Pé no Mato, and Odília e Palmeirona (Araújo, "Sou" 133; Bola Sete 27). Pires mentions an additional name of a female *capoeirista* in Bahia, Francisca Albino dos Santos, a prostitute nicknamed "Chicão," who supposedly gained recognition for challenging and attacking Pedro Porreta, a well-known male *capoeirista* in the district of Pilar (288).[2]

Pedro R. J. Abib and his assistants[3] also list three women whom they believe played *capoeira* in Bahia in the beginning of the twentieth century: Almerinda, Menininha e Chica.[4] They were considered *a malta de saia* ("the gang that wore skirts"), lived in Baixa dos Sapateiros, part of the historical center of Salvador, and formed a team of ruffians always prone to get involved in fights and other disorderly conduct (37–38). Nevertheless, the researchers acknowledge that hardly anything is known about their life story: there are big question marks about their place of origin, or even how and when they arrived in Baixa do Sapateiro and learned *capoeira* (37). They also refer to Maria Doze Homens ("Maria Twelve Men")[5] who seemed to have been better known than the others, in part because there are descriptions of her (probably from police records), portraying her as someone guarded and reticent who walked heavily, gestured coarsely, and was always in a bad mood (103). They also mention Angélica Endiabrada ("Devilish Angélica") who liked to talk and gossip, was always involved in unruly behavior, and would get into a fight easily for little or no reason (104).

Abib's research team also found references about Cândida Rosa de Jesus (better known as Rosa Palmeirão) who sold *sarapatel* (a dish made of boiled blood and viscera of hogs) in Mercado Popular (135). They characterize her as involved in "lidas capoeiristas" (*capoeiristas'* toil) and in amorous relationships with male players (135). Their research findings also include Massú, a woman who lived in the district of Muritiba, in Nazaré das Farinhas, and was considered the Queen of Capoeiragem, a beautiful woman who also had amorous relationships with *capoeiristas* (136). It is encouraging to find so many references to women who, at one point or another in their lives, may have been involved with *capoeira* groups in Bahia, Pará, and in Rio de Janeiro. While it is possible to argue that women always secured a place for themselves as bystanders in the *rodas* played on the streets of Belém, Rio de Janeiro, and Salvador, it is difficult to argue that they were involved in the game as players in any meaningful or sizeable way prior to the 1970s. Most of the allusions to those women refer to fights, their use of razors, or that they were groupies, and do not provide any substantial evidence of their participating in *rodas de capoeira*. Except for the references to their names and their unruly behavior, in the vast majority of cases, there is no knowledge of how well they played *capoeira*, or the impact they might have had. Due to the scarcity of written documentation, it is challenging to draw a clear profile of women in *capoeira* prior to the 1970s, but it is equally untimely to dismiss their participation entirely. As discussed, very little written documentation exists about the earlier stages of the game's development. Thus, it could be either hasty or anecdotal to magnify women's active participation in *capoeira* circles prior to the 1970s.

In general, the nicknames *capoeiristas* receive—as part of their integration and acceptance into *capoeira* circles—reflect their moral values, physical traits, standard behaviors, approach to the game, or way of playing. The codenames Maria Homem and Chicão, for instance, refer to their masculine traits which indicate that, for a woman to play *capoeira*, she must resemble or behave like men, or have some evil connections (Angélica Endiabrada). In the end, women faced a no-win situation: to be accepted they needed to play "like men," yet their masculine features and actions could be used derogatorily. The research that Menara Lube Guizardi and Annelou Ypeij conducted confirms this analysis. They found no evidence of women's participation in *capoeira* on a regular basis, and noticed that the few females who are on record as having played between 1900 and the 1960s were stigmatized as "masculine girls" because it was considered that they "had crossed the gender boundaries that defined them as women" ("Being" 177).

In another study about masculine archetypes and the female presence in *capoeira* groups, Guizardi discusses the expression *como si fueran hombres* that she heard in *capoeira* circles—an expression that *mestres* and other group leaders were taught by Brazilian males in Madrid—used to incite women to play hard and well, in other words, "to play like men." Her reflection on gender dynamics in those academies led her to conclude that "the gender relations and definitions tended to assume a corporal dimension" ("Como" 299). In analyzing female participation in the group, and women's interaction with male players, Guizardi ascertained that the internal hierarchy was also highly influenced by the archetype of the "normative corporal masculinity" and the "masculinization" of *capoeira* in Brazilian society ("Como" 300). To "play like a man," or to play "harder," was the measure used to establish the discourse of "equality" in those groups ("Como" 304). However, as she points out, in this context, the expression "as if they were men" suggests that even if there is a discourse of equality and inclusion, "the physical practice of capoeira continues to cultivate a corporal dynamic that considers women unfit to reach the same level of performance attained by men" ("Como" 304).

In certain types of *rodas de capoeira*, especially in *capoeira angola*, a player should not "buy the game," that is, it can be considered an "impolite" move to disturb two *capoeiristas* when they are playing, a gesture similar to someone meddling into, or interrupting, a conversation. A *capoeirista* who wants to enter the *roda* should wait until one of the players leaves the circle, as if waiting for a pause to interject in a conversation. In many *capoeira* circles, it is also considered disrespectful, or at least inconsiderate, for a player to "buy the game" when more advanced *capoeiristas*, or *mestres*, are playing. However, as previously discussed, it is not uncommon for men to interrupt women when they are playing, even if the females are more qualified than them. Guizardi calls attention to the fact that, during her fieldwork, she noticed that even when men and women have reached the same level of dexterity and knowledge, measurable, for instance, by the fact that they have the same skills—proven by the belt they wear—the men will always play first. As she concludes, even though female *capoeiristas* have proven that they are as physically skilled and mentally prepared as their male counterparts, the order in which the ritual takes place (who plays first) indicates, "in a silent way, who has the primacy in those groups" ("Como" 306).

Physical and symbolic masculine dominance still takes place. Guizardi cites instances in the groups she observed in which women were physically removed from the *roda*, or men would poke fun at them ("Como" 300–01). She mentions that, in those groups, whenever women executed a movement that would evince men's "technical faults," or when they overpowered their male counterparts by using *malícia* skillfully, male players immobilized females by holding their arms, or carried them out of the *roda* on their shoulders. When the women complained, the men disregarded the matter, considering the maneuver an innocent prank, and everyone would laugh at such a display of "playfulness" ("Como" 306). However, as Guizardi observes, "had the same thing been done to a man, it would have been considered a brutal offense, a dismissal of the code of respect in *capoeira*. Only women are removed from the *roda* in the arms of another *capoeirista* without meaning an invitation to a fight" ("Como" 306).

Violence is oftentimes a tactic male players use to frighten women and drive them away from the *rodas* and academies. Mestra Cigana (Fátima Colombiana) analyzes the calculated violence in the game, recounting an experience she had in the beginning of her career, in the 1970s, with a young man in an academy in Rio de Janeiro. The man's reaction to her being in the *roda* was so strong that he kicked her viciously out of the circle. Although physically and emotionally painful, the experience taught her a valuable lesson: she needed to learn how to apply the principles of *malícia* to the game more efficiently, and be in paramount physical shape to endure such blows. The experience also taught her that many male *capoeiristas* never fully embrace the idea of gender equality (Mestra Cigana, "Interview" by Barbosa). All types of violence against women are still common. As examples, Maria Zeneide G. da Silva reports two serious cases of aggression that took place in Belém. According to her report, in the late 1980s, a strong and excellent female *capoeirista* named Nazaré Pantoja (Grupo Dandara Bambula in Belém) had her calling in *capoeira* interrupted when a male player hit her maliciously on the knee ("Movimento" 77). The second incident took place in 2013. People in *capoeira* circles, especially women, were outraged when a pregnant female *capoeirista* was "taken down" by a male player during a *batizado* without a plausible explanation. On social media, bloggers condemned the aggression and, in analyzing the possible reasons for such a belligerent behavior, concluded that the male *capoeirista* had likely deemed it a transgression for a woman, particularly a pregnant female, to be playing *capoeira* (Silva, "Movimento" 77–78). Considering that the woman involved in the 2013 *batizado* was not a neophyte (and should not have been taken down), it is easy to understand why the aggressive gesture perplexed the *capoeira* community. This is not to say that women never play offensively; however, aggression and other types of violence are more likely to happen between two females than between a male and a female. When women play each other, they are not afraid to participate fully or let their aggressiveness manifest because they see the other women as peers. This also reflects a pattern of behavior found in society in general, a topic Nestor Capoeira discussed during a question-and-answer session with the Group Senzala. He comments that some "women players agreed that aggression and excessive competition exist between women in capoeira, but they consider this the legacy of 'a certain type of education and the position women were relegated in society and only very recently began to change'" (*Little* 181).

Marisa Cordeiro (Mestra Marisa) confides that, when she began playing *capoeira*, in the 1980s, in Grupo Cordão de Ouro (São Paulo), there were about twenty young women, yet she was the only one who continued because sexism was so prevalent at the time that the female players felt discouraged (Mestra Marisa). She believes it is one of the major reasons why women are still lingering behind men in number and rank. As she further explains:

> Naquele tempo, a maioria dos homens não dava nem mesmo a consideração de jogar com você. Às vezes, eu tinha acabado de "comprar o jogo" e eles me tiravam da roda para colocar um rapaz. As mulheres não cantavam porque eles não estavam acostumados a jogar e cantar com mulheres, porque não é a mesma entonação. As mulheres ficavam cantando no coro e batendo palmas, não lideravam o canto.[6]

> In the 1980s and early 1990s, the majority of men would not even consider playing with you. Sometimes, I had just "bought the game" and they would remove me from the *roda* so that a man could play because they were not used to playing and singing with women because it is a different type of intonation. Women could sing in the chorus, and clap, but not lead a song.

Such prejudice also relates to women playing the instruments or singing in the *roda*, two areas of participation that some still consider a male province. Carla Fernandes and Paula Silva point out that, in the male dominated groups that they observed during their fieldwork in Campinas, women were allowed to play percussion instruments (*atabaque, pandeiro*, and *agogô*) but were rarely seen playing the *berimbau* (1–8). But, it is not only in Brazil that women have faced such constraints, or similar types of discrimination. Mestra Luar do Sertão (Anne Pollack) mentions that, even in the United States, female *capoeiristas* are still warned that, to perform well, they must "sing like a man" (Mestra Luar do Sertão, 2017 "Interview" by Barbosa). Guizardi summarizes such discussions by allowing that "there is a contradiction between the pretension of equality and the practice of a 'differential equality'" ("Como" 304). The topic is also discussed in local, national, and international meetings, conferences, and workshops that attract a large female attendance, or which are organized by women.

Even though women have questioned the myths about their role in *capoeira* and have mapped new trends, those in the beginning and intermediate stages of the learning process still look for ways to validate themselves in the game. They have what appears to be an urgency to prove to themselves, and especially to their male counterparts, that they are competent, know how to play the *berimbau* and other instruments, and can sing the *cantigas* well.

Even females who have reached high levels of training (such as Paula Verdino-Pimentinha) admit that sometimes women allow themselves to feel intimidated when facing men in a *roda* because they have this ingrained belief that "males are stronger and can play better" (Delgado). They also find it important to evidence that they have dexterity, strength, and are experts in the use of *malícia*. Rosa Maria Araújo Simões believes that such a need derives from the desire to demonstrate to themselves and others that they are as good (if not better) than their male counterparts. She considers that it might also relate to the fact that women entered *capoeira* circles—as effective players—much later than men did. Such belated engagement has created a temporal and cultural phase displacement that has contributed to the belief that they are more "fragile" and less important players (Simões 99). The numeric inferiority and temporal and cultural gap to which Simões calls attention indicates that there is still a fracture in the system, and room for improvement. Mestra Janja confirms this notion by referring to the roadblocks women still encounter to earn a place in circles of *capoeira*. She discusses the efforts to overcome those obstacles as a very hard task, a tiresome job that demands constant working to convince skeptics of the value of female *capoeirista* (Mestra Janja, "Personal interview").

Women are not always taken out of the *roda* draped on a man's shoulder or with a knee injury, but there are many reports of females being pushed out of *capoeira* circles by other types of physical and symbolic violence (intimidation, for instance). Fear of looking or sounding sexist can lead male *capoeiristas* to adopt condescending attitudes. By choosing to be too lenient or "cordial" when playing with women, male *capoeiristas* impart the idea that women are fragile and delicate, and thus need to be handled with extra care. This patronizing attitude is a point that Mestra Suelly (Suellen Einarsen)[7] raised as she discussed such behaviors as another form of violence in *rodas de capoeira*. She addressed the physical and psychological domination that women encounter, the condescending attitudes, and a false sense of protection that exists in *capoeira* circles (*United Capoeira Association*, "Mestra Suelly"). She interprets the two faces of chauvinism (outright exclusion through physical or psychological violence, or a superfluous and contrived surge of gentility) as a lack of consideration and respect to the female players' talent and experience. For her, excessive courtesy is also a type of discrimination, one that can be even more dangerous exactly because it is a subtle and concealed form of condescendence. As she phrases it: "I feel uncomfortable with those aggressive, very physically intense confrontational *jogos* ... I also shy away from the debauchery of some games, when it takes on shades of patronizing and arrogance. I believe that those games are as aggressive and macho as the ones which admit a punch on the face," (*United Capoeira Association*, "Mestra Suelly"). In the same interview, she addresses her concerns about women being excluded (either by force or by unnecessary gentility), and advises females to show strength and energy in the *roda*:

> It is very frustrating to the female capoeirista to be confronted by those who don't respect or take seriously women in capoeira, sometimes assuming condescending attitudes, such as treating the female partner with inappropriate cavalierism. Or, at the other extreme but in the same category, those who want to impose their weight, disregarding the woman's technical performance to show they can dominate their female opponent anyhow. (*United Capoeira Association*, "Mestra Suelly")

As discussed in Chapters One and Three, the hegemonic notion of a woman who is delicate, soft spoken, fragile, obedient, emotional, and unfit for sports that demand dexterity and strength was widely accepted in Brazil. Therefore, members of traditional families also feared that their daughters, sisters, and wives would become less feminine by playing sports considered violent, or that they would be judged negatively for not fitting the accepted parameters of femininity. Edna Lima who, in 1990, received the title of *mestra,* and currently teaches ABADÁ-Capoeira in New York, confirms this concern. At the age of twelve she began practicing incognito, hiding her activities from the family for fear that she would be forced to abandon them. As she mentions, the gender discrepancy that she found in *capoeira* academies bewildered her: "After a week of class, noticing that there were no girls in the class, I became a bit confused and thought that perhaps *capoeira* was not for women" (Interview by Perry). Fortunately, Lima was one of the rare cases, at the time, in which her parents were open-minded, and when she confided in her mother, she was supported, even when other people would insist that it was not "suited for a girl" (Perry).

Mestra Cigana often addresses the difficulties she encountered to play *capoeira*, confirming that, with rare exceptions, until the 1970s, it was very difficult for a woman to become a *capoeira* player, and even harder to be awarded the title of *mestra*.[8] There was a general discrimination against the fight-ritual as it was still considered a hooligan's activity. In such an environment, it was unacceptable for a woman of a "good" family—that is, a socially affluent person and/or someone who had higher levels of formal education—to be involved with such an "unrefined" and tricky activity. From that perspective, only a woman lacking good moral values would disgrace herself by getting involved in *capoeira*:

> Era o maior vexame para a família ter uma mulher que fosse treinar capoeira. Ela seria considerada uma "mulher-a-toa," "va-gabunda." Uma moça de "boa família" não podia nem assistir quanto mais treinar capoeira. (Mestra Cigana)

> It was quite shameful for the family to have a woman who would practice *capoeira*; she would be considered a "fallen women" or a "slut." A girl from a "good family" could not even watch, let alone practice it.

Traditional *mestres* have often played a part in the process of exclusion of women from *capoeira* circles, in cases when they embody the figure of a patriarch, and as such, establish asymmetrical relationships with their neophytes. Lewis has argued that, regardless of the style of *capoeira* played, *mestres* share the desire to exercise authority and control over the other players. He contends that "if the capoeira master is to do his job well, he must also become an ambivalent figure, both respected and feared, and no better example of such a figure can be found than Mestre Bimba" (77). He links a *mestre*'s ambivalence, power struggle, and strategies of domination to a larger historical and cultural context, analyzing the relationship between *mestre* and student as an imitation of the master/slave relationship of colonial times in Brazil (77). He also sees the entire game as a metaphoric depiction of "the struggle of slaves against oppression and as a sample of the system of patronage in Brazilian society" (77). Thus, disciples who follow their *mestres* with reverence and blind obedience apply the principles they learned to map out their social and cultural space, and their influence in the *capoeira* circles. This might be one of the reasons why the large majority of women to whom I talked described their relationship with their *mestres* in affectionate and respectful terms, emphasizing that, during their learning process, they did not suffer discrimination or receive special treatment because of their gender. Since the majority of *mestres*—and other players who embrace *capoeira* as a lifestyle and a solo career or calling—are men, when it comes time to choose someone to carry on their lineage, they usually favor those who are more advanced or who can follow their teachings more closely. Therefore, it is not unusual that, looking forward to having someone follow in their footsteps, *mestres* end up encouraging their male students because they see in them the continuity of the work they have established.

Even though a lot has changed since the 1970s in terms of gender, in Brazil I still noticed some discrepancies in the *rodas de capoeira* and workshops that I attended. The information I collected during the conversations and interviews I had with *capoeiristas*, and other sorts of materials that I accrued during my years of field research also corroborate such conclusions. For instance, in 2001, a *contra-mestre*, in the United States, became quite irritated with a comment I made about the extra attention I was convinced he gave to male players during one of the workshops I observed. Probably, to show me how annoyed he was with my candid remark, he told me that, in *rodas de capoeira*, women are considered "frills," or "symbolic representations," because they "still do not bear the same weight men do," and "they are not taken as seriously as their male counterparts."[9] Such display of macho attitude and straightforward honesty about the makings of the "inside game," to borrow *capoeira*'s own terminology, came as a surprise to me, if only because half of the students who were taking part in that workshop were females, and some of them were also sitting at the dinner table at the time we had this verbal exchange. The female students did not react to the *mestre*'s discourse and, in this instance, appeared to have bowed to the authority that the *contra-mestre* represented. This episode reminded me of Lewis's comments that *mestres* and *contra-mestres* are figures of authority who embody not only the highest knowledge of the history, philosophy, and physical training of *capoeira*, but also a patriarchal seat of power that confers upon them the clout to make unchallenged decisions. Such attitude is a reflection of the relationships prevalent in authoritarian environments in which whoever is in command expects absolute obedience and loyalty from all.

During the silence that fell after the *contra-mestre* spoke, I searched across the table for a single sign of disapproval of his discourse. I could find none. All eyes were lowered, facing the food in front of them, probably for fear of losing their sense of belonging to the group. By silencing, they accepted the "game" as played and avoided displeasing the teacher. However, by doing so, the young women also acquiesced to the system that discriminates against them and contributed to normalize a discourse that had so explicitly belittled all female players. By pretending that nothing was out of the ordinary, the students' attitude revealed that, in many cases, women partake in the system that oppresses them because they have internalized the "rules of the game" and willingly surrendered to the process. Therefore, in my estimation, the students' excessive respect for, or fear of, the *contra-mestre* revealed an uneven gender dynamic in that *capoeira* workshop which contradicts the theory that all are equal in *capoeira*.

However, they were not alone. I, for one, must confess that, in the end, I behaved in a similar manner, and my complacency also became my complicity. Charmed by the *contra-mestre*'s knowledge of the history of *capoeira* (during a long conversation we had had the day before the workshop), and by his teaching about the "philosophy of *capoeira*" during the workshop, I had developed a high opinion of him. Several times during that weekend I had heard him instruct his students on how to avoid confrontation in the *roda* and discuss the skillful use of *malícia* as a substitute for violence. Thus, caught off-guard, I felt both intimidated by his abrupt comment and level of aggressiveness, and embarrassed about being so bold in challenging the figure of authority that I had come to admire. Feeling mortified that I had confronted him so openly in front of his students, I experienced guilt, accepted his outburst as a corrective measure, and embraced the silence that followed. Without further ado, a short time later, I also looked down at my plate. But, a few weeks later when organizing my notes and critically analyzing that experience, I thought of Bourdieu's discussion of how women contribute to their own subjugation by internalizing concepts and ideas that render them inferior, subservient, and obedient. As he discusses, "the dominated, often unwittingly, sometimes unwillingly, contribute to their own domination by tacitly accepting the limits imposed" (*Masculine* 38–39). In those circumstances, he adds, submission takes "the form of bodily emotions—shame, humiliation, timidity, anxiety, and guilt—or passions and sentiments—love, admiration, respect" (38–39).

Quite often *capoeiristas* establish metaphoric comparisons between a *roda de capoeira* and the world, drawing on the philosophy and history of the fight-ritual to teach, or learn, how to behave in the *roda* and in life. As addressed in Chapter Four, Nestor Capoeira asserts that a *roda de capoeira* resembles a miniature theater where people act out situations, play roles, and interact with other players in the same manner that they would in real life (*Roots* 18). Thus, my candid question to the *contra-mestre* had the makings of a direct, unexpected, and hurtful "kick" that did not fit the structure of a *jogo bonito*, so to speak. However, the *contra-mestre* also missed a great opportunity to teach me and his students a valuable lesson, applicable both to the *roda do jogo* and *roda da vida*. Instead of answering my "kick" with a similar swaggering "blow" that, willingly or not, belittled every female sitting at the table, and beyond, he could have applied the most important rule of *capoeira*, the use of *malícia* or *malandragem*—that subtle but powerful evasiveness so efficient in avoiding violence and direct confrontation—to respond to my comment. As someone who prides himself in his knowledge of *capoeira*, the *contra-mestre* missed a wonderful chance to showcase his ability to use *malícia*. Had he done so, he would have come out looking substantially smarter than me and more skilled in the game. He could, for instance, have communicated his dissatisfaction by humorously calling attention to the candid way I asked the question, and suggested a more subtle approach to the subject, or even proposed a more appropriate place and time to discuss the topic. He could have explained his reasons without resorting to aggressive language to refer to women and their participation in *capoeira*. In that case, he would have taught me, and his students, how to apply the philosophy of *capoeira* to conform to the metaphor of the game as part of the *roda do mundo*. Downey describes someone who uses *malícia* to avoid violence as "a cunning player" who is acutely "aware of interlocking perceptual systems" and senses the opponent's "shifting vulnerabilities" (*Learning* 144), not to humiliate the other, but rather to teach a valuable lesson. Hence, in analyzing the circumstances retrospectively, it became clear to me that neither I, nor the *contra-mestre*, were skilled players in the art of *malícia* in the game of life.

Neither Frills nor Symbolic Representations

Even if it is still not possible to accurately estimate the number of female players and their degree of participation in *rodas de capoeira* prior to the 1970s, they have had an unprecedented effective role in *capoeira* circles in the last decades. Their presence in *rodas* and work in *capoeira* associations have increased substantially, as Mestra Janja explains:

> A mulher deixou de ser vista como "novidade" nos grupos, academias e rodas de capoeira ... Novidade mesmo é o fato a sua atual representação numérica e qualitativa; ou seja, o fato delas representarem hoje cerca de 40% dos praticantes de capoeira, numa distribuição mundial, indica que tanto a capoeira, no geral, quanto os grupos, academias, mestres, contra-mestres, professores, etc., no particular, não podem mais insistir em ignorá-las, ou mesmo em reduzir seus papéis e participação na prática e nas atividades destas organizações. ("Contra-Mestre" 18)

> Women can no longer be considered a "novelty" in groups, academies, and *rodas de capoeira* ... The real novelty is their current numeric and qualitative representation; that is, the fact that nowadays they represent about 40% of the people who practice *capoeira* worldwide, which indicates that *capoeira*, in general, as well as the groups, academies, *mestres*, *contra-mestres*, instructors, etc., in particular, cannot insist on ignoring them, or in reducing their roles and their participation in the activities of those organizations.

Considering the percentage of women who are *capoeiristas*, Mestra Suelly expresses her desire to see more femininity in the way women play *capoeira*, not to change the parameters of the game, but to showcase the natural movements of the female body. She believes that instead of "imitating men," women should play the game in such a way that it would imprint a feminine touch in the *rodas* (*United Corporation Association*, "Mestra Suelly 2"). Her proposal dialogues well with the discussion that Halle Berry provided in a CBS News interview, during the advertising campaign for her 2004 film *Catwoman*. When *The Early Show* co-anchor, Rene Syler, asked her how she prepared for the role (which demanded dexterity, strength, and sensual feline movements), she responded by explaining that to master her part in that film, she underwent training in *capoeira*, "a Brazilian form of martial arts" that "incorporates gymnastics and dance" (Shetty).[10] In discussing how she benefited from *capoeira*, she explained that she gained agility, flexibility, and the physical power she needed for the role. She also concluded that *capoeira* movements helped her be in touch with her femininity and sensuality (Shetty).

If aggression and hostility have driven women, children, and elders away from *capoeira* circles, ironically, urban violence may have played an indirect role in women's engagement. While it would be an overstatement to say that they joined *capoeira* circles merely because they sought a form of self-defense, it is undeniable that the females who practice *capoeira* can feel more secure and in control of their physical and emotional space. Numerous women to whom I talked during interviews, *capoeira* workshops, conferences, and visits to academies confided that they have a keener sense of security on the streets of large cities. They feel more empowered to defend themselves if threatened (for instance, to escape a rape attempt or other forms of violence) and consider their learning *capoeira* as an additional safety measure. A personal story that Mestra Marisa shared with me stands out as a sample of how she saw the practice of *capoeira* as empowerment and protection ("Interview" by Barbosa). The incident took place in 1989, during her first stay in Chicago, when she was part of a performing company/show (*Oba, Oba: The Brazilian Musical Extravaganza*)[11] produced by Franco Fontana. (The repertoire of the show ranged from Carmen Miranda's *samba* to *bossa nova* rhythms, and also included Afro-Brazilian folk songs and dances, a *berimbau* medley, performances of *capoeira angola* and *regional*, *maculelê*, a *mulata* show, and *lambada*.)[12]

Having lived in poverty in Minas Gerais in her childhood and teenage years (at the age of seventeen she began working as a housekeeper), and struggling to make a living in São Paulo (distributing fliers on the streets, and later working as a sales person at a popular department store), in the late 1980s Mestre Marisa found a niche in Mestre Suassuna's Capoeira Academy.[13] It provided her the place and space to learn the art form and embrace her Afro-Brazilian heritage. For the first time in her life, she had a sense of "belonging" in Brazilian society. It was at this time, as she explained, that Fontana had bought the rights from Sargentelli to put together a show that would highlight Afro-Brazilian music and dance to tour the United States. In selecting *capoeiristas* for his performing company, Fontana ran into a problem: one of the best *capoeiristas* he had selected balked at the prospect of spending a lengthy amount of time in the United States without his girlfriend. Since his romantic partner also played *capoeira*, to remedy the situation, Fontana's recruiting team decided to find another female *capoeirista* and include the two women in the show as an additional novelty. In their visits to Suassuna's academy, the recruiters witnessed Marisa Cordeiro practicing and issued an invitation for her to perform in Fontana's company. In 1989, at the age of twenty-one, she joined *Oba, Oba: The Brazilian Musical Extravaganza* (Mestra Marisa, "Interview" by Barbosa).

Mestra Marisa revealed that, when in Chicago, she would often take advantage of the fact that their hotel was near Lake Michigan to run around the shore after the last performance of the day. Past ten o'clock one night, a man who had been fascinated by the "Brazilian Extravaganza" decided to accompany her to protect her from any impending harm on the streets of Chicago. Having fended for herself from an early age (her father died when she was six years old), lived in large cities like São Paulo where one needs to be careful and street-smart to navigate certain areas of the city, and having received her training in *capoeira* at Mestre Suassuna's academy, she had learned to be attentive about her surroundings, and was confident that she was well equipped to defend herself, if necessary. As she reminisced, she found it hilarious that a medical doctor who had no training in self-defense, wearing a suit and dress shoes, thought that he was better prepared to defend her from an impending attack on the streets of Chicago based on gender difference. She laughed as she recalled the tall guy trying to catch up with her as she breezed through the trails along Lake Michigan's shore, feeling empowered by her fitness, and humored by the gender dynamics of the situation. In 1991, for personal reasons, she was back in Chicago where she has lived ever since. Around 1992, she was introduced to Greg Downey (who was a student at the University of Chicago), and teamed up with him to establish a *capoeira* group as an extra-curricular activity for a student club which she still directs. It was the first step she took to create Gingarte Capoeira. Her work since then has earned her high regard as a *capoeirista* and allowed her to teach *capoeira* (as dance) at public schools in Chicago.[14]

Enlightened *mestres* have also played a substantial and positive part in helping women advance through the intricate levels of *capoeira* playing. As expressed in the documentary *Cigarra Capoeirista*, Márcia speaks about Mestre Camisa (José Tadeu Carneiro Cardoso) in tender and laudatory terms as she recalls that he was always supportive, "not just as a *mestre* figure, but as a father figure as well," and that he would be concerned about her training and education" (Leech). In the same documentary, Mestre Camisa emphasizes that women should not be treated differently or considered lesser players because of gender: "Women have the ability to reach the same levels of men in terms of technique and professionalism" (Leech). Mestra Janja defends the idea that *capoeira angola* is a welcoming space for women. In analyzing her trajectory in *capoeira* and her experience as an *angoleira*, she mentions her *mestres* (João Grande, Moraes and Cobra Mansa) in laudatory terms:

> Meus mestres nunca nos discriminaram e, mais que isto, trataram de não perder tempo inventando "fundamentos" para nos impedir de crescermos como capoeiristas, dizendo coisas que ainda hoje não compreendemos—como dizer que mulher não pode tocar berimbau, ou cantar ladainha, etc. ("Contra Mestre" 18–19)

> My *mestres* would never discriminate and did not waste time establishing certain "foundations" to inhibit our growth as *capoeiristas*, saying things that are beyond my comprehension, for instance, that women cannot play *berimbau* or sing a *ladainha*.

Several other women confirm the productive interaction they have had with their *mestres* and consider that synergy one of the main reasons why they were able to evolve in *capoeira*. Mestra Luar do Sertão, for instance, analyzes the constructive aspects of her personal experience with her Mestre Caveirinha (Marcelo Pereira). She explains that "he has brought up several women through the ranks and has given a lot of energy to them." However, she warns that this is not the norm in *capoeira*: "But, we must also consider that, even *mestres* who say 'all of my students are half women and half men,' devote most of their energy to those young guys who they perceive as taking on after them" (Mestra Luar do Sertão, 2017 "Interview" by Barbosa). It is also important to remember that a number of the women who have risen to the rank of *mestras* or *contra-mestras* are married to a *capoeira* partner or have had amorous involvement with their male *mestres*. Thus, because of that special bond, they may feel more empowered and included, but oftentimes cannot soundly make an objective judgement.

I was not able to independently verify if gender bias (as far as *mestres* are concerned) does not occur on a consistent basis in *capoeira* groups, or if female students consider that it would be defamatory to establish a clear difference between theory ("all are equal in *capoeira* circles") and practice ("there is a preference for the students who can contribute to give a continuity to the *mestres'* work"). Speaking openly about it can be tricky, especially when the *mestres* in question are legendary or quasi-legendary figures in *capoeira*. When describing individuals whose accomplishments in certain fields are larger than life, there is a tendency to forget that the process of representation does not usually account for the complexities of individual lives. It seems that the dynamics of male dominance are so ingrained in the fabric of Brazilian society and in *capoeira*, in general, that even revered *mestres* (such as Pastinha and Bimba) may not have lived up to their words, in regard to their general attitude toward women, when amorous or sexual relationships were involved.

Most followers or disciples have treated *mestres* (particularly the older ones) as revered personalities, idols, heroes, and cultural icons who deserve the utmost respect and obedience because of the knowledge they accumulated, or the status and prestige they have enjoyed in their communities. However, without losing perspective of the colossal contributions that great *mestres* have given to *capoeira*, at times, it is possible to question their approach to group socialization and situate them as human beings subject to lesser virtues. They are people who also adopt the parameters, values, and limitations of the time, place, and space in which they live and work. Even if *mestres* have great knowledge of *capoeira's* history and principles and often propagate the theory that *capoeira* is an all-inclusive martial art-dance-ritual, many of them are raised within the parameters of conservative societies and, consequently, still consider *capoeira* as a male tradition. Those individuals tend to repeat in *rodas de capoeira* the gender bias they learned in their social circles.

In some cases, the students can become so fascinated with the celebrity, or the archetypal configuration of a *mestre*, that it has a positive effect on them. Their desire to please the *mestres* and gain their admiration and respect in the groups can be an incentive for them to devote more time and attention to the game. As in any learning circle, it can also have an adverse outcome: in case they do not receive the attention they crave, when the relationship loses its intensity, or if it ends, it is not unusual for female students to be unable to differentiate the emotional attachment to the *mestre* from the art form, and give up learning *capoeira* altogether. A biased or condescending attitude of *mestres* toward students (regardless of gender) can have a negative impact on how they see themselves in the game and in life. In other words, it can curtail their sense of belonging and even shorten the period they commit to learning *capoeira*. By the same token, *mestres* who support women through the ranks have had a profoundly constructive effect on the trajectory in *capoeira*. This may be one of the reasons why, in the last two decades, women have been increasingly promoted to the levels of *mestra* and *contra-mestra*, *graduada*, *professora*, and other ranking positions.

During my field research, when I would ask female players about gender discrimination in *capoeira*, they would acknowledge having experienced or heard complaints about double standards.[15] They would also mention that it is not unusual for male players to dismiss claims of gender discrimination by referring to the large number of women currently playing *capoeira*, and to the umbrella notion often attributed to Mestre Pastinha (sometimes to Mestre Bimba), which teaches that *capoeira* welcomes all people because it "is for men, women, and children." Oftentimes players use this escape-hatch to shield themselves from accusations, and to advocate the notion that the *capoeira* circle is a ludic and inclusive space. Basing my conclusions on field and library research, I construed that there are, at least, three general types of attitudes regarding females in *capoeira*: a) some leaders still insist on treating men and women differently, subjecting the latter to double standards; b) there is also a "softer side of sexism,"[16] or the type that treats women with too much deference because they are perceived as weak and fragile; c) a healthier third segment that rejects both premises mentioned above and regards female *capoeiristas* with the same respect and consideration as men. Fortunately, if there are some *mestres*, *contra-mestres*, and instructors who insist on separating women from men, or in treating them differently, there are also those who show genuine respect and consideration for everyone engaged in the process as all the women in this study acknowledge about their *mestres*.

Agents of Cultural Transformation

Cultural, social, and political processes from the 1960s to the 1990s contributed, directly and indirectly, to females joining *capoeira* groups and participate in sports and other activities previously regarded as male turf. The Women's Liberation Movement worldwide had a substantial impact on Brazilian society and helped open previously closed doors, and secure acceptance for females in areas that were inaccessible to them until then. Women campaigned against legal and social discrepancies, and questioned antiquated moral codes by locating sites of struggle, creating modes of resistance, and changing institutional structures. The feminist discourse coincided with protests requiring major changes in political and cultural environments. Their fight was always articulated with the struggle for a return to democracy and amnesty for those involved in the political struggle (Machado). As a transition to democracy, the *abertura* period (from the late-1970s to mid-1980s) guaranteed the right of assembly and allowed less powerful groups at the time the opportunity to express their opinions more freely and voice their demands. Thus, the feminist movement worked in tandem with other minorities (blacks, indigenous, and the LGBTQ communities) to demand their rights, and worked with movements for the re-democratization of Brazil.

The changes that gradually took hold in Brazilian society played a significant role in modifying the family dynamics, and the social expectations for women. Those changes included, but were not limited to: the development of a stronger feminist movement, the modernization and legal modification of the Brazilian family, the sexual revolution which established different parameters for morality, the demographic change in the workforce and at universities, and a new constitution that abolished obsolete laws that curtailed women's rights. The cultural, political, and social improvements that took place in those decades also include the role intellectuals played by adopting and validating African-centric cultural manifestations, and the wave of "roots tourism" to Bahia, in the 1980s and 1990s. Women were able to practice *capoeira* legally in Brazil, in part, because of the changes that occurred in that period.

From the late 1970s throughout the 1980s, and even in the 1990s, feminists in Brazil defended equal rights and opportunities, raising the public's awareness that discrepancies in gender power relations are socially constructed, and therefore, could and should be dismantled. They called attention to the need to have sexual freedom and held a public debate on abortion. The different feminist groups in most regions of the country denounced inequalities in the workforce, and sexual and domestic violence; they also fought against the "defense of honor" legal practice in which men were acquitted of homicides committed against their wives or lovers. In addition, women also wanted to be engaged in any physical activity they so desired and, in 1979, the government lifted the ban that had prohibited them, since 1941, from practicing sports deemed violent and inappropriate for the feminine physique. They also entered institutions of higher education and the marketplace in record numbers, choosing careers nearly inaccessible to them in the past which made them financially and socially more independent. Such independence resulted in the ability to exercise jurisdiction over their personal spaces. In this context, conventional cultural and social configurations were overturned or redesigned.

The structure of Brazilian family became more flexible in its moral values and less restrictive in terms of its male domination which created a space for parents to support their daughters in their personal choices. As discussed in Chapter One, in 1977, the institutionalization of divorce changed the family configuration substantially. For the first time, Brazilians had the opportunity to marry legally after a separation and, for women this was an opening to rebuild their lives without the stigma previously attached to the condition of *desquitada*. Divorce seemed more modern than *desquite*, thus less stigmatized, empowering women in ways they had not experience before. The sexual revolution of the 1960s and 1970s, brought about by innovative birth control methods, allowed females to have a better control of family planning and the management of their bodies.

Other factors may also have contributed to engage women in *capoeira* playing. It is also in the 1970s and 1980s that the "*diaspora baiana*" (as L. Reis labels the group of high-ranking *capoeiristas* who made their art popular in São Paulo, Rio de Janeiro, and other state capitals) systematically began to open academies and regulate the game, hoping to attract the middle class. Numerous *mestres* immigrated to the United States and Europe to teach *capoeira*. It is in this context that families, communities, and government agencies—which had previously discouraged women from engaging in such a ruffian's activity—began to relax their grip. From then on, the number of women continued to rise in *capoeira* circles. Numerous public intellectuals, writers, musicians, and performers included *capoeira* in their creative endeavors, thus bestowing upon it the aura of respectability it deserved and, consequently validating its importance for the Brazilian society at-large (L. Reis 144–45).[17] Brazilian and foreign scholars' interest in studying and writing about *capoeira* also stands as a key factor for its fast growth around the world and the inclusion of women in those circles. Several prominent men and women in the United States and Brazil have helped popularize the practice of *capoeira* by practicing it, publishing academic books and articles, and writing theses and dissertations about it. Their efforts have contributed to validate *capoeira* and disseminate its practice in academic settings (student clubs, for instance). Additionally, *capoeiristas* organized several magazines which are dedicated exclusively to the study and practice of *capoeira*—such as *Praticando Capoeira, Coleção Grandes Mestres, Ginga Capoeira: Letras e Movimentos*, and *Revista Cordão de Ouro*—all of which have opened a space for women, by publishing interviews, profiles, and lyrics of songs composed by female *capoeiristas*, and discussing their accomplishments. Although the number of articles or the references to women in publications are still only occasional, they reveal their male peers' willingness to include them in the overall picture of *capoeira* circles.

The 1964–1985 military government's effort in promoting a nationalist agenda that included *capoeira* as a "Brazilian national gymnastic" (among other African-centric cultural manifestations) established an institutional framework that validated and popularized it, making it more acceptable to the general population. This is an aspect that Leni M. Silverstein discusses when addressing the changes that took place in the 1970s in Bahia, when the State and the Catholic Church joined forces with African-derived religious groups to showcase religious syncretism as a form of tolerance for cultural hybridity and as a trademark of racial harmony in Brazil. Focusing on the Festa do Senhor do Bonfim ("The Celebration of Our Lord of the Good End"), in Salvador, she analyses "how the cults were transformed from shunned and persecuted pagan rites into a valued cultural heritage, courted by church and state alike" (Hess and DaMatta 141). In this environment, *capoeira* and other practices of African origin became staple tourist attractions and, eventually, were widely accepted in Brazil. The steady wave of "roots tourism" to Bahia in the 1980s and 1990s also had a significant role in the proliferation of interest in *capoeira*, Candomblé ceremonies, Bahian cuisine, and *axé* music. The desire of foreigners to see and/or participate in those African-centric cultural manifestations contributed to heighten their importance in Brazil. The politics of culture that validated Bahian African-centric manifestations in the 1980s and 1990s is similar to the process of valorization that *samba* and other elements of Afro-Brazilian culture received in Rio de Janeiro in the 1920s. Vianna attributes the interest that affluent French nationals (Blaise Cendras and Darius Milhaud, in particular) had in "the exoticism of Brazilian culture" (African-derived music, religions, and cuisine), and "the ethnic miscegenation of the Brazilian people" as key factors for *samba* and *carnaval* to become fashionable in the whole country (67–76).[18]

As Fontana's *Oba, Oba: The Brazilian Extravaganza* revealed, since the mid-1980s, there was a renewed and enhanced interest in Afro-Brazilian culture at home and abroad. The euphoria of Olodum's and Ilê Aiyê's Afro-reggae beat contributed to call attention to Afro-derived cultural manifestations and increase the number of women participating in those events. Even if the inclusion of *capoeira* in "folkloric shows" has watered down the game's components, emphasizing only its performative aspects (similar to Edna Lima's *Capoeira Workout* exercise program), it also contributed to decreasing the social and moral stigma associated with *capoeira* (a foot-fight linked to ruffians and outlaws), and allowed it to be promoted as an art form.[19] The proliferation of *capoeira* academies (everywhere in Brazil, from the smallest town to the largest metropolis) also made the game look more familiar and acceptable. In many cases, those associations provided women a safe and familiar niche (as in the case of Marisa Cordeiro who found a sense of belonging in Mestre Suassuna's Cordão de Ouro). Consequently, the explosion of *capoeira* academies and groups around the world has opened doors for women to participate in the game and to change the gender dynamics in the *rodas*. In those new contexts, the martial art-ritual acquired a more positive outlook (a less violent image), gradually gaining the general the population's approval. The establishment of *capoeira* academies and working groups throughout the United States, and in other countries as well, further contributed to balancing the gender profile in *capoeira*.

Since the end of the 1970s, *mestres, contra-mestres,* instructors, and leaders of groups (many of whom are Brazilians residing abroad), have traveled with their students to Brazil for short and long stays during which time they play with locals, or participate in *capoeira* gatherings, workshops, and tournaments. In general, the international groups that travel to Brazil, especially from the United States, Canada, Australia, and northern European countries, are composed of a higher number of females which imparts the idea that, in highly industrialized nations, *capoeira* is also practiced by a large contingent of women (in a way similar to the history of women in soccer). Such information—and the positive image it conveys—has contributed to redefine the perception that women are integral participants in *rodas de capoeira.* As a result, throughout the years, the homegrown population in Brazil has had the opportunity to interact with foreign women who participate actively in the *rodas* which, at least in the 1980s and 1990s, may have influenced their views, and played a part in enforcing an attitude of respect in *capoeira* circles. This holds true especially in smaller urban centers—as in the case of several cities in the Recôncavo Baiano, in the state of Bahia—where foreign tourism was less frequent than in larger urban sites in the 1980s and 1990s. However, it does not mean that those who teach or study *capoeira* in the United States and other industrialized countries are automatically more open-minded, or more inclined to respect gender equality than in Brazil. It means that, a stronger feminist movement in those countries has allowed for an environment in which women feel comfortable demanding their rights more effectively.

Mestres, contra-mestres, instructors, and group leaders have grown accustomed not only to having females in their classes, but also to taking them more seriously. In some cases, women who have risen to high-ranking positions are more sensitive to gender inequalities and not only demand their rights, but also serve as role models. Women have become quite sensitive to the lyrics of some songs, especially the ones that include derogatory themes or expressions. The irony, though, is that since the songs are always sung in Portuguese (regardless of the country where *capoeira* is played) and many students outside the realm of Portuguese-speaking countries may only have rudimentary levels of Portuguese, it is more difficult to detect the gender bias embedded in the figurative language of the traditional lyrics. Consequently, their singing can contribute to perpetuate discrimination that would otherwise be rejected.

In the new millennium, the internet made the dissemination of information so fast and affordable that it has opened opportunities to broadcast events, share information about meetings, advertise *capoeira* groups and academies, and showcase profiles of *mestres* and *contra-mestres* to unprecedented large numbers of people around the globe. The use of mass communication venues (mobile phones, web pages, blogs, YouTube, and other forms of internet usage and social media) have also made it easier to publicize new songs and create a sense of a larger *capoeira* community. These changes have allowed the population in general to see that this martial art-dance-ritual is a common practice, and that good gender interaction can enhance its trajectory worldwide. A stellar example of how women have used the internet to advertise their accomplishments and to support each other is the blog created by Joaninha Mandingueira (from Canada) who kept an ongoing, lively conversation from 2007 to 2009. She did research on women in *capoeira*, collected information about nine *mestras* and *mestrandas,* and posted biographies, interviews, and video recordings of their playing or teaching *capoeira*. Her blog sustained an energetic discussion of Feminism and *capoeira* and contributed to highlight female advancement and accomplishments.[20]

In addition to the changes in Brazilian society that have contributed to normalize the practice of *capoeira* for women, individual lifestyles and personal interests have also led females to join *capoeira* circles. Numerous interviews and conversations I conducted in the United States and in Brazil, as well as several references I found in personal blogs, websites, testimonials, interviews, and academic publications indicate that a number of women were initially interested in *capoeira* because of their prior knowledge of dance, yoga, and other disciplined systems of exercise that promote control of the body and mind. For instance, Mestra Suelly (who was instrumental in helping develop the United Capoeira Association and now runs the Berkeley chapter with Mestre Acordeon) embodies a perfect example of the transition from dance to *capoeira*. She confirms that her training in modern dance helped her better understand *capoeira*'s movements and more easily learn a new corporal language. In a statement about her, Mestre Acordeon recalls that, when she joined his academy, in 1982, he noticed immediately that she was well acquainted with dance movements ("Making").

Mestra Edna Lima is another *capoerista* who was involved in other types of physical trainings in addition to learning *capoeira*. Lima was introduced to the world of *capoeira* when she was 12 years old in Brasília (where she was Mestre Tabosa's student and learned different styles of *capoeira*). She later joined Mestre Camisa's ABADÁ-Capoeira Group and, in 1997, both Mestre Camisa and Grand Mestre Camisa Roxa awarded her the title of *mestranda*. In 1999, Lima also earned a black belt in Shotokan and a degree in Physical Education, and in 2013, she was promoted to the level of *mestra* of *capoeira* in Rio de Janeiro. She is currently a signature name sought after to lead *batizados* and teach workshops,[21] and has accumulated an impressive number of national and international prizes and awards.[22] In an interview conducted with Lima in 2004 to highlight her 30th anniversary in *capoeira*, Lydia Alicea presented a profile of her as a *capoeirista* and as a martial artist: "What impressed me about Mestra Lima was not just her many accomplishments and vast experience or knowledge, or that she is one of the few high ranking female martial artists in the world today. Mestra Lima truly manifests the evolution of what Capoeira is today, what it represents to its followers as an art, and where it is headed in the future" (Interview). In addition to teaching *capoeira*, in 2004, Lima developed an exercise regimen (*Capoeira Workout* DVD). Her set of exercises does not use the circle formation (a basic element in a *roda de capoeira*), and has eliminated the traditional instruments (*berimbau, agogô, pandeiro, atabaque*) and the warm up time. It replaced the traditional songs and music of *capoeira* with Afro-reggae music (Bergamo 58). Her workout program received high praise and harsh criticism. Those in favor consider *Workout* an excellent venue to popularize *capoeira*'s movements, while those against it argue that those aerobic exercises distort the core principles of *capoeira*. They claim it strips the game of its ritualistic elements since it does not include the original songs and instruments which make *capoeira* stand out in comparison to other martial arts (Esteves 123–24).

Even if the majority of the girls, young women, and adult females who are interested in *capoeira* have had prior experience with other dance or exercise forms, there are also a number of them who had had no previous familiarity with any martial art or dance when they began learning *capoeira*. In some cases, an inverse movement occurs: the involvement with *capoeira* may lead students to find other related activities in order to validate the time and energy they have invested in learning the fight-dance-ritual. This is an aspect that Mestra Cigana detailed when specifying the challenges she had to overcome. From her perspective, it seemed illogical that after so many years of training, and after having received the title of *mestra* in *capoeira regional*, she was denied the opportunity to teach it in an academic setting. Realizing that she needed to comply with curricular rules, she earned a college degree in Educação Física ("Physical Education/Sports Education") and secured a position at a private high school where she was allowed to teach *capoeira* as a curricular discipline. Her accomplishment was a great step toward normalizing *capoeira* in schools as a respectful physical activity. Even if on a small scale, she acted as a surrogate for the writer Coelho Neto who, in the beginning of the twentieth century, advocated for Brazilian schools to adopt *capoeira* as part of their Physical Education program (as discussed in Chapter Three).

As in many professions or career choices in which there is a personal calling, or a strong vocational element (similar to what happens to priests, teachers, artists, social workers, activists, musicians, writers, scientists, researchers, and athletes), those professionals usually dispense unparalleled dedication to their trade and put large amounts of time coaching people, perfecting their activities, or mastering their trade to optimize results. Therefore, to achieve a high level of mastery, *mestres* and other full time instructors of *capoeira* have to be entirely committed to training, studying, and living *capoeira*. For social, historical, and cultural reasons, fewer women attain higher levels of "graduation" because they have less time and fewer opportunities to spend a lot of time inside a *roda*, in actual playing mode. Fewer opportunities to practice can limit the acceleration of progress toward achieving higher ranks. Many women complain that it is a no-win situation. Pregnancy and responsibilities related to maternity, and motherhood, and chores regarding the management of a household, all of which are time-consuming, can put a woman in a disadvantaged position. Many women raise this question—especially in Brazil where men are less culturally inclined to participate in the daily routine of child raising and domestic chores—arguing that it is hard to compete with their male counterparts at the higher levels of *capoeira* training. These and many other personal and professional aspects can deprive them of the time and opportunity to dedicate themselves exclusively to running an academy or teaching and practicing *capoeira*. In some cases, to follow their calling, females have adopted the *capoeira* lifestyle wholeheartedly and have given up the idea of constituting a traditional family.

That was Mestra Cigana's experience. She belongs to a generation of women in Brazil who often married in their late teens in part because they hoped to have more freedom and power of decision. But it did not work out as she planned. When she decided to learn *capoeira*, her husband opposed it because, in the late 1960s and early 1970s, it was just not something a respectable married woman—and a mother—would conceive of doing. Forced to choose between her family and *capoeira*, she chose the latter. When fighting to keep custody of her young son, she lost the battle exactly because she was a *capoeirista* and her lifestyle was considered "questionable" at best (Mestra Cigana). As she emphasized, *capoeira* was stigmatized not just as a masculine activity performed by thugs and outlaws, but also as a violent practice not suitable for women of a *boa família* ("good family").[23] In some ways, Mestra Cigana's life options resembled the choices Chiquinha Gonzaga made in the nineteenth century. Both decided to carve a future on their own terms, making personal and professional choices that were unusual for their time: Gonzaga chose music over marriage, and Mestra Cigana opted for *capoeira*.

In the early 1970s, Mestra Cigana pioneered efforts to free her peers from the ideological and social constraints of a male-oriented *capoeira* environment.[24] She paved the way for prospective generations of women *capoeiristas* by challenging Brazilian cultural rules so that she could unrestrictedly dedicate her entire adult life to learning and teaching *capoeira*. She completely embraced the *capoeira* environment, training, and lifestyle, and associated herself with several *mestres de capoeira* in Bahia, Pará, Rio de Janeiro, and São Paulo, including Mestre Bezerra (José Bezerra da Silva from the state of Pará) and Mestre Canjiquinha (Washington Bruno da

Silva from Bahia) who took her under their wings and gave her proper training. In the 1970s, she joined Mestre Canjiquinha's group, and in 1980 was conferred the title of *mestra* by him in Rio de Janeiro (Mestra Cigana). Her *capoeira* codename (Mestra Cigana) was later awarded to her by Mestre Leopoldina (Dermeval Lopes de Lacerda) to represent aspects of her nomadic and un-conventional lifestyle and seductive way of playing *capoeira*. She distinguishes herself as the first woman to receive the title of *mestra* in Brazil (in 1980), and direct the Federação de Capoeira do Rio de Janeiro ("*Capoeira* Federation in Rio de Janeiro"). In addition, she played a major role in masterminding the creation of the Federação Nacional de Capoeira ("National Federation of *Capoeira*").

As she confided, a major difficulty she encountered in *capoeira* circles at the time was sexual harassment, which is one of the reasons she gives for her frequently changing groups. She explained that, when she began playing *capoeira*, a large amount of players were womanizers and, for the most part, prostitutes and street vendors were the only women associating with them. It was not un-common for *capoeiristas* to assume that, if a woman joined them, it was because she was promiscuous. In *City of Women*, Lande confirms this point when she reports a conversation she had with Edison Carneiro, in 1947, in which he told her that numerous Candomblé priestesses had reservations about *capoeiristas* because they thought they did not "believe in God," and they were heavy drinkers, thugs, and lawbreakers (92). Reiterating Lande's 1947 reporting that women in Candomblé did not endorse *capoeiristas'* promiscuous and lawless lifestyle, in 1995, Browning writes that she also heard derogatory comments about *capoeiristas*. As she reports, a priestess in Candomblé despised Mestre Pastinha's be-havior toward females: "His big dim useless eyes had an expression of exquisite tenderness, despite a curious half-smile. My mother of saints said, 'Ha! Everybody thinks Pastinha was such a sweet guy. I knew him and he was a woman-user and a dirty, manipulative son of a bitch like the rest of them'" (106). In his recollections of his days in Bahia, when he was Mestre Bimba's student, Mestre Acordeon speaks of women and their relationship with *capoeiristas* as groupies. He recalls one female, in particular, "Maria Lucia, a most beautiful mulatta who practically lived in Mestre Bimba's school. In her languid arms many of us healed the pains of our bodies and souls in wonderful nights of love" (120). Hence, the comments by Lande, Browning, and Mestre Acordeon corroborate Mestra Cigana's grievances about the way she was treated in *capoeira* circles throughout the country (she was met with physical and symbolic violence, other players ignored or downplayed her abilities, and disrespected her). As she recollects, it was not until the 1980s, and beyond, that even women, including some Afro-Brazilian females, would consider *capoeira* a respectable activity and/or would join groups or academies (Mestra Cigana).

Mestra Márcia Cigarra is another female *capoeirista* who has overcome challenges to become an internationally known personality (as Katya Wesolowski details in the 2007 documentary, *Cigarra Capoeirista*). In tracing Márcia Treidler's personal and professional trajectory, Wesolowski mentions that "it was not until the late seventies and early eighties [that] women started training in capoeira more frequently in Rio, and Márcia is really part of that first wave."[25] In discussing her *capoeira* nickname, Treidler explains that Mestre Camisa (the founder of ABADÁ-Capoeira) called her "Cigarra" ("Cicada") on the occasion of her *batizado* because she can "sing really loud and strong" (Leech). Mestra Cigarra also speaks tenderly of her negotiations with her mother, in the mid-1970s, to have permission to learn *capoeira*. As she reminisces, she was the only woman in the *capoeira* center that she attended (CEMB: Centro Educacional Mestre Bimba), and the other players did not welcome her when she first began ("they did not really like me," she says). However, as she became more accomplished, they became friendlier.[26] Wesolowski attributes Mestra Cigarra's acceptance by her male peers to the fact that she "would play as an equal; she wanted them to play fiercely with her as they did with each other, and the men, little by little, accepted her as an equal" (Leech). Mestra Cigarra immigrated to the United States in 1991 and has taught *capoeira* in the Bay Area since then.[27] In an effort to provide public service, in 1997, she fashioned the Brazilian Cultural Center, the first organization of its kind in the Bay Area to promote cultural legacies from her country of origin. She is also the artistic director of ABADÁ-Capoeira International.[28] Like Mestra Cigarra, some of the best known female *capoeiristas* in the United States practice *capoeira regional* or its variants (ABADÁ, for instance).[29] In fact, the better known female *capoeiristas* in the United States are not *angoleiras*, in part because *regional* has been on the international market for a longer time and, to some degree, because its highly structured graduation system allows the students to appreciate their progress through the ranks in a more measurable way.

In Brazil, women who train in the *capoeira angola* variant have also become quite successful as role models. For instance, the *angoleiras* Mestra Janja (Rosângela Araújo) and Mestra Paulinha (Paula Cristina da Silva Barreto) have combined their knowledge of *capoeira* with their social and intellectual visibility[30] to engage in public service. Their work with communities in Salvador and in other geographical areas of Brazil has reaped benefits. In 1995, they established the Instituto Nzinga de Estudos da Capoeira Angola e Tradições Educativas Banto no Brasil (INCAB; "Nzinga Institute of *Capoeira Angola* and Bantu Educational Traditions in Brazil"),[31] and, in 1999, assembled a *berimbau* orchestra in São Paulo. In selecting a name for the institute that would house and transmit information about *capoeira angola* and Bantu traditions in Brazil, Mestra Janja and the co-founders Mestra Paulinha and Mestre Poloca (Paulo Roberto Guimarães Barreto) established an association between *capoeira*'s cultural survival and the resistance that Nzinga, the Angolan queen represented.[32] By choosing the name Nzinga for the institute and the orchestra, they empowered women *capoeiristas* by directing attention to female warriors and emphasizing women's competence in leadership roles. All chapters of the Instituto Nzinga address the rights of children and adolescents, raise consciousness about race and gender issues, fight discrimination, and develop a sense of empowerment in the Afro-Brazilian communities where they are located.

Therefore, Mestra Janja and Mestra Paulinha reveal that women can and should play *berimbau* in *rodas de capoeira*, not only because they can play well, but also because they assembled and directed an entire *berimbau* orchestra. They stand as great examples of how women have worked to promote *capoeira angola* and showcase their creativity, strength, and organizational skills. In addition to conducting the Nzinga Berimbaus Orchestra, Mestra Janja also works as an editor of the magazine *Toques de Angola* ("*capoeira angola* beats") and has taken a leadership role in preparing new generations to continue the traditions set by Mestre Pastinha and his followers. As a distinguished *mestra* who has dedicated several decades of her life to learning and teaching *capoeira*, she serves as a very positive role model. By working with grassroots movements, teaching *capoeira angola*, writing about it, and composing new songs, Mestra Janja and her peers have contributed extensively to change the dynamics of the fight-ritual and increase female visibility in *rodas de capoeira* worldwide. Mestra Janja and Mestra Paulinha have emulated some of Nzinga's intrepid personality traits as they continue to fight for more recognition for *capoeira angola* and have developed programs to galvanize Afro-Brazilians' pride in their heritage.

In Brazil, the number of *mestras* and *contra-mestras* continues to expand. In August of 2018, Mestra Alcione, who teaches *capoeira* in Belo Horizonte, became the first woman in Minas Gerais promoted to the rank *mestra*. At the end of the Twenty-Seventh International Meeting of Capoeira Angola which took place in Salvador (January 15–20, 2019), two other women became *mestras*: Gegê (Andressa Siqueira from São Paulo) and Rosinha (Rosa Simões from Bauru); Mestre Pé de Chumbo (Gidalto Pereira Dias) awarded them the title. In addition to Mestras Janja and Paulinha who are signature names in Salvador, other *mestras* participated in the event, namely, Mestra Elma (who received the title in 2004 from Mestre Patinho and has taught *capoeira* in São Luís, Porto Alegre, and Florianópolis), and Mestra Jararaca (Valdelice dos Santos de Jesus, who received the title from Mestre Curió in 2008). Maria Zeneide Gomes da Silva reports that during a *capoeira* colloquium organized by the Movimento Capoeira Mulher (MCM) in Belém do Pará, on November 22, 2016, Mestra Janja spearheaded the idea of honoring the *capoeirista* Pé de Anjo (Sílvia Leão) by conferring to her the title of *mestra* (in memoriam), in recognition of her fifteen years of work to promote and teach *capoeira* in Pará (169–73). The certificate was signed by members of the organization and participants in the event. Mestre Bezerra (a highly esteemed figure in *capoeira* circles) supported the decision.[33]

Ever since *capoeira* was taken from the streets to the sheltered environment of academies and fitness centers, women have often worked as aides, and lent helping hands to organize federations, maintain records, and promote gatherings. In short, time and again, they have supported their husbands, lovers, boyfriends, brothers, or fathers in *capoeira* settings, similar to what *baianas* and *quitandeiras* used to do on the streets of Salvador and Rio de

Janeiro. Based on this factor, Frederico J. Abreu claims that women have given a sustained contribution to *capoeira* because, even if they have not participated formally (on a large scale) in the *rodas*, they have lent their organizational skills to the group with which they are affiliated ("Personal interview").[34] Guizardi's research corroborates Abreu's discussions by reporting that she amassed substantial evidence that women gave a significant contribution to the internal configuration of the groups as well as to the events they organized. For her, not only have women had an important organizational function in the academies, but they have also held several other similar positions in which there is no masculine participation (302).

While juggling a profession with the practice of a sport, martial art, or an artistic interest is not an exclusive female domain, the point is that, in looking at the demographics and the social and familial roles women usually play, the statistics show that, in comparative terms, there are more men than women who are able to dedicate themselves exclusively to the teaching or learning of *capoeira*, a situation similar to positions of power occupied at executive levels in private sectors of business, academia, and government. It does not mean that females cannot, or do not reach high levels of mastery. A host of women, including the ones cited in this study, has successfully combined teaching *capoeira* with holding other professions, and balancing the roles of motherhood, womanhood, and wifehood. However, it means that, despite the feasibility of keeping a balance between their ability to practice *capoeira* full time and their active engagement in personal activities, as in many other professions, the effort required can discourage many women from persisting in the practice of *capoeira*. Consequently, fewer women than men can rise to the level of *mestra* because of time and familial constraints. Nevertheless, in all styles of *capoeira*, the superior performance and success of female players also indicates that women have made a concerted effort to achieve high ranks and be fully engaged in *capoeira*. Some of them also successfully manage to sustain a parallel professional career and, in many cases, attend to the needs of their families. Some have made personal choices that do not include the standard roles women have played. Regardless of gender, a student's advancement through *capoeira* ranks depends on lifestyle, personal choices, and the personal commitment he or she makes. However, as the testimonies of several women cited in this study reveal, the degree of support, or lack thereof, that individuals receive from their *mestres* can significantly impact the trajectory of their involvement with *capoeira*.

Although women have already overcome many barriers and crossed several borders in *capoeira*, this is still a transitional phase for them. Unlike the pioneer female *capoeiristas* of the nineteenth and twentieth centuries who, because of their social status and how women were viewed at the time, had no higher ground from where to challenge societal parameters and/or their male counterparts, modern *capoeiristas* are in a very different position. They are gradually establishing themselves in the masculine universe of *capoeira* and instituting their own configuration as players and leaders. To set the process in motion, they have formed strong coalitions by organizing regional, national, and international meetings, and have developed a renewed interest in promoting each other's accomplishments. They have also consistently participated in meetings that include both sexes which give them an opportunity to showcase their abilities. Considering that now many women actively participate in *capoeira* circles and have taken a leadership role, in the future, it will be easier to evaluate the impact that the gender dynamics have had on groups and academies led by women. Once a substantial number of females have established a consistent program of their own initiative and have "graduated" new generations of players, it will be possible to determine more clearly the actual position they hold in the large scheme of this globalized cultural practice.

Chapter Six

Women in Brazilian Popular Music and *Capoeira* Songs

Representations of Women in Song Lyrics

The musical renewal that *bossa nova* represented, from the end of the 1950s through the 1960s, paved the way for the rise of an assorted group of musical rhythms. Composers blended several national rhythms and musical styles (elements of *bossa nova, bolero, sertaneja* music, Northeastern music, and other genres) and incorporated foreign influences (from jazz, rock, reggae), creating a final product that defies categorization and is usually known as "Música Popular Brasileira" or MPB (McGowan and Pessanha 78).[1] As Chris McGowan and Ricardo Pessanha asserted, Brazilian popular music "is intensely eclectic, varying greatly in style from artists to artists," even when the songwriters share a musical tradition and trademarks which include captivating melodies, exquisite harmonies, a diversity of rhythms, and the passion for poetic lyrics (77).[2] Charles A. Perrone also highlights those characteristics, particularly in reference to the compositions that appeared between 1965 and 1985 (from the height of *bossa nova* to the period post-*Abertura*). He underscores the complex word play and the "manipulation of formal features" of the lyrics of Brazilian songs (*Seven* 91). To avoid censorship, he stresses, lyricists used "the subtlety of phrase, ambiguity, metaphor, and allegory" as a concerted effort to dissimulate historical references and complaints about political conditions (*Seven* 91).

In tracing the history of the MPB acronym, John J. Harvey identifies 1966 as the year when the term began to be used "to denote folk-based material of protest songs performed at televised festivals that had become quite important" (108). Being selected to participate in those competitions and winning a prize could contribute substantially to launch a successful musical career.

Therefore, those televised festivals turned out to be stages of national reach that inspired young musicians and composers to produce new songs. Although different in many aspects, for the most part, two elements connect the MPB songbook: a) the proliferation of protest songs in direct ratio to the intensification of the military regime's repression (especially in the late 1960s and 1970s); and b) the traditional representation of women. Even if substantially more sophisticated than songs written before the 1960s (in terms of melody, rhythm, harmony, form, timbre, and the poetic erudition), for the most part, the lyrics of MPB songs also describe females stereotypically. Their rendition of women's personality and behavior remain remarkably similar to depictions of women in *samba-canção*, *sambolero* (rhythms of *samba* and *bolero* combined), and *marchas*, all of which were extremely popular until the advent of *bossa nova* in the late 1950s (Noel Rosa, Ismael Silva, Ataulfo Alves, Lupicínio Rodrigues, Lamartine Babo, and Dorival Caymmi are some of the most revered songwriters of the period).[3]

An analysis of the repertoire of songs, regarding gender dynamics, reveals that in building a canon of feminine aesthetics, songwriters reiterated typical views of Brazilian society. Traditional songs of the 1930s and 1940s describe females as unreliable, unfaithful, and untrustworthy individuals who entice discord and conflict. They also portray women as males' possessions, inferior beings, objects of sexual pleasure, or obstacles to men's welfare. By comparison, when depicting men, the lyrics of songs reserve for them positive roles such as guardians of moral virtue and custodians of respectable norms of behavior. They also describe men as victims of female selfishness, greed, and deceit. The traditional songs, composed between the 1930s and 1950s, reveal social and cultural mechanisms that chastise women for not sporting a certain look, describe the ideal woman for an amorous relationship, and encourage females to act altruistically. Those songs represent striking examples of the gender dynamics of the Brazilian cultural environment and have inspired and influenced generations of songwriters who continue to perpetuate such themes.

Most of the traditional *capoeira* chants can be traced to folkloric songs or the lyrics of popular music (such as *modinha* and *samba*), thus they also repeat the themes found in those types of songs. *Malandragem* ("roguery"), for instance, is a very common topic in Brazilian popular music in the 1930s and 1940s, and in traditional *capoeira* chants. There was also a proliferation of songs that celebrated *malandragem* "as a world view and survival strategy," and rejected formal employment because some sectors of the popular classes refused "to submit to the discipline and monotony associated with the world of wage labor" (Oliven, "Imaginary" 172). To evidence that, Ruben George Oliven cites a 1931 *samba*, "O Que Será de Mim?" ("What Will Become of Me?"), composed by Ismael Silva:

> Se eu precisar algum dia
> De ir pro batente
> Não sei o que será
> Pois vivo na malandragem
> E vida melhor não há.
> (173)

> If one day I am
> Forced into drudging work
> I don't know what will become of me
> Because I live in *malandragem*
> And there is no better life than that.[4]

Although Oliven limits his inquiry to the repertoire of songs from the 1930s–1950s, his conclusions about representations of women in Brazilian popular music are relevant to the analysis of other contemporary lyrics and to *capoeira* songs. His discussions of the 1933 song, "Caixa Econômica" ("Savings Bank") by Orestes Barbosa and Antônio Nássara offers a telling illustration of the mindset of the time when popular songs would often rant against work, women, and money. The lyric voice refutes the accusation that he is lazy, and gaslights by shifting the blame to a woman, accusing her of having a "predatory character," and describing her as an "insatiable consumer" (Oliven, "Imaginary" 174). The following stanzas offer insights into the lyric voice's defense argument and his strategic counterattack:

> Você quer comprar o seu sossego
> Me vendo morrer num emprego
> Pra depois então gozar
> Esta vida é muito cômica
> Eu não sou Caixa Econômica

Que tem juros a ganhar
E você quer comprar o quê, hem?

Você diz que eu sou moleque
Porque não vou trabalhar
Eu não sou livro de cheque
Pra você ir descontar
Se você vive tranquila
Sempre fazendo chiquê
Sempre na primeira fila
Me fazendo de guichê. [5]
(Oliven, "Imaginary" 174)

You want to secure peace and quiet
Watching me kill myself at work
Just so you can enjoy yourself
Life is quite comical
I am not the Savings Bank
Which has interest to collect
And what is it you want to buy, hum?
You say I am a bum
Because I don't go to work
I am not a checkbook
For you to get your cash
Always in the front row
Always playing chic
If you live without worries.
(Oliven's translation)

In summarizing the psychological profile of men in the lyrics of Brazilian popular music, Oliven notices that it is one of the few cultural fields in which lyricists project a weak image of themselves by expressing their suffering: "While in most other kinds of public discourse a man seeks to convey an image of strength and superiority vis-à-vis the opposite sex, in music he may be frank about his anxieties and fears, his weaknesses and pains, his desires. Quite often, what emerges is the picture of a fragile and helpless creature who seems to have suffered irremediable losses" ("Imaginary" 180–81). Oliven further analyzes songs by Lupicínio Rodrigues, Noel Rosa, and Ataulfo Alves to discuss the dynamics of gender in the construction of Brazilian identity, categorizing those songs into two axes: *a economia do trabalho* ("the economy of work"), and *a economia do afeto* ("the economy of affection"). The songs he examines also typify females according to the supporting roles they play. If they are self-effacing and highly supportive, they are considered either *mulheres-âncora* ("anchor-women") whose role in life is to strengthen men's power, or *mulheres-bússolas* ("compass-women") who should guide and protect their men (Oliven, "A mulher" 52–54, 57).

As discussed in the first part of this study, under the Vargas regime, several segments of society (including educational, medical, religious, and social organizations) joined forces to regulate women's behaviors, choices, and obligations. Females were considered mostly as household administrators, mothers, and child bearers who should avoid ostentatious and frivolous behavior. Very much in tune with the conservative morality of the time, the song "Ai, Que Saudade da Amélia" ("Oh, How I Miss Amélia"), composed in 1942 by Ataulfo Alves and Mário Lago, [6] became a classic representation of the ideal of womanhood in Brazil.

> Nunca vi fazer
> Tanta exigência
> Nem fazer o que você me faz.
> Você não sabe
> O que é consciência.
> Nem vê que eu sou um pobre rapaz.
> Você só pensa em luxo e riqueza,
> Tudo o que você vê, você quer.
> Ai, meu Deus, que saudade da Amélia!
> Aquilo sim é que era mulher.
> Às vezes passava fome ao meu lado,
> E achava bonito
> Não ter o que comer.
> Quando me via contrariado
> Dizia: "meu filho, o que se há de fazer?"
> Amélia não tinha a menor vaidade,
> Amélia é que era mulher de verdade.

> I've never seen anyone
> Make so many demands
> Or do what you do to me.
> You don't know
> What a conscience is.
> You can't see I'm a poor guy.
> You think only of luxury and riches,

> Everything you see, you want.
> Oh God, how I miss Amélia!
> That one was a real woman.
> At times she went hungry by my side,
> And thought it was charming
> Having nothing to eat.
> And when I was upset
> She'd say, "My child, what can be done?"
> Amélia wasn't vain at all,
> Amélia, that one was a true woman.

"Ai, Que Saudade da Amélia" reveals that a "good-natured" woman should be passive, loving, caring, and predisposed to any sacrifice (without complaining) for the good of her man. The song compares and contrasts two females (supposedly his past and present lovers), and the lyric voice uses a distressed tone to create a negative profile of the second lover. To accomplish that, the lyricist uses a clever maneuver: instead of berating her, he praises Amélia whom he describes as a model of virtue because she demands no riches or luxury. The approach pays off because he comes out looking supportive of well-behaved women (like Amélia) and victimized by unscrupulous women (like his current companion). Feeling trapped in a relationship with a woman who does not conform to the ideal role that Amélia played in his life, he reminisces about bygone days and Amélia's abnegation, contrition, and unselfish behavior (the "anchor-women" to which Oliven refers). In line with the religious and conservative apparatus of the time, Alves and Lago repeated the idea that men sought women who were self-effacing, undemanding, loving, and hard workers. If a man ended up in the companionship of a woman who did not have those qualities, he could suffer catastrophic consequences.

Lupicínio Rodrigues's songs emblematize another pillar of Brazilian popular music prevalent in the 1940s whose characterization of women contributed to disseminate myths and create an unfavorable profile of the feminine psyche. The themes of his songs and the messages they convey share with traditional *capoeira* songs a gender bias and a derogatory perception of women. In discussing the concept of masculinity and representations of the feminine in his songs, Maria Izilda S. de Matos and Fernando A. Faria notice that his lyrics are peppered with gender double standards. For Rodrigues, males are essentially sincere and generous

beings imbued with noble moral values, while females are snob-
bish, aloof, cruel, rude, mean, malicious, sharp-tongued, phony,
unpredictable, and self-centered individuals (Matos and Faria
107–30; 134, 146–52). His songs often categorize unfaithfulness
as a female personality trait, arguing that such conduct causes
male resentment, suffering, and desire for revenge. In "Vingança"
("Vengeance"), one of Rodrigues's best-known songs, the lyricist
explains the causes of his emotional distress. He mentions that his
lover shamed and demoralized him by betraying him with a close
friend of his ("me fazer passar esta vergonha com um companheiro"). The lyric voice curses his former lover for having violated his
trust and, feels somewhat vindicated that, according to his friends'
accounts, she is living in misery and drinking heavily in public
spaces, probably feeling remorseful for what she did to him.[7] The
lyric voice believes justice had been done, as the following excerpt
from "Vingança" indicates:

> Eu gostei tanto, tanto
> Quando me contaram
> Que a encontraram
> Bebendo e chorando
> Na mesa de um bar.

> I was thrilled
> To learn
> That they found her
> Drinking and crying
> At a bar table.

In the lyrics of songs of the period, men do not invoke their
right to the "defense of honor" theory or suggest killing women
as in the lyrics of *capoeira* songs. They prefer to seek sympathy by
describing themselves as helpless victims of women's mean deceitful nature as the stanza from "Vingança" reveals:

> Ela há de rolar como as pedras
> Que rolam na estrada
> Sem ter nunca um cantinho de seu
> Para poder descansar.

> And she shall roll like rocks
> That roll on the road

Never having a place of her own
Upon which to rest.

Rodrigues reaches the end of the song with a pseudo-philo-sophical punch line created by the masterful use of the polyvalent nature and multifaceted aspects of the word *vergonha*. Throughout the lyrics of the song, he referred to all the negative meanings of *vergonha* (it can convey the idea of dishonor, disgrace, stigma, abashment, and mortification) which he attributes to the harm his unfaithful lover has caused him. In the last three lines, however, he resorts to another meaning of *vergonha* (*dignidade*; "dignity") to showcase his moral superiority. Those verses reveal that, even though the woman shamed him, as a greater human being, he still has dignity, a quality he inherited from his father.

O remorso talvez seja a causa
Do seu desespero
Me fazer passar esta vergonha
Com um companheiro
E a vergonha
É a herança maior
Que meu pai me deixou.

Remorse may be the reason
She feels so desperate
To put me through such shame
With a friend of mine
And self-respect
Is the greatest inheritance
That my father bequeathed to me

The convergence between the lyrics of *samba* and *capoeira* chants is not unusual. Lewis attributes the fact that *samba* and *capoeira* borrow songs back and forth from each other to the no-tion that they "may have had a common origin in slave *batuques*" (172). Composed by Geraldo Gomes and Harold Torres, and recorded by the group Namorados da Lua in 1946, the *samba-canção* "Se Essa Mulher Fosse Minha" ("If That Woman Were Mine"), became a staple *cantiga* in *rodas de capoeira*. The lyrics instruct that the most efficient way to control an insubordinate woman is by beating her up, rationing her food, and removing her from the *rodas de samba* and *capoeira* as if she were an animal being tamed, or a prisoner subject to torture:

Se essa mulher fosse minha,
Eu ensinava a viver.
Dava feijão com farinha
A semana inteirinha pra ela comer
Se essa mulher fosse minha,
Eu tirava da roda, já, já
Dava um surra nela
Que ela gritava: "chega!"
(Public domain; qtd. in Mestre Burguês)

If that woman were mine,
I would teach her how to live.
I would give her beans with flour
The entire week for her to eat.
If that woman was mine,
I would quickly take her from the *roda*
And would beat her up
Until she cried: "enough!"

A host of lyrics of *capoeira* songs also deride women, classifying them as unfaithful, treacherous, and wicked human beings who can easily destroy the opposite sex.[8] A good example is the use of the word *cobra,* an ambiguous term that can refer to a viper or a garden snake. It carries a positive connotation when it is used to describe someone who excels in a field of expertise or performs a task well (similar to "he is a killer," in English). Yet, it can also describe someone who is mean, despicable, or dangerous. A snake is the most celebrated animal in *capoeira* chants because it represents flexibility and can have a precise, sly, and lethal attack. Mestre Acordeon observes that "good *capoeristas* attack like a snake with a quick draw, sharp bite, and an even faster withdrawal" (158). When used as a metaphor for the game's makeup it connotes power, precision, and astuteness, in which case the word *cobra* has a positive meaning. The ambiguity of the term *cobra* is obvious in the metaphoric connotations it has in *capoeira* songs and how it is used to describe the players' attitudes and behaviors. When addressing male *capoeiristas,* the lyrics of songs use the word *cobra* to commend the players' agility in strategic movements of attack and defense, and their accurate and powerful strikes.

Capoeiristas also argue that they emulate the reptile's behavior, attacking only when threatened. They often compare their ability to hurt someone to a snake's venom, an imagery that also conveys the duality of the ritualistic elements of *capoeira* (especially if considered that a snake's poison can kill, but can also be used as an antidote to neutralize the poison).[9] This duplicity highlights a state of alertness and the dialectics of *capoeira*, a duality that Browning analyzes, in a different (but pertinent) context, as "the basic tension of the game—not a struggle *between* positive and negative forces but rather the exploration of what is negative, painful, or malicious *within* the ostensibly positive, whole, and benignant" (108; italics in the original). A case in point is "A Cobra Me Morde" ("The Snake Bites Me"), a chant that makes strategic comparisons between a snake's accurate airstrike and the players' flexibility, dexterity, and acuity. The lyrics also address the deceptive and malicious aspects of a *capoeira* circle in which a player can emulate the flexibility and the precision of the serpent (to play a *jogo bonito*) but can also embody the viper's aggressive conduct. *Capoeiristas* simultaneously praise the serpent's qualities (it is fearless and daring, attacking only in self-defense, or when it feels threatened), and fear the wicked and venomous snake, capable of causing harm. However, even when the song describes a snake as harmful, if the player is a male it does not refer to his lack of moral virtues or describe his character flaws. The song "A Cobra Me Morde" illustrates this point:

> Esta cobra te morde,
> Ô, sinhô São Bento! (Coro)
> Ôi, o bote da cobra,
> Ôi, a cobra mordeu,
> O veneno da cobra,
> Ô, a casca da cobra,
> Ô que cobra danada,
> Ô que cobra malvada.
> (Public domain; qtd. in Rego 94–95)

> This snake bites you
> Oh, Lord Saint Benedict! (Chorus)
> Oh, the snake's strike,
> Oh, the snake bit me,
> Oh, the snake's venom,
> Oh, the snake's skin,
> Oh, what a damned snake,
> Oh, what a mean snake.

In "O Calado É Vencedor" ("The Silent Man Wins"), the lyric voice takes a different stand and becomes substantially more accusatory, describing the "viper" as a greedy, selfish, and opportunistic female. The song compares women to serpents, describing them as evil, unscrupulous, and coldblooded individuals who can have a pernicious and malevolent influence on a man's life. Attempting to lend credibility to the thematic concept of the song, the lyricist resorts to biology to explain viciousness as a genetic blueprint ("tem sangue de peçanha"), and to justify depicting females as amoral and unscrupulous creatures who dishonor and shame men. The lyrics also resort to pseudo-theories of character development, that is, women's alleged propensity to squander (as in the phrase *ela deixa o rico na miséria*, which is also in dialogue with "Ai, Que Saudade da Amélia"):

> O calado é vencedor.
> Para quem juízo tem,
> Quem espera ser vingado
> Não roga praga em ninguém.
> A mulher é como a cobra,
> Tem sangue de "peçanha,"
> Deixa o rico na miséria,
> Deixa o pobre sem vergonha.
> (Public domain; qtd. in Bola Sete 117)

> The silent one wins.
> He who has wisdom, .
> He who hopes to be avenged
> Never curses anyone.
> A woman is like a venomous snake,
> With poisonous blood,
> She leaves a rich man penniless,
> And strips a poor guy of his dignity.

In *capoeira* circles, men are also depicted as astute human beings who can trick the police, dupe bullies, and fight bravely in war.[10] A number of *capoeira* songs also describe men who are annoyed by the fact that they have to work rather than laze, loaf, or play around, in other words, *vadiar*, which in the *capoeirista* vocabulary is synonymous with "to play." *Malandragem* or *vadiagem* ("idleness, indolence") also connote social parasitism, but in *capoeira* chants and in the lyrics of popular songs those words are stripped of any negative symbolism. Even when the lyrics refer to *malandragem* or *vadiagem* they do not sound derogatory. On the contrary, those personality traits become synonymous with the art of mastering evasion which represents the playfulness of *capoeira*. That is why the ambivalent concepts of *malandro* (rouge, con man, or smart person) and *vagabundo* (drifter, hobo, a laidback person) often define a *capoeira* player. *Malandro* is also characterized as a street-smart individual, a sort of a charming con man who plays small tricks, takes advantage of women and situations, outsmarts others, and is proud of it. The only character trait that could be mildly perceived as negative is that *malandros* dislike work and despise a humdrum life. *Malandragem* or *vadiagem* become metaphors of the game itself (in the case of *capoeira*), or reveal personality traits that carry the meaning of wisdom, prudence, and flexibility (both in *capoeira* and the MPB songbook).[11] Used in *capoeira*, or in the lyrics of songs, *malandragem* or *vadiagem* convey positive qualities when referring to men, describing them as smart and judicious.[12]

Similar to Rodrigues's songbook, numerous lyrics of *capoeira* songs depict men as emotional victims of women's deception. Female jealousy (and how it impacts the lives of men) is a topic frequently found both in the lyrics of *samba* and *capoeira*. To build their case, songwriters essentialize femaleness by describing jealousy as a feminine trait, a character flaw, and a plague that threatens the well-being of a man. While traditional songs condemn female jealousy, they do not seem to scrutinize the causes that lead women to be jealous or distrust men. They do not comment, for example, on male infidelity or masculine covetous attitudes. Jealousy is considered the worst feminine trait in part because conventional Brazilian culture glamorizes male infidelity. In the case of *capoeira* songs, Lewis believes that women are jealous because men can be unfaithful and promiscuous: "it relates somewhat to the tradition of male *capoeiristas* having many lovers and frequenting houses of prostitution" (173).[13]

The double standard is obvious. If a female is jealous, the song represents her as disproportionally disgraceful, incensed, and revolted. As for a jealous man, his jealousy constitutes a socially acceptable expression of emotion because women are deemed unreliable and cannot be trusted. Thus, when a jealous man is mentioned in a song, he is described in positive terms since male jealousy is interpreted as a case of zealous vigilance. The *corrido* "Casa de Palha É Palhoça" ("A House Made of Straw Is a Straw Hut") is a typical example of a song that sees female jealousy as a mental illness, so annoying and contemptible a condition that a man can only wish for her death. Such rhetorical rawness incites misogyny and insults women:

> Casa de palha é palhoça,
> Se eu fosse fogo queimava.
> Toda mulher ciumenta,
> Se eu fosse a morte matava.
> (Public domain; qtd. in Bola Sete 112)

> A straw house is a straw hut,
> If I were fire, I would burn.
> Every jealous woman,
> If I were death, I would kill her.

Unlike the lyrics of popular music, numerous *capoeira* songs make no attempt to hide their brutal intent. They teach cruelty and catalogue ways of controlling and disciplining "unruly" women more efficiently. Some *capoeira* songs prescribe punishments intended to penalize/teach women, and hopefully protect men against their jealousy. In the song "Quatro Coisas Neste Mundo" ("Four Things in This World") the lyricist offers a classical example. He curses women's alleged jealousy, analyzing it as an irritating character trait, and a sickening combination of possessiveness and obsessive suspicion which, in his opinion, can bedevil men, and drive them insane. The lyricist itemizes four things that can consume a man: a leaky roof, a bad horse, a whimpering child, and a jealous woman. To spare his fellow friends from having to deal with unfortunate circumstances, he teaches them how to remedy every one of those situations: retile the roof, sell the horse, rock the baby, and batter the woman:

> São quatro coisas no mundo
> que ao homem consome:
> uma casa pingando,
> um cavalo "chotão,"
> uma mulher ciumenta,
> um menino chorão.
> Tudo isso ele dá jeito

a casa ele retelha,
o cavalo "negoceia,"
o menino acalenta,
a mulher ciumenta cai na peia.
(Public domain; qtd. in Mestre Reinaldo)

There are four things in the world
that drain a man:
a leaky roof,
an old, unstable horse,
a jealous woman,
a crying kid.
He can fix them all:
he can re-tile the roof,
he can sell the horse,
he can quiet the kid,
and beat up the jealous woman.

The song "Xique-xique, Moçambira" also expresses scorn, contempt, and misogyny by inciting men to beat women up and discard them as undesirable objects. The references to the words that mean cacti (*moçambira, mandacaru, palmatória,* and *xique-xique*) infer a resemblance between a thorny cactus and a difficult woman. *Palmatória* also means ferule, a tool that was often used to punish recalcitrant slaves or misbehaving and inattentive school children. The double meaning of the word *palmatória* (cactus and ferule) can be interpreted as a reference to a "prickly" woman and suggests a method to control her.

Xique-xique, moçambira
Mandacaru, palmatória.
A mulher quando não presta,
O homem manda embora.
(Public domain; qtd. in Bola Sete 92)

Xique-xique, moçambira
Mandacaru, palmatória.
When the woman is useless,
The man sends her away.

Conversely, the songs that mention mothers and/or grand-mothers, or "unselfish" women, that is, females who never complain about *malandragem* or *vadiagem*, describe those females as a source of support and emotional security. Those songs, particularly the ones that invoke the Virgin Mary, showcase these types of women as the supreme representation of the maternal figure. One outstanding example in *capoeira* is the *cantiga* "Valha-me, Nossa Senhora" ("Help Me, Our Lady"), a public-domain song that portrays the saint as a symbol of divine power, a refuge, and a guiding source. To impart the idea that, in the past, the singer endured many shortcomings (in *capoeira* circles and in life), and would not like to revisit those moments, he pleads for Mary's divine protection to overcome his conflicts and distresses. To describe his feelings, the lyric voice provides a list of past and present metaphorical elements with which he associates himself in a *roda de capoeira*.

Valha-me, Nossa Senhora,
Mãe de Deus de Nazaré
A vaca mansa dá leite
A braba dá quando qué
A mansa dá sossegada
A braba levanta o pé
Já fui barco, fui navio
E hoje sou iscalé
Já fui linha de meada
Hoje sou carreté
Já fui menino, sou home
Só me falta ser mulhé
Valha-me, Nossa Senhora
Mãe de Deus de Nazaré.
(Public domain; qtd. in Bola Sete 98)

Help me, Our Lady,
Mother of God of Nazareth
The tamed cow gives milk
The untamed cow only when she wants
The tamed one gives quietly
The untamed one raises its foot
I was a boat, I was a ship
And today I am a small boat
I was thread of a skein
Today I am a spool
I was a boy, I am a man
The bottom line is to be a woman
Save me, Our Lady,
Mother of God of Nazareth.

The lyric voice compares the players to dairy cows, water transport, sewing materials, and categorizes them by gender (male/female). Such allegorical references allow him to elaborate on his different performances in *capoeira* circles. He places the cows/players in two contrastive categories: tamed/untamed, and feeble/feisty. As for him, when he played well, he felt like a ship; when he did not, he considered himself a small boat. Sometimes he performed so skillfully that he compared himself to a connecting thread; in contrast, when he played poorly, he resembled an empty spool. He also explains that when he performs well he feels like a man; his fear is that he could sink so low as to be compared to a woman. By suggesting an order of importance by the size of the objects (ship/small boat), the degree of usefulness or worth of the material (thread/spool), and the gender (man/woman), he establishes a hierarchy and endows the first element of the duality with the power to signify a positive outcome or constructive characteristic (ship/thread/man) and, by contrast, diminishes the importance of the second element (small boat/spool/woman). In some ways, the contrastive elements and the significance assigned to the first element of the duality reveal the "con of the text"[14] and highlight the privileged realms of the patriarchal context. The implication is that, even when he feels small, or empty, he still has a purpose and some degree of significance. To fall to the level of a woman, however, would strip him of any social or cultural standing. Thus, ironically, he invokes the Virgin Mary, seeking her assistance and protection, because she embodies the supreme representation of both the "anchor-woman" and the "compass-woman" as Oliven would argue.

In traditional *cantigas de capoeira*, male *capoeiristas* promote their dominance and purported supremacy by behaving in arrogant and condescending ways, or strategically positioning themselves at a vantage point in the *roda*. To illustrate that, Letícia Reis directed my attention to the fact that, time and again, some songs describe women as gossips and, by contrast, depict male players as reserved people who avoid hearsay and do not get involved in idle chatter (Reis, "Personal interview"). The public domain song "Conversa de Comadres" ("Midwives' Chat"), corroborates her opinion. Presented in the format of a dialogue, it offers a good example of references to females as slanderers and the double standards applied to gender dynamics in *capoeira* circles. The expression *conversa de comadres* carries an ambiguous meaning as it suggests female friendship and comradery, but also refers to a woman who has a "big mouth," namely, talks excessively, or likes intrigue and gossip, as the following verses illustrate:

> —Minha comadre, até você falou
> de mim, minha comadre?
> —Eu não falei, minha comadre.
> —Falou que eu vi, minha comadre.
> —Eu não vou na sua casa, minha comadre,
> —Pra você não ir na minha, minha comadre.
> —Você tem a boca grande, minha comadre,
> —Vai comer minha farinha, minha comadre.
> (Public domain; qtd. in Bola Sete 149)

> —My friend, even you gossiped
> about me, my friend?
> —I did not, my friend.
> —Yes you did, I saw you, my friend.
> —I don't visit you, my friend,
> —So that you won't visit me.
> —You have a big mouth, my friend,
> —You're going to eat my manioc flour, my friend.

"Conversa de Comadres" is presented in the form of a call-and-response dialogue, a technique in which both players identify each other as *comadre* (meant to be a pejorative word).[15] As discussed in Chapter Four, *capoeira* songs include a host of figures of speech (particularly metaphor, metonymy, inversion, irony, and symbol) that function as small linguistic puzzles, often to teach the rules of the game, or to present several layers of meaning that can be understood as an analysis of the game. In "Conversa de Comadres," the lyric voice uses some of these literary devices. For instance, he closes his argument by vowing to outsmart the other player (*vai comer minha farinha*). One of the verses refers to the player's *boca grande* ("big mouth") which is an allusion to the his "gluttony," that is, as a metaphor for the players's arrogance. It suggests that the competitor attempts to accomplish too much despite his lack of knowledge and experience, inferior physical dexterity, and other limitations. The opposing player refutes such display of power and attempted intimidation because he believes he is also daring and knowledgeable in the art of playing *capoeira* and could use *malícia* (*comer minha farinha*) to trick the opponent and gain control of the game. The allusion to "my house" also becomes a figurative reference to the physical and energetic space one secures in a *roda de capoeira*, and a warning for the opponent not to attempt to take him down or invade his personal space.

However, considering that, in "Conversa de Comadres," the lyric voice initiates the song with the complaint that the other has defamed him (*você até falou de mim*), his "big mouth" can also be interpreted as a reference to gossip. In this case, by calling the other player a *comadre*, he classifies him as someone who is prone to chattiness (a derogatory quality characteristically associated with women in traditional circles of Brazilian society). The reference to *comadre* (and not *compadre*, the masculine counterpart) alludes to a player who behaves like a "woman," that is, a man whose lack of experience, fragility, and vulnerability characterize him as an easy human target. The gender reference in "Conversa de Comadres" exemplifies a popular thought process in which identifying a man as a female can diminish him. In other words, the lyrics of the song imply that a *comadre*-player is an emasculated man whose effeminate characteristics render him inferior and justify the use of violence against him. The song's several layers of meaning contribute to vilify women whether by stereotyping them as gossipmongers, or by using the word *comadre* to assign an inferior characteristic to a player who is considered a weaker or less experienced *capoeirista*.

In the masculine discourse of conservative circles of Brazilian society, from an early age, males learn that to be respected in their communities as "real" men, they should express anger, rage, fury, resentment, and hatred. They could also retaliate, be impatient, show contempt, and use physical and psychological violence. It is also necessary to curb, mask, or suppress tender sentiments because those feelings and emotions are subjective, uncontrollable, and dangerous. They perceive sensibility and tenderness, for instance, as feminine characteristics that reveal a softer side of a person's character which, eventually, could be construed as weakness and vulnerability. A sensitive, caring, and thoughtful man would be branded a "sissy," or be considered an undervalued human being. Therefore, to be called a woman was the worst slur a man could receive in those social circles. Most traditional *cantigas de capoeira* adopt this point of view as exemplified in the song "Valha-me, Nossa Senhora."

The Verbal Codes of Difference

Male control over women's bodies is another theme commonly used in both *capoeira* songs and Brazilian popular music. The lyrics of those songs associate moral superiority with the power to impose and enforce norms of conduct. "Marina," a 1947 song by Dorival Caymmi illustrates well the processes of representation and normative concepts of femininity, gender dynamics, and relations of power. The poetic voice uses several rhetorical techniques to shame or intimidate a woman with whom he has a relationship, and to convince her to avoid using makeup and display a "natural" look. In developing his arguments, the lyric voice deploys various approaches to convince her to listen to him: first, he criticizes her; then threatens to leave her if she does not follow his demand; and finally resorts to using manipulative psychological devices to sugarcoat his intentions (he emphasizes their emotional bond and praises her looks) as the following verses reveal:

> Marina, morena
> Marina, você se pintou
> Marina, você faça tudo
> Mas faça um favor
> Não pinte esse rosto que eu gosto
> Que eu gosto e que é só meu
> Marina, você já é bonita
> Com o que Deus lhe deu
> Me aborreci, me zanguei
> Já não posso falar
> E quando me zango, Marina,
> Não sei perdoar
> Eu já desculpei tanta coisa
> Você não arranjava outro igual
> Desculpe, Marina morena,
> Mas estou de mal, de mal com você.

> Brunette Marina,
> Marina, you've put make up on
> Marina, you can do anything
> But do me a favor.
> Don't paint that face I love
> That I love, and is only mine.
> Marina, you're already pretty
> With what God gave you.
> I became so annoyed and angry

That I cannot even speak
and when I get upset, Marina,
I do not know how to forgive
I have forgiven so many things
You couldn't find a man like me.
I am sorry, brunette Marina,
But I am cross with you.

In a similar fashion, the *cantiga de capoeira* "A Mulher pra Ser Bonita" ("To Be a Beautiful Woman") reveals the type of tradition in which men feel entitled to interpret the rules of conduct for women and dictate the norms of how they should groom their bodies. Both Caymmi's "Marina" and "A Mulher pra Ser Bonita" emphasize the conservative parameters of the time which prescribed a "natural" look for virtuous women, while stigmatizing makeup as a seductive trick to which vulgar women resorted to attract sexual partners.

A mulher pra ser bonita, Paraná,
Não precisa se pintar, Paraná.
A pintura é do demônio, Paraná.
Beleza é Deus quem dá, Paraná.[16]

To be beautiful, Paraná,
A woman doesn't need makeup.
Makeup is an evil thing, Paraná.
Beauty comes from God, Paraná.

With the advent of *bossa nova*, several lyricists such as Vinicius de Moraes, Antônio Carlos Jobim, João Gilberto, and Carlinhos Lyra featured women in their verses in a more poetic and lyric style. One of the best-known songs of the period, "Garota de Ipanema" ("The Girl from Ipanema") by lyricists Moraes and Jobim, emphasizes beauty, sensuality, and the ephemeral traces of desire:

Olha que coisa mais linda
Mais cheia de graça
É ela, a menina que vem
E que passa
Num doce balanço
Aa caminho do mar
Moça do corpo dourado

Do sol de Ipanema
O seu balançado
É mais que um poema
É a coisa mais linda
Que eu já vi passar

Tall and tan
And young and lovely,
The girl from Ipanema
Goes walking
And when she passes,
Each one she passes goes "ah"
When she walks,
She's like a *samba*
That swings so cool
And sways so gentle
That when she passes
Each one she passes goes "ah"
And when she passes, each one goes "ah"
(Translation by Norman Gimbel)

Carlinhos Lyra's "Minha Namorada" ("My Girlfriend") offers another sample of the mindset of the 1960s. Embedded in the melodic softness and beauty of *bossa nova* songs was the concept of the "eternal feminine" and the misconstruction of possession as an endearing concept:

Se você quer ser minha namorada
Ah, que linda namorada
Você poderia ser.
Se quiser ser somente minha
Exatamente essa coisinha
Essa coisa toda minha
Que ninguém mais pode ser ...
Você tem que me fazer um juramento
De só ter um pensamento
Ser só minha até morrer ... (Lyra)[17]

If you want to be my sweetheart
Ah, what a beautiful sweetheart
You could be.
If you want to be just mine
Exactly this little thing
This thing all mine
That no one else could be ...

> You must avow
> To have only one thought
> To be mine until you die ...

In terms of their thematic content, the lyrics of some *capoeira* chants may also praise the "eternal feminine"; however, there are some dissimilarities in terms of how the feminine mystique is expressed. In *capoeira* songs, the language is often more direct and abrupt than in the lyrics of *bossa nova* songs. Traditional *capoeira* songs tend to boast about masculine power and ridicule or vilify women. A telling example is the *corrido* "Minha Mãe Sempre Dizia" ("My Mother Would Always Tell Me") in which the male poetic voice uses two strategies to accomplish his goal: he complains against women, describing them as the worst cause of men's distress and, paradoxically, invokes his own mother's "wisdom" to validate his argument. To dismiss his culpability, the lyric voice praises the essentialist virtues that motherhood conveys (abnegation and goodness, for instance), and highlights the acumen that he learned from his mother. Such a maneuver aspires to prevent the listener from passing judgment on him (he is purportedly repeating what he learned from his mother) and, by quoting her, he invokes her "wisdom" and highlights female complicity. Thus, he transfers any criticism about his behavior to the way she raised him.

> Minha mãe sempre dizia
> Que a mulher matava homem.
> Agora acabei de crer:
> Quando não mata, consome.
> (Public domain; qtd. in Bola Sete 101)

> My mother used to tell me
> That women could kill men.
> Now I've got proof of that:
> When they don't kill, they drain you.

While references to women in Brazilian popular music are common, the lyrics of Chico Buarque de Hollanda's stand out because he is the composer/lyricist of the post-1960s generation who best continued the tradition developed by Noel Rosa, Ataulfo Alves, and other songwriters of the 1930s and 1940s. He became widely popular as a songwriter and composer after his success with "A Banda," in 1966, when he won the Viola de Ouro prize

for best composition at the second MPB Festival. He has diversified his creative endeavors and also sustained his popularity as a
playwright and a novelist. The lyrics of his songs have been studied in Brazilian academic settings as poetry and he has received
highly esteemed prizes for his poetic erudition as a lyricist and a
novelist.[18] Perrone credits Hollanda's popularity to the fact that
"his musical appeal cuts across class lines" and "his songs are both
'popular' in their musical foundations and themes and 'erudite' in
their refinement and lyrical tones" (*Masters* 1). Even if the lyrics
of Hollanda's songs present a poetic sophistication rarely found
in Brazilian Popular Music, thematically speaking, a substantial
number of his songs describe females in ways remarkably similar
to the images created in songs of the first four decades of the
twentieth century. In discussing the lyrics of *sambas* composed
in that period, Manoel Tosta Berlinck lists three types of women
often found in that repertoire of songs: *domésticas* (females who
are confined to the private space of their homes); *piranhas* (those
who are promiscuous and mingle in masculine public spaces); and
oníricas (the idealized type of females). This same categorization
can be applied to describe women in Hollanda's songbook. The
difference between his songs and those of his predecessors is that,
in describing women who are considered *piranhas*, quite often the
lyric voice sympathizes with their trials and tribulations.

Similar to the songs of the 1930s and 1940s, Hollanda's
songbook also describes females who transgress the social order, seek erotic pleasure during *carnaval* ("Ela Desatinou"; "She
Acted Wildly"), or who are sexy *sambistas* ("Morena de Angola";
"Angolan Brown Woman"). In tandem with the thematic choices
of his predecessors, several of his lyrics address separation and
unrequited love. In those cases, he depicts men as generous partners who are unattached to material possessions. In "Trocando in
Miúdos" ("To Put It Simply"), for instance, the lyric voice tells his
female companion, when they are breaking up, that she can take
anything she wants as long as she leaves his two favorite possessions: a musical record by Noel Rosa and a book by Pablo Neruda.
There are also women who leave without an explanation, abandoning their children, and causing great pain (as in "Madalena Foi
Pro Mar"; "Madalena Went Off to Sea").

To make a case that Hollanda is not the only lyricist of his
generation to accuse women of being difficult or exploiting men,

Adélia Bezerra de Meneses cites Caetano Veloso's sexist statement that "no one can figure out what women want" (15). Nonetheless, as she discusses, Hollanda is the songwriter/composer of his generation who paid more attention to women, representing them in a variety of ways, some of which impart a very traditional masculine perception of the "eternal feminine," or the "feminine mystique" (Meneses 15–16). She also underlines another thematic characteristic of his songs: how nagging females—especially those who despise *malandragem* and *vadiagem*—constantly pester men to find some work. This theme seems plucked from the *samba-canção* songbook of the 1930s and 1940s.[19] Similar to the characterization of women in *capoeira* chants and popular songs from the 1930s and 1940s, in Hollanda's repertoire of songs, jealous female characters are described as unpredictable and controlling individuals who want to impose order in their men's lives by convincing them to abandon their bohemian lifestyle.[20] A case in point is Hollanda's 1967 song, "Logo Eu" ("Why Me?"), in which the lyric voice complains about his companion:

> Essa morena quer me transtornar
> Me condena
> Me faz cena
> Diz que já me viu na esquina
> A namorar.
> (Vol. II)

> This brunette woman is driving me insane
> She accuses me
> Makes scenes
> Says she saw me around the corner
> Flirting.

"Logo Eu" is the prototype of a number of songs in Hollanda's repertoire that addresses quotidian topics and male entrapment. It describes an irritating woman who victimizes her companion by constantly telling him to act more responsibly. For the lyric voice, married life equals confinement and represents a dull routine of obligations and commitments (the prison-house of marriage, so to speak). In his complaints, the lyric voice expresses his concerns that his companion may victimize him even further by depriving him of the company of his best friends.

Diz que é pra eu deixar de férias
Pra largar a batucada
E pra pensar em coisas sérias
E qualquer dia
Ela ainda vem pedir, aposto
Pra eu deixar a companhia
Dos amigos que mais gosto.

She tells me to drop the vacation mode
Stop playing *samba*
And think of more serious things
And one of these days
I can bet she will ask me
To stop seeing
My best friends.

To stress his point of view and present an additional rationale in his defense, the lyric voice skillfully maneuvers the opinion in his favor and pleads for sympathy. He makes his case by revealing that he is not only a goodhearted and responsible individual, but also a hard-working man, a good provider, and a stellar amorous companion who fulfills his professional and marital obligations. In light of the fact that his companion does not seem to recognize any of those qualities, he strives to gain the listener's sympathy by expressing his lament:

Logo eu, bom indivíduo
Cumpridor fiel e assíduo
Dos deveres do meu lar
Logo eu, bom funcionário
Cumpridor dos meus horários
Um amor quase exemplar
À minha amada
E tem mais isso
Estou cansado quando chego
Pego extra no serviço
Quero um pouco de sossego
Mas não contente
Ela me acorda reclamando
Me despacha pro batente
E fica em casa descansando.

> Why me, a good fellow
> Faithful and timely
> In keeping up with my obligations
> Why me, such a good worker
> Always keeping my schedule
> An almost exemplary love
> For my beloved woman
> And there is more
> I am tired when I arrive home
> I do overtime at work
> I want some peace
> But unsatisfied
> She wakes me up
> And sends me back to work
> While she rests at home.

In 1971, Hollanda launched "Cotidiano" ("Daily Life") as part of his album *Construção*. Its opening verse attests to the monotony of domestic life and sets the tone for why the lyric voice wants change: *Todo dia ela faz tudo sempre igual* ("Every day she does it the same way"). The song was so popular that it was selected as the opening soundtrack of Edi Lima's *telenovela*, *Como Salvar Meu Casamento* ("*How to Save My Marriage*"). The *telenovela* addressed the efforts a female character makes to keep her twenty-three-year marriage alive when her husband begins a love affair with a younger woman because he is tired of the domestic routine. Thus, Hollanda's repertoire includes a wide range of songs that perceive women in a domestic setting—cooking, taking care of a man, attempting to make him go to work, but also placing him in an environment that suffocates and paralyzes him emotionally. He also describes women who behave frantically when abandoned (as in "Pedaço de Mim"; "A Part of Me"), or who seem to have an infinite capacity to sit home and wait for men to return from their travels or escapades.

Composed in 1976, the song "Mulheres de Atenas" ("Athenian Women") epitomizes his perception of domesticity, very much in sync with views of older tunes in Brazilian popular music. The opening verse, also used as a refrain, suggests that females should take the Athenian model to heart: *Mirem-se no exemplo daquelas mulheres de Atenas*. And then, the lyric voice characterizes the reasons why they should serve as prototypes: Athenian women live for their husbands (*Vivem pros seus maridos*); they do not cry when afflicted (*Quando fustigadas não choram*); and, they stay home embroidering while waiting for the husbands to return from their conquering adventures (*Sofrem por seus maridos / Quando eles embarcam, soldados / Elas tecem longos bordados*). In some sense, "Mulheres de Atenas" reveals not only a close intertextual dialogue with Penelope's "stellar" behavior (in Homer's *Odyssey*), but also with Ataulfo Alves's "Ai, Que Saudades da Amélia," both of whom are women who represent the model of virtue that such a vision of ideal womanhood characterizes.

Hollanda's fourth collection, launched in 1970, included "Essa Moça Tá Diferente" ("This Young Woman Has Changed"), a song that summarizes the cultural transformations taking place in Brazilian society. Perrone refers to the songwriter's use of slang "to make ironic observations about the modernization of popular music and about the shifts in cultural values that affected him" (10). Even though this song exemplifies the changes that began taking shape in the 1970s in Brazil, and got into full swing in the 1980s, it also resembles a lament for bygone times. The poetic voice complains that the young woman has displayed non-conforming behavior by adopting modern trends and new musical choices.

> Essa moça tá diferente
> Está pra lá de pra frente
> Está me passando pra trás
> Essa moça tá decidida
> A se supermodernizar
> Ela só samba escondida
> Que é pra ninguém reparar.
> (Vol. IV)

> This young woman is acting strange
> She is quite trendy
> She is leaving me behind
> She is determined
> To become ultramodern
> She only dances *samba* secretly
> So that no one sees it.

The lyricist also establishes a contrast between the man who embodies a romantic type and believes in the power of rhymes and gives roses to win a woman's heart, and the young woman who seems determined to change her lifestyle and social parameters.

The male voice uses all his skills to win her back, but she remains unimpressed by his efforts and romantic overture:

> Eu cultivo rosas e rimas
> Achando que é muito bom
> Ela me olha de cima
> E vai desinventar o som.
> Faço-lhe um concerto de flauta
> E não lhe desperto emoção
> Ela quer ver o astronauta
> Descer na televisão
>
> Essa moça é a tal da janela
> Que eu me cansei de cantar
> E agora está só na dela
> Botando só pra quebrar.
>
> I cultivate roses and rhymes
> Thinking that it is so nice
> She looks down on me
> And goes to invent new sounds.
> I do a flute concert for her,
> And I do not raise any emotions in her
> She wants to see the astronauts on television
> landing on the moon.
>
> This is the young woman
> That I got tired of singing
> And now she is so full of herself
> Just rock and rolling.

In synchrony with the discourse of the 1930s and 1940s, quite often Hollanda confines the women of his songs to the private space of the house. Restricted to the safety of the domestic environment, they have a glimpse of the outside world from the opening of a window ("Ela e Sua Janela," "Januária," and "Carolina" are some other examples). Such a representation of women's domesticity finds a counterpart in the novelistic tradition of the nineteenth century and beginning of the twentieth century. On a positive note, the lyric voice (representing the lyricist) seems to be exercising a degree of self-criticism when he acknowledges that he has consistently described women framed by a window. The song also signals the change in perception regarding private and public spaces in Brazil to which DaMatta refers as *o mundo da casa* ("the realm of home"), and *o mundo da rua* ("the realm of the street") as he outlines the fundamental spatial differences that marked the gender codes for so long in Brazil (*O Que* 23). For DaMatta, these two spaces divided Brazilian social life. While the street was considered a masculine space (stressful, dangerous, and full of temptation), home was the place where there was calm and security, and represented moral fortitude (*O Que* 23–25). In recognizing the social changes that had taken place, the lyricist may also be acknowledging that the generation of women of the 1970s, and beyond, no longer wanted to be framed by windows, or be subjected to physical or social confining spaces. They do not want to experience the world vicariously and have tiny windows of opportunity. The generation of "ultramodern" women to which he refers in "Essa Moça Tá Diferente" prefers to experience the outside world fully and unrestrictedly.

Even though Hollanda composed most of his songs that address women and their lifestyles in the period between the 1960s to the 1980s, as Janaína de Assis Rufino underscores, he never abandoned the subject entirely (69). A case in point is the 2017 album *Caravanas*, which he released after a six-year hiatus in his musical career. In the lead song ("Tua Cantiga"; "Your Song"), a male voice tells the object of his infatuation that he would do anything for her. The tiniest of her sighs would get him to her side to comfort her (*Basta dar um suspiro / Que eu vou ligeiro te consolar*). If she wanted, he would follow her anywhere (*Deixa cair um lenço / Que eu te alcanço em qualquer lugar*). He would even leave his wife and children to follow her on his knees (*Largo mulher e filhos / E de joelhos vou te seguir*). This is an example of the lyrics of a song that romanticize male infidelity by focusing on his burning passion. While the poetic stretches, tensions, and absolute precision of wording of his verses are captivating, as far as his views on women, the lyricist seems stuck in the past.

There is no qualm that Hollanda and Veloso are highly sophisticated songwriters and innovators of Brazilian Popular Music whose talents are greatly appreciated at home and abroad. Perrone, for instance, considers Veloso to be "the most imaginative, versatile, and controversial popular composer" of his generation who "is known as the poet laureate of Brazilian song and as a 'trend setter' [whose] importance in Brazil can be compared with that

of Bob Dylan and John Lennon in the Anglo-American sphere"
(*Masters* 47). In his praise for Hollanda's works as a composer and
a poet-songwriter, Perrone mentions "the careful manipulation of
sound effects, subtlety of imagery and idea, reliance on metaphor
and symbol, and depth of perception of emotional, psychological,
and social phenomena" (*Masters* 1). Therefore, when the two of
them joined forces in 1972 to perform at a live show and produce
an album, they received high acclaim. In *Chico e Caetano Juntos*,
the two of them sang a version of one of Veloso's songs, "Você Não
entende Nada" ("You Don't Understand a Thing") which was followed by Hollanda's song "Cotidiano" ("Quotidian Life"), probably because they shared a similar theme. Veloso's song expresses
the monotony of married life (from a man's point of view):

> Quando chego em casa
> Nada me consola
> Lágrimas nos olhos
> De cortar cebola
> Você é tão bonita
> Você traz a Coca-Cola, eu tomo
> Você põe a mesa
> Eu como, eu como, eu como, eu como
> Você tem que entender
> Que eu quero é correr mundo
> Eu quero é ir embora.

> When I get home
> Nothing comforts me
> Watery eyes
> From cutting onions
> You're so pretty
> You bring a Coke, I drink
> You set the table
> I eat, I eat, I eat, I eat
> You have to understand
> That I want to travel the world
> I want to go away.

In the vocal rendition of the song "Você Não Entende Nada,"
Hollanda and Veloso changed the normal pause in two of the
verses to stress the gastronomic-sexual association so common
in Brazil. "*Eu como, eu como, eu como, eu como / Você tem que
entender*" becomes "*Eu como, eu como, eu como, eu como você /*

Tem que entender." The cultural ambiguity is also expressed in the grammatical ambivalence they created because, in the context of that rendition of the song, *você* was used both as the subject and object of the sentences at stake. By repeating the word *como* and placing an emphatic pause after the word *você*, they transmuted the subject (the woman) into their coveted object of desire (woman-food-sex). By changing the status of the verb *comer* from an intransitive verb (*eu como*; "I eat") to the category of a transitive verb (*eu como você*; "I eat you") they achieved the desirable effect of suggesting intercourse and stressing gender domination. The evidence that both artists intended to conflate the meanings of eating and having sex can also be confirmed by watching a recording of the live show in which they exchanged looks and smiles right before the punch line, which drew loud cheers from the crowd. Although a clever maneuver to connect with their fans, the intentionality of the sexist pun seems disconcerting when analyzed from a critical perspective.

Therefore, even politically liberal and intellectually sophisticated men in Brazil do not escape the pervasively sexist constraints of Brazilian culture that relate women to gastronomic images and constrict men to the confinement of their chauvinist ideologies. As the live performance of the song "Você Não Entende Nada" reveals, even the most innovative composers and songwriters in Brazil—whose creative endeavors, intellectual acumen, progressive political views, and sensitive analyses of race and class are admired nationwide and internationally—are not immune to the deep-seated disregard for gender equality in Brazilian culture. In this sense, their opinions about women are similar to the views the male characters express in the novels written by female authors in the first decades of the twentieth century (as analyzed in Chapter One). The metaphoric association between eating and having sex as presented in the rendition of the song "Você Não Entende Nada" echoes the gastronomic-sexual connections also found in popular culture and literature (as discussed in Chapter Two).

But Hollanda and Veloso are not alone. Numerous other songs in different musical genres and periods have also denigrated women, especially by objectifying them as male possessions, making explicit sexual references to them, or describing them as foodstuff. In the 1980s, when Brazil was undergoing substantial political, cultural, and social changes (including a robust feminist movement),

Alceu Valença composed and recorded "Morena Tropicana" (a play on words that meant "Tropical Sugar Cane Brunette") in which he compares a woman's body to the juicy tropical fruits of Northeast Brazil. Even though the song's sexual discursivity establishes an image of the young woman who is prized as an object of visual and gustative pleasure, such a derogatory opinion of women was not a roadblock to the song's commercial success. The expressive invitation for a sexual encounter is embedded in the metaphors of savoring the *morena*'s body-fruit-honey. The reference to *fruta de vez* (an almost ripened fruit) infers that the *morena tropicana* is underage. Valença's comparisons also resemble the culinary associations/sexual connotations present in Brazilian literature, televised performances, and other lyrics of songs discussed in the previous chapters:

> Da manga rosa
> Quero gosto e sumo
> Melão maduro, sapoti, juá
> Jaboticaba, teu olhar noturno
> Beijo travoso de umbu cajá
> Pele macia, Ai! Carne de caju!
> Saliva doce, doce mel,
> Mel de uruçu
> Linda morena
> Fruta de vez temporana
> Caldo de cana caiana
> Vem me desfrutar!
> Morena Tropicana
> Eu quero teu sabor (...)
> Vou te desfrutar!

> From the rose mango
> I want taste and juice
> Ripe melon, sapoti, juá
> *Jaboticaba*, your night eyes
> A bitter kiss like *umbu cajá*
> Soft skin, Ah! Cashew pulp!
> Sweet saliva, sweet honey,
> *Uruçu* bee honey
> Beautiful brunnette
> A fruit not quite ripened
> Juice from the caiana sugar cane
> Come enjoy me!
> Tropicana brunette

I want to taste you (...)
I am going to savor you.

As referenced throughout this study, regardless of age, race, and social class, Brazilian men share similar views regarding gender. Even if composers of *samba, bossa nova,* and MPB have different styles and methods of composition, they impart analogous perceptions when women are the thematic subjects of their songs. For instance, the iconic Afro-Brazilian composer and lyricist, Martinho da Vila, represents the working-class neighborhood of Vila Isabel, a community nestled in the outskirts of Rio de Janeiro. His 1975 *samba* hit, "Você Não Passa de uma Mulher" ("You Are Nothing but a Woman"), can give some insights into the mentality of the time. The misogynist list of arguments, descriptions, and perceptions about womanhood listed in "Você Não Passa de uma Mulher" reveals a bitter compilation of derogatory terms that berate women of all ages, social class, or intellectual expertise. In some ways, the list of traits he compiles resembles the songs of the 1930s and 1940s, and the traditional *cantigas de capoeira.* The difference is that, in other songs, the lyricists usually present the reasons why they are complaining about women (even if their complaints seem to be skewed perceptions of the facts), while in "Você Não Passa de uma Mulher," there is no explanation as to why women are considered lazy, deceitful, unfaithful, and unreliable beings. The lyric voice of Vila's song fits the profile of a man who shows contempt, prejudice, and hostility for all kinds of women, and belittles and objectifies females for the sake of disenfranchising them:

Olha a moça inteligente,
Que tem no batente
O trabalho mental.
QI elevado e pós-graduada
Psicanalizada, intelectual
Vive à procura de um mito,
Pois não se adapta
A um tipo qualquer.
Já fiz seu retrato:
Apesar do estudo,
Você não passa de uma mulher.

> Look at the intelligent girl,
> Whose job requires
> Mental work.
> A high IQ and graduate studies,
> Psychoanalyzed and intellectual
> In search of a myth,
> Because you do not adapt
> To anyone.
> I've pictured you:
> Despite your studies,
> You are nothing but a woman.

In making his argument that women belong to an inferior class of people, the lyricist uses the refrain ("Você não passa de uma mulher") as a closing argument to each and every category he presents. For him, they are foodstuff, gustative items to be savored, objects of sexual desire, and individuals subjected to the caste system of womanhood. According to him, even when they are dainty, rich, pretty, and/or intelligent, and regardless of their accomplishments, they still are considered "lesser beings" because of their gender.

> Mulher preguiçosa,
> Mulher tão dengosa, mulher
> Refrão: Você não passa de uma mulher.
> Mulher tão bacana e
> Cheia de grana, mulher
> Olha que moça bonita!

> Lazy woman,
> Such a dainty woman.
> Refrain: You are nothing but a woman
> A woman so splendid and
> Loaded with money, woman.
> What a beautiful young woman!

For the lyric voice, a "real" woman is someone who cooks, cleans, and takes care of him (which thematically resembles the songs of the 1930s and 1940s and some of Hollanda's songs). The most disturbing parts of his lyrics are the ones in which he addresses young women and girls and talks about savoring their bodies as gastronomic delicacies. Vila's chauvinistic assessments are in sync with ideological precepts and belief systems codified in Brazilian culture that have institutionalized sexism and mistrust for women. They derive from religious views, philosophical concepts, legal structures, and pseudo-scientific studies.

> Olhar dispersivo,
> anquinhas maneiras.
> Um prato feitinho
> pra garfo e colher.
> Menina-moça também é mulher
> Pra ficar comigo
> Tem que ser mulher (tem, mulher).
> Fazer meu almoço e
> Também meu café (só mulher).

> A scattered look
> hips easy to be handled.
> A plate ready to be eaten
> with fork and spoon.
> Teenagers are also women
> To be with me
> You must be a woman (you must, woman).
> Prepare my lunch and
> Also my coffee (only a woman).

It seems that the glorification of sexual violence is a recurrent theme in Brazilian Popular Musc in this new millennium. The 2015 song, "Turbinada" ("Turbocharged") by the composers Zé Ricardo e Thiago, is a good example that the lyrics of songs have grown more sexualized even in the trendy genre of *música sertaneja* or *sertanejo* (a style that originated in rural Brazil and has increasingly grown in popularity since the 1990s).

> À noite bombando,
> Ela chega arrasando
> Não vai prestar.
> Eu chamei meu amigo
> E disse pra ele
> Essa que eu vou pegar!
> Quando eu vi,
> Eu já tava puxando seu braço
> E tome, tome amasso
> Meu Deus do Céu!
> Nossa! Eu acho ela top
> Nossa! Eu acho ela boa demais

Tá doido, é a mais gostosa
Turbinada na frente e atrás
Ah, se eu pegar você e, tum
Vai me prometer, hum hum
Que vai ser só minha.

At night she is a crowd pleaser
She makes a killer arrival
This is not going to be good.
I called my friend
And I told him
I am going to grab that one!
When I realized,
I was already pulling her arm
And making out
My heavenly God!
Wow! I find her the best
Wow! She's extremely sexy
My goodness, she is the sexiest
She had a front and back makeover.
Ah, if I catch you and, tum
You are going to promise me, hum hum
That you are going to be only mine.

The references to grabbing, pulling, and the comparison between a woman and a turbocharged engine reveals the lyricists's contempt for females. Since Zé Ricardo e Thiago are quite popular musicians, the song also serves as a sample of how females continue to be considered mere objects of masculine lust. But considering that the composers are also very popular with females, those fans contribute to their own domination and disrespect, as Bourdieu would suggest. Their complacency and acceptance of the status quo are also their complicity.

In the new millennium, lyricists seldom refer to women as fruits to be savored, or suggest they should be home preparing breakfast, or waiting for men with "sugar and affection." However, the gender dynamics have not changed much. The sexualized lyrics of the songs, references to violence, and the erotic dance movements of *baile funks* are as sexist and disturbing as the references to women in Vila's "Você Não Passa de uma Mulher." In this aspect, the lyrics of *capoeira* chants diverge from the songbook of contemporary Brazilian popular music. Contrary to the repertoire of Brazilian popular songs whose lyrics seem to have grown more sexualized, new *capoeira* songs are significantly more sensitive to gender discrimination, and mostly make historical references, contextualize *capoeira* as an art form, or praise *mestres* and Afro-derived cultural practices. When contemporary *capoeira* songs refer to women, it is to acknowledge their participation in the *roda* or, if there are references to love affairs, they do not sound distasteful or misogynistic. Even though older *capoeira* songs continue to be sung, new generations of *capoeiristas* are gradually changing the lyrics of chants.

Several *cantigas de capoeira* also make sexual references to women, especially those songs borrowed from the *samba* repertoire; however, as Lewis contends, those references are often perceived as a joking interplay and not taken too seriously (175). A most conspicuous example he offers is the song "Dona Maria do Caboatá,"[21] from which he quotes two verses, one of which tenders a male player inviting a woman to take off her skirt and go to bed with him ("tira a saia e vamos deitar"). However, even when there are sexual references in *cantigas de capoeira*, the language of those songs does not advocate sexual harassment or other types of sexual mistreatment. While contemporary styles of Brazilian songs have increasingly become more sexualized and violent in tone, the opposite has happened in *rodas de capoeira* in which blatantly erotic references are not common (when the lyrics of a song refer to an amorous encounter it usually issues an invitation to a *morena* to join the men in bed).

The *Bonafide* Place and Space of Women in *Capoeira* Chants

Enlightened *mestres*, *contra-mestres*, and *professores* have exercised caution in selecting chants for their *rodas*, avoiding those that denigrate the female image or boast chauvinistic attitudes. The majority of progressive *capoeiristas* believe that pejorative *cantigas* are out of tune with the contemporary cultural environment, arguing that such lyrics contradict the philosophical principles of *capoeira* which usually preach inclusion and equality: *Capoeira é pra homem, criança e mulher. Só não aprende quem não quer* ("*Capoeira* is for men, children and women. Anyone willing to learn can do so").[22] The traditional version of the song "Ilha de Maré" ("Tide Island") is a good example of how men and women have changed the lyrics of some *capoeira* chants to correct and/

or curb attitudes of superiority as far as gender references are concerned. In the second stanza of the original version, the poetic voice describes the functions that males have in a *roda de capoeira*, and in life, and contrasts them with the spatial and ideological position that women occupy in *capoeira* and society. The song uses the metaphors of a musical instrument (tambourine) and singing and clapping to establish the gender roles; namely, males play tambourine and form part of the inner circle (meaning that they have a central position in the *roda*), while females sing and clap, and occupy a peripheral area (the outer loop), a space from which they can watch the development of the *roda*.

> Minha mãe 'tá me chamando,
> Oh! Que vida de mulher!
> Quem toca pandeiro é homem,
> Quem bate palmas é mulher.[23]

> My mother's calling me,
> Oh! What a woman's life!
> Men play tambourine,
> Women clap their hands.

Lewis refers to this song to offer his testimony of gender bias in *rodas de capoeira* by describing his personal experience in Bahia in the 1980s when he was warned not to clap because that was a woman's role (174). Although the song continues to be intoned in *capoeira* circles and some stereotypes still seem to go unquestioned, there are signs of constructive changes. A case in point is how Mestre Bola Sete has rewritten "Ilha da Maré" to omit the reference to women singing and clapping hands, and men playing the tambourine.

> Minha mãe 'tá me chamando,
> Oh! Que vida de mulher!
> Capoeira tá na roda
> Só vou lá quando puder.
> (Public domain; qtd. in Bola Sete 90)

> My mother's calling me,
> Oh! What a woman's life!
> The capoeirista is playing now
> I will only go there when I can.

The quantitative and qualitative presence of women in *capoeira* has contributed to alter the male/female rapport in the *roda*. Females have questioned the narrowmindedness and prejudice in some conventional lyrics, and have challenged the old parameters by refusing to sing certain songs, amending or upgrading the lyrics of the traditional tunes, and/or writing their own chants. In this new environment, practitioners of *capoeira* reexamine the traditional songs that vilify women and replace them with new *ladainhas*, *chulas*, and *corridos*. The *corrido* "Dendê de Aro Amarelo" ("Yellow Palm Oil") illustrates how women have put certain values in check by changing the phrasing to acknowledge their presence as players in the *rodas*. The original lyrics state:

> Oi dendê, oi dendê,
> Dendê de aro amarelo
> Vou dizer a dendê:
> "Sou homem, não sou mulher."
> (Public domain; qtd. in Bola Sete 142)

> Hi, palm oil, palm oil
> Yellow palm oil
> I am going to tell palm oil
> "I am a man, not a woman."

A sample of the rewritten version reverses the gender order of the last verse: "*Eu sou mulher / Não sou homem*" ("I am a woman / not a man"). However, because such an inversion simply transposes the gender bias and does not change hierarchical roles, to make it more inclusive, Mestra Janja teaches her students to sing the last sentence as follows: "*Tem homem, tem mulher*" ("There are men and women in *rodas de capoeira*").

One of the most discussed topics in the new *cantigas* is the presence of women in *capoeira* as players, and their singing *ladainhas* or playing the *berimbau*. Noticing that women would not sing *ladainhas* in the *rodas* she attended in Brazil, Carolina Soares decided to compose *ladainhas* and other types of *cantigas*. Although she is not a *capoeirista*, as a musician, she has contributed to highlight the positive image of women in the *capoeira* environment by recording several songs on the topic, singing frequently at *rodas* and *batizados*, and participating in similar events. Soares's efforts to write new songs and publicize the active presence of women in *rodas* have contributed in a positive way to open more space for them, and improve their image in *capoeira* circles. By showcasing the lively contribution that female *capoeiristas* have given as performers, teachers, and instrumentalists, she has questioned the belief that women are frills, tokens, or symbolic representations. A case in point is the *ladainha* "Mulher na Roda" ("A Woman in the *Roda*") which she composed and recorded in São Paulo as part of her repertoire of songs that stress *capoeira*'s cultural importance. By making a clear reference to the traditional version of the song "Ilha da Maré," "Mulher na Roda" uses intertextual references to challenge traditional concepts and highlight women's triumphs and the positive changes that have taken place in *capoeira* circles.

Coro: Mulher na Roda
Não é pra enfeitar
Mulher na roda
É pra ensinar
Ê, ela treina com destreza
E respeita o educador
Mostrando delicadeza
E também o seu valor
Já passou aquele tempo
Que era só bater pandeiro.
Bater palma e cantar coro
Pra poder ganhar terreno.
Não precisa de espaço
Pois ela já conquistou.
Hoje cantar bem na roda
Não é só pra cantador.

Chorus: A woman in the *roda*
Is not a frill
Women teach
In the *capoeira* circle
She trains with dexterity
And respects the teacher
Showing softness
But also her value.
It's a bygone time when
She should only play tambourine,
Clap hands and sing in the chorus
To make some headway.
She no longer needs space
Because she's already conquered it.
Nowadays, to sing well in the roda
Is not just for male singers.

Considering *capoeira*'s development, its various phases, styles, and international reach, it is encouraging to see that reassuring transformations have already taken shape both in the representation of women in songs and in the attitudes of male *capoeiristas*. A significant number of males and females have written new songs, many of which question double standards and ideological precepts. Such questioning has promoted a greater equilibrium between masculine and feminine energy in the *rodas de capoeira*. In such an environment, the traditional songs dishonoring or discriminating against women have become increasingly dissonant. A good example is the *ladainha* "Balança, Roseira" ("Swing, Rosebush") which was composed by male and female *capoeiristas* in Belém do Pará. Mestre Abil wrote the first stanza and the refrain, while his female students from the Movimento Capoeira Mulher (MCM) penned the other stanzas (Silva 126). The song highlights important changes, including female participation in writing the *ladainha*. In addition, as underscored in the following selected stanzas, the cooperative venture between a *mestre* and his female students took place in Belém, which reveals the steady increase in number and accomplishments of women in *capoeira* outside the traditional circles of Bahia, Rio de Janeiro, and São Paulo. "Balança, Roseira" reveals that contemporary female *capoeiristas* have put a process of cultural mediation in place by establishing a better interaction and negotiating a sound space for themselves inside and outside *capoeira* circles.

> A mulher na capoeira
> É bonita de se vê
> Vou pegar meu berimbau
> Vou tocar só pra você.
> O que meu mestre me ensinou
> Eu agora vou fazer
> Com mandinga e malícia
> Jogo de dentro pra valer.
>
> Refrão: Balança roseira
> Tem mulher na capoeira
> Balança a roseira
> Ela é valente, ela é guerreira.
> [...]
> Hoje é dia de festa
> E as meninas vão jogar
> Conquistando seu espaço
> Na capoeira do Pará.

A woman in *capoeira*
Is beautiful to watch
I'll go get my *berimbau*
Just to play for you.
What my mestre taught me
I am going to do now
With mandinga and malícia
Inside game for real.

Refrain: Swing, rosebush
There are women in *capoeira*
Swing, rose bush
She is valiant, she's a warrior.
[...]
Today is a festive day
Young women are going to play
Conquering their space
In Pará's *capoeira*.

In "Ela Joga Capoeira" ("She Plays *Capoeira*"), a *ladainha* composed by Mestre Acordeon and Mestra Suelly (and recorded by her), there is also an emphasis on the presence and active participation of women in *rodas de capoeira*. Set in Salvador, the song makes references to elements of Bahian culture; namely, the lagoon where washer women and *capoeiristas* would gather (Lagoa do Abaeté), Maria Doze Homens (an allegedly renowned *capoeirista* from Bahia), Candomblé, and Mestres Bimba and Pastinha (the two major pillars of *capoeira*'s foundation). The lyricists also recycle some concepts about the philosophy and history of *capoeira* to add cultural and thematic weight to their song. Another important fact is that Mestre Acordeon and Mestra Suelly joined forces to remind their followers that the great *mestres* believed *capoeira* should be an all-inclusive game.

Na Lagoa do Abaeté
Ora meu Deus (Refrão)
Encontrei Dona Sinhá
Tava lavando o abadá
Pra dançá no Candomblé.
Ela joga capoeira,
Todos sabem como é
Joga homem e menino

E também joga mulher.
Mestre Pastinha falou
E Mestre Bimba confirmou
Todos podem aprender
General também doutor.
Sou mulher, eu sou Maria,
Capoeira de valor
Doze Homems me chamavam,
É melhor saber quem sou, camará.

In Abaeté Lagoon
Praise be God (Refrain)
I found Dona Sinhá
Washing her abada
To dance in Candomblé.
She plays *capoeira*,
Everyone knows how it is
Men and children play
And so do women.
Said Mestre Pastinha
And Mestre Bimba confirmed
Everyone can learn (praise be God)
Generals and doctors.
I am a woman, I am Maria,
A valued *capoeira* player
I was nicknamed Twelve Men.
You'd better know who I am, my friend.

The *cantigas* that focus on female *capoeiristas* offer a sharp contrast with the traditional songs that celebrate masculine strength and domination. The *ladainha* "Força Guerreira" ("Female Warrior Strength"), by Ively Mayumi Nagaye Viccari, describes women in terms of endurance, courage, resistance, strength, and empowerment. It follows a didactic tradition in which *ladainhas* comment on the history of *capoeira*, make references to slavery and to cultural resistance, or discuss the etymology of the word *capoeira*, its origin, development, and philosophy. However, "Força Guerreira" also adds to the conventional themes of *ladainhas* by referring to forms of female cultural and historical resistance. In this sense, as warriors, women *capoeiristas* have emulated the courage and strategies of other powerful women. The song also showcases the importance of focusing on strengths and prerogatives as the following selected verses indicate:

Força guerreira, que não só
Pelo físico, mas pela intuição
E energia interna
Aflorada quando necessário
Para defender o alimento
De seu filho, de sua linhagem
De seu povo, de toda sua espécie.

Female warrior strength, is not just
Physical, but also intuitive
And an inner energy
It blossoms when necessary
To defend her child's
Sustenance and her people's
Lineage and the entire species.

The lyrics of songs that are composed, or rewritten, by women (or by men who understand the need to create a balance in *capoeira* circles) can potentially ensure the type of impact that Gonzaga's song ("Ó, Abre Alas"; "Oh, Clear the Way") had and still has on *carnaval* festivities in Brazil. For instance, the parade that each *samba* association presents during *carnaval* uses the title/refrain of Gonzaga's *marchinha* to reference the float and opening wing that initiates the Brazilian Mardi Gras extravaganza. They function as an introduction to the thematic construct selected by each *samba* association for a given year's competition. The "Abre Alas" float and wing showcase the members' creativity, resourcefulness and, oftentimes, their pride in their African heritage. That might be one of the reasons why Gonzaga's *carnaval* song ("Ó, Abre Alas") is still popular. Its refrain asking to "clear the way" has the makings of a motto that resonates well with disenfranchised segments of the population. As Gonzaga's *marchinha* reveals, composing songs with new thematic focus is a crucial step in changing gender discrepancies. When lyrics of songs are carefully crafted to avoid repeating stereotypes, they become one of the most effective ways to balance gender dynamics. In the case of *capoeira* circles, they can make a difference because those songs propagate quickly (they are posted on websites, intoned in *rodas*, workshops, *batizados*, and recorded and sold at academies and by retailers that have a wide international reach). Female composers and lyricists can use their *capoeira* songs to neutralize double standards, in which case, they are bound to accomplish what Rita Flesky has theorized (in another context) as the need to overcome "women's estrangement within a male-defined environment," and the determination to accomplish, at least partially, an "individual liberation from existing ideological and social constraints" (124).

Coda

Although women in Brazil have already moved up the social, political, and economic ladder, and have gained unprecedented rights and prerogatives, the concept of gender equality is a misguided assessment of the current reality. Such is the theoretical position Milestone and Meyer take in *Gender and Popular Culture* as they acknowledge that, in contemporary modern societies, women have succeeded in attaining gender equality in many respects. They cite equal opportunities, comment on anti-discrimination legislation, and discuss key legal mechanisms that are meant to "ensure, at least theoretically, that women have the same rights and opportunities as men, both at home and in the workplace" (214). They also mention changes in lifestyle and cultural blueprints which have led a record number of women to be employed outside their homes while men have become more involved in raising children. Despite all those achievements, as Milestone and Meyer notice, not everyone has embraced those changes (214). This is also a position that Louis Menand takes when analyzing the emphasis on certain words in the media, blogs, and other forms of communication. He discusses the extraordinary resurgence of the search for the meaning of the word "feminism" in the United States, in 2016 and 2017. He considers that search as a sign that women have not shattered as many social and political glass ceilings as publicized by a new generation that has profited from previous waves of Feminism. Menand was intrigued by the fact that people still "needed to be told what 'feminism' means." In a sarcastic note, he writes that "Upon, searching, these people would have learned from Merriam-Webster's that the definition of 'feminism' is 'the theory of the political, economic, and social equality of the sexes'" (15). And he concludes, playing with the double meaning of the word "theory": "Some number of them were probably relieved to learn that it is still just a theory" (15).

263

As discussed throughout this study, and more specifically in analyzing Brazilian women in *capoeira, carnaval,* and soccer, and their representation in popular music and literature, there is still a misconception about what it means to be a feminist in Brazil. Women of all walks of life—black, *morenas, pardas,* white, rich, poor, urban, or rural—still have to fight for their rights as far as the political, economic, and social equality of the sexes is concerned. News of the impeachment of Brazil's first female president, in 2016, and the rise of a rightwing and misogynist candidate to the presidency in 2018, was a backlash against women's rights. Peter Beinart addresses these issues as he discusses the connection between "male dominance" and "political legitimacy" (12).[1] He analyzes how the global rise of authoritarian governments has created a setback for women's rights since those in power have worked relentlessly to curtail women's opportunities and empowerment and have progressively taken away rights that females had previously accrued (12). In his discussions of the topic, Beinart mentions the then newly elected president of Brazil, Jair Messias Bolsonaro, who "linked his counterrevolution to a counterrevolution against uppity women" (13). Comparing Bolsonaro's campaign to Donald Trump's, Beinart refers to the masses of people at Trump's rallies shouting, "Lock her up," when referring to Hillary Clinton, and "crowds at Bolsonaro's rallies chant[ing] that they would feed dog food to feminists" (13). In 2015, Bolsonaro told Maria do Rosário Nunes, a congresswoman from the opposition party (PT-RS), that he would not rape her because she was not worthy of it (Beinart 13).[2] The video recording of their heated verbal exchange reveals that he also insulted her by repeatedly calling her a *vagabunda* (a bum, loafer, or tart), and hit her shoulder several times to forcefully push her away from him. Another congressman had to intervene to avoid what could have accelerated into an appalling fight, or greater physical intimidation.[3] Bolsonaro, who has also made damaging remarks about Feminism, berated female journalists, and targeted other disenfranchised groups (the LGBTQ community, indigenous groups, and Afro-Brazilians).[4] to express their dissatisfaction with the status quo, since 2015, Brazilian women have raised a series of public protests because of the increase in domestic violence and sexual abuse.

Violence against women is still a common occurrence in Brazil and in many other parts of the world. It is not a thing of the past for a woman to be disregarded or mocked when reporting rape, sexual assault, or other types of brutality. It is telling that, although currently Brazil has a comprehensive legal structure that guarantees justice and protection for women, only roughly one quarter of those who suffer violence or sexual assault have the courage to report them, and one in every four Brazilian males places the blame on females for being raped or assaulted (Santos and Grelin 35–39). Gruesome violence still makes the daily news in Brazil. For instance, on January 25, 2019, William Bonner, the anchor of *Journal Nacional*, Globo Network's news hour, reported a case of domestic violence in Rio de Janeiro and a vital gesture of resistance by Elaine Maria Santana who was shot in the head by her husband. Still alive, but unable to speak, she managed to dab her finger in the blood running from her head and write the name of her assailant on the hospital cot. Five days later, the same anchor mentioned another woman, this time in Pernambuco, who was beaten so brutally by her former husband that he found the video too graphic to be displayed in its entirety. Bonner introduced the material by reminding viewers that, as equally disturbing, was the fact that the footage had been recorded by a ten-year-old child who witnessed the brutal occurrence.[5] Those are not isolated cases of the brutality taking place in the large urban centers of Brazil. Media reports are peppered with accounts of *femicídos* (murder of women), rapes, and other types of vicious behavior that occur in the most diverse locations of the country.

Violence against women is also common in public spaces. A case in point is the wave of rapes that took place in Rio de Janeiro in 2013, shocking the country and the international community. One gang rape, in particular, made headlines around the world because it was perpetrated twice by the same men. First, they "abducted and raped a working-class woman in a transit van as it wended through densely populated areas" (Romero). Even though she reported the crime, the police failed to investigate, and a week later, the same men raped a twenty-one-year-old American student, in the same van, "pummeling her face and beating her male companion with a metal bar" (Romero). Because of the international attention the case received, the authorities in Rio de Janeiro suspended the use of private vans which are widely used as an alternative to public transportation because of a lack of reliable city transit. The statistics indicate that unreported cases of

domestic violence and sexual assaults are even higher in economically challenged segments of society because most women do not
believe that the police will investigate the complaints and protect
them. A large number of females are also afraid that the perpetra-
tors may retaliate.

It is challenging for those who depend financially on their partners to search for other alternatives, especially if they have children.
In some cases, an internalized sense of low self-esteem may prevent
them from seeking other solutions, or they fall into the trap of
hoping that an abusive relationship will turn into an emotionally satisfying marital life. As a result, the unregistered incidents
foster impunity and lawlessness, and create a sense of hopelessness
in the victims. The numbers show that women of color are even
more likely than white females to experience domestic violence
and sexual abuse (Instituto DataFolha 8). However, as discussed
in Chapter One, in the segment "Mapping Asymmetries: The
'Defense of Honor' Discourse," notwithstanding of social class
or race, females have not received dependable and encompassing
institutionalized protection from domestic and sexual violence. It
was not until 1991, after nearly two decades of hard-fought battles
from feminists and sympathizers with their cause against the
"defense of honor" argument, that the Supreme Court in Brazil
ruled that a man could "no longer kill his wife and win acquittal
on the ground of 'legitimate defense of honor'" (Brooke B00016).
However, even two decades later, lawyers continue to use the
"defense of honor" argument to defend their male clients who are
accused of femicide. Such disregard for women's constitutional
rights led José Antônio Dias Toffoti, a judge on Brazil's Supreme
Court, to issue a preliminary injunction, on February 26, 2021,
reiterating that it is unconstitutional to use the "defense of honor"
argument to justify femicide. The news that Doca Street died in
December 2020 a free man at the age of seventy-three earned him
a brief commentary on the news: he was identified as the man who
killed Ângela Diniz in 1976. The reporters forgot to mention that
she was only thirty-two years old then, and he was acquitted on
the grounds that he was defending his "honor," even though he
was legally married to another woman.

Television networks and other media sources have played a
positive role by drawing attention to the dire need to change
behavior patterns regarding gender issues in Brazil. In that line of

thinking, on March 8, 2019, to commemorate the International Day of Women, Globo Television Network launched a campaign meant to educate its alleged seventy million viewers about gender respect. The didactic tone of the voice-over message—created and directed by Sérgio Valente, Mariana Sá, and Leandro Castilho—alerted viewers to the distinction between fighting for equal rights and attempting to eliminate gender differences. The fact that the network felt the need to raise awareness about women's rights indicates the level of misinformation and misogyny which is still prevalent in Brazilian society. It also reinforces Menand's concern that people, in general, even in industrialized countries, are still striving to understand what Feminism is about. Attempting to educate Brazilian viewers about the need to embrace and respect gender differences, Globo's campaign catchphrases explained what Feminism means:

> Os homens não são todos iguais. Nem as mulheres. Quando as mulheres lutam por igualdade, elas não querem ser iguais aos homens. Querem, sim, direitos iguais, deveres iguais, oportunidades iguais, divisões de tarefas iguais, cargos iguais, salários iguais e respeito à diferença. Porque a diferença, sim, é sempre benvinda. A desigualdade nunca. Tudo começa pelo respeito.

> Men are not all the same. Neither are women. When women fight for equality, they do not want to be like men. What they want are equal rights, equal opportunities, equal division of labor, equal jobs, equal salaries, and respect for the differences. Because difference is always welcome, inequality is not. Everything begins with respect.

However, the Brazilian ambiguity is ubiquitous, and is often found in the double standards by which television networks operate. For instance, Rede Globo openly criticizes violence and regressive gender dynamics during its prime time news but follows those criticisms with programs that promote old-fashioned patterns of behavior. The plots of *telenovelas*, for instance, undermine women's place in society by reinforcing patterns of behavior and morality that conform to ideals set in the nineteenth and early twentieth centuries. Those popular programs usually sanction a mentality that celebrates women's abnegation, their capacity to forgive their husbands' infidelity, and complete surrender to the role of a mother as the ideal of femininity. In the case of Afro-Brazilian women, Globo often casts them as sexy cooks (good in bed and in the kitchen), puts emphasis on miscegenation (by always portraying racially-mixed couples), and in some cases, reinforces the myth of the racial democracy.

The current political scenario also reveals Brazil's ambiguous and ambivalent position in defining the country's role in a fast-changing world: it has adopted many positive changes while simultaneously keeping old prerogatives. It may be that, in the national imaginary, the traditional segments of society feel that embracing new assertions and abandoning outdated perspectives (in politics as well as in gender policies), can disrupt the pre-established concept of social order. Even if there are current laws that protect women, and special police units in place to help females fight violence, those police units are small in number. There are only eight of them in the whole country, and they are based in large urban centers and not uniformly distributed (as reported by Instituto DataFolha which is housed in the headquarters of the newspaper *Folha de São Paulo*). The staggering number of sexual assaults, rapes, and domestic violence in Brazilian society has unleashed a series of demonstrations by concerned citizens. For instance, on May 12, 2015, marchers on the streets of São Paulo protested against male chauvinism and violence perpetrated on women in Brazil (Hargreaves). The situation was so critical that, in 2015, the Brazilian congress passed legislation sharply increasing punishment for violence against females. Currently, the laws to protect women are comprehensive, but, enforcing those laws—before tragedy strikes—has not always taken precedence over other pressing issues.

Brazil's gender paradoxes are also noticeable in the political arena. Rousseff was twice elected president by popular vote (in 2010 and 2014) and, in December 2015, was suspended from office for six months while Congress decided her political fate. She was impeached and subsequently removed from office in August 2016. Electing a woman for president of the largest democratic republic in Latin America was a stride forward for women's rights, a point Sabrina Fernandes makes as she highlights the symbolic importance of that election because it alluded "to the power of a politics of possibility" which gave hope to other women (122). However, as she concludes, the changes were not dramatic or steady: "the constant portrayal of Rousseff [both on mainstream and unconventional media] as a masculine leader, and her lack of consistency in addressing women's issues and tackling gender inequality from a more radical position place[d] her in a 'double-bind'" (122). While Rousseff's election to the presidency of Brazil contributed to increase the number of women running for public offices, and to pass protective laws more easily, such progress did not radically change the public mentality or substantially diminish the rates of violence against women.

Rousseff was ousted on the grounds of fiscal irresponsibility, breaking budgetary laws, and criminal administrative misconduct. The process of her impeachment reveals the ambivalent and ambiguous social and political arena, since the crimes of which she was accused were also committed by several male politicians who remained in power.[6] I am not suggesting that Rousseff was innocent or merely a victim of misogyny. What I criticize is the double standards applied to impeach her. Of special significance were the votes from those who have been accused of having ties to corrupt schemes, money laundering, embezzlement of public resources, and other crimes investigated by the Polícia Federal (the Brazilian FBI). One of those votes, and the rationale presented, seemed utterly hypocritical because it was cast by Fernando Collor de Mello, former president of Brazil (1990–1992), who resigned to avoid an impeachment trial by the Brazilian Senate on allegations of corruption, influence peddling, and disastrous economic plans. He was acquitted of criminal charges but became disqualified to hold an elected office for eight years. In 2006, he returned to politics, was elected senator for his state, Alagoas, and reelected in 2014. His explanation of why he was casting a vote to impeach Rousseff ("fiscal irresponsibility") was significantly representative of the politics of gender in the Brazilian Senate (and House of Representatives as well). The vote cast by Bolsonaro, who was a congressman at the time, revealed not only his disregard for Rousseff as a politician and a woman, but also his contempt for human rights. He prefaced his vote by dedicating it to Colonel Carlos Alberto Brilhante Ustra who, in 2008, was condemned for his advocacy for, and excessive practice of, torture during the military dictatorship, including ordering and supervising the brutalization that Rousseff endured as a political prisoner in the 1970s (Christofeletti).[7]

Yet, not all is so bleak in Brazil. As discussed in Chapter Six, since the1970s, some positive changes have happened for women in Brazil ranging from improvements in the family structure to direct participation in the country's political life, and the support of protectionist laws. Since the country returned to a democracy in 1985, lawmakers have attempted to correct gender inequalities. For instance, in an effort to repair damages and advance women's causes, on August 7, 2006, the Brazilian Congress enacted law number 11.340, popularly known as Lei Maria da Penha, and on September 22, 2006, then-President Luiz Inácio Lula da Silva signed it into law. It is a groundbreaking legislation on domestic violence that takes its name from Maria da Penha Maya Fernandes who underwent physical and psychological abuse from her husband for a sustained period of fourteen years, and was battered so violently that she was left a paraplegic (OMCT 75).[8] In 2013, then-president Dilma Rousseff signed legislation requiring hospitals to provide treatment for HIV and other sexually transmitted diseases to rape victims. In 2015, she signed another law establishing new and stricter penalties for the killing of women and girls. She also increased the incarceration period for *femicídio* to a minimum of twelve years, a substantially stricter sentence than before. Even if the changes she implemented during her presidency were not radical, those bills made a difference in the advancement of women's causes in Brazil. Despite the fact that a deep-seated male chauvinism is still embedded in the fabric of society, women have taken substantial strides in Brazil.

Progressive choices that governmental entities and leaders make often work as vehicles of empowerment for minorities. To emphasize that, throughout *The Ripple Effect: Gender and Race in Brazilian Culture and Literature*, I have made a concerted effort to present interdisciplinary topics and diversified theoretical analyses that connect past and contemporary events. This study also finds common denominators that interconnect Brazilian culture and literature vis-à-vis gender and race issues. It uses *capoeira* as a lynchpin and a critical paradigm to discuss several cultural art forms (such as *carnaval*, soccer, popular songs) and literary texts. *The Ripple Effect* also informs readers about a number of misconceptions embedded in the slippery variables of Brazilian national identity, and analyzes the ambiguities, ambivalences, double standards, and inequalities prevalent in Brazil's cultural, social, political, and legal systems. To disclose the complexities and nuances of Brazilian cultural identity (which is forthright and violent at times, suggestive and romantic at others, and always showcasing the appearance of cordial relations), this study highlights the aesthetics of literary texts and cultural contexts and probes into the country's "ambiguous process of modernization" (Caulfield's expression) as discussed in the Introductory Remarks.

Notes

Introductory Remarks

1. I borrow the expression from Caulfield who uses it to describe the moral values and norms of conduct in the period comprised between 1914 and 1940 in Brazil.

2. *Marchinha* (meaning "little march") is a genre of music that has a binary compass. It originated from Portuguese popular street marches. See McCann, pp. 1–3, 236–37.

3. The Portuguese version of the song was reprinted in Diniz, p. 160.

4. The Week of Modern Art in 1922 is the hallmark of Brazilian Modernism. The modernists' contributions to the literary and artistic environment extended beyond that period and had enduring repercussions, lasting roughly until the 1960s. Avant-garde literary and artistic tendencies had been introduced in Brazil since 1912, when Oswald de Andrade returned from his trip to Europe talking about Marinetti and Futurism. Lasar Segal's painting exhibition in 1913, and Anita Mafalti's exhibitions in 1914 and 1917 also contributed to prepare the Brazilian public for the new perceptions of art highlighted in the Week of Modern Art.

5. Hess uses this expression to present Roberto DaMatta's analysis of *jeitinho brasileiro*.

6. For analyses of *jeito* or *jeitinho brasileiro*, see also L. Barbosa, "The Brazilian Jeitinho"; DaMatta, *Carnivals* pp. 93–105; Levine, "The Brazilian Way."

7. The word *propaganda* means both advertisement and propaganda.

8. For music and citizenship, see also Avelar and Dunn.

9. The novel was first published in 1958, and translated into English as *Gabriela, Clove and Cinnamon*, in 1962, and has had several adaptations to television and film.

10. For additional discussions on the "ideology of whitening" and the "myth of the racial democracy," see Dávila, Florestan, Guimarães, Hellwig, Htun, A. Nascimento, Nogueira, Roosevelt, Silva, Skidmore, Twine, and Winant.

11. The book was translated to English as *A Brazilian Tenement* in 1976, and retranslated as *The Slum* in 2000.

12. This poem was originally published in 1925, in the volume *Pau-Brasil*. The word *capoeira* can refer to both a player and the game. When referring to a player it is used in the masculine form.

13. Other texts in Brazilian literature that makes references to *capoeira* are Amado's *Capitães da Areia, Jubiabá, Tenda dos Milagres*, and *A Morte e a Morte de Quincas Berro d'Água*. For discussions of some of these texts, see the chapter "Pedrito, sete mortes e a ficção amadiana" in *Capoeira, Identidade e Gênero* by Josivaldo Pires de Oliveira and Luiz Augusto Pinheiro Leal. See also Manuel Antônio de Almeida's *Memórias de um Sargento de Milícias*

(1854–1855) which discusses at length the role Major Vidigal (based on a real historical figure) plays in his relentless prosecution of *capoeira* players. See Rego, p. 353.

Chapter One: Mapping Asymmetries

1. See Lobato, "A propósito," which became better known as "Paranoia ou Mistificação."

2. See Campos, R. Cobra, Coelho, Duarte, Ferreira, Ferreira-Pinto, Foster, Guedes, Marchant, Mott, Owen, Quinlan and Sharpe, Risério, Sharpe, Unruh, and Valente.

3. See also Mott, pp. 89–104; Quinlan and Sharpe, pp. 27, 140; Ferreira, p. 35; and R. Cobra, p. 6.

4. For in-depth discussions of Eugenics in Brazil, see Besse, pp. 68, 69, 93, 99, 100, 111, 124, 126, and 229.

5. I borrow Ruthven's expression (p. 72). She used it, in an unrelated context, to discuss dismantling androcentric assumptions.

6. "O amor físico é tão necessário à mulher como o comer e beber."

7. Courteau refers to her 1930s novels, *O quinze*, *João Miguel*, and *Caminho das pedras*.

8. I adopt Kolodny's expression used in an unrelated context in the article "Dancing through the Minefield."

9. For the expression, see Leich, p. 146.

10. Fear of being classified as *corno* still runs rampant in contemporary Brazilian society, particularly in the Northeast and in smaller towns. A case in point is the popularity of the prize-winning 2003 film, *Lisbela e o Prisioneiro*, based on Osman Lins's 1964 play of the same name.

11. For information about honor killing in Brazil and the legal system from 1890 to 1940, see Caulfield, pp. 41–44.

12. See Bourdieu, *Masculine*, p. 50, for a theoretical sample of these discussions.

13. Before divorce was institute, in 1977, there was a procedure called *desquite* which conceded a legal separation, but not the legalization of another union.

14. Even though divorce became legal in Brazil, it came with an additional clause which specified that couples needed to be separated for at least one year before filling for a divorce (Priore 231). This policy lasted until 2010 when the sixty-sixth amendment to Brazil's Constitution removed that condition.

15. For a list and discussion of other crimes, see Priore, pp. 211–13.

Chapter Two: The Erotic and Exotic Lure

1. See, for instance, Hobbs's *A Chosen Exile;* and Larsen's *Passing.*

2. Degler used the term. See *Neither Black nor White.*

3. For further discussions of preference for mulattoes over blacks in the United States, see E. B. Reuter's 1917 study.

4. For the expression "race is in the eye of the beholder," see also Gates Jr., *Brazil: A Racial Democracy?*

5. Brazilians inherited such concept from Portugal where, as a controlling measure, from the sixteenth to the eighteen centuries, it was meant to prevent non-whites from holding positions in public offices, the military, and ecclesiastic posts in Portugal's overseas colonies. In special cases, the person could ask for the punishment to be waived (*dispensa do defeito de cor*), a topic that Ana Maria Gonçalves addresses extensively in her novel *Um Defeito de Cor* (2009).

6. The song was published in 1939. For information about Barroso, discussion of the song, and the impact it had, see McCann, pp. 67–77.

7. See publications by Hellwig, Twine, Guimarães, and Htun.

8. There were, however, a few dissident opinions about the absence of a racial system of caste in Brazil. A case in point is W. E. B. DuBois who saw contradictions and ambiguities in the Brazilian system of race relations in the country. See Hellwig, pp. 31, and 34.

9. Guimarães argues that Arthur Ramos (in 1941) and Roger Bastide (in 1944) introduced the term that Freyre later used during the series of lectures that he gave in Portugal in 1946 (121–24).

10. He discusses poems by Gregório de Matos Guerra and the following works: Manuel Antônio de Almeida's *Memórias de um Sargento de Milícias*; Bernardo Guimarães's *A Escrava Isaura*; Aluísio de Azevedo's *O Cortiço*; João Felício dos Santos's *João Abade;* "A Estória de Lélio e Lina" by João Guimarães Rosa; and *Gabriela, Cravo e Canela* by Jorge Amado (pp. 45–63).

11. See, for instance, Jorge Amado's *Gabriela, Cravo e Canela* which had several adaptations to television, including two by Globo Television Network in 1975 and 2012.

12. For samples, see beer commercials for Antarctica and Kaiser as discussed by Bacchi and in Casadei. See also Ferreira and Medeiros for black women protesting against racism and violence. Women counter-attacked by reacting against a series of advertisements, especially, against a slogan Kaiser produced in 2003. Printed on coasters and distributed in bars throughout Brazil, it read: "Mulher e Cerveja: Especialidade da casa" ("Woman and Beer: The House Specialty"). In a joint action with other feminist organizations, CLADEM (Latin American and Caribbean Committee for the Defense of Women's Rights) filed a public complaint and action against the beer maker and won the litigation.

13. To keep her popularity afloat, when *O Clone* ended, Couto reproduced the racial-gastronomic model of the *telenovela* by publishing a book of recipes (*Receitas de Botequim*; *"Bar Food Recipes"*) and giving numerous interviews about her cooking abilities, and her role as Sargentelli's *mulata* (she was one of the first mestizo women hired to dance in his shows).

14. At the age of twenty-four, she was considered old for the *mulata* show and Sargentelli secured an audition for her with Bandeirantes Television Network. She later worked for Globo. See Dalevi's article.

15. See "O bumbo silenciou" in *Tribuna do Norte*.

16. For sex tourism in Bahia, see Williams.

17. Composed in 1929 with the original name "Mulata" by Irmãos Valença, it was popularized by Lamartino Babo in 1931 and, since then, it became a staple *carnaval marchinha.*

18. For Sargentelli's shows in night clubs, see Heuman's documentary (*Brazil: The Heart of South America*), and the film directed by Porto (*As granfinas e o camelô*).

19. The name of Sargentelli's show, loosely translated, means "Wow, Wow," and indicates pleasant sensation and triumph. He sold the rights to Franco Fontana to produce the show "Oba, Oba: The Brazilian Extravaganza" and tour in the US and Canada from 1989 to 1992.

20. Giacomini's research discloses that the organizers of those courses received technical assistance from SENAC, the National Chamber of Commerce, and RIOTUR, Rio de Janeiro's official tourism agency.

21. For similar and different views on *mulatas, passitas,* and *carnaval,* see also research by Corrêa, Daveli, Dias Filho, Giacomini, Gilliam, Gomes, Gonzalez, Rector, and Rosa.

22. This expression is a play on words with the title of Bhabha's essay, "Signs Taken for Wonders," adapted to fit the context of this analysis.

23. For an excellent chronology of Brazilian *carnaval* festivities, see Diniz, pp. 239–44.

24. I borrow the expressions from Parker, pp. 8 and 53, used in another context.

25. José Bonifácio de Oliveira Sobrinho (Boni) and Hans Donner, both from Globo, were jurors at the beauty pageant, and invited her to audition for the role of Globeleza in a *carnaval* vignette that Globo Television Network had devised (Valenssa, "Personal interview").

26. I borrow and adapt the expression from Butler, p. 372.

27. The expression is from Butler, p. 379, used in another context.

28. The song was composed by Jorge Aragão and Franco Lattari for Globo and played during the *carnaval* season to advertise Globo's broadcasting of the *samba* parades and other events. See also Bergallo and Duarte, p. 64; Petrini, pp. 126–27; and C. F. Rosa, pp. 73–74.

29. See the reference to Caminha's letter in Simões and Gonzaga, pp. 18, 26, 43, 58.

30. The book is a special edition that is not paginated. The estimated pages on which Donner addresses the development of Globeleza are pp. 154–65, and 182–85.

31. The photos of Valenssa included in that calendar and the pictures of her that grace sixteen pages of his autobiography resemble the style of photos found in *Playboy Magazine.* See Donner (n.p.).

32. Donner explains that he produced that video recording for a foreign public (n.p.).

33. I borrow Donaldson's discussion of *piccaninny,* pp. 66–88, used in reference to Portuguese colonization, and adapt it to this context.

34. I borrow Toplin's expression, p. 141 and adapt to this case.

35. After she lost her Globeleza job, she joined the Igreja Universal do Reino de Deus for ten years. See Bergallo and Duarte, pp. 129–33.

36. For an analysis of representations of *parda* women in Brazilian literature, see Sant'Anna, *Canibalismo* pp. 20–60; and Hanchiau's article.

37. The book was translated to English as *A Brazilian Tenement* in 1976, and retranslated as *The Slum* in 2000.

38. See Vaz, pp. 581–97, for a detailed and comparative analysis of nineteenth-century tenements, twentieth-century *favelas* (slums), and modern apartment living in Rio de Janeiro.

39. See the audio CD *Gozos da Alma* by Geraldo Carneiro (track 5).

40. Directed by Carlos Diegues, the film was an adaptation of the novel *Memórias do Distrito de Diamantina* ("*Memoirs of the District of Diamantina*") by José Feliciano dos Santos.

41. It was composed by Afro-Brazilian Jorge Ben Jor. Motta also recorded this song.

42. Motta's complaints seem to be confirmed by the fact that when the now defunct television network Manchete produced and aired a *telenovela* based on Chica da Silva's life, the network cast Taís Araújo, a beautiful light-skinned Afro-Brazilian, to play the leading part.

43. The title of the book establishes an intertextual dialogue with Césaire Aimé's *Notebook of a Return to the Native Land*.

44. See Coelho, Fry, Hanchard, and Schemo.

45. In Brazil, quite often, it was assumed that black people would be performing menial jobs, and it was not uncommon for them to be directed to such entrances or access routes, even if they were not workers. Such a way of mischaracterizing racism went unchallenged until the end of the twentieth century when scholars, politicians, and activists questioned such ambiguous cases of prejudice that had been accepted as normal.

46. Cf. with Freyre, *Casa grande e senzala*, p. 104: "Branca para casar, mulata para foder, negra pra trabalhar."

47. The word *malê* derives from the Yoruba *imalê*, referring to African slaves who adopted Islam's doctrine.

48. The song was composed by Da Gama, Toni Garrido, and Lasão, and recorded by the popular group Cidade Negra.

49. The lyrics of the song make a metonymic reference to *mulata* Globeleza, by mentioning the sound "Pirlimpimpim" which Globo emits to enter and leave the air waves.

Chaper Three: Women in Soccer

1. See Santiago's endorsement, on the back cover of Coutinho's book.

2. See Biazzi and Franchesci Neto, Escher et al., Guedes, Levine, and Eakin for comments on the globalization of the sport, and the role *futebol* plays in Brazilian culture.

3. In 2010, Marcioni Scarinci coordinated a project that catalogued a large sample of poems and lyrics of songs ("Futebol e Poesia"), comprising 57 pages, published on Antônio Lisboa Carvalho de Miranda's website.

4. Pereira contends that, as early as 1908, Coelho Neto had already shown signs of an embryonic interest in soccer, as part of the sport culture that was emerging in Brazil (198).

5. Some of those terms survived until the 1960s when Portuguese translations and or spellings became popular (*gol, time, pênalti*).

6. The musicians, lyricists, and composers Milton Nascimento and Lô Borges pay homage to those small, *mestiço*, and politically insignificant neighborhood soccer associations of the 1920s by naming their 1972 LP album *Clube da Esquina*.

7. See C. Rosa, pp. 23–24, for analyses of the choreography of soccer, *capoeira*, and *samba*.

8. See also the works of Lyra Filho and Guedes.

9. Eakin, pp. 175–83, has summarized several discussions on race and *futebol-arte* which have been historically associated with black or *pardo* players such as Carlos Alberto, Fausto, Friedenreich, Garrincha, Leônidas, Pelé, and Ronaldo. For the concept and references to *futebol-arte*, see also Souza, Vilela and Petta.

10. This is discussed in the video recordings and voiceover narrations presented in the exhibition hall of the Museu de Futebol in São Paulo ("Sala Rito de Passage"), addressing the fatalistic day when fans in the newly built stadium Maracanã fell silent and wept when Uruguay won by one penalty kick goal.

11. The fact that volleyball and basketball were not stigmatized as "violent," and/or forbidden for women seems to confirm the concept discussed by Marcos Alves Souza.

12. See Vargas, Getúlio, Presidência da República, Casa Civil, *Diário Oficial*, Decreto-Lei nº 3.199.

13. Milestone and Meyer contrast "public patriarchy" with "private patriarchy"; the latter exercises control over a woman's body in a domestic setting (either by using violence or other forms of limiting women's ability to come and go). The traditional notions of public (male) and private (female) spaces, is extensively discussed in DaMatta's works. I adapt those concepts to the discussion of banning women from playing soccer and *capoeira*.

14. Even a player like Marta Vieira Silva—whose fast moves, dexterity, and incredible capacity to dribble and score have earned her auspicious comparisons with the best male players in Brazil—has not received the financial support she deserves. See Hughes, "The Best Player on Earth Is Looking for a Job."

15. See BBC SPORT, "Women Footballers Blast Blatter."

16. I adapt this expression from Grosz, p. 241.

17. For general comments on the body as a commodity, see Goldenberg.

18. As noticeable during the 2019 FIFA Women's World Cup, it seems that many players still feel the need to wear makeup during the games.

19. The Brazilian Football Confederation (CBF) had already withdrawn her name from the list of referees in the Brazilian Championship after she disallowed a legitimate goal in the semi-finals of the Brazilian Cup.

20. I conducted research at the museum (display rooms and library) in July 2018. The information I present here is based on the permanent collections that were on display then. I am not aware if any changes have been implemented since then.

21. This section is organized by "Walls," alphabetized and catalogued in numbers. On "Wall B," there are pictures and copies of written records of women in France, the United States, and England playing soccer and/or rooting for their teams as spectators.

22. Exhibit number 195 is a picture of a woman playing soccer in England in 1906, and number 201 is a reproduction of a watercolor in which a female is playing soccer in France in the early twentieth century.

23. I was unable to find additional information about the women who played soccer in the circus (their race and social class, for instance, if they earned a stipend, how their families reacted, and how they were selected for those performances).

24. Circo Irmãos Queirolo arrived in Rio de Janeiro in 1917, and Antolin Garcia founded the Circo Garcia in Campinas in 1916.

25. He was born Izydor Spurgin, in Russia, 1882–1968.

26. I refer here to the private versus public space as discussed by DaMatta.

27. Tradição, Família e Propriedade ("Tradition, Family and Property") is a civil organization founded in 1960 by the Catholic leader Plínio Corrêa de Oliveira.

28. The information about her life and career was provided by her during an interview I conducted with her in New York, on April 13 and 14, 2016. It is also based on materials she made available (newspaper clippings, photos, and certificates) from her private collection.

29. She also studied Journalism and Physical Education. As a teenager, she led an eclectic lifestyle; including participating in beauty contests (she was Rainha do Cruzeiro Futebol Clube, Rainha do Exército de Minas Gerais, Miss Fotogênica, and Rainha do Carnaval de Minas Gerais). The fact that both the media and Campos find it important to highlight her participation in beauty pageants underscores the need to emphasize her femininity.

30. Campos had a free pass into their headquarters because her father was a retired military man in Belo Horizonte's armed forces, and she had been Rainha do Exército.

Chapter Four: *Capoeira: Jogo Bonito, Jogo de Dentro, Jogo de Fora*

1. I use "spatiality" in this study as is appears in Lefebvre's *Production of Space.*

2. The word *capoeira* also means brushwood, dense woodland, and shrubbery. For a detailed and enlightening analysis of *capoeira's* etymology and meanings, see Rego, pp. 17–29.

3. To avoid the label of a "sport," most high ranking *capoeiristas* usually reject the idea of lobbying to have *capoeira* included in the Olympic Games. See Nichols's article on the subject.

4. While in some studies the word *roda* is accurately translated as "ring,"

I elected to use the word "circle" to avoid any association with violent and/or competitive sports (such as boxing) in which the term "ring" is used.

5. The word *axé*, which was originally connected with Afro-Brazilian religions, became a trademark for any spiritual or positive vibrations in Bahia and was appropriated by the music industry in the 1980s, giving rise to the musical style called *axé* music.

6. See Downey, "Interação," a pamphlet inserted in the CD *Capoeira Angola: Grupo de Capoeira Angola Pelourinho*, pp. 1–22. Although there are two versions of Downey's text (in English and in Portuguese), the sentence I quoted in this study was omitted from the English version; therefore, I translated it. Compare pp. 12 and 21–22 of the pamphlet.

7. See his article "Jogo Bonito: A Brief Anatomy of *Capoeira*."

8. See Pelé's autobiography.

9. Those movements can be organized as follows: "Defensive Movements," "The Basic Kicks," "Bimba's Sequences," "Cintura Desprezada," "Takedowns," "Other Kicks and Movements," and "The Language of Angola" (Nestor Capoeira, *Little* pp. 60–140; *Fundamentos* pp. 158–207; *Street-Smart* pp. 275–99). Mestre Bola Sete also presents a classification, explanation of movements, and learning techniques in *capoeira angola* (*Capoeira* pp. 47–88).

10. For a full description of all the instruments used in *capoeira*, see Rego, pp. 70–88.

11. For references to the *berimbau*, see also Rugendas, p. 197; and Debret, p. 253.

12. There are many variations in the lyrics of traditional songs published in songbooks, magazines, books, or found on covers of CDs and websites.

13. See also Roger Bastide, pp. 22, 23, 252–53.

14. For references to the *mandinga* groups in Africa, see also works by Edward E. Curtis IV, Harold G. Lawrence. For *mandinga* in *capoeira*, see Sérgio Gonzalez Varela. See João José Reis's book for a detailed account of the 1835 slave uprising in Salvador, Bahia, during Ramadan. It was led by Muslim slaves who belonged to an ethnic group from the Mali Empire, known in Brazil as Malês. As Reis informs, the Malê group was credited with sorcery powers; they were also respected by their peers because they knew how to read and write. The white population also feared them because they resisted adopting Roman Catholicism.

15. For a definition of the term *corpo fechado* and other explanations, as well as for an account of the stories, myths and legends surrounding famous *capoeiristas* and their *corpos fechados* see Almeida, p. 150; Browning, pp. 118–19; Downey, pp. 136–52; and Talmon-Chvaicer, pp. 106–07.

16. For a profile of Besouro, see the film *Besouro*, directed by João Daniel Tikhomiroff.

17. For *timbuera* as "castanha de caju" ("cashew nut") see L. Barbosa p. 152.

18. From the native Brazilian language Tupi, *timbuera* means "nut that produces itself."

19. See also Lewis, p. 111.

20. For an extensive explanation of how to "close/open the body" in a *capoeira* game and discussions about gestures, postures, and (in)vulnerability, see Downey, *Learning* pp. 136–52.

21. Samples of *bolsas de mandinga* can still be found in the National Archive of Portugal that houses early eighteenth century Portuguese Inquisition records. See J. Souza, pp. 130–41, 161, 178, 192–93, 200, 206, 209–10, 223, 255.

22. "Popular" Catholicism should be understood in contrast to "official" Catholicism (dogmatic and concerned with sacraments and rites). Popular Catholicism is rooted in Spanish and Portuguese traditions, and is based on the devotion to saints, pilgrimages, processions, blessings, promises, and *novenas* (a series of prayers). For further details, see Oliveira's *Religião e dominação de classe*.

23. In contemporary usage, a scapular is a sacramental object, usually measuring roughly two inches by three inches, made of two small panels of material (wool, silk, and others) that are joined by a loop of string. See Herbermann, pp. 508–14.

24. Unknown composer. Mestres Limão and Nataniel recorded it. www.capoeira-music.net. Accessed May 8, 2017. The lyrics of the song were also published online by Victor de Miguel Borrego (Rasca) who compiled a songbook for the group Capoeira Libertação (Málaga and Granada, Spain). See capoeiralibertacao.weebly.com. Accessed June 25, 2015.

25. See the novel by Jô Soares, *Xangô de Baker Street* and its English version (*A Samba for Sherlock*), the film *O Xangô de Baker Street*, directed by Miguel Faria Jr.; the *telenovela Carmen* by Glória Peres, and the play *O dia em que comi a Pomba Gira* by Milton Levy.

26. The description of Pomba Gira as a gypsy and a seductive, sexually attractive, and powerful entity, and her itinerant lifestyle may have played a part in the selection of the codename Cigana that Mestre Leopoldina selected for Fátima Colombiana.

27. See, for instance, drawings, paintings, and/or travel accounts of Debret, Graham, and Rugendas.

28. For a reproduction of the drawings and the statement that accompanies Neves's drawings of *capoeira* and *N'Golo*, see Assunção, pp. 48–51.

29. See L. Reis, "A 'gymnastica' brasileira," a chapter of her book on *capoeira*, particularly pp. 60–69, 82–100.

30. The following songs address violence and/or talk about killing or death: "Essa dança mata," "Quando eu bato, eu quero ver cair," "Quem vem lá," "Meia hora só," "Sei, sim senhor," "Canarinho da Alemanha," and "Na batalha do Mugunge." For other examples of popular songs included in *capoeira* circles, see Rego, pp. 89–125; and Almeida, pp. 96–99.

31. As Talmon-Chvaicer, pp. 56–60, points out, the *capoeira* groups described in the novel were actually based on Guayamos and Nagoas, two factions which represented the alliances and merging of several neighborhood *capoeira* groups.

32. For a detailed analysis of this dynamic, see Rego, pp. 291–317.

33. An a*rrastão* (literally a dragnet, a fishing technique) is a form of stealing in urban areas in which a group of individuals surrounds a location and mugs the people, and, sometimes, also perpetrating some type of violence. It was first noticed in the 1980s. In the 1990s it made the international news because of assaults on tourists in Copacabana, and in 2015 it terrorized some touristic areas of Rio de Janeiro.

34. See also *Veja*, May 11, 1998, p. 31.

35. I borrow the expression from Browning, p. 114.

36. For similar information, see Williams, pp. 67–69.

37. For further analyses of Bimba's accomplishments as well as critiques of *capoeira regional*, see Rego, pp. 31–33, 282–87; Almeida, pp. 31–37; Lewis, pp. 59–61, 70, 100–01, 149–50; Downey, *Learning* pp. 173–77. See also Abreu, *Bimba é bamba*, and Sodré, *Mestre Bimba*.

38. For a discussion of styles attributed to specific *mestres*, see Almeida, pp. 134–37.

39. See also Taylor, pp. 43–50.

40. For excellent comparative studies of *capoeira angola* and *regional*, see L. Reis, pp. 75–124; and Merrell, pp. 9–19, 270–75. For an informative account of his first-hand experience with *capoeira* as a student of Mestre Bimba's and as a teacher of *capoeira*, see Almeida, pp. 31–54. For a list of similarities and differences, see Esteves, p. 126; for contrast in ideology and critiques see Downey, *Learning* pp. 63–73, 175–77.

41. This statement is based on personal interviews with Letícia Vidor de Souza Reis and Rosângela Araújo in São Paulo, Fátima Colombiano, in Rio de Janeiro, and Paula Barreto and Frederico Abreu in Salvador. All interviews were originally conducted in 2002 and 2003. Subsequent conversations with them in 2006 and 2008 updated their information.

42. A telling example is Quilombhoje (a name derived from the fusion of the words *quilombo*, the name of settlements of escaped slaves in colonial and imperial Brazil, and *hoje* which means today). It became the group's trademark, and the name of a journal, the group's primary venue of literary publication, and gateway to advocate an intellectual space for Afro-Brazilian writers. For a detailed studied of Quilombhoje, see Oliveira's *Writing Identity*.

43. For similar critiques, see Downey, *Learning* pp. 173–75.

Chapter Five: Women in *Capoeira*

1. As referenced, Pires (291) found that information in a criminal process against Manuel de Santana ("Ano 1900. Caixa 215. Doc. 13, p. 16. Arquivo Público do Estado da Bahia"). His research indicates that the woman got into a verbal fight with another washer woman over a stolen piece of clothing. Manuel de Santana interfered, attacking her physically; she attempted self-defense with *capoeira* kicks, he used a machete and hurt her hand; and they both had to go to the police station; their names were registered in the police records.

2. Pires refers to page 232 of Waldeloir Rego's 1968 book, *Capoeira Angola*, as his source of information about Chicão's behavior and her beating up Pedro Porreta. However, I could not confirm this information because the only reference to Porreta in Rego's work appears on page 266, where he mentions Porreta's name and describes him as "a symbol of disorder." There is also no reference to any woman called Chica, Chicão, or Francisca in Rego's work.

3. Abib coordinated a group of seven researchers who contribute to the book *Mestres e capoeiras famosos da Bahia*, published in 2009.

4. Chica and Chicão (referred in other studies) seem to be the same person.

5. She is probably the same woman that Araújo and Rego refer to as Maria Homem.

6. Henceforth, all information included in this study about Marisa Cordeiro is based on intermittent conversations I have had with her since 2006, and on a long interview I conducted with her in Chicago (10–11 April, 2016), and materials she made available to me from her personal files and memorabilia.

7. She was the first woman born in the United States to be awarded the title of *mestra* (she received it in 1990).

8. Unless otherwise indicated, all biographical information about Mestra Cigana is based on a personal interview I conducted with her in Rio de Janeiro, on May 24, 2003.

9. A conversation I had with Eric Johnson, Contra-Mestre Pererê, 15 Oct. 2001.

10. See Bergamo's "Roda de gringo."

11. In Chicago, "Oba, Oba: The Brazilian Musical Extravaganza" ran at the Shubert Theater for four and a half months. The program was a concession Fontana had from Sargentelli in which he combined Sargentelli's show of *mulatas* and expanded it to create a variety show (Brazilian popular music and dance), featuring fifty-two Brazilians. The San Francisco show counted on Marta Sargentelli as Assistant Choreographer, carrying on her father's tradition.

12. Sid Smith questioned the production value of "Oba, Oba: The Brazilian Musical Extravaganza" and gave it a mixed review: he considered half of the show "delightful" because it conjured up "in simple and unaffected ways, another world and culture, one poundingly underscored by gorgeous musical beats." Yet, he also raised objections about the overall content and staging of the musical and dance program, writing that the "latest installment of the Brazilian variety extravaganza" combined "folk fest, circus act and skin show," and tried "too hard the rest of the time to dazzle, whoop it up and pander, assaulting the audience with Vegas razzmatazz and cruise-ship, night-life mentality and showmanship."

13. He is one of the most respected *mestres* of his generation and founder of "Capoeira Grupo Cordão de Ouro—Mestre Suassuna." See www.grupocordaodeouro.com.br/. Accessed April 4, 2016.

14. See also her website, www.gingartecapoeira.org/our-group. Accessed May 30, 2019.

15. Mestre Janja makes similar comments. See "Sou discípulo" pp. 96–98, and 135–53.

16. I borrow the expression from Schrobsdorff, p. 55. She used it to discuss "verbal slights" in relation to the way the media addressed the Olympic gold-medal gymnasts.

17. In Salvador, *capoeira* was highly regarded as an important component of the Bahian/Brazilian cultural heritage. It appears in Jorge Amado's novels, Carybé's drawings, and songs by Dorival Caymmi and Gilberto Gil. In the 1980s there was a new wave of Afro-Brazilian music promoted by African-centric *carnaval* and activist groups such as Ilê Aiyê, Olodum, and Filhos de Ghandi. In Rio de Janeiro, famous lyricists such as Vinicius de Moraes (who was also a diplomat and a celebrated poet) and virtuoso musicians and composers (Baden Powell, for instance) lent their names and prestige to the game by composing highly popular songs that contributed to legitimize the *capoeira* game-fight. For samples of lyrics of MPB songs about *capoeira*, see Mestre Acordeon, pp. 98–103. The interest in promoting African-centric cultural manifestations also extended to other parts of Brazil. In São Paulo, some prominent cultural and academic figures (including university professors, sociologists, psychiatrists, writers, musicians, and dancers) embraced *capoeira*, and thus contributed to its popularity (L. Reis, pp. 144–45).

18. An example of this interest is illustrated in Mário de Andrade's *Macunaíma*, in which he mentions a visit several intellectuals of the period to the house of worship of Tia Ciata (in Rio de Janeiro) and how after the ceremony Macunaíma and other "macumbeiros," namely, "Jaime Ovalle, Dodô, Manu Bandeira, Blaise Cendrars, Ascenso Ferreira, Raul Bopp, Antônio Bento" left the place in the early hours of the morning, after a night of samba dancing, eating, and raucous fun.

19. For a criticism of cultural shows because they oversimplify multifaceted and complex cultural practices of African origin to satisfy tourist curiosity, see Esteves, pp. 112–14.

20. I visited her site (mandingueira.ca/category/female-mestres/) in 2018. She featured the following women *capoeiristas* on her site: Part 1: Mestra Edna Lima; Part 2: Mestra Suelly; Part 3: Mestranda Márcia Cigarra; Part 4: Contra-Mestra Marisa Cordeiro; Part 5: Mestra Janja; Part 6: Mestra Paulinha; Part 7: Contra-Mestra Susy; Part 8: Mestra Jararaca; Part 9: Contra-Mestra Cristina. Since then, Marisa Cordeiro (in 2001) and Márcia Cigarra (2009) have been promoted to the levels of *mestras*.

21. Her website lists her as "five-time Brazilian Champion, four-time US Champion, four-time Pan-American Champion, two-time Ozawa International Champion, and Black Belt Magazine Hall of Fame." www.ednalima.com/html/edn.html. Accessed May 30, 2019.

22. For further details, see *ABADÁ Capoeira*. See also Chatman's article.

23. The expression "good family" does not necessarily relate to moral issues but rather indicates how financially and socially affluent the family is. The understanding is that someone from a higher social class also has moral fortitude.

24. Unless other sources are mentioned, all references to Mestra Cigana and her professional and personal accomplishments in this study are based on an interview I conducted with her in Rio de Janeiro in 2003.

25. The documentary interweaves Mestra Cigarra's own account of her life story and trajectory in *capoeira*, with students' testimony, samples of performances, and intermittent comments by Wesolowski who was instrumental in helping Mestra Cigarra open her first *capoeira* academy in the United States (Leech).

26. As discussed in the video recording, *Márcia Capoeirista*, her dedication and passion for *capoeira* paid off: it did not take long for her to earn a yellow, orange, and blue ribbon which only a few women before her had received. The cord levels in ABADÁ-Capoeira are: natural, yellow, orange, blue (graduado), green (graduado), purple (instrutor), brown (professor), red (mestrando), red/white (mestre), white (mestre).

27. Mestra Cigarra had visited the United States as a guest instructor a couple of times before 1991, when Jennifer Walsh managed to raise funds from the San Francisco Foundation to get the first studio space for her where she opened the ABADÁ-Capoeira San Francisco and has lived there since then (Leech).

28. Some of Mestra Cigarra's outstanding awards and accomplishments include: KPIX Jefferson Award (2016) for teaching *capoeira*; ABC 7 Profile Excellence Award for her contribution to cultural diversity in the Bay Area (2014); title of *mestra* conferred by Mestre Camisa (2013); first place in ABADÁ-Capoeira Female Competition (Rio de Janeiro, 2010); recognition by Flyaway Productions: 10 Women Campaign Award, for her work as a "Bridge-Builder" in San Francisco communities (2009); and the KQED Latino Heritage Award (2007) for outstanding achievements as a teacher, leader, role model (Leech).

29. Highly visible examples include the Brazilian born women who had settled in the United States (Edna Lima, Márcia Cigarra, and Marisa Cordeiro).

30. They are university professors at the Universidade Federal da Bahia (UFBA).

31. It is the first organization of *capoeira angola* founded by women and it has expanded housing units in São Paulo, Salvador, and Brasília, and established subsidiary institutes in Maputo, Mexico City, London, and Marburg.

32. Unless otherwise indicated, all references to Mestra Janja and her professional and personal accomplishments are based on an interview I conducted with her in São Paulo in 2002, and on several phone and internet exchanges between 2006 and 2016.

33. However, M. Silva (174–75) also addresses the retaliations the group received for having bestowed the title of *mestra* on Pé de Anjo. As she reports, the misogynist debates that took place on social media, following the event, were highly disrespectful not only to Mestra Pé de Anjo, but to women *capoeiristas* everywhere in the world.

34. This information is based on the interviews I conducted with him in

Salvador, Bahia (July 13, 2003), and additional conversations we had in July and August, 2006.

Chapter Six: Women in Brazilian Popular Music and *Capoeira* Songs

1. Arguing for an all-encompassing definition of MPB, Martha de Ulhôa Carvalho traces its roots to "the 1930s sambas that were performed by Radio Nacional" (171). For her, "romantic music" and "samba-canção" (a softer and slower type of *samba* that puts emphasis on the lyrics) should be included in the definition of MPB because they are "just as much Brazilian popular music as MPB and bossa nova" (175).

2. See also works by Avelar and Dunn, McCann, and Perrone, listed in the Bibliography.

3. For an overview of the period, see McGowan and Pessanha, pp. 31–35; 201–02.

4. Oliven translated this song. For more details, see "Imaginary" 173.

5. For the complete lyrics of the song and the soundtrack, see "Letras," www.letras.com.br/orestes-barbosa/caixa-economica. Accessed May 9, 2017.

6. For the lyrics, see Ataulfo Alves; for a discussion of Alves's success and compositions, see Cabral's book; the first chapter is about this song.

7. At the time, bars were spaces for men. Virtuous women would shy away from them.

8. These songs are still present in *rodas de capoeira*, and continue to be taught by *mestres* and *contra-mestres* both inside and outside Brazil.

9. The *caxixi* (the instrument that accompanies the *berimbau*) reinforces the iconic image of a snake/*capoeira* player as it produces a jingling sound comparable to the noise a rattlesnake emits when it is ready to attack.

10. There are several references in *capoeira* songs to the "Paraguayan War," the War of the Triple Alliance that Argentina, Brazil, and Uruguay fought against Paraguay from 1864 to 1870. See Rego, pp. 197–98, 248; Assunção, pp. 103–04.

11. See also Moreira da Silva's *O Último Malandro*, recorded in 1958, and Chico Buarque's 1987 *Ópera do Malandro*. Walt Disney also created a Brazilian *malandro*, the parrot Zé Carioca who befriended Donald Duck.

12. Oliven addresses the concept *of malandragem* and *malandro* at length in "The Imaginary of Brazilian Popular Music," pp. 169–207.

13. See also Mestre Acordeon, p. 120.

14. I borrow the expression from Donaldson, pp. 52–53, used in a different context.

15. The words *comadre* (female) and *compadre* (male) do not have an exact equivalent in English. In Iberian and Latin American families, the terms originally meant co-parents; they still signal a special bond established when a child is baptized; they are also used to indicate a cordial relationship and strong comradery.

16. Public domain; sang by *capoeirista* Sereia. www.youtube.com/watch?v=_oHT2j9YCAs. Accessed May 30, 2019.

17. The song was first recorded in 1965 in the album *Vinicius: Poesia e Canção.*

18. In 2010 he received the Prêmio Jabuti, the highest honor in Brazilian literature, and in 2019 he was awarded the Camões Prize, the most important award given to writers of the Portuguese-speaking countries for his song lyrics, novels, and plays.

19. Meneses cites the song "Emília" by Haroldo Lobo and Wilson Batista (in which the lyric voice describes his ideal woman as someone who knows how to cook and do other house chores). She also mentions "Levanta, José" ("Get Up, José"), a song by Donga and Haroldo Lobo about a woman who gets up at five in the morning to prepare breakfast for her man and then tries to get him up to force him to go to work (Meneses, p. 45, n. 7).

20. For the theme of jealousy in Hollanda's song, see also Meneses, pp. 43–52.

21. Legend goes that Dona Maria do Camboatá (her name is a reference to the city where she lived which was located about a 100 miles north of Salvador, Bahia) was a fearless participator in *capoeira* games in the late nineteenth and early twentieth centuries. Variations in the lyrics of songs are common. This is the only reference I found to this song in which sexual references are made. The other lyrics discuss her as a bossy woman who plays *capoeira*.

22. The saying is sometimes attributed to Mestre Pastinha, other times to Mestre Bimba. See, for instance, Mestre João Pequeno and Mestre Miguel Machado, "Os erês curumins," and Mestre Paulo dos Anjos, "Três mestres."

23. Quoted to me by Letícia Vidor de Souza Reis, during an interview. See also Lewis, p. 173 in which he offers an account of his own experience in *rodas de capoeira* in Brazil.

Coda

1. The surge of the Me Too Movement, in 2017, galvanized public revelations of high profile male sexual misconduct in the United States and impacted women's desire to tell their stories as a form of protest across the globe. Brazilian women also shared those concerns.

2. Following a court ruling, on June 13, 2019, in a "note of retraction" President Jair Bolsonaro issued a public apology to Maria do Rosário Nunes. The judge also ordered him to pay her R$ 10,000 in reparation for "moral damages." See the article by Maia and Santos.

3. The incident happened in 2014. For a video recording of their interaction, see www.youtube.com/watch?v=h1Q108j7Y0. 2 Dec. 2, 2018.

4. For instance, he signed executive orders that affect their sense of community, identity, and livelihood (preventing the identification and demarcation of new lands, and vowing to confiscate land already owned by Afro-Brazilians since the abolition of slavery). See also "Brazil's Sad Choice" by the Editorial Board of *The New York Times.*

5. See g1.globo.com/pe/pernambuco/noticia/2019/01/24/mulher-leva-tiro-na-cabeca-e-denuncia-marido-escrevendo-nome-dele-com-sangue-em-maca.ghtml. Accessed Jan. 24, 2019.

6. Including Michel Temer, the vice president, who took over when she was removed from office and, on March 21, 2019, was arrested as part of a larger corruption investigation.

7. For additional information about Ustra, see Christofoletti's article.

8. For more details on the "Maria da Penha Law," see Spieler and Nandi.

Bibliography

"A herdeira natural das feministas das décadas de 60 e 70." *Revista Época*, vol. 100, 2000, p. 1.

Abib, Pedro Rodolpho Jungers, coordinator. Prefácio by Frederico José Abreu. *Mestres e capoeiras famosos da Bahia*. EDUFBA, 2009.

Abreu, Frederico José. *Bimba é bamba: A capoeira no ringue*. Instituto Jair Moura, 1999.

———. Personal interview. 3 Aug. 2004.

Abrahão, Bruno Otávio, and Antônio Jorge Soares. "O que o brasileiro não esquece nem a tiro é o chamado frango de Barbosa: Questões sobre o racismo no futebol." *Movimento*, vol. 15, no. 2, 2009, pp.13–31.

Alicea, Lydia. "An Interview with Mestranda Edna Lima." *MartialForce.Com: Online Magazine*. www.martialforce.com/edna_lima_story.htm. Accessed 30 May 2019.

Almeida, Manuel Antônio de. *Memórias de um sargento de milícias (1854–1855)*. W.M. Jackson, 1963.

Alves, Ataulfo and Mário Lago, composers. "Ai, que saudades da Amélia." *Ataulfo Alves e seus sucessos*. Sinter, 1966.

Amado, Jorge. (1937) *Capitães da Areia*. Record, 1995.

———. (1945) *Bahia de todos os santos: Guia das ruas e mistérios da cidade de Salvador*. Record, 1975.

———. (1958) *Gabriela, Cravo e Canela*. Companhia das Letras, 2012.

———. (1959) *A morte e a morte de Quincas Berro D'água*. Record, 1993.

"Ana Paula Oliveira será capa de 'Playboy' em julho." *O Estado de São Paulo*, 18 Jun. 2007. www.estadao.com.br/esportes/futebol/noticias/2007/jun/18/295.htm. Accessed 10 May 2014.

Andrade, Carlos Drummond. "Futebol." *Quando é dia de futebol*. Companhia das Letras, 2014, p. 13.

Andrade, Mário de. *Macunaíma: O herói sem nenhum caráter*. Critical edition. Edited by Telê Porto Ancona. CNPq, 1988.

Andrade, Oswald de. "Cannibalist Manifesto." Translated by Leslie Bary. *Latin American Literary Review*, vol. 19, no. 38, 1991, pp. 38–47.

———. "O Capoeira." *Pau Brasil*. 2nd edition. Globo / Secretaria da Cultura, 1990, p. 87.

Assis, Joaquim Maria Machado de. *Obra completa. Poesia, crônica, crítica, miscelânea e epistolário*. Volume III. 2nd edition. Edited by Afrânio Coutinho. General introduction by J. Galante de Sousa. José

Aguilar, 1962, pp. 442–44.

Assunção, Matthias Röhrig. *Capoeira: The History of an Afro-Brazilian Martial Art*. Routledge, 2005.

Austern, Linda Phyllis and Naroditskaya, Inna, editors. *Music of Sirens*. Indiana UP, 2006.

Avelar, Idelber. "Revisões da masculinidade sob ditadura: Gabeira, Caio e Noll." *Estudos de Literatura Brasileira* Contemporân*ea*, vol. 43, 2014, pp. 49–68.

Avelar, Idelber, and Christopher Dunn, editors. *Brazilian Popular Music and Citizenship*. Duke UP, 2011.

Azevedo, Aluísiode. *The Slum*. Translated with a foreword by David Rosenthal. Afterword by Affonso Romano de Sant'Anna. Oxford UP, 2000.

Azevedo, Thales de. *Democracia racial: Ideologia e realidade*. Editora Vozes, 1975.

Bacchi, Karina. Comercial de cerveja Antarctica. "Bar da Boa: Sou boa, gostosa e todo mundo adora." www.youtube.com/watch?v=qQ4-TksZoUQ. Accessed 29 May 2019.

Barbosa, A. Lemos. *Pequeno vocabulário tupi-português com quarto apêndices: Perfil da língua tupi, palavras compostas e derivadas, metaplasmo, síntese bibliográfica*. Livraria São José, 1951.

Barbosa, Lívia Neves de H. "The Brazilian *Jeitinho*: An Exercise in National Identity." *The Brazilian Puzzle: Culture on the Borderlands of the Western World*. Edited by David Hess and Roberto DaMatta. Columbia UP, 1995, pp. 35–48.

Barbosa, Maria José Somerlate. "Capoeira: A gramática do corpo e a dança das palavras." *Luso-Brazilian Review*, vol. 42, no. 1, 2005, pp. 78–98.

———. "A mulher na capoeira." *Arizona Journal of Hispanic Cultural Studies*, vol. 9, 2005, pp. 9–28.

———. Women Novelists in the Early Decades of Brazilian Modernism." *Chasqui: Revista de Literatura Latinoamericana*, vol. 32, no.1, 2008, pp.3–24.

———. "As aves que aqui gorgeiam não gorgeiam como lá: As abordagens raciais no Brasil e nos Estados Unidos." *Afro-Hispanic Review*, vol. 29, no. 2, 2010, pp. 237–62.

———. "A representação da mulher nas cantigas de capoeira." *Portuguese Literary and Cultural Studies*, vol. 19/20, 2011, pp. 463–77.

Bastide, Roger. *African Religions in Brazil*. Johns Hopkins UP, 1978.

———. *O candomblé da Bahia: Rito nagô*. Translsation by Maria Isaura

Pereira de Queiroz. Companhia das Letras, 2001.

Beinart, Peter. "The Global Backlash against Women." *The Atlantic*, vol. 323, no. 1, 2019, pp. 11–15.

Belira, Célia Abicalil. "A imagem fotográfica e a estética da gravidez." *Mulher: Cinco séculos de desenvolvimento na América: Capítulo Brasil.* Edited by Sylvia Auad. CREZ/MG / IA/MG, 1999, pp. 411–23.

Benhabib, Sheyla. "The Liberal Imagination and the Four Dogmas of Multiculturalism." *The Yale Journal of Criticism*, vol. 12, no. 2, 1999, pp. 401–13.

Bergallo, Laura e Josiane Duarte. *Valeria Valenssa: Uma vida de sonhos.* Tinta Negra, 2015.

Bergamo, Giuliana. "Roda de gringo: A capoeira entra para o cardápio de grandes academias de ginástica dos Estados Unidos." *Veja*, 2004, p. 58.

Berkenbrock, Volney J. *A experiência dos orixás: Um estudo sobre a experiência religiosa no Candomblé.* Vozes, 1997.

Berlinck, Manoel Tosta. "Sossega Leão! Algumas considerações sobre o samba como forma de cultura popular." *Revista Contexto Educação*, no.1, 1976, pp. 101–14.

Besse, Susan K. *Restructuring Patriarchy: The Modernization of Gender Inequity in Brazil, 1914–1940.* North Carolina UP, 1996.

Bhabha, Homi K. "Signs Taken for Wonders." *The Post-Colonial Reader.* Edited by Bill Ashcroft, et al. 2nd edition. Routledge, 2006, pp. 38–43.

Biazzi, Alessandro e Franchesci Neto, Virgílio. "Futebol e política externa brasileira: Entre o político-identitário e o comercial." *Revista Digital*, vol. 11, n. 104, 2007, n.p.

Bishop-Sanchez, Kathryn. *Creating Carmen Miranda: Race, Camp, and Transnational Stardom.* Vanderbilt UP, 2016

Bittencourt, Adalzira. "Sua Excia.: A presidente da República no ano 2500." *Visões do passado, previsões do futuro. Ercília Nogueira Cobra: Virgindade inútil* e *Virgindade anti-higiênica. Adalzira Bittencourt: A Sua Excia.: A presidente da República no ano 2500.* Edited and annotated by Susan Quinlan and Peggy Sharpe.Tempo Brasileiro / Editora da UFG, 1996, pp. 153–212.

Boaventura, Maria Eugênia. *A vanguarda antropofágica.* Ática, 1985.

Borrego, Victor de Miguel (Rasca), organizor. "Sereia." Songbook for the group Capoeira Libertação. capoeiralibertacao.weebly.com/capoeira-libertaccedilatildeo.html. Recorded by Mestres Limão e Nataniel. www.capoeira-music.net/all-capoeira-songs/all-capoeira-corridos-songs-o/o-sereia-o-sereia/. Accessed 8 May 2017.

Bourdieu, Pierre. *Masculine Domination*. Translated by Richard Nice. Polity, 2001.

Bretas, Marcos Luiz. "Navalhas e capoeiras: Uma outra queda." *Ciência Hoje*, vol. 10, no. 59, 1989, pp. 56–64.

Brooke, James. "'Honor' Killing of Wives Is Outlawed in Brazil." *The New York Times*, published 29 March 1991, p. B00016, www.nytimes.com/1991/03/29/us/honor-killing-of-wives-is-outlawed-in-brazil.html. Accessed 12 Sept. 2016.

Browning, Barbara. *Samba: Resistance in Motion*. Indiana UP, 1995.

Bruhns, Heloisa Turini. *Futebol, carnaval e capoeira: Entre as gingas do corpo brasileiro*. Papirus, 2000.

Burdick, John. *Blessed Anastacia: Women, Race, and Popular Christianity in Brazil*. Routledge, 1998.

Burns, E. Bradford. *A History of Brazil*. 3rd edition. Columbia UP, 1993.

Butler, Judith. "Desire." *Critical Terms for Literary Study*. Edited by Frank Lentricchia and Thomas McLaughlin. Chicago UP, 1995, pp. 369–86.

Cabral, Sérgio. *Ataulfo Alves: Vida e obra*. Lazuli Publisher / Bookwire Brazil Distribuição Ltda. 1 Aug. 2016. Kindle edition.

Campos, Léa. Personal interview. 24 and 25 Apr. 2016.

Capoeira, Nestor. *A Street-Smart Song: Capoeira Philosophy and Inner Life*. Snake Blue Books, 2006.

———. *Capoeira: Os fundamentos da malícia*. 6th edition. Editora Record, 2000.

———. *Roots of Dance, Fight, Game*. North Atlantic Book, 2002.

———. *The Little Capoeira Book*. Translated by Alex Ladd. Revised edition. Blue Snake Books, 2003.

Carneiro, Geraldo. "Rita Baiana." *Gozos da Alma*. Biscoito Fino, 2011.

Carvalho, Martha de Ulhôa. "Tupi or Not Tupi MPB: Popular Music and Identity in Brazil." *The Brazilian Puzzle: Culture on the Borderlands of the Western World*. Edited by David J. Hess and Roberto A. DaMatta. Columbia UP, 1995, pp. 159–79.

Casadei, Carol. "As garotas Kaiser." www.youtube.com/watch?v=BMr6zI_3I--k. Acessed 29 Jan. 2018.

Cascudo, Luís da Câmara. *Folclore do Brasil: Pesquisas e notas*. Fundo de Cultura, 1967.

———. *Made in África*. Global, 2001.

———. *Geografia dos mitos brasileiros*. Global, 2010.

Castello Branco, Humberto. "Decreto-Lei n. 4.638." Diário Oficial da União, section 1, 28 May 1965. www2.camara.leg.br/legin/ fed/ declei/1940-1949/decreto-lei-3199-14-abril-1941-413238- norma-pe.html. Accessed 7 Nov. 2013.

Caulfield, Sueann. *In Defense of Honor: Sexual Morality, Modernity, and Nation in Early-Twenty-Century Brazil.* Duke UP, 2000.

Caymmi, Dorival. "Marina." *The Essential Dorival Caymmi.* DRG Records. 18 Nov. 2014.

Certeau, Michel de. *The Practice of Everyday Life.* Translated by Steven F. Rendall. California UP, 1984.

Chatman, Catharine. "Too Beautiful to Be a Fight and Much Too Graceful to Be Dangerous." *The New York Times*, 22 Dec. 2000, p. E50.

Chauí, Marilena. *Conformismo e resistência: Aspectos da cultura popular no Brasil.* Brasiliense, 1986.

Christofoletti, Lilian. "Juiz condena Ustra por sequestro e tortura." *Folha de São Paulo*, 10 Oct. 2008, www1.folha.uol.com.br/fsp/brasil/ fc1010200834.htm. Acessed 03 jan. 2016.

Cidade Negra. "Mucama." *Sobre todas as forças.* Sony Music, 1994.

Cobra , Rubem Queiroz. "Ercília, culta e destemida modernista brasileira." Cobra Pages, 2000, pp. 1–12.

Cobra, Ercília Nogueira. "Virgindade inútil: Novela de uma revoltada," e "Virgindade anti-higiênica." *Visões do passado, previsões do futuro. Ercília Nogueira Cobra: Virgindade inútil e Virgindade anti-higiênica. Adalzira Bittencourt: A Sua Excia.: A presidente da República no ano 2500.* Edited and organized by Susan Quinlan and Peggy Sharpe. Tempo Brasileiro / Editora da UFG, 1996, pp. 41–94; 103–39.

Coelho, Nelly Novaes. "Cecília Meireles," "Gilka Machado," "Francisca Júlia," "Henriqueta Lisboa." *Dicionário crítico de escritoras brasileiras.* Editora Escrituras, 2002.

Coelho Neto, Henrique Maximiliano. "O nosso jogo." *Melhores crônicas Coelho Neto.* Selectino and preface by Ubiratan Machado. Global, 2009, pp. 89–94.

Conceição, Sônia Fátima da. "Passado Histórico." *Cadernos negros: Os melhores poemas.* Fundo Nacional da Cultura / Ministério da Cultura, 1998, p. 118.

Connell, Raewyn W., and Messerschmidt, James W. "Hegemonic Masculinity: Rethinking the Concept." *Gender and Society*, vol. 19, no. 6, 2005, pp. 829–59.

Contins, Márcia e Goldman, Márcio. "O caso da Pomba-Gira: Religião e violência. Uma análise do jogo discursivo entre Umbanda e sociedade." *Religião e Sociedade*, vol. 11, no. 1, 1984, pp. 103–32.

Corrêa, Mariza. "Sobre a invenção da mulata." *Cadernos Pagu*, no. 6–7, 1996, pp. 35–50.

Costa, Sérgio. "A construção sociológica da raça no Brasil." *Estudos Afro-Asiáticos*, vol. 24, no.1, 2002, pp. 35–61.

Courteau, Joanna. "A feminização do discurso nacional na obra de Rachel de Queiroz." *Hispania*, vol. 84, no. 4, 2001, pp. 749–57.

Coutinho, Edilberto. *Bye, Bye, Soccer*. Translated by Wilson Loria. Host Publications, 1994.

Couto, Solange. *Receitas de Botequim*. Editoras Melhoramentos / Caras, 2002.

———. "O bumbo silenciou. Morre o sambista Sargentelli." Interview. *Tribuna do Norte*, www. tribunadonorte.com.br/anteriores/020414/brasil.html. Accessed 27 Jan. 2018.

Cristino, Fernanda da Rosa. "Ilegítima defesa da honra." Âmbito Jurídico, vol. XI, no. 54, 2008. www.ambito-juridico.com.br/site/index.php?n_link=artigos_leitura_pdf&artigo_ id=2966. Accessed 12 Sept. 2016.

Curtis IV, Edward E. *The Call of Bilal: Islam in the Africana Diaspora*. North Carolina UP, 2014.

Dalevi, Alessandra. "In Praise of *Mulatas*." *Brazzil*, 6 April 2002, www.brazzil.com/ pages/p06apr02.htm. Accessed 12 jan. 2018.

DaMatta, Roberto. *Relativizando: Uma introdução à antropologia social*. Editora Rocco, 1990.

———. *Carnivals, Rogues, and Heroes: An Interpretation of the Brazilian Dilemma*. Translated by John Drury. Notre Dame UP, 1991.

———. *O Que Faz o Brasil, Brasil?* Rocco, 1993, pp. 93–105.

———. "Sport in Society: An Essay on Brazilian Football." *VIBRANT*, vol. 6, no. 2, 2009, pp. 98–120.

Dávila, Jerry. *Diploma of Whiteness: Race and Social Policy in Brazil, 1917–1945*. Duke UP, 2003.

Debret, Jean Baptiste. *Viagem pitoresca e histórica ao Brasil, 1816–183, excertos e ilustrações*. Edições Melhoramentos, 1971.

Degler, Carl N. *Neither Black nor White: Slavery and Race Relations in Brazil and the United States*. Wisconsin UP, 1971.

Delgado, Julie. "Female Champion of Capoeira Teaches in New York: Interview with Graduada Pimentinha," *Planeta Capoeira Magazine*, 25 July 2002, www.capoeira.com/ planetcapoeira/view. Accessed 20 Aug. 2002.

Desch-Obi, M. Thomas J. *Fighting for Honor: The History of African Martial Art Traditions in the Atlantic World.* South Carolina UP, 2008.

Dias Filho, Antônio Jonas. "As mulatas que não estão no mapa." *Cadernos Pagu,* vol 6, no. 7, 1996, pp. 51–66.

Donaldson, Laura E. *Decolonizing Feminisms: Race, Gender, and Empire Building.* North Carolina UP, 1992.

Diniz, Edinha. *Chiquinha Gonzaga: Uma história de vida.* Record / Rosa dos Tempos, 1999.

Donner, Hans. *Hans Donner e seu universo.* Special edition. Editora Escala Ltda, 1996.

Diário Oficial da União. Seção 1, 18 April 1941. www2.camara.leg.br/ legin/ fed/declei/1940-1949/decreto-lei-3199-14-abril-1941-413238-norma-pe.html. Accessed 7 Nov. 2013.

Downey, Greg. "The Interaction of Music and Dance in *Capoeira.*" *Capoeira Angola: Grupo de Capoeira Angola Pelourinho.* Smithsonian / Folkways Records, 1996, pp. 11–13.

———. "Apresentação." *Capoeira Angola: Grupo de Capoeira Angola Pelourinho.* Smithsonian / Folkways Records, 1996, pp. 15–23.

———. "Domesticating an Urban Menace: Reforming Capoeira as a Brazilian National Sport." *The International Journal of History of Sport,* vol. 19, no. 4, 2002, pp. 1–32.

———. *Learning Capoeira: Lessons in Cunning from an Afro-Brazilian Art.* Oxford U P, 2005.

Downing, Ben. "Jogo Bonito: A Brief Anatomy of *Capoeira,*" *Southwest Review,* vol. 81, no. 4, 1996, pp. 545–62.

Dunn, Christopher. *Contracultura: An Alternative Arts and Social Transformation in Authoritarian Brazil.* North Carolina UP, 2016.

Duranti, Alessandro. *Linguistic Anthropology: A Reader.* Blackwell, 2001.

Eakin, Marshall C. *Becoming Brazilians: Race and National Identity in Twentieth-Century Brazil.* Cambridge UP, 2017.

Editorial Board. Opinion. "Brazil's Sad Choice." *The New York Times,* 21 Oct. 2018, www.nytimes.com/2018/10/21/opinion/brazil-election-jair-bolsonaro.html. Accessed 22 Oct. 2018.

Ellison, Fred P. *Brazil's New Novel: Four Northeastern Masters, José Lins do Rego, Jorge Amado, Graciliano Ramos, Rachel de Queiroz.* California UP, 1954.

Escher, Thiago de Aragão, and Reis, Heloisa Helena Baldy. "A relações entre futebol globalizado e nacionalismo: O exemplo da Copa do Mundo de 2006." *Revista Brasileira de Ciências do Esporte,* vol. 30, 2008, pp. 41–55.

Esteves, Acúrsio Pereira. *A "capoeira" da indústria do entretenimento do corpo, acrobacia e espetáculo para "turista ver."* A. P. Esteves, 2004.

Evleshin, Catherine, "Capoeira at the Crossroads." *UCLA Journal of Music Ethnology*, vol. 71, no. 10, 1986, pp. 7–17.

Faria Jr., Miguel, diretor. *O Xangô de Baker Street*. Sky Light Cinema, 27 Sept. 2001.

Faustino, Roberto, diretor. *Escolas de samba: O espetáculo. (A Documentary of Rio's Carnival)*. Gravadora Escola de Samba Ltda., 2002.

Fernandes, Carla Cristiane, e Silva, Paula C. da. "Um estudo sobre a participação feminina na capoeira em Campinas/SP." *Educação Física em Revista*, vol, 2, no. 2, 2008, pp. 1–8.

Fernandes, Florestan. *A integração do negro na sociedade de classes*. Dominus Editora, 1965.

———. *O negro no mundo dos brancos*. Difusão Europeia do Livro, 1972.

Fernandes, Sabrina. "Dilma Rousseff and the Challenge of Fighting Patriarchy Through Political Representation in Brazil." *Journal of International Women's Studies*, vol. 13, no. 3, 2012, pp. 114–26.

Ferreira, Débora Ribeiro de Sena. *Pilares narrativos: A construção do eu e da nação na prosa de oito romancistas brasileiras*. Editora Mulheres, 2004.

Ferreira-Pinto, Cristina. *O Bildungsroman feminino: Quatro exemplos brasileiros*. Editora Perspectiva, 1990.

Filho, Mário. (1947) *O negro no futebol brasileiro*. 4th edition. Mauad, 2003.

Flesky, Rita. *Beyond Feminist Aesthetics: Feminine Literature and Social Change*. Harvard UP, 1989.

Foster, David William. "The Feminization of Social Space in Patrícia Galvão's *Parque Industrial*." *Brasil / Brazil: Revista de Literatura Brasileira / A Journal of Brazillian Literature*, vol. 33, 2005–2006, pp. 23–46.

Foucault, Michel. *Madness and Civilization: A History of Insanity in the Age of Reason*. Translated by the French by Richard Howard. Vintage Books, 1988.

Franchesci Neto, Virgílio, "Futebol e política externa brasileira: Entre o político-identitário e o comercial," *Revista Digital*, vol. 11, no. 104, 2007, n.p.

Freire Filho, João, and Hershmann, Micael. "Funk Music Made in Brazil: Media and Moral Panic." *Brazilian Popular Music and Citizenship*. Edited by Idelber Avelar and Christopher Dunn. Duke UP, 2011, pp. 221–39.

Freyre, Gilberto. *The Masters and the Slaves: A Study in the Development of Brazilian Civilization*. Translated by Samuel Putman. California

UP, 1986.

———. "Foot-ball mulato." *Diário de Pernambuco*, 17 June 1938, p. 4.

———. Prefácio à primeira edição. "O negro no futebol brasileiro." *O negro no futebol brasileiro* de Mário Filho. Mauad, 2003, pp. 24–26.

Fry, Peter. "O que a Cinderela negra tem a dizer sobre a 'política racial' no Brasil." *Revista USP*, vol. 28, 1995–1996, pp. 122–35.

Furtado, Júnia Ferreira. "Chica, a verdadeira." *Nossa História*, vol. 1, no. 2, 2003, pp. 14–21.

Galvão, Patrícia Rehder. (1933) *Parque industrial*. Preface by Geraldo Galvão Ferraz. Introduction by Flávio Loureiro Chaves. 3rd edition. Mercado Aberto / EDUFSCar, 1994.

———. *Industrial Park: A Proletarian Novel*. Translated by Elizabeth and K. David Jackson. Translators' Preface. Afterword by K. David Jackson. Nebraska UP, 1993.

Gates Jr., Henry Louis. *The Signifying Monkey: A Theory of Afro-American Literary Criticism*. Oxford UP, 1988.

Gates Jr., Henry Louis, et al. "Brazil: A Racial Paradise?" *Black in Latin America*, Public Broadcasting Service, 2011.

Giacomini, Sônia Maria. *Mulher e escrava: Uma introdução histórica ao estudo da mulher negra no Brasil*. Vozes Ltda., 1988.

———. "Aprendendo a ser mulata: Um estudo sobre a identidade da mulata professional." *Entre a virtude e o pecado*. Edited by Albertina de Oliveira Costa and Cristina Brushini. Rosa dos Tempos / Fundação Carlos Chagas, 1992, pp. 213–46.

Gil-Montero, Martha. *Brazilian Bombshell: The Biography of Carmen Miranda*. Penguin Publishing, 1989.

Gilliam, Angela. "The Brazilian Mulata: Images in the Global Economy." *Race and Class*, vol. 40, no. 1, 1998, pp. 57–69.

———. "Women's Equality and National Liberation." *Third World Women and the Politics of Feminism*. Edited by Chandra Talpade, et al. Indiana UP, 1991, pp. 215–36.

Gomes, Camila. "Emissora confirma que Nayara Justino não será Globeleza em 2015." *Folha de São Paulo*, 15 Oct. 2014. www.folha.uol.com.br. Accessed 20 Oct. 2016.

Gomes, Mariana Selister. "A (des) construção do Brasil com um paraíso das mulatas." *Revista Eletrônica de Turismo Cultural*, vol. 4, no. 2, 2010, pp. 48–70.

Goldenberg, Mirian, org. *O corpo como capital: Estudos sobre gênero, sexualidade e moda na cultura brasileira*. Estação das Letras / Cores Editora, 2007.

Gonzalez, Lélia. "Racismo e sexismo na cultura brasileira." *Ciências Sociais Hoje*, vol. 2, 1983, pp. 223–44.

Graham, Maria (Lady Maria Callcott). *Journal of a Voyage to Brazil, and Residence There, during Part of the Years 1821, 1822, 1823*. Cambridge UP, 2010.

Graham, Richard. "Technology and Culture Change: The Development of the Berimbau in Colonial Brazil." *Latin-American Music Review*, vol. 12, no. 1, 1991, pp. 1–20.

Grosz, Elizabeth, "Bodies-Cities." *Sexuality and Space*. Edited by Beatriz Colomina. Princeton U School of Architecture, 1992, pp. 241–54.

Guedes, Simoni Lahud. *O Brasil no campo de futebol: Estudos antropológicos sobre o significado do futebol brasileiro*. U Federal Fluminense, 1998.

Gonçalves, Ana Maria. *Um defeito de cor*. Record, 2009.

Guimarães, Antônio Sérgio Alfredo "Racial Democracy." *Imagining Brazil*. Edited by Jessé Souza and Valter Sinders. Lexington Books, 2005, pp. 119–39.

Guizardi, Menara Lube "'Como si fueran hombres': Los arquetipos masculinos y la presencia femenina en los grupos de capoeira de Madrid." *Revista de Antropologia Experimental*, no. 11, 2001, pp. 299–315.

Guizard, Manara Lube, and Ypeij, Annelou. "'Being Carried Out": Women's Bodies and Masculinity Inside and Outside the *Capoeira* Ring." *Gender and Conflict: Embodiment, Discourse and Symbolic Practices*. Edited by Georg Freks, et al. Ashgate Publishing, 2014, pp. 175–92.

Hahner, Jude E. *Emancipating the Female Sex: The Struggle for Women's Rights in Brazil, 1850–1940*. Duke UP, 1990.

Hanchard, Michael. "Black Cinderella?" Race and the Public Sphere in Brazil." *Racial Politics in Contemporary Brazil*. Duke UP, 1999, pp. 59–81.

Hanchiau, Núbia. "A representação da mulata na literatura brasileira: Estereótipo e preconceito." *Cadernos Literários*, vol. 7, 2002, pp. 57–64.

Harding, Rachel E. *A Refuge in Thunder: Candomblé and Alternative Spaces of Blackness*. Indiana UP, 2000.

Hargreaves, Melanie. "Brazil Tough Laws on Violence against Women Stymied by Social Norms." 12 May 2015. www.theguardian.com. Accessed 28 Sept. 2018.

Harper, Nick. "Stuart Hall". *The Guardian*, London, 2 May 2003, www.theguardian. com/football/2003/may/02/newsstory.sport11. Accessed 31 Aug. 2016.

Harvey, John J. "Cannibals, Mutants, and Hipsters: The Tropicalist Revival." *Brazilian Popular Music and Globalization.* Edited by Charles A. Perrone and Christopher Dunn. Routledge, 2002, pp. 106–22.

Hayes, Kelly E. *Holy Harlots: Femininity, Sexuality, and Black Magic in Brazil.* California, UP 2011.

Hellwig, David J. *African-American Reflections on Brazil's Racial Paradise.* Temple UP, 1992.

Herbermann, Charles George et al., editors. *The Catholic Encyclopedia: An International Work of Constitution, Doctrine, Discipline, and History of the Catholic Church.* The Encyclopedia Press, Inc., 1912, pp. 508–14.

Hess, David J., and DaMatta, Roberto A. *The Brazilian Puzzle: Culture on the Borderlands of the Western World.* Columbia UP, 1995.

Heuman, Michael, and Heuman, Susie, directors. *Brazil: Heart of South America.* Narrated by Bruce Robertson. International Video Network, 1988, 55 min.

Hite, Shere. *The Hite Report: A National Study of Female Sexuality.* MacMillan Publishing Company, 1976.

Hobbs, Allyson. *A Chosen Exile: A History of Racial Passing in American Life.* Harvard UP, 2016.

Holanda, Sérgio Buarque de. "O homem cordial." *Raízes do Brasil.* José Olympio, 1956, pp. 139–51.

Hollanda, Francisco Buarque de. *Chico Buarque de Hollanda.* LP. vol. I, RGE, 1966.

———. *Chico Buarque de Hollanda.* LP. vol. II, RGE, 1967.

———. *Chico Buarque de Hollanda.* LP. vol. III, RGE, 1968.

———. *Chico Buarque de Hollanda.* LP. vol. IV, RGE, 1970.

———. *Construção. LP. Philips,* 1971.

———. *Caetano e Chico juntos ao vivo,* 7 Jan. 1972. Verve Reissues. Universal Music Ltda., 11 Sept. 2007.

———. *Caravanas.* Biscoito Fino. 1 Sept. 2017.

Holloway, Thomas H. "O 'saudável terror': Repressão policial aos capoeiras e resistência dos escravos no Rio de Janeiro no século XIX." *Estudos Afro-Asiáticos,* vol. 16, 1989, pp. 129–40.

Hughes, Rob. "The Best Player on Earth Is Looking for a Job." *The New York Times,* 11 Jan. 2011, www.nytimes.com/2011/01/12/sports/soccer/12iht-SOCCER12.html. Accessed 12 Jan. 2016.

Hulet, Claude Lyle. *Brazilian Literature 3: 1920–1960, Modernism.* Georgetown UP, 1975.

Htun, Mala. "From Racial Democracy to Affirmative Action: Changing State Policy on Race in Brazil." *Latin American Research Review*, vol.
39, no. 1, 2004, pp. 60–89.

Instituto Brasileiro de Geografia e Estatística (IBGE). "What Color Are
you?" *The Brazil Reader: History, Culture, Politics*. Edited by Robert
M. Levine and John J. Crocitti. Duke UP, 1999, pp. 386–90.

Instituto DataFolha e Fórum Brasileiro de Segurança Pública. "Visível e in-
visível: A vitimização de mulheres no Brasil." Mar. 2017, pp. 1–43.
www.forumseguranca. org.br/publicacoes/visivel-e-invisivel-a-viti-
mizacao-de-mulheres-no-brasil. Accessed 28 Dec. 2018.

Jobim, Antônio Carlos, and Moraes, Vinicius de. "A Garota de Ipanema."
Translated as "The Girl from Ipanema" by Norman Gimbel. *Antônio Carlos Jobim Songbook*. Verve Records, 1995.

Johnson, Paul Christopher. *Secrets, Gossips, and Gods: The Transformation of
Brazilian Candomblé*. Oxford UP, 2002.

Johnson, Randal. "Brazilian Modernism: An Idea Out of Place?" *Modernism
and Its Margins: Reinscribing Cultural Modernity from Spain and
Latin America*. Edited by Anthony L. Geist and José B. Monleón.
Garland Publishing, 1999, pp.186–214.

Kirby, Kathleen M. *Indifferent Boundaries: Spatial Concepts of Human Subjectivity*. The Guildford Press, 1996.

Knijnik, Jorge. "Visions of Gender Justice: *Untested Feasibility* on the Foot-
ball Fields of Brazil." *Journal of Sport and Social Issues*, vol. 37, no.
1, 2012, pp. 8–30.

Kolodny, Annette. "Dancing through the Minefield: Some Observations on
the Theory, Practice, and Politics of a Feminist Literary Criticism."
Critical Theory since 1995. Edited by Hazard Adams and Leroy
Searle. UP Florida, 1986, pp. 499–512.

Lande, Ruth. *City of Women*. The McMillan Company, 1947.

Larsen, Nella. *Passing*. Knopf, 1929.

Lawrence, Harold G. "Mandinga Voyages across the Atlantic." *Journal of
African Civilizations*, vol. 8, no. 2, 1986, pp. 202–47.

Leech, Marla Renée, director. *Cigarra Capoeirista*. Produced by Marla Renée
Leech and Jennifer Walsh. Edited by Dale G. Nabeta. San Francisco Art Commission and Individual Art Commission, 2007.

Lefebvre, Henri. *The Production of Space*. Wiley-Blackwell, 1992.

Leich, Vincent B. *Cultural Criticism, Literary Theory, Post-structuralism*. Columbia UP, 1992.

Lemos Barbosa, A. *Pequeno vocabulário tupi-português com quarto apêndices:
Perfil da língua tupi, palavras compostas e derivadas, metaplasmo,*

síntese bibliográfica. Livraria São José, 1995.

Lesnoff-Caravaglia, Gari, editor. *The World of the Older Woman.* Human Sciences, 1984.

Lever, Janet. *Soccer Madness.* Chicago UP, 1983.

Levine, Robert M. "Sport in Society: The Case of Brazilian *Futebol.*" *Luso-Brazilian Review,* vol. 17, no. 2, 1980, pp. 233–52.

———. "The Brazilian Way." *Brazilian Legacies.* Routledge, 1997, pp. 80–110.

Lewis, John Lowell. *Ring of Liberation: Deceptive Discourses in Brazilian Capoeira.* UP Chicago, 1992.

Levy, Milton. *O dia em que comi a Pomba Gira.* Teatro Bibi Ferreira, 2 May–28 Nov. 2015.

Ligeiro, Zeca. "Candomblé Is Religion-life-art." *Divine Inspiration.* Organized and photographed by Phylls Galembo; translated by Brian F. Head; foreword by David Burne. New Mexico UP, 1993, pp. 97–117.

Lima, Edi. *Como salvar meu casamento.* Rede Tupi de Televisão, Jun. 1979–Feb. 1980.

Lobato, Monteiro. "A propósito da exposição Malfatti." *Estado de São Paulo,* 20 dez. 1917, n.p.

Lopes, Nei. *Novo dicionário banto do Brasil, contendo mais de 250 propostas etimológicas acolhidas pelo dicionário Houaiss.* Pallas, 2003.

Lucinda, Elisa, "Mulata Exportação." *O semelhante.* Rob Digital, 1997.

Lyra, Carlos. "Minha Namorada." *Pure Bossa Nova.* Verve International, 2008.

Lyra Filho, João. *Introdução à Sociologia de Desportos.* Bloch / Instituto Nacional do Livro, 1973.

McCann, Bryan. *Hello, Hello Brazil: Popular Music in the Making of Modern Brazil.* Duke UP, 2004.

Machado, Liz Zanotta. "Brazilian Feminisms in Their Relations with the State: Contexts and Uncertainties." *Cadernos Pagu,* no. 47, 2016.

Maia, Gustavo, e Santos, Jussara. "Cumprindo decisão judicial, Bolsonaro pede desculpas a Maria do Rosário em rede social." *Jornal O Globo,* 19 June 2019. oglobo.globo.com. Accessed 19 June 2019.

Main, Oleander. *The Summer of Pomba Gira.* Xlibris, 2009.

Marchant, Elizabeth A. "Lúcia Miguel Pereira and the Era(c)ing of Brazilian National Literature." *Critical Acts: Latin-American Women and Cultural Criticism.* Florida UP, 1999, pp. 18–45.

Marino, Katherine M. *Feminism for the Americas: The Making of an Interna-*

tional Human Rights Movement. North Carolina UP, 2019.

Martins, Wilson. *The Modernist Idea: A Critical Survey of Brazilian Writing in the Twentieth Century*. Greenwood P, 1979.

Matos, Maria Izilda S. de and Fernando A. Faria. *Melodia e sintonia em Lupicínio Rodrigues: O feminino, o masculino e suas relações*. Bertrand Brasil, 1996.

McGowan, Chris and Ricardo Pessanha. *The Brazilian Sound: Samba, Bossa Nova, and the Popular Music of Brazil*. Temple UP, 2008.

Menand, Louis. "Words of the Year." *The New Yorker*, 8 Jan. 2017, p. 15.

Meneses, Adélia Bezerra de. *Figuras do feminino na canção de Chico Buarque*. 2nd edition. Ateliê Editorial, 2001.

Merrell, Floyd. *Capoeira and Candomblé: Conformity and Resistance through Afro-Brazilian Experience*. Markus Weiner Publishers, 2005.

Mestra Cigana (Fátima Colombiana). Personal interview. 25 May 2005.

———. "Interview with Mestra Cigana." Translated into English by Shayna McHugh. *Praticando Capoeira*, vol. 1, no. 4, 2011.

"Mestra Edna Lima." ABADÁ-Capoeira New York. www.ednalima.com/html/edn.html. Accessed 30 Jan. 2005;

———. "Interview by Susan Perry." *Aikido Today Magazine*, no. 40, n.d, n.p. www.ednalima.com/EDNA_MEDIA/aikido.html. Accessed 30 May 2019.

———. "An Interview with Mestranda Edna Lima." Interviewed by Lydia Alicea. *MARTIAL FORCE.COM: Online Magazine*. www.martial-force.com/edna_lima_story.htm. Accessed 15 Aug. 2011.

Mestra Janja (Rosângela Costa Araújo). "'Sou discípulo que aprende, meu mestre me deu lição': Tradição e educação entre os angoleiros baianos (anos 80–90)." Doctoral dissertation. Universidade de São Paulo, 1999.

———. "Contra-Mestre Janja." *Cordão Branco: A Revista dos Mestres*, vol. 1, no. 1, 2001, pp. 18–21.

———. Personal interview. 13 and 14 July 2002.

———. "Entrevista com Contra-Mestra Janja." Interview by Danilo Clímaco. *Toques D'Angola*, vol. 1, 2003, pp. 8–9.

Mestra Luar do Sertão (Anne Pollack). Personal interview. 29 June 1999 and 17 July 2017.

"Mestra (Márcia Treidler) Cigarra." ABADÁ Capoeira San Francisco. www.abada.qorg/mestra-marcia-cigarra/. Accessed 30 May 2019.

Mestra Marisa (Marisa Cordeiro). Personal interview. 10 and 11 April 2016.

Mestra Paulinha (Paula Cristina da Silva Barreto). Personal interview. 14

June 2004.

Mestre Acordeon (Bira Almeida). *Capoeira: A Brazilian Art Form.* North Atlantic Books, 1986.

———. "Mestra Suelly: The Making of a Mestra." Translation by Fogueirinha. www.capoeira.bz/mestreacordeon/articles/mestrasuelly.html. Accessed 30 May 2019.

Mestre Acordeon (Bira Almeida), and Mestra Suelly (Suellen Einarsen). "Ela joga capoeira—Zum Zum Zum." *Capoeira Voices II.* Ubirajara G. Almeida, 2009.

Mestre Barrão. "Essa Arte." www.letras.com/mestre-barrao/436144. Accessed 10 Sept. 2016.

Mestre Bola Sete (José Luiz Olveira Cruz). *Capoeira Angola: Do mestre ao iniciante.* EDUFBA / Pallas, 2003.

Mestre Burguês (Grupo Muzenza de Capoeira). "Se essa mulher fosse minha." *Capoeira Muzenza,*1991.

Mestre João Pequeno, e Mestre Miguel Machado. "Os erês curumins." *Revista Ginga Capoeira: A Revista dos Mestres,* vol. 2, no. 11, 2001, n.p.

Mestre Moraes. "Se Essa Mulher Fosse Minha." mestremoraes-gcap.blogspot. com. Accessed 16 July 2010.

Mestre Paulo dos Anjos. "Três mestres." *Revista Ginga Capoeira: A Revista dos Mestres,* vol. 3, no. 22, 2002, n.p.

Mestre Reinaldo. "Quatro Coisas Neste Mundo." *Revista Ginga: A Revista dos Mestres de Capoeira,* ano 3, no. 22, 2002, n.p.

Mestre Valdemar. "Quatro coisas neste mundo." www.youtube.com/watch?-v=wug At3GGZq0. Accessed 20 abr. 2019.

Milestone, Katie, and Meyer, Anneke. *Gender and Popular Culture.* Polity, 2012.

Moehn, Frederick. "We Live in Two Countries: Audiotopias of Postdictatorship Brazil." *Brazilian Popular Music and Citizenship.* Edited by Idelber Avelar and Christopher Dunn. Duke UP, 2011, pp. 109–30.

Moraes, Enny Vieira, e Dias, Maria Odília Leite da Silva. "Diferentes corpos se apresentam: Fragmentos da história do futebol feminino no Brasil." *Caderno Espaço Feminino*, vol. 22, no. 2, 2009, pp. 183–204.

Moreno, Rita. "Valeria Valenssa: Que beleza!" *Raça Brasil*, vol, 2, no. 6, 1996, pp. 44–46.

Mott, Maria Lúcia de Barros. "Biografia de uma revoltada: Ercília Nogueira Cobra." *Cadernos de Pesquisa*, vol. 58, 1986, pp. 89–104.

Motta, Zezé. *Xica da Silva.* Warner Music Brazil Ltda, 1981.

Museu do Futebol. "História e curiosidades do futebol brasileiro." Portal.

Arquivos e coleções permanentes. www.museudofutebol.org.br/. Accessed 10 May 2019.

Nandi, Aline, et al. "The Maria da Penha Law as Public Policy Assistant to Women Victims of Violence." *Scholedge International Journal of Multidisciplinary & Allied Studies*, vol. 1, no.2, Nov. 2014, pp. 30–39.

Nascimento, Abadias do. *"Racial Democracy" in Brazil, Myth or Reality?: A Dossier of Brazilian Racism.* Translated by Elisa Larking do Nascimento; Foreword by Wole Soyinka. 2nd edition, revised and expanded. Sketch Publishing, 1977.

———. *O genocídio do negro brasileiro: Processo de um racismo mascarado.* Editora Perspectiva, 2016.

Nascimento, Edson Arantes do (Pelé), with Robert L. Fish. *My Life and the Beautiful Game: The Autobiography of Pelé.* Foreword by Shep Messing. Photos by Joe Greene. Garden City, 1977.

Nega Gizza. *Na Humildade.* Zâmbia / DumDum Records, 2002.

Neschling, John and Carneiro, Geraldo. "Rita Baiana." *Gozos da alma.* SESC Rio Som, 2011.

Nichols, Peter. "Rio 2016: Never Mind Golf and Rugby, Bring on Olympic Kabbadi and Capoeira." *The Guardian*, www.theguardian.com/commentisfree/2012/aug/13/rio-2016-olympics-golf-rugb. Accessed 31 Aug. 2016.

Nogueira, Oracy. "Preconceito racial de marca e preconceito racial de origem." *Tempo Social: Revista de Sociologia da USP*, vol. 19, no 1, 2006, pp. 287–308.

Oliveira, Emanuelle K. F. *Writing Identity: The Politics of Contemporary Afro-Brazilian Literature.* Purdue UP, 2007.

Oliveira, Josivaldo Pires de and Luiz Augusto Pinheiro Leal. *Capoeira, identidade e gênero: Ensaios sobre a história social da capoeira no Brasil.* EDUFA, 2009.

Oliveira, Pedro Assis Ribeiro de. *Religião e dominação de classe: Gênese, estrutura e função do Catolicismo romanizado no Brasil.* Vozes, 1985.

Oliven, Ruben George. "A mulher faz e desfaz o homem." *Ciência Hoje*, vol. 37, 1987, pp. 54–62.

———. "The Imaginary of Brazilian Popular Music." *Vibrant (Virtual Brazilian Anthropology)*, vol. 8, no.1, 2001, pp. 169–207

OMCT. (World Organization against Torture). "Violence against Women in Brazil. A Report to the Committee on Economic, Social and Cultural Rights." www.omct.org/files/2004/ 07/2409/eng_2003_02 _brazil.pdf. Accessed 15 Dec. 2018.

Ortiz, Renato. *Cultura brasileira e identidade nacional.* Editora Brasiliense, 1985.

——. *A morte branca do feiticeiro negro: Umbanda e sociedade brasileira.* Editora Brasiliense, 1991.

Owen, Hilary. "Discardable Discourses in Patrícia Galvão's *Parque industrial.*" *Brazilian Feminisms.* Edited by Solange Ribeiro de Oliveira and Judith Still. Nottingham UP, 1999, pp. 68–84.

Parker, Richard G. *Bodies, Pleasures and Passions: Sexual Culture in Contemporary Brazil.* Beacon P, 1991.

Pereira, Edimilson de Almeida. *Caderno de Retorno. As coisas arcas: Obra poética 4.* Funalfa Edições, 2003.

Pereira, Leonardo Affonso de Miranda. *Footballmania. Uma história social do futebol no Rio de Janeiro.* Nova Fronteira, 2000.

Pereira, Lúcia Miguel. *Amanhecer,* 1938. José Olympio Editora, 1979.

——. *Em Surdina.* Ariel Editora, 1933.

——. *Maria Luiza.* Schmidt Editor, 1933.

Perrone, Charles A. *Letras & letras da música popular brasileira.* Elo, 1988.

——. *Masters of Contemporary Brazilian Song: MPB 1965–1985.* Texas UP, 1989.

——. *Seven Faces: Brazilian Poetry since Modernism.* Duke UP, 1996.

Petrini, Paulo. "Um estudo crítico sobre as vinhetas da Rede Globo." *Acta Scientiarum. Human and Social Sciences,* vol. 26, no. 1, 2004, pp. 123–33.

Pfister, Gerturd. "The Medical Discourse on Female Physical Culture in Germany in the 19th and 20th Centuries." *Journal of Sport History,* vol. 17, no. 2, Summer 1990, pp. 183–98.

Pinho, Patrícia de Santana. *Mapping Diaspora: African American Roots Tourism in Brazil.* North Carolina UP, 2018.

Pires, Antônio Liberac Cardoso Simões. "Uma 'volta ao mundo' com as mulheres capoeiras: Gênero e cultura negra no Brasil (1850–1920)." *Mulheres negras no Brasil escravista e do pós-emancipação.* Edited by Giovana Xavier, et al. Selo Negro, 2012, pp. 282–96.

Porto, Ismar, diretor. *As granfinas e o Camelô.* Vydia Produções Cinematográficas, 1977.

Prandi, Reginaldo. *Herdeiras do axé: Sociologia das religiões afro-brasileiras.* Editora HUCITEC, 1996.

Pravaz, Natasha. "Imagining Brazil: Seduction, Samba, and the Mulata's Body." *Canadian Women Studies / LesCahiers de la Femme,* vol. 20, no. 1, 2000, pp. 48–55.

————. "Brazilian *Mulatice*: Performing Race, Gender, and the Nation." *Journal of Latin American Anthropology*, vol. 8, 2003, pp. 116–46.

Priore, Mary del. *Mulheres no Brasil colonial.* Editora contexto, 2000.

————. *Histórias Íntimas: Sexualidade e Erotismo na História do Brasil.* Editora Planeta, 2011.

Queiroz, Rachel de. *O quinze*, 1930. Livraria José Olympio Editora, 1966.

Queiroz Junior, Teófilo de. *Preconceito de cor e a mulata na literatura brasileira.* Ática, 1975.

Quinlan, Susan, and Peggy Sharpe. "Duas modernistas esquecidas: Adalzira Bittencourt e Ercília Nogueira Cobra;" "Notas." *Visões do passado, previsões do futuro. Ercília Nogueira Cobra: Virgindade inútil e Virgindade anti-higiênica. Adalzira Bittencourt: A Sua Excia.: A presidente da República no ano 2500.* Edição anotada por Susan Quilan e Peggy Sarpe. Tempo Brasileiro / Editora UFG, 1996, pp. 13–222.

Rachum, Ilan. "Woman Suffrage and National Politics in Brazil: 1922–1937." *Luso-Brazilian Review*, vol, 14, no. 1, 1997, pp. 118–34.

Rector, Monica. "Nudity in Brazilian Carnival." *The American Journal of Semiotics*, vol. 6, no. 4, 1989, pp. 67–77.

Rego, Waldeloir. *Capoeira Angola: Ensaio sócio-etnográfico.* Itapoã, 1968.

Reis, João José. *Slave Rebellion in Brazil: The Muslim Uprising of 1835 in Bahia.* Johns Hopkins UP, 1993.

Reis, Letícia Vidor de Sousa. *O mundo de pernas para o ar: A capoeira no Brasil.* Brasil, 1997.

————. Personal interview. 12 July 2002.

Risério, Antônio. "Pagu: Vida-obra, obravida, vida." *Patrícia Galvão: Vida-obra.* Edited by Augusto de Campos. Brasiliense, 1987, pp. 18–30.

Rodrigues Filho, Mário. *O negro no futebol brasileiro.* 2nd edition. Civilização Brasileira, 1964.

Romero, Simon. "Public Rapes Outrage Brazil, Testing Ideas of Image and Class." *The New York Times*, 24 May 2013, p. A1.

Roosevelt, Theodore. "Brazil and the Negro." *Outlook,* 1914, pp. 409–11.

Rosa, Cristina F. *Brazilian Bodies and Their Choreographies of Identification: Swing Nation.* Palgrave MacMillan, 2015.

Rosa, Renato, organizador. "Di Cavalcanti: O enamorado da vida." www. dicavalcanti.com.br/ apresentacao.htm. Accessed 18 Jan. 2018.

Rufino, Janaína de Assis. "As minhas meninas: Constituição e complexidade discursivas das personagens femininas no cancioneiro de Chico Buarque." Edited by Jarbas Vargas Nascimento et al. *Língua, litera-*

tura e ensino. Blucher, 2015, pp. 67–74.

Rugendas, Johann Moritz. *Viajem pitoresca através do Brasil*. Livraria Martins, 1940.

Ruthven, K.K. *Feminist Literary Studies: An Introduction*. Cambridge UP, 1984.

Sadlier, Darlene. "Modernity and Femininity in 'He and She' by Júlia Lopes de Almeida." *Studies in Short Fiction*, vol. 30, no. 4, 1993, pp. 575–83.

Sant'Anna, Affonso Romano de. *Música Popular e Moderna Poesia Brasileira*. Vozes, 1980.

———. *O canibalismo amoroso: O desejo e a interdição em nossa cultura através da poesia*. Brasiliense, 1985.

———. "Mulher." *Que país é este?* Editora Rocco, 1990, pp. 90–95.

Santos, Joel Rufino dos. *A história política do futebol brasileiro*. Brasiliense, 1981.

Santos, Mafoane Odara Poli, e Grelin, Daniela Marques. "Violências invisíveis: O não óbvio em evidência". Instituto DataFolha e Fórum Brasileiro de Segurança Pública, pp. 35–39. www.forumseguranca. org.br/publicacoes/visivel-e-invisivel-a-vitimizacao-de-mulheres-no-brasil. Accessed 15 Feb. 2019.

Sargentelli, Oswaldo. *Ziriguidum*. Letras & Letras, 1993.

Scarinci, Marcioni, coordenador. "Futebol e Poesia." *Poemas sobre Futebol. Poesia dos Brasis. Poetas de Brasília. Poesia Ibero-americana. Poesia visual*, 2010. www.Antôniomiranda.com.br/poesia_brasis/rio_de_janeiro/futebol_e_poesia.html. Accessed 30 May 2019.

Schaffer, Matt. "Bound to Africa: The Mandinka Legacy in the New World." *History in Africa*, vol. 32, 2005, pp. 321–69.

Schemo, Diana Jean. "The Elevator Doesn't Lie: Intolerance in Brazil." *The New York Times*, 22 Aug. 1995, p. A:4.

Schrobsdorff, Susanna. "A Distressing Summer of Workplace, Sexism Reminds Us How Far We Have to Go." *Time Magazine*, 5 Sept. 2016, p. 55.

Sharpe, Peggy. "Construindo o caminho da nação através da obra de Júlia Lopes de Almeida e Adalzira Bittencourt." *Letras de Hoje*, vol. 33, 1998, pp. 39–49.

Shetty, Raksha. "Feline Fatale: Halle Berry." Interview. *CBS News, The Early Show*, 20 July 2004. www.cbsnews.com/stories/2004/07/20/earlyshow/leisure/ celebspot/main630707.shtml. Accessed 4 Aug. 2011.

Silva, Ana Paula da. "King Pele: Race, Professionalism and Football in Brazil." *National Black Law Journal,* no. 29, 2009, 1–20.

Silva, Maria Zeneide Gomes da. "Movimento capoeira mulher: Saberes ancestrais e a práxis feminista no século XXI em Belém do Pará." Doctoral dissertation. Universidade Federal do Estadual Paulista, 2017.

———. "Identidade de gênero: Mandingas, malícias e o jogo de poder nas rodas de capoeira paraense." *Gênero na Amazônia,* no. 7–12, jun.-dez. 2007, pp. 73–84.

Simões, Rosa Maria Araújo. "Capoeira: Um convite ao jogo feminino." Doctoral dissertation. Universidade Estadual Paulista, 1999.

Simões, Henrique Campos (textos, leituras e notas), e Gonzaga, Reinaldo Rocha (arte e ilustração). *O achamento do Brasil: A carta de Pero Vaz de Caminha a El-Rei D.Manuel sobre o achamento do Brasil, em quadrinhos.* EGBA / EDITUS, 1999.

Skidmore, Thomas. "Toward a Comparative Analysis of Race Relations since the Abolition in Brazil and the *United* States." *Journal of Latin American Studies,* vol. 4, no 1, 1972, pp.1–28.

———. *Black into White: Race and Nationality in Brazilian Thou*ght. Oxford UP, 1974.

———. "Bi-Racial U.S.A. vs. Multi-Racial Brazil: Is the contrast Still Valid?" *Journal of Latin American Studies,* vol. 25, no. 2, 1993, pp. 373–86.

Smith, Sid. "Oba, Oba: The Brazilian Musical Extravaganza." *The Chicago Tribune,* 20 Dec. 1991, n. p.

Soares, Carlos Eugênio Líbano. *A capoeira escrava e outras tradições rebeldes no Rio de Janeiro (1808–1850).* 2nd edition, revised and expanded. UNICAMP / Centro de Pesquisa em História Social da Cultura, 2002.

———. *A negregada instituição: Os capoeiras na Corte Imperial, 1830–1850.* Editora Access, 1999.

Soares, Jô (José Eugênio). *Xangô de Baker Street.* Companhia das Letras, 2011.

Sodré, Muniz. *Mestre Bimba: Corpo de Mandinga.* Editora Manati, 2002.

Sokolove, Michael. "Kicking Off." *The New York Times,* 1 Apr. 2009, p. MM23. archive.nytimes.com/www.nytimes.com/2009/04/05/magazine/05marta-t.html. Accessed 30 May 2019.

Souza, Jair. *Futebol-arte.* Editora SENAC / Empresa das Artes, 1998.

Souza, Marcos Alves. "Gênero e Raça: A nação construída pelo futebol brasileiro." *Cadernos Pagu,* vol. 6–7, 1996, pp. 109–52.

Spieler, Paula. "The Maria da Penha Case and the Inter-American Commission on Human Rights: Contributions to the Debate on Domestic Violence against Women in Brazil." *Indiana Journal of Global Legal Studies,* vol. 8, no. 1, 2011, pp. 121–43.

Squeff, Enio, and Wisnik, Miguel. *Música: O nacional e o popular na cultura brasileira.* 2nd edition. Brasiliense, 1983.

Street, Doca. *Mea culpa: O depoimento que rompe 30 anos de silêncio.* Planeta, 2006.

Taffarel, Celi Nelza Zulke, e França, Teresa Luiza de. "A mulher no esporte: O espaço social das práticas esportivas e de produção do conhecimento científico." *Revista Brasileira de Ciências do Esporte,* vol. 15, no. 3, 1994, pp. 235–46.

Talmon-Chvaicer, Maya. *The Hidden History of Capoeira: A Collision of Cultures in the Brazilian Battle Dance.* Texas UP, 2008.

Taylor, Gerard. *Capoeira: The Jogo de Angola from Luanda to Cyberspace.* Blue Snake Books, 2007.

Telles, Edward. *Racismo à brasileira: Uma nova perspectiva sociológica.* Relume Dumará, 2003.

Tigges. Gabriela P. C. Rust. "The History of Capoeira in Brazil." Doctoral dissertation. Brigham Young University, 1992.

Tikhomiroff, João Daniel, director. *Besouro.* Walt Disney Pictures, 2009.

Toplin, Robert Brent. "Reinterpreting Comparative Race Relations." *Journal of Black Studies,* vol. 2, no. 2, 1971, pp. 135–55.

Twine, France Windance. *Racism in a Racial Democracy: The Maintenance of White Supremacy in Brazil.* Rutgers UP, 1998.

United Capoeira Association. "Mestra Suelly." (Suellen Einarsen), 3 May 2001. wwwcapoeiraarts. com/articles/suellyangola.html. Accessed June 2003.

———. "Mestra Suelly 2." (Suellen Einarsen). 3 May 2001. www.capoeira-arts.com/articles/suellyangola.html. Accessed in June 2003.

Unruh, Vicky. "A Refusal to Perform: Patrícia Galvão's Spy on the Wall." *Performing Women and Modern Literary Culture in Latin America.* UP Texas, 2006, pp. 195–221.

Valenssa, Valeria. *Aprenda a sambar com Valeria Valenssa.* Directed by Otto Weiser and Hans Donner. PlayArte Pictures Ltda., 1997.

———. Personal interview. 30 May 2003.

———. "Valéria Valenssa comenta na mudança na vinheta Globo." *Extra,* 10 Jan. 2017. extra-globo.com. Accessed 15 jan. 2017.

Valente, Sérgio, et al. "Semana da mulher na Globo." Campanha "Semana da Mulher na Globo," Mar. 2019. redeglogo.globo.com/novidades/

noticia/confire-camapnha-da-globo-pra-o-dia-internacional-da-mulher.ghtml. Accessed 16 mar. 2019.

Vallado, Armando. *Iemanjá: A grande mãe africana do Brazil.* Pallas, 2002.

Varela, Sérgio Gonzalez. "Mandinga: Power and Deception in Afro-Brazilian Capoeira." *Social Analysis,* vol. 57, no. 2, 2013, pp. 1–20.

Vargas, Getúlio. (Presidência da República, Casa Civil.) "Decree-Law no. 3.199." *Diário Oficial da União,* Seção 1, 16 abril 1941, p. 7452.

Vaz, Lilian Fessler. "Dos cortiços às favelas e aos edifícios de apartamento—a modernização da moradia no Rio de Janeiro." *Análise Social,* vol. 29, no. 127, 1994, pp. 581–97.

Verger, Pierre Fatumbi. *Orixás, deuses iorubás na África e no Novo Mundo.* Translated by Maria Aparecida da Nóbrega. Corrupio, 1997.

Vianna, Hermano. *The Mystery of Samba: Popular Music and National Identity in Brazil.* Translated by John Charles Chasteen. North Carolina UP, 1999.

Viccari, Ively Mayumi Nagaye. "Força Guerreira." *Revista Ginga: A Revista dos Mestres de Capoeira,* vol. 23, no. 11, 2002, n.p.

Vila, Martinho da. "Você Não Passa de uma Mulher." *Maravilha de Cenário.* RCA Victor, 1975. www.letras.com/martinho-da-vila/47333/. Accessed 16 Jan. 2016.

Vilela, Caio e Petta, Eduardo. *O futebol-arte do Oiapoque ao Chuí.* Preface by Zico. Grão Editora, 2013.

Walby, Sylvia. *Theorizing Patriarchy.* Blackwell Publishers, 1990.

Webb, Jen, at al. *Understanding Bourdieu.* Sage Publication, 2002.

Williams, Darlyle. *Culture Wars in Brazil: The First Vargas Regime, 1930–1945.* Duke UP, 2001.

Winant, Howard. *Racial Conditions: Politics, Theory, Comparisons.* Minnesota UP, 1994.

Wisnik, José Miguel. "The Riddle of Brazilian Soccer: Reflections on the Emancipatory Dimensions of Culture." *Review: Literature and Arts of the Americas,* issue 73, vol. 39, no.2, 2006, pp. 198–209.

———. *Veneno remédio: o futebol e o Brasil.* Companhia da Letras, 2008.

"Women Footballers Blast Blatter." *BBC Sport.* Published 16 Jan. 2004. news.bbc.co. uk/go/pr/fr/-/sport2/hi/football/3402519.stm. Accessed 15 Jan. 2016.

Zé Ricardo, e Thiago. "Turbinada." *Onde Tudo Começou,* 2015.

Index

About the Book

In *The Ripple Effect: Gender and Race in Brazilian Culture and Literature*, Barbosa adopts a comparative, multilayered, and interdisciplinary line of research to examine social values and cultural mores from the first decades of the twentieth century to the present. By analyzing the historical, cultural, religious, and interactive space of Brazil's national identity, *The Ripple Effect* surveys expressive cultures and literary manifestations. It uses the martial art-dance-ritual *capoeira* as a lynchpin to disclose historical ambiguities and the negotiation of cultural and literary boundaries within the context of the ideological construct of a mestizo nation. The book also examines laws governing gender in Brazil and discusses honor killings and other types of violence against women. *The Ripple Effect* appraises the contributions that some iconic female figures have made to the development of Brazil's distinctive cultural and literary production. Drawing on more than fifteen years of field, archival, and scholarly research, this work offers new interpretative venues, and broadens the critical focus and the methodological scope of previous scholarship. It reveals how literature and other arts can be used to document cultural norms, catalog life experiences, and analyze complex constructions of social values, ideas, and belief systems.

About the Author

Maria José Somerlate Barbosa is Professor Emerita in the department of Spanish and Portuguese at the University of Iowa. She specializes in Brazilian literary and cultural studies. Her scholarly production is interdisciplinary and her book-length publications include *Clarice Lispector: Spinning the Webs of Passion* (translated to Portuguese and published in Brazil as *Clarice Lispector: Desfiando as Teias da Paixão*) which addresses gender as related to identity formation, age, class, race, and the body politic. Her book, *Recitação da Passagem: A Obra Poética de Edimilson de Almeída Pereira* ("*The Middle Passage: The Poetic Works of Edimilson de Almeída Pereira*") focuses on themes related to the experiences of the African diaspora. She is also the contributing editor of *Passo e Compasso: Nos Ritmos do Envelhecer* ("*In the Rhythms of Growing Old*"), a collection of critical essays on cultural and literary representations of age/aging in the Portuguese-speaking countries. Barbosa served as vice president and president of the American Portuguese Studies Association, on the executive committee of the Brazilian Studies Association, and as a member of the Modern Language Association's Luso-Brazilian subdivision.

9 781612 498522